STAR WARS

COMPLETE LOCATIONS

STAR WARS

COMPLETE LOCATIONS

WRITTEN BY
KRISTIN LUND (EPISODE I), SIMON BEECROFT (EPISODE II),
KERRIE DOUGHERTY (EPISODE III), JAMES LUCENO (EPISODES IV–VI),
JASON FRY (EPISODES VII–VIII, *SOLO: A STAR WARS STORY*), AND EMILY
SHKOUKANI (EPISODE IX, *ANDOR*, *ROGUE ONE: A STAR WARS STORY*,
THE MANDALORIAN)

CONSULTATION BY
CURTIS SAXTON

ILLUSTRATED BY
RICHARD CHASEMORE, HANS JENSSEN, KEMP REMILLARD,
MAXIM DEGTYAREV, SOFIAN MOUMENE, AND JOHN R. MULLANEY

ADDITIONAL ILLUSTRATIONS BY
ROBERT E. BARNES, RICHARD BONSON, GREG KNIGHT, CHRISTIAN PICCOLO,
CHRIS TREVAS, ALEX IVANOV, MASAHIKO TANO, ROGER HUTCHINS,
BILL LE FEVER, AND JON HALL

FOREWORD BY
DOUG CHIANG

FOREWORD

Since I was eight years old, I have been fascinated with creating fantastic worlds and understanding how they are built. My earliest drawings were filled with diagrams of structures and rocket-ship constructions. All of my spaceships had interiors. It wasn't enough just to draw the outside, I needed to make sense of the inside. Little did I know that this fascination with details would lead to a long career in film design, where I would have the opportunity to create and shape the worlds and locations of *Star Wars*. That career has now spanned more than 25 years.

I grew up in the suburbs of Michigan, in a new residential development that was surrounded by acres of wild woods. Those woods were a playground that fueled my growing imagination. I spent entire weekends exploring them. A fallen tree became an ancient city. I imagined that the layers of decaying wood were buildings of alien construction. During the winter months, I would explore the frozen creeks behind our house. The layers of thick ice, when held close to my eyes, formed complex shapes that became a miniature crystalline metropolis. Later, at home, I would draw the things I had seen and embellish them even further, inventing stories and crafting exotic reasons for why they were built.

When I wasn't outside, I would spend hours inside looking through an encyclopedia, marveling at its cut-away view of the pyramids. Or getting lost within NASA illustrations of space stations and future moon bases. One of my fondest memories during this time was building a model kit of a cut-away submarine. I had often wondered where the bathrooms were on a submarine. Or where the crew's beds were.

That summer, construction began across the street on several new homes. Over the course of many months, I saw foundations dug and skeletal frames of houses erected. Before my eyes, in slow motion, I learned about the different parts of a house. That was my first real-life cross-section experience, and it transformed how I approached my drawings. I realized that the inside was just as interesting as the outside, and perhaps more important.

Twenty-three years later, I found myself working on the new *Star Wars* films with George Lucas. My childhood fascination to figure out how things functioned was about to pay off. That first year at Skywalker Ranch was the most significant for me. Because I didn't know how the environments and locations that I was designing would be used in the film, I imagined them as real, believable places, places that worked from the inside as well as the outside. That year of early exploration gave me the opportunity to design locations in their entirety. I didn't approach them as movie sets. Instead, I wanted the sets to have a logic for why they looked the way they did.

One of the keys to designing successful film environments in this manner was to take a real location and twist it by 20 percent to make something new. This approach to cinematic design turns the ordinary into the extraordinary, while anchoring it in reality. The podrace course was a wonderful example. George wanted each terrain to be recognizable and distinct. To achieve this, we combined and condensed real locations and exaggerated the scale to add that 20 percent extra to make it unique. Topographical maps were made for George to stage the race. Canyons and plateaus were configured to create memorable landmarks. Using this map, we timed out the race to see how many laps could be completed in eight minutes at speeds of up to 600 miles per hour. This determined the length of the course. Obstacles were then added to dull sections while other areas were simplified for visual clarity.

Other times we built detailed cardboard models to work out a location. These simply constructed card models were very elaborate in form. For the Naboo starfighter hangar, the card models allowed us to figure out how the hangar would be connected to the power generator room. That connection became important when George staged his climactic fight between Darth Maul and Qui-Gon Jinn. For *Star Wars: The Force Awakens*, we made many detailed card models of Starkiller Base, the Resistance base, and Maz's castle, as well as Rey's AT-AT desert home.

Lucasfilm has always been at the forefront of advancements in storytelling, whether it be the use of massive practical sets and models or groundbreaking visual effects and technological advancements. That tradition continues, including innovations like Stagecraft where LED screens are utilized to create feature-film-quality realistic backgrounds in real time for shows like *Star Wars: The Mandalorian* and *Star Wars: Andor*.

In *Star Wars: Complete Locations*, everything comes to life in exquisite detail. Not only have the artists remained faithful to the film designs, they have expanded upon them, often improving the designs by resolving discontinuities and errors that we didn't figure out. Each artist took fragments of sets and transformed them into real places. Their extraordinary illustrations are accurate, or as accurate as they can be for "a galaxy far, far away." Looking at their work, I marvel at their ingenuity and admire their clever solutions. We can see where Watto sleeps, or what's inside the Hoth rebel base.

This book stands as the definitive blueprint for *Star Wars* locations. I delight in them today. Even though I'm familiar with many of these, I still enjoy immersing myself, getting lost within these pages for hours. I am that eight-year-old kid again, exploring the woods behind my house.

D. CHIANG

Doug Chiang
Senior Vice President and Executive Design Director, Lucasfilm

CONTENTS

Introduction	8
Planet Profiles	14
THE REPUBLIC ERA	18
Naboo	20
Naboo Locations	22
Otoh Gunga	24
Droid Control Ship	26
Theed Hangar	28
Tatooine	30
Mos Espa	32
Watto's Junkshop	34
Anakin's Hovel	36
Mos Espa Circuit	38
Mos Espa Arena	40
Coruscant	46
Federal District	48
Galactic Senate	50
Jedi Temple	52
The Invasion of Naboo	54
Defense of Naboo	56
Grass Plains Battle	58
Generator Battle	60
The City of Theed	62
Coruscant Under Crisis	64
Speeder Chase	66
Risky Pursuit	68
Outlander Club	70
Jedi Temple Operations	72
Naboo Retreats	74
Kamino	76
Tipoca City	78
Military Complex	80
Return to Tatooine	82
Spaceports	84
Geonosis	86
Droid Factory	88
Execution Arena	90
Republic Army	92
Separatist Forces	94
Battle of Geonosis	96
Hangar Duels	98
Coruscant Battle	100
Jedi Temple Complex	102
Palpatine's Office	104
Utapau	106
Pau City	108
Kashyyyk	110
Wookiee Tree	112
Battlefronts	114
Mustafar	116
Mustafar Mines	118
Mustafar Duel	120
Polis Massa	122
Medcenter	124

THE IMPERIAL ERA	126	Echo Base	162	Resistance Base	200
Corellia	128	Dagobah	168	First Order Military	202
Conveyex Heist	130	Yoda's House	170	Starkiller Base	204
Kessel Mines	132	Cloud City	172	Ahch-To	208
Ferrix	134	Processing Vane	174	Fathier Chase	210
Narkina 5	136	Jabba's Palace	176	Crait	212
The Imperial Senate	138	Jabba's Throne Room	178	Battle of Crait	214
Jedha	140	Battle of Endor	180	Sith Citadel	216
Vader's Castle	142	Ewok Village	182	Death Star Ruins	218
Scarif	144	Death Star II	184		
Trials on Tatooine	146	Emperor's Lair	186	Index	220
Lars Homestead	148	Executor Command Tower	188	Acknowledgments	224
Tosche Station and Ben's House	150				
Mos Eisley	152	THE NEW REPUBLIC	190		
The Cantina	154	Nevarro	192		
The Death Star	156	Jakku	194		
The Great Temple	158	Rey's Home	196		
Battle of Hoth	160	Maz's Castle	198		

INTRODUCTION

THE *STAR WARS* SAGA is the story of the Skywalkers—a family whose members hold the fate of the galaxy in their hands and whose destiny is played out against a background of political upheaval, revolt, and rebellion. Old institutions crumble and harsh new tyrannies arise as Anakin Skywalker, a young man powerful with the Force, seeks his destiny as the Chosen One of the Jedi Order, only to succumb to the dark side and become an instrument of evil. His children, Luke and Leia, born of his overpowering love for Padmé Amidala, must save their father and the galaxy from the darkness of the Empire in order to restore true balance to the Force and democracy to the star systems.

GALACTIC GOVERNMENTS

With more than a million inhabited worlds, the galaxy is divided into varying alliances and power blocs, the most important of which is the Galactic Republic. The Republic endures, in one form or another, for millennia, but eventually collapses from internal corruption. Adroitly manipulating this disorder, Supreme Chancellor Palpatine, secretly a Sith Lord, seizes emergency powers and transforms the Republic into the Empire, with himself as ruler. The Empire dominates the galaxy for more than two decades, suppressing all dissent and ruthlessly punishing disorder. Eventually, the regime in turn collapses in the face of a determined rebellion, and a New Republic rises to inherit the galaxy. But the descendants of the Empire will not forgive or forget what they see as a despicable betrayal, and beyond the New Republic's borders they ceaselessly plot their return to power. Calling themselves the First Order, their surprise attack, when it finally comes, is overwhelming. The New Republic is decimated in a single strike, and the vastly outnumbered fighters of General Leia Organa's Resistance must hold the line. Discovering that their true enemy is none other than a reborn Emperor Palpatine, the free peoples of the galaxy unite to face him, destroying him and his forces in a climactic battle at Exegol.

THE CLONE WARS
The brutal conflict that comes to be known as the Clone Wars erupts in the aftermath of a political upheaval in the Galactic Senate. A Separatist Alliance of disaffected star systems attempts to withdraw from the Republic, triggering a vast and deadly war that rages for three years. In its final stages, the Jedi Order is falsely accused of treason and wiped out, the Separatist leaders are destroyed, and the Republic is transformed into the evil Galactic Empire.

THE GALACTIC CIVIL WAR
After years of tyrannical Imperial rule, scattered sparks of rebellion across the galaxy combine into a full-scale revolt. Dubbed the Alliance to Restore the Republic, but better known as the Rebel Alliance, this group of brave freedom fighters wages desperate battles against the mighty Imperial military. The Alliance's first great victory sees the destruction of the Death Star—the Empire's most powerful weapon. After many years of struggle and hardship, the rebels finally confront the Emperor at Endor, destroying the newly constructed second Death Star and seemingly killing Palpatine.

THE RISE OF THE FIRST ORDER
For a time, there is peace. The New Republic tries to rebuild a scarred and traumatized galaxy. But evil is never easily vanquished, and in the Unknown Regions, dark forces rise again, determined to destroy all that the Rebellion had fought to achieve. Guided in secret by the resurrected Emperor, the First Order spends decades patiently gathering its forces. Those who see this threat for what it is are branded delusional or warmongers, and are driven to create a new force willing to do what the Republic is not, known as the Resistance. The ensuing war is brief, as the New Republic quickly falls and the Resistance is almost wiped out. The Emperor nearly re-conquers the galaxy, and only by the narrowest of margins is victory snatched from the jaws of defeat.

MAJOR TRADE ROUTES OF THE GALAXY
1. Perlemian Trade Route
2. Corellian Run
3. Corellian Trade Spine
4. Rimma Trade Route
5. Hydian Way

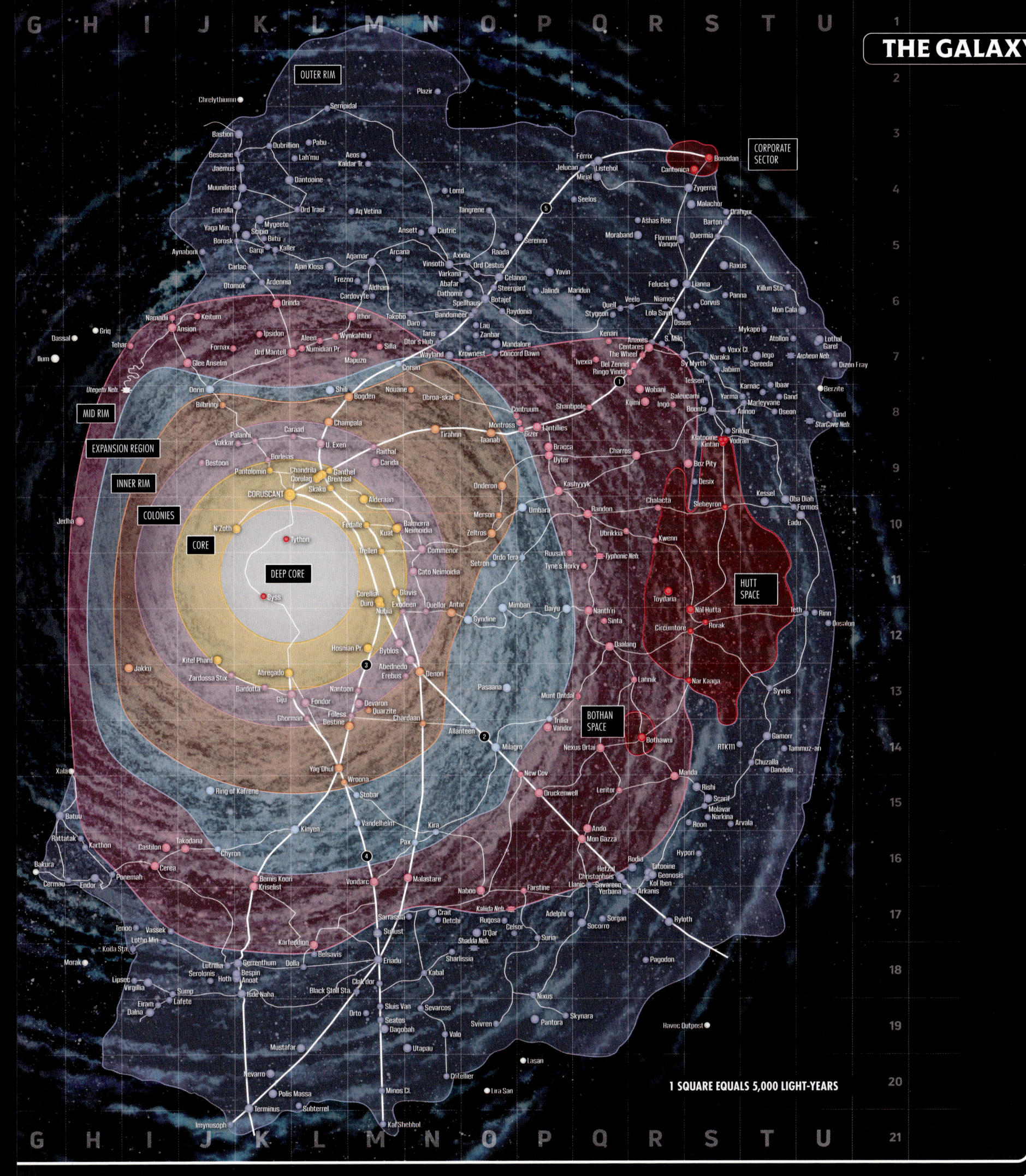

THE GALAXY CONTINUED

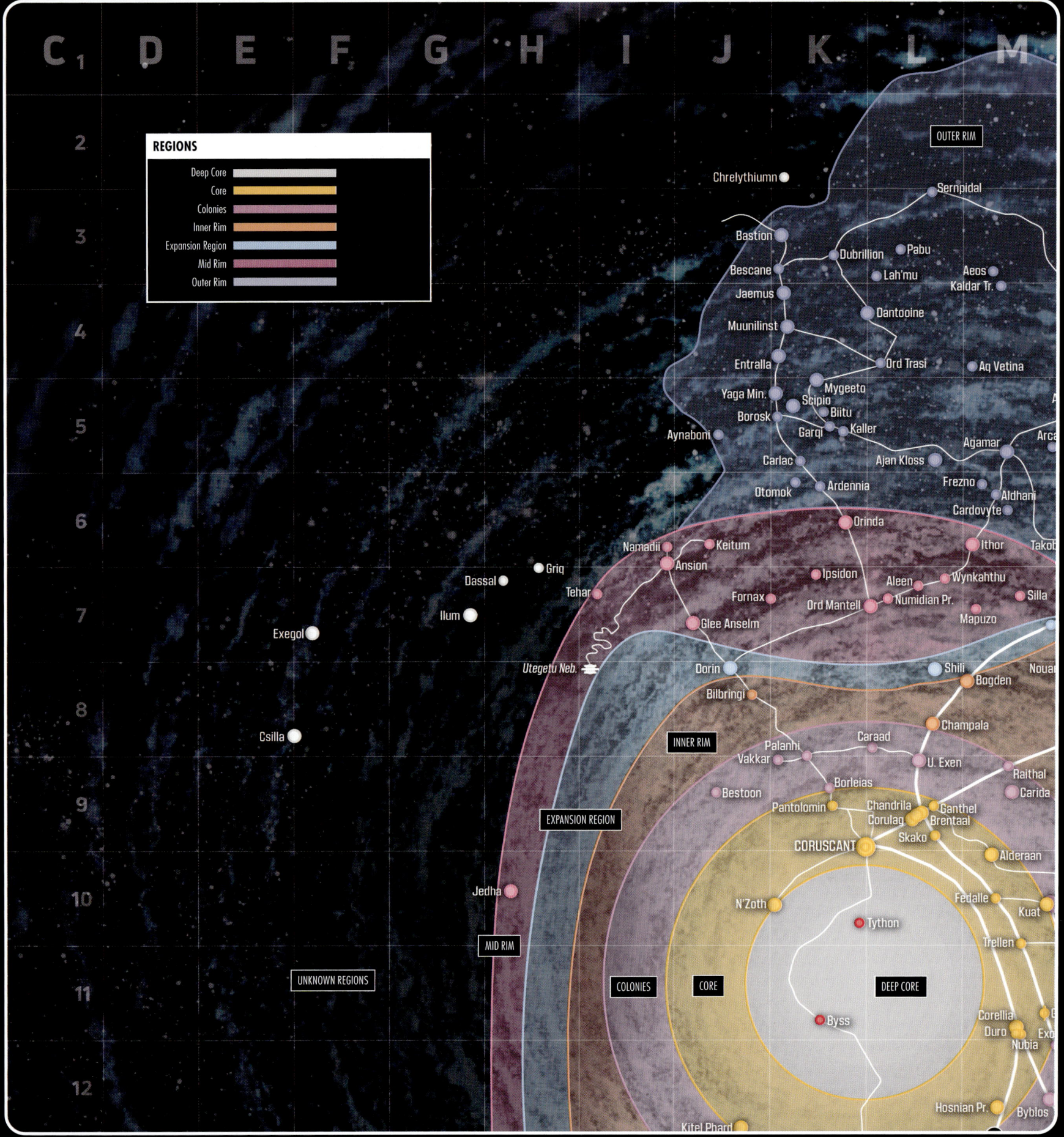

1 SQUARE EQUALS 5,000 LIGHT-YEARS

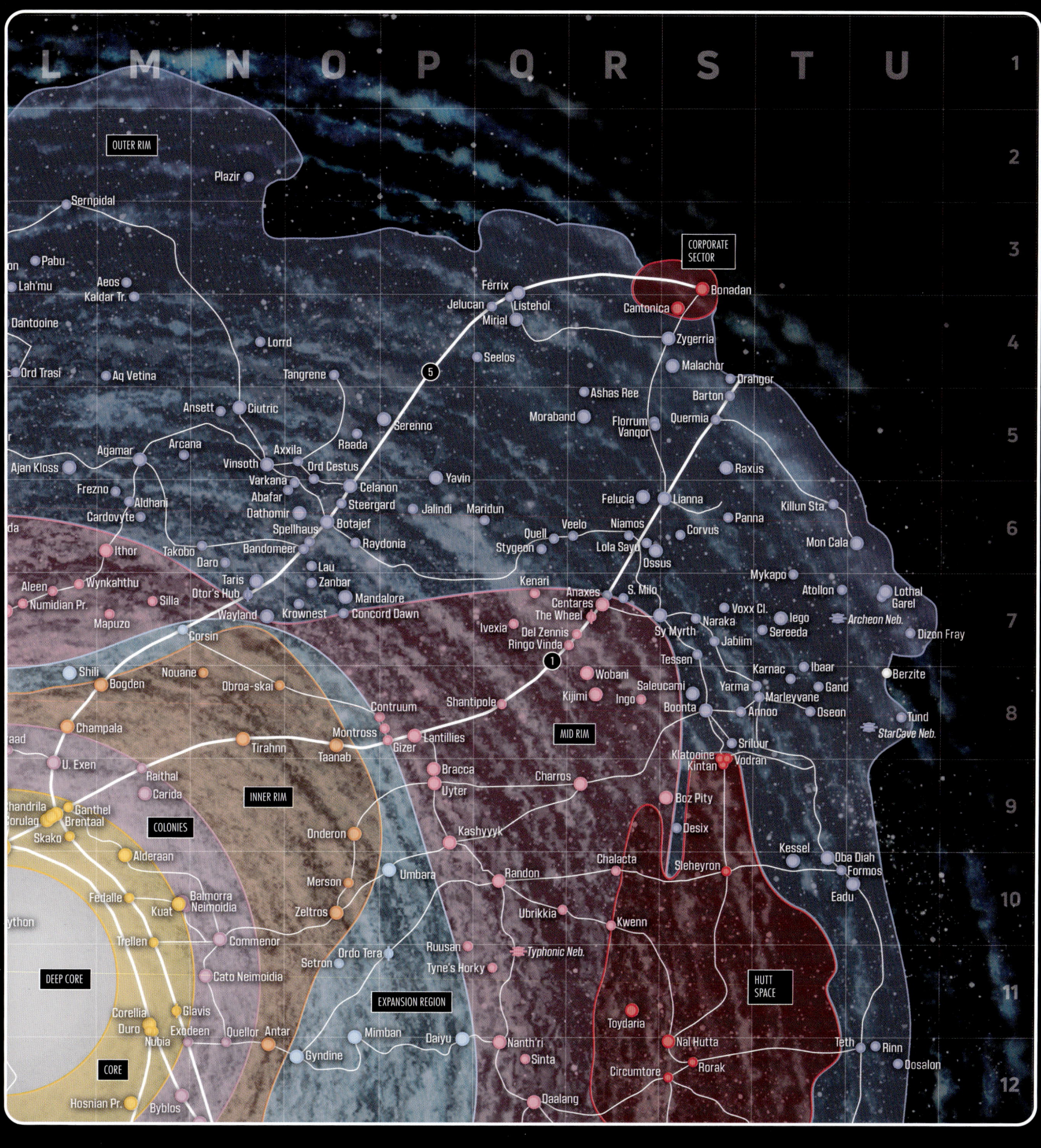

THE GALAXY CONTINUED

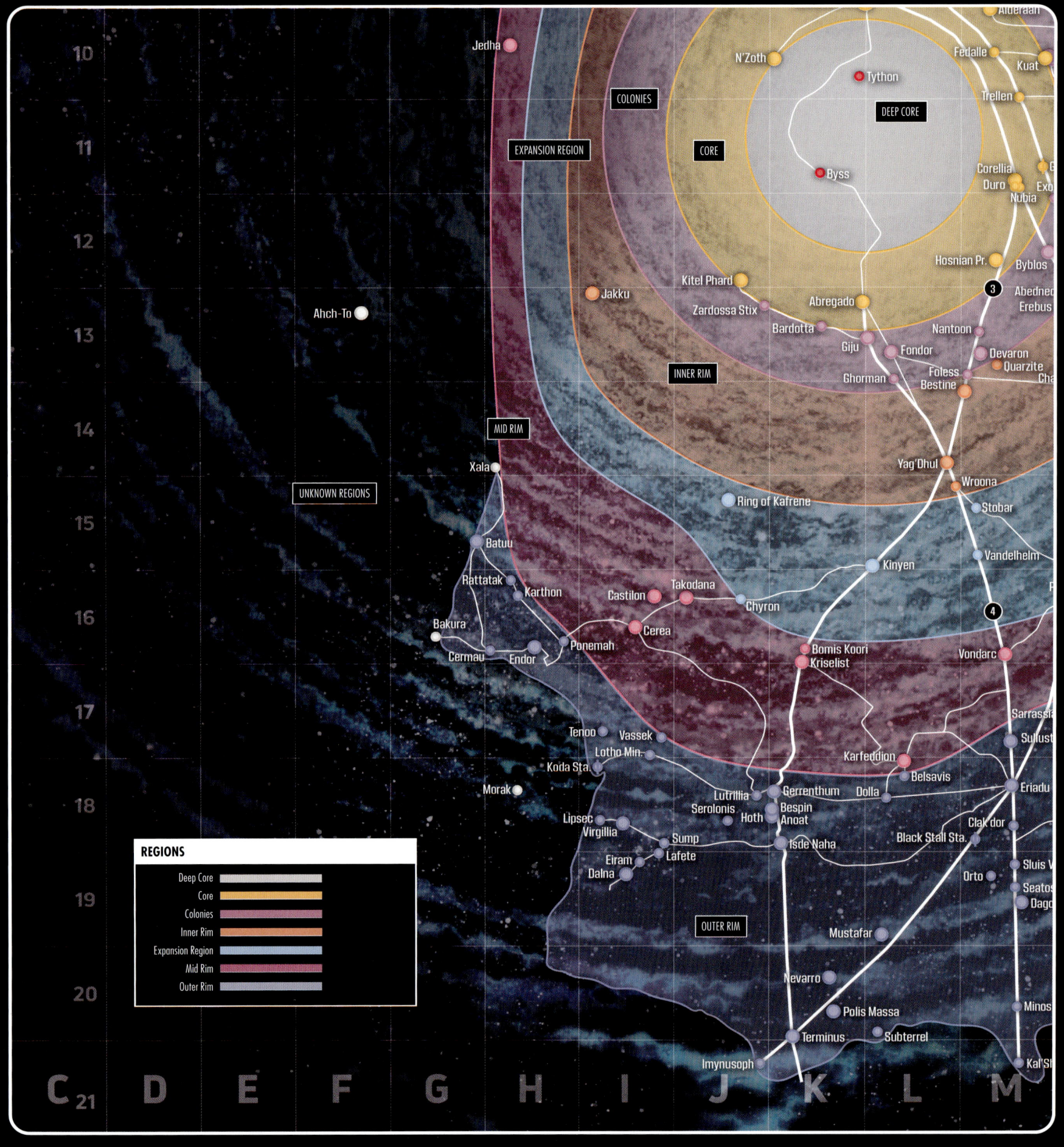

1 SQUARE EQUALS 5,000 LIGHT-YEARS

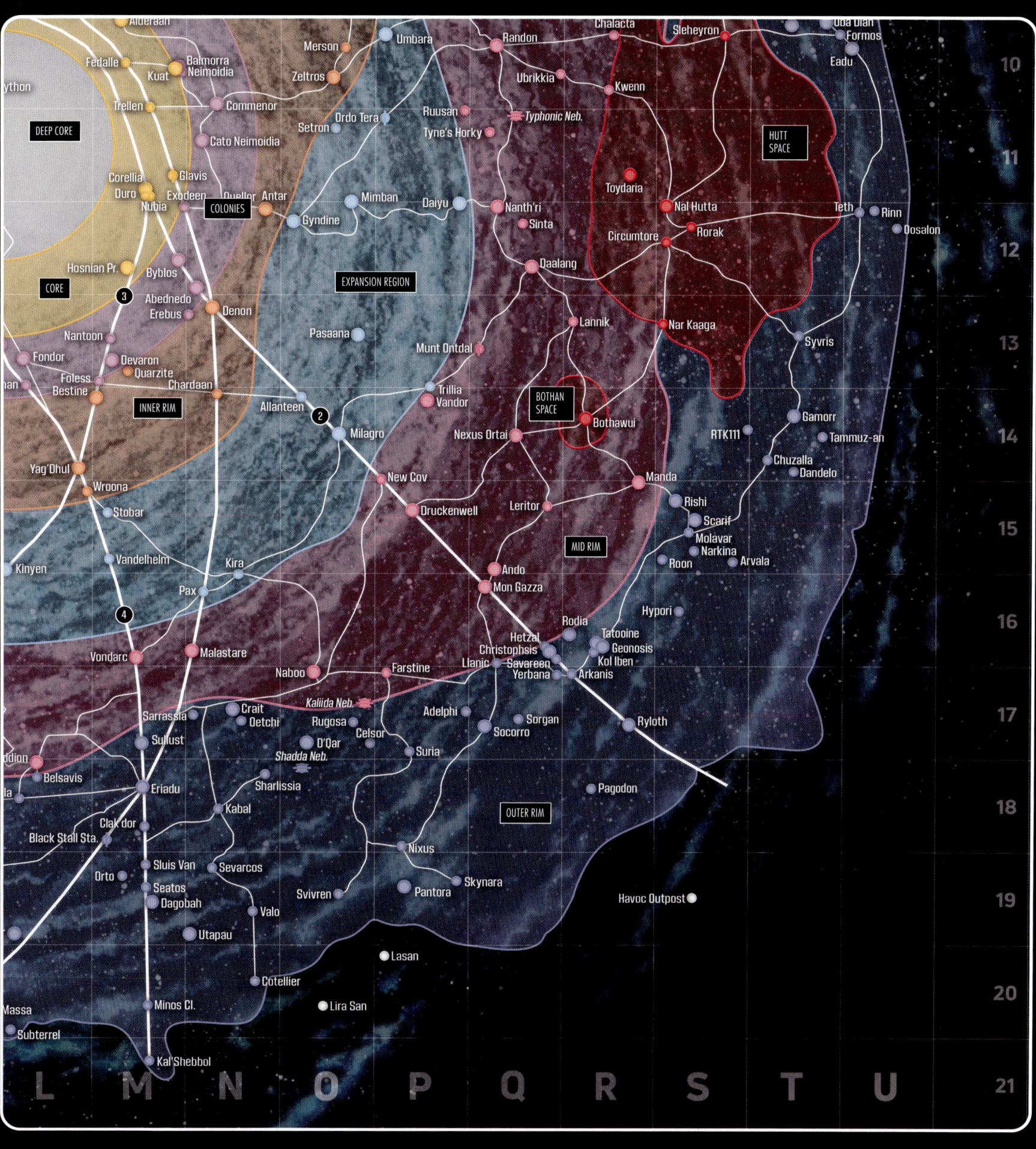

PLANET PROFILES

THE GALAXY IN WHICH the Republic and its successors exert their sway teems with life. There are hundreds of millions of worlds harboring intelligent beings and countless millions more where they are now extinct or never arose. An almost bewildering assortment of planetary environments—from frozen wastes to blistering deserts, from swamp-and-forest worlds to volcanic hells and verdant paradises, from world-oceans to world-cities—form the backdrop to the Skywalker saga and the battle for control of the galaxy. This struggle for peace and justice thrusts some worlds into prominence because of the events that take place there or the heroes and villains they produce.

> "If there's a bright center to the universe, you're on the planet that it's farthest from."
>
> — LUKE SKYWALKER

NABOO

Considered a jewel of the Mid Rim, Naboo is a trading hub and cultural nexus for a swath of star systems in surrounding sectors. The planet is home to both amphibious indigenous Gungans and the human descendants of Core Worlds colonists, an uneasy situation that's driven centuries of resentment, strife, and occasional conflicts.

Galactic Region: Mid Rim

Diameter: 12,120 km (7,531 miles)

Principal Terrain: Mountains, plains, swamps

Number of Moons: 3

Length of Year: 312 days

Population: 4.5 billion

Grid Square: O-17

TATOOINE

Located in the Outer Rim, Tatooine is often derided by young and impatient residents as a hopeless desert backwater world. The reality, however, is more interesting—its location on a major Rim route near the mighty Corellian Run has made it an entrepôt for both legal trade and more questionable transactions.

Galactic Region: Outer Rim

Diameter: 10,465 km (6,503 miles)

Principal Terrain: Desert

Number of Moons: 3

Length of Year: 304 days

Population: 200,000

Grid Square: R-16

CORUSCANT

As the capital of multiple galaxy-spanning civilizations during the vast sweep of galactic history, Coruscant is a glittering ecumenopolis in the heart of the Core. The ancient city-world has become a potent symbol: to some, a promise of the galaxy's optimistic potential and endless excitement; to others, an indictment of its rapacious greed and shocking inequality. On Coruscant, wealth increases with altitude: the lowermost levels are abandoned to darkness and inhabited only by the lost and desperate; above, one finds lawless underlevels where the wise are eternally wary; next come sprawling blocks inhabited by countless middle-class workers; and finally one reaches soaring towers that are sanctuaries for the galactic elite.

Galactic Region: Core Worlds

Diameter: 12,240 km (7,605 miles)

Principal Terrain: Urban

Number of Moons: 4

Length of Year: 365 days

Population: 1 trillion+

Grid Square: L-9

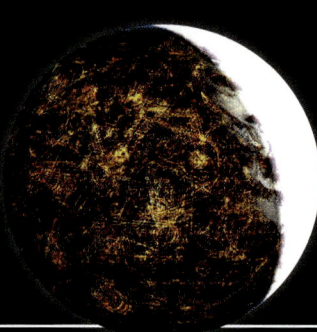

KAMINO

Kamino is a storm-wracked waterworld circling an aging star, which straggles on the outskirts of the satellite galaxy known as the Rishi Maze. For centuries, the Kaminoans have been known for their superlative skill as cloners and their studied disinclination to ask questions of wealthy clients who have made the difficult trek to reach their homeworld and seek their services.

Galactic Region: Extragalactic

Diameter: 19,270 km (11,974 miles)

Principal Terrain: Ocean

Number of Moons: 3

Length of Year: 463 days

Population: 1 billion (none in Imperial era)

Grid Square: N/A

GEONOSIS

An Outer Rim neighbor of Tatooine, Geonosis is a world whose spectacular rings stand in stark contrast to its harsh surface, which is plagued by meteor showers and radiation storms. Life that survives here does so by sheltering underground; the most successful such species is the insectile Geonosians, bipeds who cluster together in hive-colonies hollowed out of hardy rock spires. These winged beings are born into a rigid caste system encompassing all from anonymous drones to queens who rule in secret from catacombs deep below the surface. Order and obedience have made Geonosians superb engineers and assembly-line workers, designing armies of droids made in their own image as well as secret weapons of far greater power.

Galactic Region: Outer Rim

Diameter: 11,370 km (7,065 miles)

Principal Terrain: Canyons, deserts

Number of Moons: 15

Length of Year: 256 days

Population: 1 billion (none in Imperial era)

Grid Square: R-16

UTAPAU

Utapau's surface is plagued by scouring hyperwinds that have forced its inhabitants into sinkholes that pierce the crust and descend kilometers to a globe-spanning sub-crustal ocean. The vertical cities built within these shafts are home to both the squat Utai, who evolved underground, and their distant kin, the tall, angular Pau'ans who once called the surface home.

Galactic Region: Outer Rim

Diameter: 12,900 km (8,016 miles)

Principal Terrain: Plains, sinkholes

Number of Moons: 9

Length of Year: 351 days

Population: 95 million

Grid Square: N-19

KASHYYYK

Kashyyyk is a verdant Mid Rim trade hub covered by mighty wroshyr trees. Its native Wookiees have a deep connection with their planet, seeking to live in harmony with the peace-loving lifeforms of its gentle treetops, as well as the half-legendary terrors of its lightless depths.

Galactic Region: Mid Rim

Diameter: 12,765 km (7,932 miles)

Principal Terrain: Forests, seas

Number of Moons: 3

Length of Year: 381 days

Population: 56 million

Grid Square: P-9

MUSTAFAR

A tiny volcanic world, Mustafar is a superheated ball of black basalt and glowing magma that spews from its unstable interior. These hellish conditions are the product of a gravitational tug-of-war between two neighboring gas giants, which generates tidal forces that threaten to pull Mustafar apart. Somehow intelligent life has evolved here in the form of two closely related insectoid species. The Mustafarians' legends claim their home was a garden world before being ruined by dark side energies.

Galactic Region: Outer Rim

Diameter: 4,200 km (2,610 miles)

Principal Terrain: Mountains, volcanoes

Number of Moons: 1

Length of Year: 412 days

Population: 20,000

Grid Square: L-19

CORELLIA

Corellia is a founding world of the Republic, and its intrepid explorers, hyperspace scouts, canny merchants, wily smugglers, and daring pilots have shaped galactic history, with two of the galaxy's mightiest trade routes bearing the Corellian name. But while Corellia's contributions to galactic civilization are storied, the planet's glory days were long ago; by the last centuries of the Republic most Corellians with the means to do so sought to escape their homeworld. Corellia remains an industrial powerhouse, with its shipyards renowned for producing vehicles with unmatched speed and efficiency, but it has become a grim, polluted planet. Coronet City, its capital, is a collection of overcrowded favelas in which the poor seek protection from criminal gangs and are trapped in endless cycles of poverty, violence, and despair.

Galactic Region: Core Worlds

Diameter: 11,000 km (6,835 miles)

Principal Terrain: Terrestrial

Number of Moons: 3

Length of Year: 329 days

Population: 3 billion

Grid Square: M-11

VANDOR

Frigid and mountainous, Vandor is a sparsely settled world far from the galaxy's major trade routes, most notable for its herds of shaggy kod'yoks. Scattered outposts such as Fort Ypso cater to ranchers, skinners, homesteaders, and the kind of eccentrics eternally drawn to the frontier. The Empire establishes garrisons on Vandor, mining iridium, harvesting kod'yok meat and hides, and trans-shipping cargo via conveyex lines built to snake through Vandor's mountain passes.

Galactic Region: Mid Rim

Diameter: 12,500 km (7,767 miles)

Principal Terrain: Terrestrial

Number of Moons: 2

Length of Year: 435 days

Population: 25,000

Grid Square: P-14

KESSEL

Both beautiful and blighted, Kessel is a planet of contrasts. Its royal family dwells in luxury in the planet's lush, warm southern hemisphere, giving no thought to conditions in the northern hemisphere, which is dominated by mining operations controlled by criminal gangs. The dim, polluted mines have become infamous in the galaxy, worked by desperate contract laborers, prisoners, and enslaved beings. Kessel produces both coaxium and spice, which has medicinal uses but is mostly sold as a powerful narcotic. The Empire ignores the enormous illegal profits generated while monitoring what comes out of the mines and supplying new laborers to replace those who die or go insane. During the Imperial era, the Pykes control the mines; after the Empire's fall, rival syndicates fight a bloody turf war for control of Kessel.

Galactic Region: Outer Rim

Diameter: 7,200 km (4,474 miles)

Principal Terrain: Terrestrial

Number of Moons: 3

Length of Year: 322 days

Population: 10,000

Grid Square: T-10

FERRIX

The Morlana system sits at the intersection of several hyperspace lanes and boasts several inhabited worlds. Morlana One is a grim industrial planet whose people live lockstep to the dictates of their corporate masters, but neighboring Ferrix is a vibrant society notable for industrious, opportunistic shipbreakers and grapplers who make their living extracting useful components from junked starships and equipment. This recycling economy is the heart of a web of industries and communities, ranging from the salyards and social clubs of Ferrix City to homesteads and farms located farther out in the flatlands. While not inherently rebellious—disorder plays havoc with the cycles of the workday—Ferrixians are tough and independent, taking pride in their traditions and balking at being told what they can and can't do.

Galactic Region: Outer Rim

Diameter: 7,914 km (4,917 miles)

Principal Terrain: Terrestrial

Number of Moons: 1

Length of Year: 462 days

Population: 1.5 million

Grid Square: Q-4

NARKINA 5

The industrial quarries of the ocean moon Narkina 5 catch the eye of the Empire and are transformed into prisons where inmates toil in workrooms beneath the watchful gaze of Imperial guards, with their days spent in service to pitiless production quotas. Finished components are then shipped off to nearby Outer Rim worlds such as Rothana and Scarif to feed the Imperial war machine. It's an axiom of galactic economics that droids are cheaper labor than organic beings, but the Empire has changed the equation by treating its prisoners as disposable. Narkina 5's inmates watch their remaining incarceration time dwindle day after dreary day, unaware that they will never be released but simply shuttled to another level and a new set of workrooms. On Narkina 5, all sentences are for life.

Galactic Region: Outer Rim

Diameter: 988 km (614 miles)

Principal Terrain: Terrestrial

Number of Moons: N/A

Length of Year: 223 days

Population: Information restricted

Grid Square: S-15

JEDHA

A sandy, unassuming moon, Jedha is deeply bound up with the history of not just the Jedi Order but also a spectrum of other Force traditions. For millennia, adherents of these ancient faiths have sought answers in Jedha's Holy City, making the moon a destination for pilgrims and an occasional flashpoint when doctrinal disputes flare into open conflict. In the last centuries of the Republic, the moon's popularity wanes and it becomes a backwater reachable only by circuitous, often unreliable hyperspace routes. Pilgrimages go from difficult to dangerous after the Empire occupies Jedha, stripping it of kyber deposits and cracking down on ancient Force traditions and any related displays of spirituality. This crackdown reaches a shocking climax when the Empire test-fires the Death Star at Jedha, devastating the moon.

Galactic Region: Mid Rim

Diameter: 11,263 km (7,000 miles)

Principal Terrain: Desert

Number of Moons: N/A

Length of Year: 420 days

Population: 11.3 million

Grid Square: H-10

SCARIF

A tranquil world dotted with tropical islands, Scarif lies deep in the Outer Rim, too far from the Core for its wealth of dense minerals to be transported efficiently to shipyards such as Kuat or Corellia. The Empire has used Scarif's remoteness to its advantage, turning the planet into an incubator for military research it wishes to keep from the eyes of the Senate. The stronghold known as the Citadel hides many Imperial secrets, including the plans for the dreaded Death Star.

Galactic Region: Outer Rim

Diameter: 9,112 km (5,662 miles)

Principal Terrain: Ocean

Number of Moons: 0

Length of Year: 287 days

Population: 475,000

Grid Square: S-15

PLANET PROFILES CONTINUED

YAVIN 4
Yavin 4 is the largest of the dozens of moons orbiting the gas giant Yavin. A pristine, emerald-green world, its landmasses are thick with purple-barked Massassi trees, named for the ancient civilization that once inhabited the moon but vanished eons ago, leaving behind towering stone monuments. Nothing in the system is of interest to mining companies or gas prospectors; when Yavin suddenly becomes a turning point in galactic history, few have ever heard of it or its necklace of moons.

Galactic Region: Outer Rim
Diameter: 10,200 km (6,338 miles)
Principal Terrain: Jungle
Number of Moons: N/A
Length of Year: 4,818 days (planet)
Population: Negligible—scattered homesteads
Grid Square: P-6

HOTH
Isolated and ice-bound, Hoth's desolate surface is dominated by massive glaciers riddled with caverns and pierced by crystalline geysers. Yet despite its brutal climate and frequent meteor impacts, Hoth isn't lifeless: herds of tauntauns wander its icy plains, hunted by hulking, white-furred wampas. Hoth lies near the Corellian Trade Spine, but is rarely visited because navigational hazards make it difficult to reach. As a result, it's a tempting bolthole for the Outer Rim's pirates, smugglers, refugees, and rebels, but all soon discover the difficulty of survival on Hoth makes it a questionable sanctuary.

Galactic Region: Outer Rim
Diameter: 7,200 km (4,474 miles)
Principal Terrain: Frozen plains, mountains
Number of Moons: 3
Length of Year: 549 days
Population: None (no permanent settlements)
Grid Square: K-18

DAGOBAH
A mysterious, mist-shrouded swamp world dotted with lakes and lagoons, Dagobah is a cauldron of life, brimming with exotic flora and fauna fighting to survive in an eat-or-be-eaten ecosystem. The planet's teeming life makes it a nexus for the power of the living Force, celebrated as one of the purest places in the galaxy by seekers lucky enough to find it. But few ever do: Dagobah sits amid a tangle of obscure hyperspace lanes and is missing from most star charts and starship navicomputers. Its Force energies and obscurity make it an ideal place of exile for Yoda following the near-destruction of the Jedi Order.

Galactic Region: Outer Rim
Diameter: 14,410 km (8,954 miles)
Principal Terrain: Swamps, bogs
Number of Moons: 0
Length of Year: 341 days
Population: None
Grid Square: M-19

BESPIN
Separated from its two sister gas giants by the asteroid belt Velser's Ring, Bespin is a primary source of naturally occurring tibanna gas, a prized substance that amplifies energy output when exposed to cohesive light. Bespin has no landmasses, but its upper atmosphere hosts a thin envelope of breathable air, known as the Life Zone. Within this beautiful expanse float exquisite orbital cities and sleek gas-mining facilities, with places such as Cloud City simultaneously pursuing galactic tourism and tibanna harvesting.

Galactic Region: Outer Rim
Diameter: 118,000 km (73,322 miles)
Principal Terrain: Gas giant
Number of Moons: 2
Length of Year: 5,110 days
Population: 6 million (located entirely on hovering gas mining facilities)
Grid Square: K-18

FOREST MOON
The Endor system lies at the edge of known space, dominated by a silver-banded gas giant with nine moons. The largest of its satellites, known simply as the Forest Moon, is a temperate world brimming with life, including the forest-dwelling Ewoks and Duloks, long-legged Yuzzums, and legendary Gorax.

Galactic Region: Outer Rim
Diameter: 4,900 km (3,045 miles)
Principal Terrain: Forests, savannas, mountains
Number of moons: N/A
Length of Year: 402 days (planet)
Population: 30 million+
Grid Square: H-16

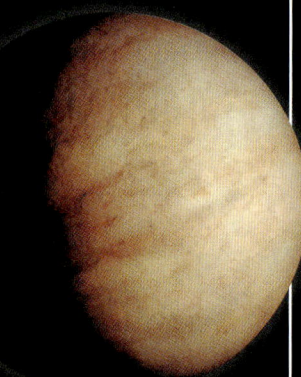

NEVARRO
A volcanic world located on a spur of the Hydian Way, Nevarro is covered with a mix of lava fields and more hospitable terrain. The planet is little regarded during the Imperial era but later gains an unseemly reputation as a haven for smugglers, bounty hunters, and pirates, as well as being home to ordinary civilians seeking a peaceful life. After a brief occupation by forces loyal to Moff Gideon's Imperial remnant, Nevarro enters a new era under the leadership of Magistrate Greef Karga, who thinks the planet's proximity to major routes could turn it into a trading port independent of the New Republic. Pirate attacks imperil this attempt at a new beginning; when a band of Mandalorians repels the pirates, Karga is quick to offer them land grants in hopes of shoring up Nevarro's security needs.

Galactic Region: Outer Rim Territories
Diameter: 8,006 km (4,975 miles)
Principal Terrain: Terrestrial
Number of Moons: 2
Length of Year: 345 days
Population: 4 million
Grid Square: K-20

JAKKU
Jakku was once a verdant world, but some past calamity turned it into a barren globe of scorched badlands and marching dunes. Located in the galaxy's Western Reaches near the uncharted frontier, Jakku is all but uninhabited during the war between the Empire and the Rebel Alliance; few know that the forlorn planet was the site of a secret Imperial research base used as a jumping-off point for exploring the galaxy's Unknown Regions. A year after the destruction of the second Death Star at Endor, an Imperial task force engages a New Republic fleet above Jakku, with wreckage from the battle crashing onto the planet. The surviving Imperial forces then vanish into the unknown.

Galactic Region: Inner Rim
Diameter: 6,400 km (3,977 miles)
Principal Terrain: Desert
Number of Moons: 2
Length of Year: 352 days
Population: Unknown (fewer than 25,000)
Grid Square: I-13

TAKODANA
Located on the border of the galaxy's Mid Rim, the forested world of Takodana has long been a crossroads for bold scouts traveling beyond the frontier, and a base for treasure hunters and prospectors… as well as pirates who prey on them. For centuries, Maz Kanata has run a legendary bar and hostel in an ancient castle by the shores of a Takodana lake, collecting travelers' tales and turning a profit from all who pass through her doors.

Galactic Region: Mid Rim
Diameter: 12,100 km (7,519 miles)
Principal Terrain: Forests, plains, seas
Number of Moons: 0
Length of Year: 215 days
Population: Less than 1 million
Grid Square: J-16

D'QAR

A lush jungle planet located in the Outer Rim, D'Qar is discovered by Alliance scouts in the final days of the Galactic Civil War and briefly houses a rebel outpost. But the war moves on and D'Qar is all but forgotten—which makes it perfect when, years later, Leia Organa breaks with the New Republic and seeks a secret headquarters for her Resistance movement. From D'Qar, Leia keeps tabs on the First Order, employing the service of daring fighter pilots, a network of droids programmed as spies, and sympathetic politicians and military officers within the New Republic.

Galactic Region: Outer Rim

Diameter: 10,400 km (6,462 miles)

Principal Terrain: Jungles, plains

Number of Moons: 2

Length of Year: 415 days

Population: None (No permanent settlements)

Grid Square: O-17

ILUM/STARKILLER BASE

Hidden in the galaxy's Unknown Regions, Ilum is a small, frozen world sacred to the Jedi Order and site of the rite of passage known as the Gathering, in which younglings find kyber crystals for their lightsabers. After the fall of the Jedi, the Empire secures Ilum and strip-mines its kyber crystals to create focusing lasers for the Death Stars' superlasers. When the First Order flees into the Unknown Regions, it completes Ilum's desecration by transforming it into Starkiller Base, a mobile weapons platform of terrifying destructive power.

Galactic Region: Unknown Regions

Diameter: 660 km (410 miles)

Principal Terrain: Forests, snow, mountains

Number of Moons: 2 (later 0)

Length of Year: 301 days (original)

Population: Originally 5,200, later classified

Grid Square: G-7 (original location)

AHCH-TO

Deep in the Unknown Regions lies lonely Ahch-To, whose heaving seas are broken by scattered islands, one of them the site of the very first Jedi Temple. Luke Skywalker and Lor San Tekka find Ahch-To after years of searching, and Luke hopes its secrets will help him restore the Jedi Order. Instead, it becomes his place of exile, where the Jedi Master cuts himself off from the Force and lives as a hermit.

Galactic Region: Unknown Regions

Diameter: 7,212 km (4,481 miles)

Principal Terrain: Ocean

Number of Moons: 1

Length of Year: 304 days

Population: Unknown

Grid Square: F-13

CANTONICA

The desert world Cantonica, located in the distant Corporate Sector, is a little-known shadowport for petty criminals until monied interests transform a dusty, sleepy town into Canto Bight—a glittering casino city on the shores of an artificial sea. This new playground for the galaxy's super-rich serves as a refuge from the Galactic Civil War and the growing tensions between the New Republic and the First Order. Here, magnates of megacorporations, arms dealers, and the scions of noble houses gather at gaming tables and fathier races, playing sabacc and hazard toss, and sipping rare vintage wines from long-dead worlds. Cocooned in luxury, they give little thought to the struggles of the galaxy beyond the occasional glance at a datapad to recalculate their net worth.

Galactic Region: Corporate Sector

Diameter: 11,440 km (7,108 miles)

Principal Terrain: Desert

Number of Moons: 2

Length of Year: 206 days

Population: 850,000

Grid Square: S-4

CRAIT

The pale, highly reflective surface of Crait has fooled many an explorer gazing down at the planet from orbit: the white expanse below them isn't ice and snow, but salt flats broken by halite steppes. Red crystalline rhodochrosite lies just below the salty crust, attracting a mining consortium to the planet. Decades later, the miners are long gone, but their abandoned facility is fortified for use as a possible rebel base during the fight against the Empire, with Leia Organa keeping Crait in reserve as a bolthole for the Resistance. This facility becomes the site of the group's last stand after First Order forces pursue them from D'Qar, with Leia's freedom fighters sharing the abandoned mine base with a skulk of furtive, crystal-furred vulptices as the projected form of Luke Skywalker faces down the entire First Order.

Galactic Region: Outer Rim

Diameter: 7,400 km (4,598 miles)

Principal Terrain: Terrestrial

Number of Moons: 0

Length of Year: 525 days

Population: None

Grid Square: N-17

EXEGOL

Deep in the Unknown Regions lies Exegol, a gloomy planet known only to scholars of the dark era when the Sith ruled the galaxy. Veiled by clouds of crimson gas and dust, Exegol is a dry, dismal world scoured by lightning and pierced by deep fissures. After the Sith's long-ago defeat, their fortress worlds were abandoned and interdicted, visited only by mad pilgrims and foolhardy seekers of dark lore. But Exegol escaped this purge, with Sith Eternal cultists turning a forbidding bastion rising from its barren plains into a dark-side locus. After many generations, their lonely vigil is rewarded: Darth Sidious makes Exegol his redoubt, envisioning it as the throne world of a restored Sith dominion and secretly constructing a fleet to serve as the instrument of his retribution and ensure the triumph of his Final Order.

Galactic Region: Unknown Regions

Diameter: 13,649 km (8,481 miles)

Principal Terrain: Barren

Number of Moons: 0

Length of Year: 210 days

Population: Unknown

Grid Square: F-7

KEF BIR

One of nine moons circling the gas giant Endor, IX3244-C—known as Kef Bir in Ewokese—is the Empire's first choice as sanctuary for the second Death Star's construction, but is rejected in favor of the nearby Forest Moon. After the battle station's destruction, a slice of its hull plunges into Kef Bir's oceans, where it is slowly chewed away by salt and waves. A band of First Order deserters lives on the Ocean Moon, tending orbaks and raiding the wreckage on sea skiffs.

Galactic Region: Outer Rim

Diameter: 3,725 km (2,315 miles)

Principal Terrain: Ocean

Number of Moons: N/A

Length of Year: 402 days

Population: 40

Grid Square: H-16

THE REPUBLIC ERA

Under the authority of the Galactic Republic and its brave defenders, the Jedi Knights, the galaxy largely exists in harmony, but darkness brews in places unknown. Even during the era of the High Republic, when the galaxy is at its most prosperous, peace is rivaled by wickedness. Raiders known as the Nihil wreak havoc across the stars before the Jedi and Republic get the situation under control. Many years later, a handful of outlying planets secede from the Galactic Republic and form their own union: the Confederacy of Independent Systems, or the Separatists, who believe the Republic prioritizes systems closer to the Core, neglecting the rest of them. Tensions between the two escalate until a battle on Geonosis—fought by the Republic's newly created clone army and the Separatists' droid army—breaks out. The eruption of the Clone Wars, spreading from the Core to the Outer Rim, sends the galaxy into chaos unseen for a millennium.

As the two factions struggle for footholds throughout the galaxy, capturing strategic locations becomes a priority, such as Christophsis for its resources and Umbara for its proximity to supply routes. While these factions wage war, all along, the galaxy's true enemy hides in plain sight on the Republic capital-world of Coruscant. There, Supreme Chancellor Palpatine has risen to power under the guise of democracy. In reality he is the Sith Lord Darth Sidious, descending from a lineage of darkness, pulling the strings of not only the Republic, but the Separatists too. His goal is simple: unlimited power. When the Jedi finally determine the truth and go to apprehend the Sith, a bigger plot unfolds wherein the Jedi are marked as traitors to the galaxy while Palpatine continues his ruse as a seemingly innocent politician. The prodigy Jedi Anakin Skywalker falls to the dark side, rising as Sidious' apprentice, Darth Vader. And across the stars, valiant Knights of the Order succumb to the Great Jedi Purge, which sees the merciless execution of nearly every single one of them. As the Republic's twilight comes to a close, the galaxy is reorganized into an Empire with Palpatine as its incumbent leader. Meanwhile, on a planetoid called Polis Massa, twins are born—and with them, hope.

NABOO

NABOO IS A BIZARRE, GEOGRAPHICALLY UNIQUE WORLD LOCATED along a major galactic trade route near the Outer Rim. The planet's serene surface of sweeping hills and rolling seas is deceptive: beneath it lies a shadowy underwater world of winding caverns and tunnels inhabited by gigantic, ferocious sea creatures. This immense labyrinth runs through the entire planet, becoming increasingly rocky and dense in the lower strata. The planet's center seethes and bubbles with eruptions of exotic plasmic energy. Over millennia these eruptions form new caverns and tunnels, and influence surface features such as mountains. The planet's two primary civilizations, the Naboo and the Gungans, rely on this plasma power, although they collect and use it in different ways.

The Naboo royal residence, Theed Palace, perches on top of a tremendous cliff with panoramic views of the surrounding countryside.

SECRETS OF OTOH GUNGA

When the amphibious Gungans were forced to retreat underwater in a fierce struggle for territory thousands of years ago, they stumbled upon a secret that enabled them to live there permanently. In deep waters, they came across a strange life-form known as locap that burrows into porous rock and siphons out plasma. The Gungans found that they were able to extract plasma from the plant using special harvesting bongos (Gungan submarines) equipped with a front-mounted siphon. This natural source of energy has many uses in Gungan life, including the creation of their unique bubble cities. Plasma-based technology allows powerful hydrostatic fields to be generated around basic frameworks, keeping water out but allowing individuals to pass through.

CULTURED CITY

Supreme Chancellor Palpatine's shuttle hovers over the elegantly domed buildings of Theed, his home city and the capital of Naboo. From this vantage point Palpatine can admire the city's unified, harmonious style, the result of extensive rebuilding after the upheavals of the ancient past. Theed's sophisticated culture has produced many able and admired galactic politicians, not least of whom is Palpatine himself, who learned much about the mechanics of government and the subtleties of power during his early years here. Naboo's reputation for peace and tolerance in the moral wilderness of the galaxy's rim lent Palpatine credibility as a young politician. The Naboo now feel secure in a galaxy ruled by this willful individual, however remote and inscrutable he has become.

NABOO LOCATIONS

THE DIVERSE TERRAIN OF NABOO teems with luscious plant and animal life. Whether it's the rich, green plains and insect-ridden swamps of the surface or the dark, fish-rich depths of the oceans, Naboo offers fruitful existences to those inhabitants who live in harmony with the planet. Several Gungan and Naboo chroniclers have advanced the theory that the mysterious and now long-dead civilization whose ruins dot the countryside failed to respect this balance and were destroyed by their greed.

The Gungan capital city of Otoh Gunga is hidden deep in the Naboo swamps, in the depths of Lake Paonga.

- Cliff edge
- Gungan sentry posts
- Gallo Mountains
- Gungan sacred place
- Trade Federation landing site
- Jar Jar Binks' adopted homelands
- Great Grass Plains
- Site of Great Grass Plains Battle
- Theed
- Underwaterway leads into Solleu River, which runs through Theed
- Caves of Eleuabad, one of the most notorious locations of sando aqua monsters
- Water-filled underwaterways
- Continental slope
- Lianorm Swamp stretches over an area of 85 square kilometers (34 square miles)
- Lake Paonga
- Otoh Gunga
- Entrance to underwaterways from Lake Paonga

NABOO UNDERWATERWAYS

Underneath the surface of Naboo, a tremendous maze of passages and caves, created by movements of unstable plasmic energy in the interior, provides the Gungans with transport routes through the planet. Navigating these underwaterways requires immense skill since they are home to ferocious creatures. A single wrong turn can spell certain death. In spite of the risks, fleets of Gungan trading subs constantly voyage through these routes; overland travel on fambaas or kaadu is slower and more arduous for this amphibious species.

SACRED PLACE

Hidden in the swampy foothills of the Gallo Mountains, the sacred place is a haven of worship for the Gungans and a sanctuary in times of trouble. Scattered around are giant statues and a vast, ruined temple, relics of a long-extinct species of Naboo inhabitants. The Gungans acknowledge these mysterious beings as their planet's elders. Yet archaeologists are mystified as to the relevance of these crumbling remnants: are they giant representations of the species themselves or are they massive icons devoted to their gods?

- Dense foliage cuts off site from outside world
- Temple ruins
- Tangled roots of cambylictus trees

SOLLEU RIVER

Although the cultures of the Naboo and the Gungans are different in many ways, both share a close relationship with water. The Naboo capital, Theed, is virtually a floating city, nestling on the banks of the mighty Solleu, a river fed by underground tributaries flowing through the planet interior. However, unlike the amphibious Gungans, the Naboo believe the meditative and restorative qualities of flowing water are best appreciated from dry land.

FUNERAL TEMPLE

The Theed Funeral Temple is located in a tranquil spot on the edge of the city. Its open-air design and numerous windows frame a magnificently carved stone platform. Nearby stands the Livet Tower containing an eternal flame, whose never-ending light reminds the Naboo of their own mortality and their duty to lead harmonious lives. Naboo funeral custom dictates that the body of the deceased be cremated within two days of death. In this way, it is believed, the life force of the dead is returned to the planet. Once the ashes are collected, they are carried onto the bridge between the temple and the Livet Tower and cast into the Solleu River before it plunges over the cliff.

TURRET ROOM

As active members of the Galactic Republic, the Naboo regularly entertain dignitaries from other worlds in lavish, hand-crafted suites of rooms within Theed Palace. When the Jedi High Council arrives for the funeral of Qui-Gon Jinn its members make use of a turret room in which to mourn privately and celebrate the life of their fellow Jedi. This serene chamber is attached to a small temple where Naboo monarchs pay homage to the great rulers of the past. The temple and chamber were built by the first ruler of the Great Time of Peace, King Jafan, who helped reestablish peace on Naboo. It is here that Yoda warns Obi-Wan Kenobi of the grave dangers he foresees in training Anakin Skywalker as a Jedi.

Grazing kaadu — *Gungan sentry*

GUNGAN SENTRY POST

The huge statue heads that dot the edges of the Lianorm Swamp at the foothills of the Gallo Mountains provide lookouts for Gungan sentries. These soldiers scan the Great Grass Plains using farseein (Gungan electrobinoculars). Before the Battle of Naboo, a sentry spies the Naboo head of security, Captain Panaka, and a group of volunteers crossing the Great Grass Plains from Theed.

Anakin

OTOH GUNGA

ANCHORED TO AN UNDERWATER CLIFF DEEP IN LAKE PAONGA, Otoh Gunga is home to nearly one million inhabitants. Like all Gungan underwater cities, Otoh Gunga's central district is a dense cluster of bubbles made up of elegant city squares, noisy cantinas, oval-shaped sacred bubbles, and an Ancient Quarter, whose fragile bubbles now only faintly glow. Radiating outward are the Otoh Villages, where most Gungans live and work. At the furthest edges are satellite clusters, some of which have been cast out from other cities and are trying to attach themselves to Otoh Gunga.

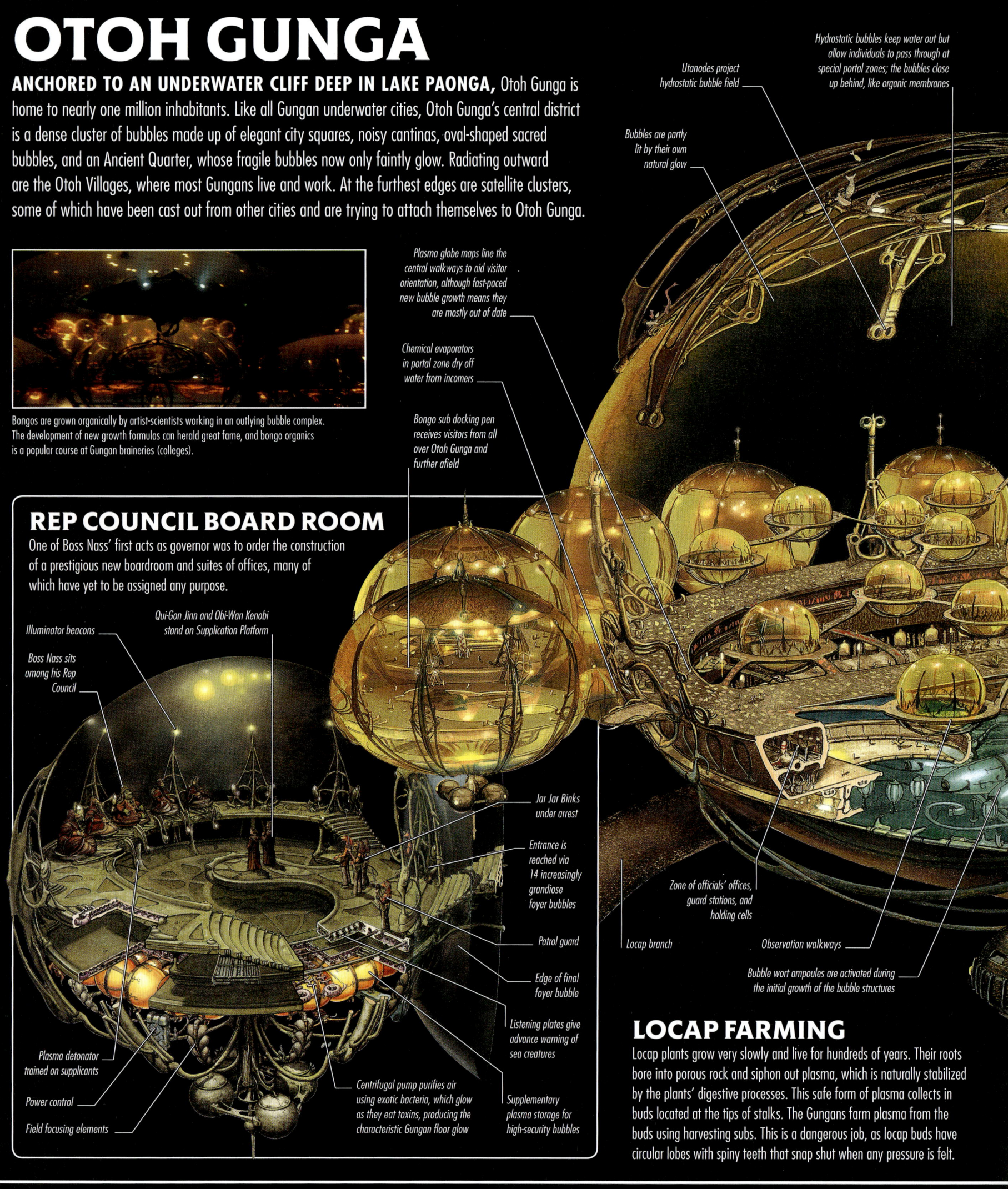

Bongos are grown organically by artist-scientists working in an outlying bubble complex. The development of new growth formulas can herald great fame, and bongo organics is a popular course at Gungan braineries (colleges).

REP COUNCIL BOARD ROOM

One of Boss Nass' first acts as governor was to order the construction of a prestigious new boardroom and suites of offices, many of which have yet to be assigned any purpose.

- Illuminator beacons
- Boss Nass sits among his Rep Council
- Qui-Gon Jinn and Obi-Wan Kenobi stand on Supplication Platform
- Plasma detonator trained on supplicants
- Power control
- Field focusing elements
- Centrifugal pump purifies air using exotic bacteria, which glow as they eat toxins, producing the characteristic Gungan floor glow
- Jar Jar Binks under arrest
- Entrance is reached via 14 increasingly grandiose foyer bubbles
- Patrol guard
- Edge of final foyer bubble
- Listening plates give advance warning of sea creatures
- Supplementary plasma storage for high-security bubbles
- Plasma globe maps line the central walkways to aid visitor orientation, although fast-paced new bubble growth means they are mostly out of date
- Chemical evaporators in portal zone dry off water from incomers
- Bongo sub docking pen receives visitors from all over Otoh Gunga and further afield
- Utanodes project hydrostatic bubble field
- Hydrostatic bubbles keep water out but allow individuals to pass through at special portal zones; the bubbles close up behind, like organic membranes
- Bubbles are partly lit by their own natural glow
- Zone of officials' offices, guard stations, and holding cells
- Locap branch
- Observation walkways
- Bubble wort ampoules are activated during the initial growth of the bubble structures

LOCAP FARMING

Locap plants grow very slowly and live for hundreds of years. Their roots bore into porous rock and siphon out plasma, which is naturally stabilized by the plants' digestive processes. This safe form of plasma collects in buds located at the tips of stalks. The Gungans farm plasma from the buds using harvesting subs. This is a dangerous job, as locap buds have circular lobes with spiny teeth that snap shut when any pressure is felt.

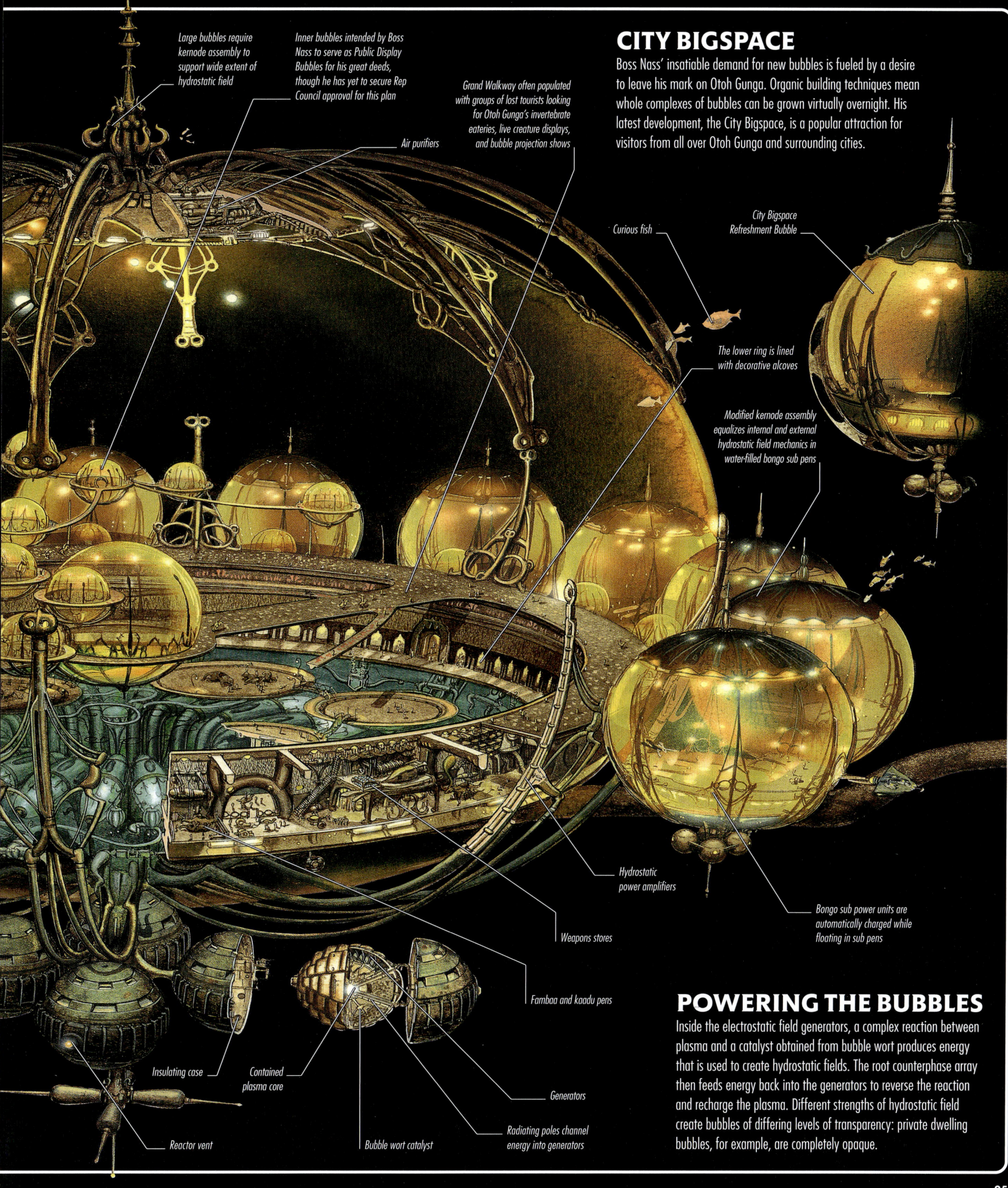

CITY BIGSPACE

Boss Nass' insatiable demand for new bubbles is fueled by a desire to leave his mark on Otoh Gunga. Organic building techniques mean whole complexes of bubbles can be grown virtually overnight. His latest development, the City Bigspace, is a popular attraction for visitors from all over Otoh Gunga and surrounding cities.

POWERING THE BUBBLES

Inside the electrostatic field generators, a complex reaction between plasma and a catalyst obtained from bubble wort produces energy that is used to create hydrostatic fields. The root counterphase array then feeds energy back into the generators to reverse the reaction and recharge the plasma. Different strengths of hydrostatic field create bubbles of differing levels of transparency: private dwelling bubbles, for example, are completely opaque.

DROID CONTROL SHIP

DROID CONTROL SHIPS ARE TRADE FEDERATION *Lucrehulk*-class vessels augmented with enormous transmitters that allow them to remotely control entire droid invasion forces from orbit. One of these massive converted cargo ships, the *Vuutun Palaa*, is the centerpiece of the Neimoidian flotilla sent to blockade the peaceful planet Naboo. Trade Federation officials are confined aboard this huge craft for months on end, leading to frayed nerves and petty backbiting. Increasingly paranoid Neimoidians rarely stray far from the command bridge for fear that a colleague will engineer some advantage in their absence or form conspiracies against them.

The signal to begin activation of the droid army is given via the pilot's manual controls.

Control signal computer relays commands to droid army

Pilot in navigation station controls ship systems via datagoggles and hand-operated instrument panels

CONTROL SHIP BRIDGE

Dominated by the throne-like pilot navigation station, the Control Ship bridge is a well-guarded location on a tower at the heart of the spacecraft. Droid pilot operatives are stationed at navigation computers on an underfloor. In this small, confined environment, Trade Federation officials frequently seek the relative privacy of the shadowy corners to scheme against each other, nominally out of earshot (though actually inviting and welcoming attention and suspicion). They communicate with trade partners via a viewscreen situated in a port at one side of the bridge.

Jedi emerge from circulation vent

SECRET ARMY

Usually piled high with cargo, the cavernous hangars in the control ship have been cleared to allow for the transport and mobilization of a droid invasion army in complete secrecy. The most recent customs officials from the Galactic Republic to venture on board the ship were persuaded that the suspicious-looking components they saw had no military function, but were a shipment of the latest, expensive binary load-lifters. However, the Jedi who emerge from a circulation vent are under no illusions about what they are witnessing.

CONFERENCE ROOM
The Control Ship's centersphere contains 50 conference rooms. As these rooms are used for trade negotiations, they are specially adapted to place clients at a disadvantage. The adaptations include variable gas emitters and remote-operated "concentration deficit" chairs, which make it difficult for individuals to think clearly.

AIR TRAFFIC CONTROL
The flow of traffic in and out of the ship is monitored from droid stations that overlook the hangars. Despite their slow reaction times, droids now oversee many ship functions. Replacing paid employees and expensive protocol droids with enslaved low-maintenance droids partially offsets the massive costs of assembling the droid army.

BLAST DOORS
While the Jedi face fearsome droidekas, the Neimoidian viceroy and his aides cower in the bridge behind triple blast doors. In status-obsessed Neimoidian society, even doors assert social standing, and these bridge doors are particularly elaborate—reminding ship employees of the superiority of its high-level occupants. However, the doors are not as impenetrable as they look, as Qui-Gon Jinn proves when he burns through them with his lightsaber.

Cargo bay

Row of MTTs (Multi Troop Transports)

Cargo containers moved aside to make space for droid army

THEED HANGAR

SITTING ATOP THE CLIFF EDGE in the city's central district, the elegant Theed hangar is a well-guarded military airbase for the N-1 starfighter fleet and Queen Amidala's Royal Starship. The neighboring power generator supplies the spacecraft in the hangar with plasma energy through underground conduits. Equipped with air traffic control, tactical computer stations, and a secret subterranean tunnel link to the palace, the location plays a pivotal role in the Battle of Naboo, becoming a rallying point for the eventual uprising.

Anticipating no resistance from the peace-loving Naboo—let alone two experienced Jedi—battle droids leave the Royal Starship operational and ready to fly.

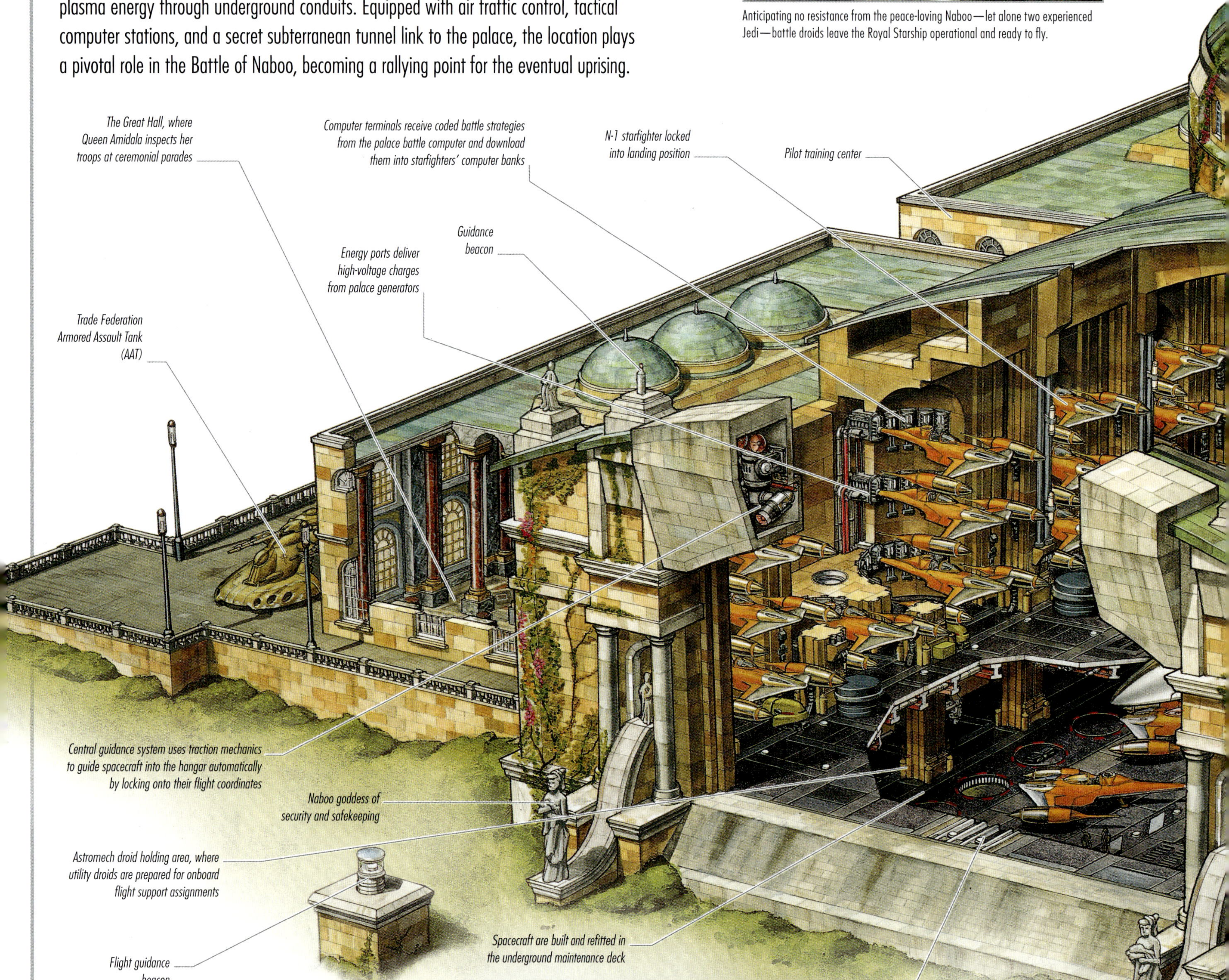

The Great Hall, where Queen Amidala inspects her troops at ceremonial parades

Computer terminals receive coded battle strategies from the palace battle computer and download them into starfighters' computer banks

N-1 starfighter locked into landing position

Pilot training center

Guidance beacon

Energy ports deliver high-voltage charges from palace generators

Trade Federation Armored Assault Tank (AAT)

Central guidance system uses traction mechanics to guide spacecraft into the hangar automatically by locking onto their flight coordinates

Naboo goddess of security and safekeeping

Astromech droid holding area, where utility droids are prepared for onboard flight support assignments

Flight guidance beacon

Spacecraft are built and refitted in the underground maintenance deck

Electromag rails generate grav field to reduce speed of incoming spaceships inside hangar

GUIDANCE SYSTEMS

The volunteer pilots of the Royal Naboo Security Forces are trained to use both onboard flight computers and air traffic control to navigate their fighters into the hangar. However, some veteran pilots are fond of boasting to their juniors that they can gauge the entrance by observing how the wind is affecting the nearby waterfalls.

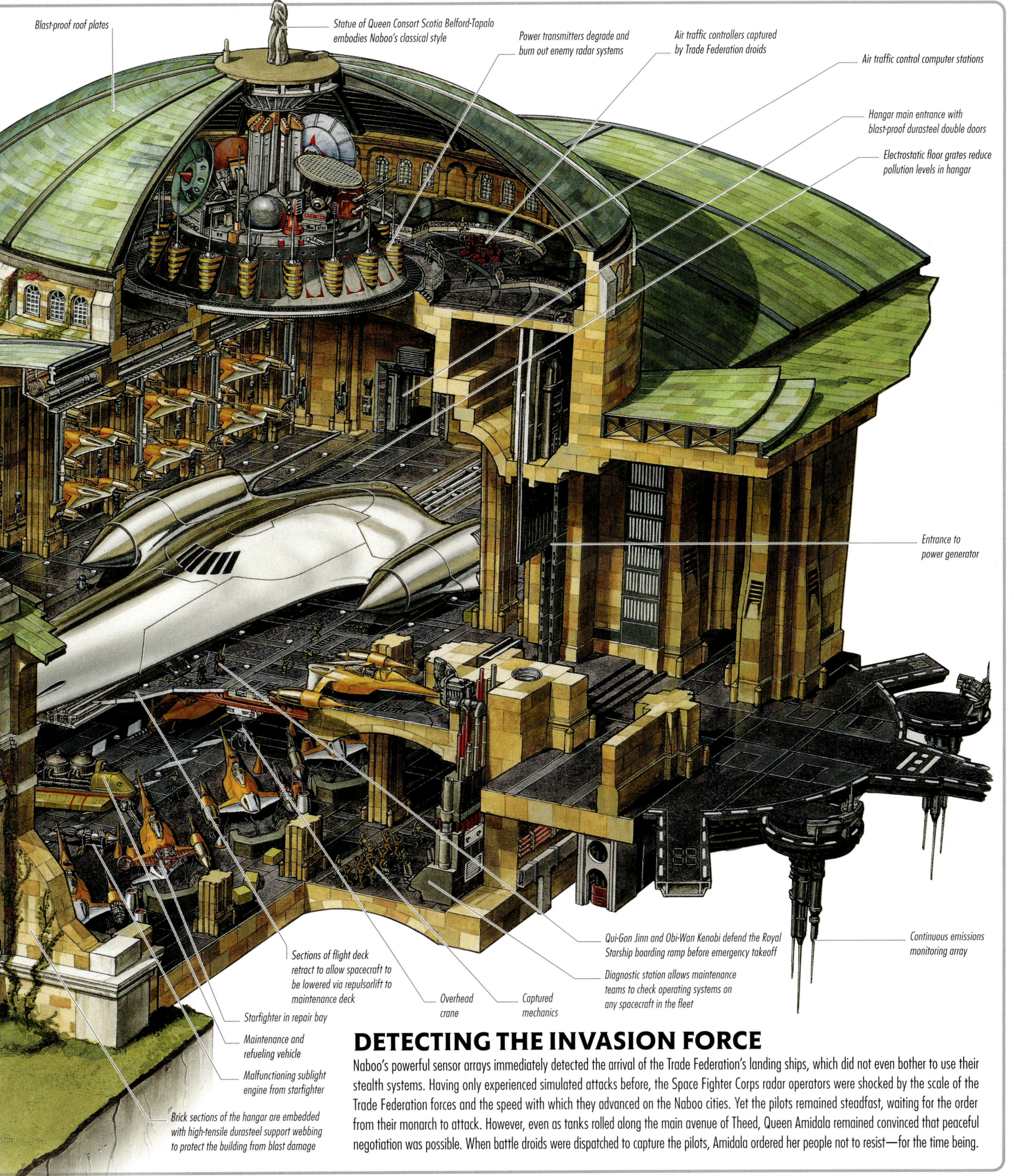

DETECTING THE INVASION FORCE

Naboo's powerful sensor arrays immediately detected the arrival of the Trade Federation's landing ships, which did not even bother to use their stealth systems. Having only experienced simulated attacks before, the Space Fighter Corps radar operators were shocked by the scale of the Trade Federation forces and the speed with which they advanced on the Naboo cities. Yet the pilots remained steadfast, waiting for the order from their monarch to attack. However, even as tanks rolled along the main avenue of Theed, Queen Amidala remained convinced that peaceful negotiation was possible. When battle droids were dispatched to capture the pilots, Amidala ordered her people not to resist—for the time being.

TATOOINE

A VAST YELLOW GLOBE baked by the heat of its twin suns, Tatooine is a testament to the tenacity of life. Its indigenous life-forms, from dewbacks, eopies, and krayt dragons to Jawas and Tuskens, must all find ways to survive in the harsh desert wastes. More recent immigrants have found a way to eke out a living as well: the first settlers were poor laborers employed by mining corporations that believed Tatooine was rich in ore and minerals. It wasn't, and when the mining venture failed, the workers and their equipment were abandoned—but their descendants and more recent arrivals have survived through moisture farming and trade. Tatooine sits at a nexus of Outer Rim trade routes, and is a frequent stopover for smugglers moving goods to or from Hutt Space, as well as outlaws, mercenaries, and those seeking to disappear. Much of its economy is controlled by the Hutt clans, and Republic law is but a rumor.

TOWN AND COUNTRY

Tatooine's few settlements are separated from each other by vast expanses of desert. The poor standards of living and harsh conditions on Tatooine mean that little distinguishes one town from another. Yet Mos Espa's location near Tatooine's famous podrace arena gives it a distinctive feel. Along with the usual spacers, its cafés and cantinas buzz with podrace crews, visiting fans, and professional gamblers. By contrast, rural Tatooine is a lonely world of small moisture farms. These use simple vaporators to collect the tiny amounts of water in the air, which is sold as a commodity and used to irrigate underground plantations.

Tatooine is so fiercely lit by its twin suns that it appears from a certain distance to be a star itself. The planet is uninhabitable save for one relatively cool area of its northern hemisphere.

THE SECRETS OF THE STONES

Characterized by gigantic, top-heavy rocks that rise eerily from the sand, Mushroom Mesa is one of the most astonishing features of Tatooine's desert wasteland. Many observers have noted the humanoid faces that appear in some of the stones: a freak accident of wind erosion or ritual objects carved by alien hands—no one knows. Some observers believe the secret lies with the Tuskens, who, they note, avoid the Mesa as if it were cursed. Tatooine's more recent settlers are less superstitious: Mos Espa's famous podrace circuit now runs directly through the stones.

The activities of Tatooine's settlers disrupt the traditional hunting patterns of the indigenous Tuskens. This has resulted in intense periods of frustrated violence, with the fearsome Tuskens attacking other species in random raids, and taking potshots using stolen blasters as weapons.

MOS ESPA

MOS ESPA IS A ROUGH, lawless town and one of Tatooine's largest spaceports. Powerful gangsters have ruled the city for generations—wringing out profits from areas such as the Workers' District and the upper sprawl and leaving the poor to eke out a living by scavenging, stealing, or gambling. The wealthy openly disregard galactic law by owning enslaved beings, with these unfortunates dwelling in cheap lodgings built by long-gone mining corporations for their workers. The authorities rarely visit these precincts, which allows the enslaved to provide safe havens—for a price—for outlaws on the run.

Although the food is guaranteed to be undercooked and stringy, Sebulba often hangs out at Akim's Munch, a street café where his fans can see him and pay their respects. However, the hot-tempered Dug is just as keen to meet opponents and enemies.

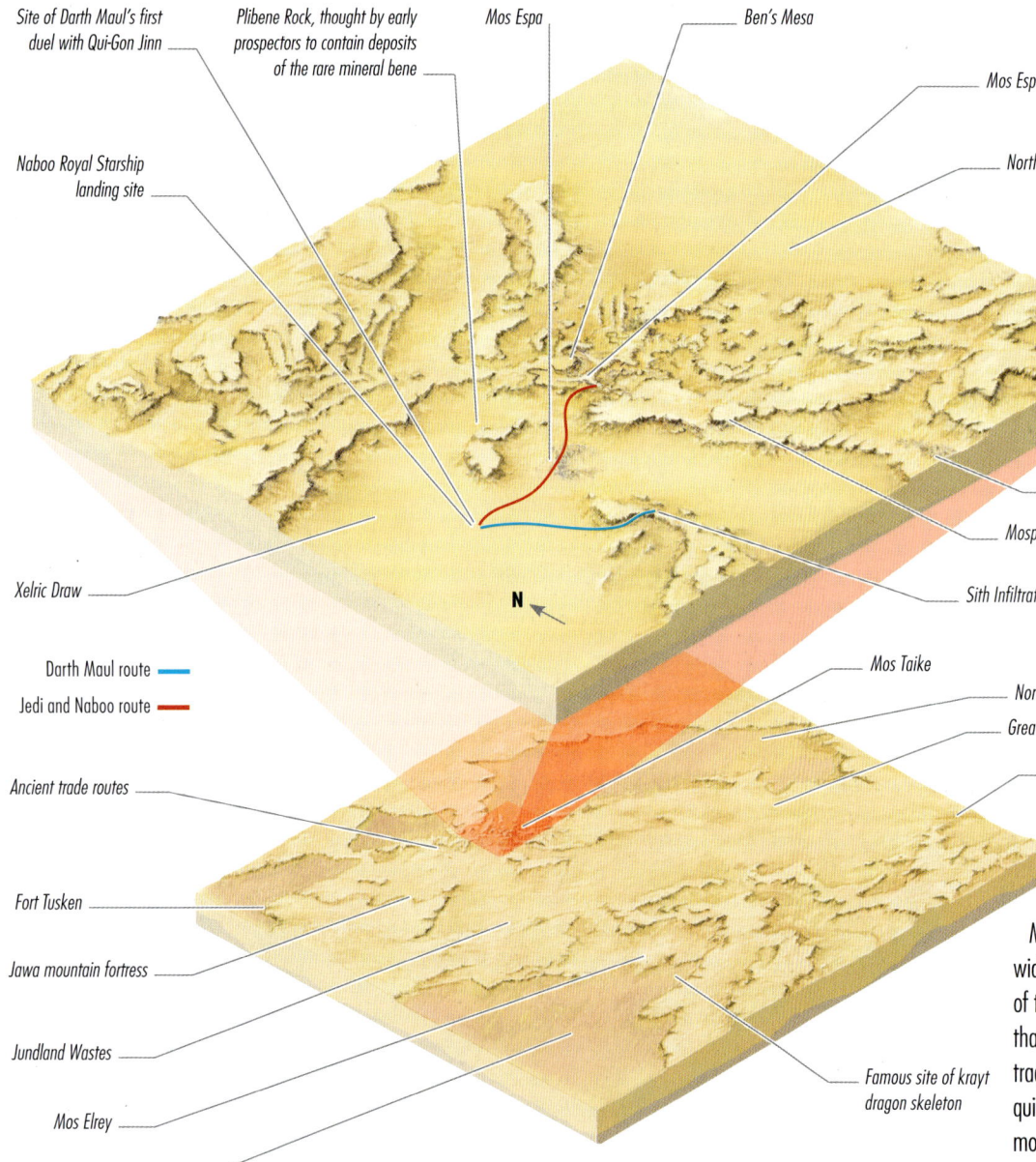

DESERT SETTLEMENT

Mos Espa is strategically situated in the Xelric Draw, a shallow, wide-mouthed canyon that splits the Mospic High Range on the edge of the Northern Dune Sea. The Xelric Draw is an ancient trading route that links the northern settlements to those further south. Since all traders must pass this way, Mos Espa's marketplace developed quickly. Settlements off the main trade route tend to be even more lawless and hostile toward traders of any species.

HOVEL BACKYARDS

Anakin Skywalker works on his podracer behind the slave quarters, safe in the knowledge that Watto never ventures here. As an owner of enslaved beings, Watto is expected to maintain such hovels. But repairs are rarely done before structures actually begin to collapse, and are then patched up by droids the Toydarian deems expendable.

MOS ESPA ARENA

Many offworlders from the Outer Rim associate Mos Espa with its famous podraces, held at the enormous arena in the desert outside the city. The thrill of the races can be addictive, and fans new to the sport soon find Tatooine-style gambling to be an expensive pursuit.

URBAN LABYRINTH

Mos Espa's market is thronged with dealers selling used parts roughly repaired, scrounged, or stolen. With no discernable building codes, new streets and buildings are tacked on whenever needed. Visitors to this labyrinth risk losing their way and their valuables.

GOVERNING GANGSTERS

Mos Espa's city hall is a stately building designed by the noted Tynnan architect Pisc Dowdrena. But the sense of civic pride and duty suggested by the architecture goes no deeper than its exterior: Mos Espa's mayors work not for the city's downtrodden people but for the gangsters who are its true rulers, serving as mediators for minor underworld disputes, organizers of cleanup efforts after sandstorms and spasms of gang violence, and figureheads who keep interfering outsiders at bay and investigate whether they should be bought off or made to disappear.

PORT OF ILL REPUTE

Mos Espa boasts many attractions for jaded tourists with deep pockets and shallow scruples: gamblers seek out its podraces, pit fights and casinos, then rub elbows with rakes in its nightclubs and cantinas. New arrivals touch down in Mos Espa's sprawling spaceport, located on a plateau above the crater that houses the city center. Here they soon find themselves shaken down for "security services." An outlander who refuses to hire one or more protection racket to guard their ship will almost certainly return to find parts missing—if the ship is still there at all.

WATTO'S JUNKSHOP

EVEN AMONG MOS ESPA'S ODD ASSORTMENT OF BUILDINGS, Watto's junkshop stands out. Originally a simple, squat dome, the money-minded shopkeeper added the unusual bell-shaped top himself after his first highly successful deal (with a wealthy Hutt clan leader). Recalling the muck nests of Watto's native Toydaria, the distinctive top attracts customers and provides Watto with a safe perch.

SUCCESS STORY

Watto's shop is one of the most successful parts dealerships in Mos Espa. His secret is simple: inflated prices, stolen stock, slave labor, and no questions asked. Watto spends little time behind the counter, letting droids do most of the work.

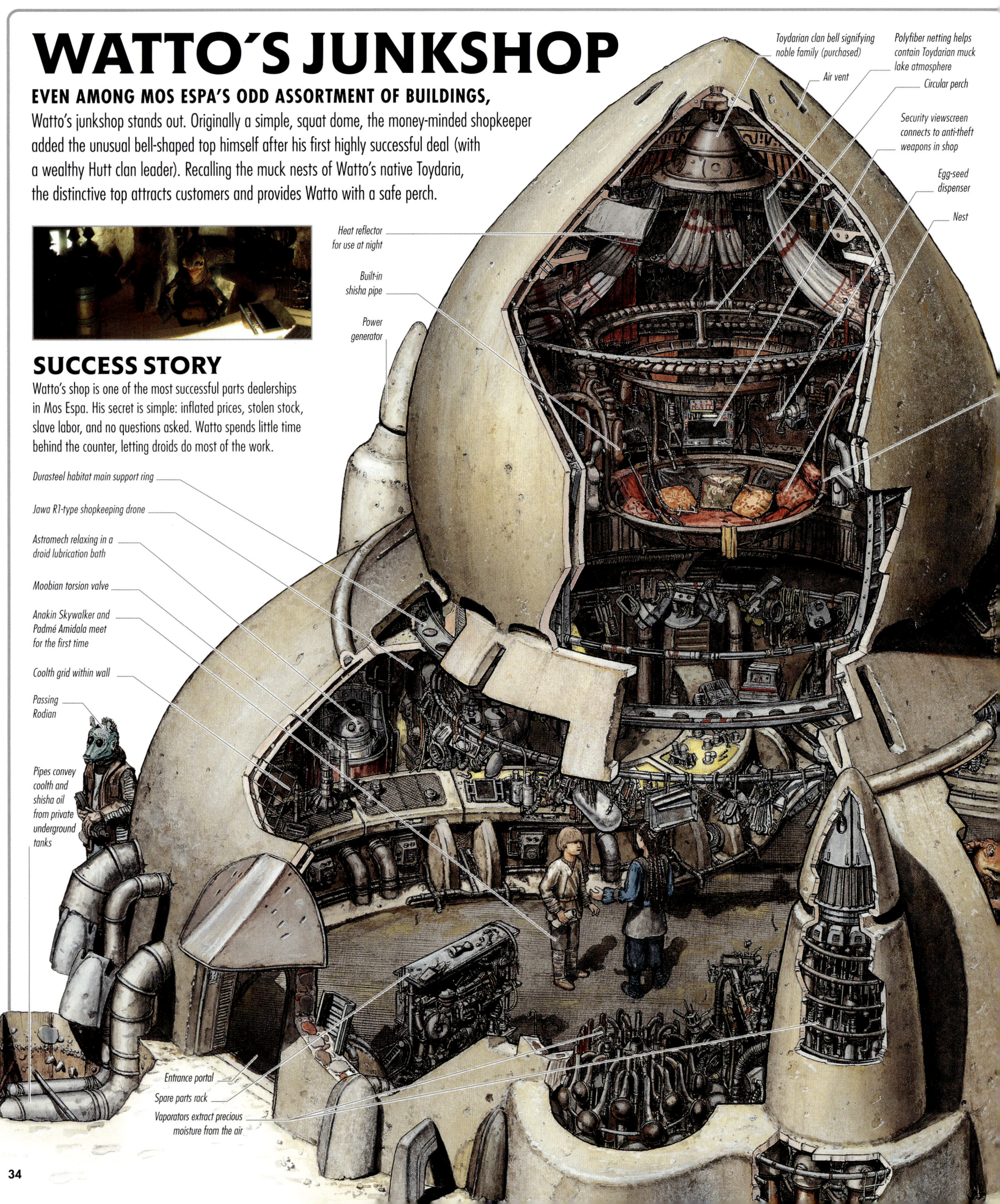

- Toydarian clan bell signifying noble family (purchased)
- Air vent
- Polyfiber netting helps contain Toydarian muck lake atmosphere
- Circular perch
- Security viewscreen connects to anti-theft weapons in shop
- Egg-seed dispenser
- Nest
- Heat reflector for use at night
- Built-in shisha pipe
- Power generator
- Durasteel habitat main support ring
- Jawa R1-type shopkeeping drone
- Astromech relaxing in a droid lubrication bath
- Moobian torsion valve
- Anakin Skywalker and Padmé Amidala meet for the first time
- Coolth grid within wall
- Passing Rodian
- Pipes convey coolth and shisha oil from private underground tanks
- Entrance portal
- Spare parts rack
- Vaporators extract precious moisture from the air

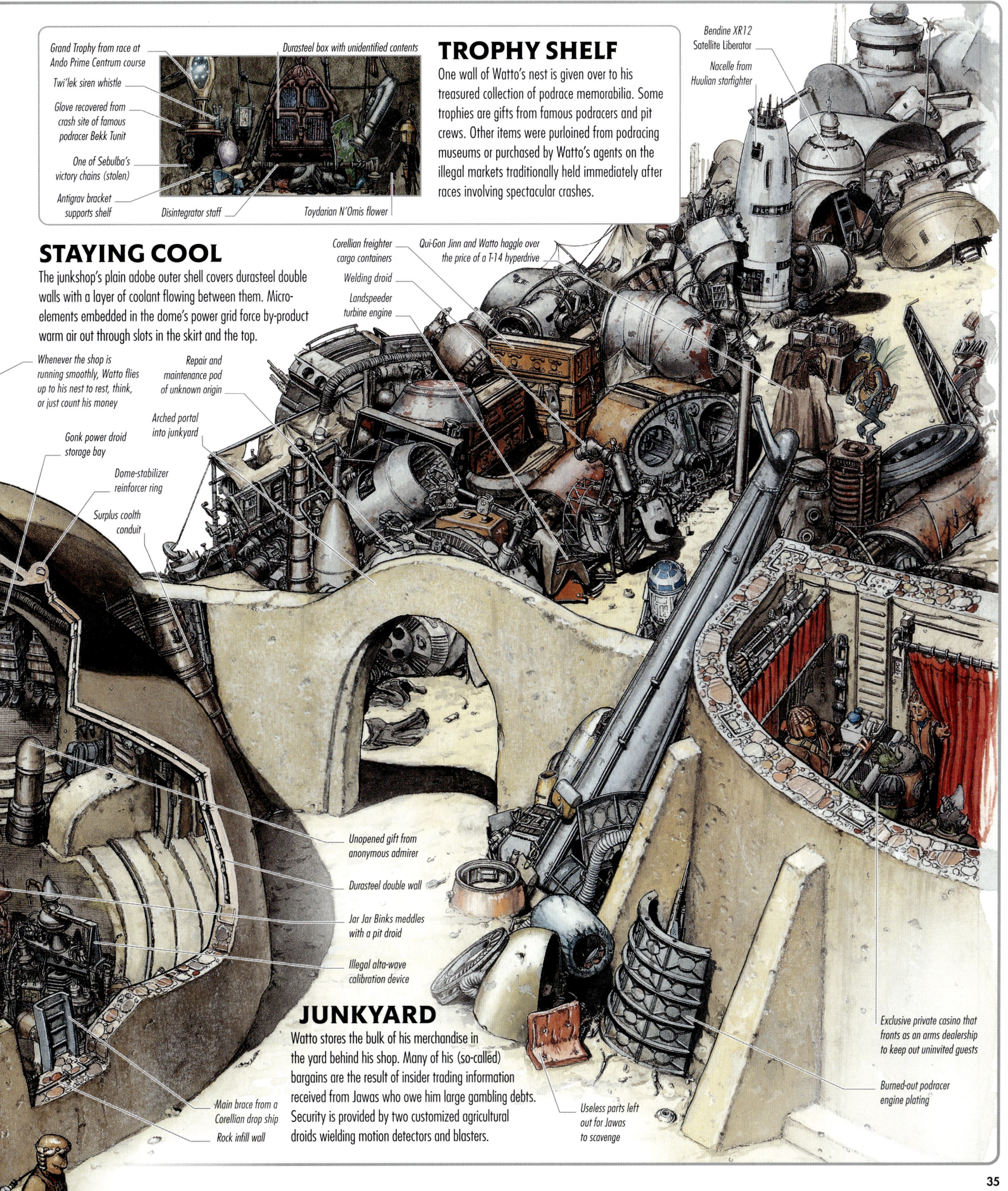

TROPHY SHELF

One wall of Watto's nest is given over to his treasured collection of podrace memorabilia. Some trophies are gifts from famous podracers and pit crews. Other items were purloined from podracing museums or purchased by Watto's agents on the illegal markets traditionally held immediately after races involving spectacular crashes.

- Grand Trophy from race at Ando Prime Centrum course
- Durasteel box with unidentified contents
- Twi'lek siren whistle
- Glove recovered from crash site of famous podracer Bekk Tunit
- One of Sebulba's victory chains (stolen)
- Antigrav bracket supports shelf
- Disintegrator staff
- Toydarian N'Omis flower
- Bendine XR12 Satellite Liberator
- Nacelle from Huulian starfighter

STAYING COOL

The junkshop's plain adobe outer shell covers durasteel double walls with a layer of coolant flowing between them. Micro-elements embedded in the dome's power grid force by-product warm air out through slots in the skirt and the top.

- Whenever the shop is running smoothly, Watto flies up to his nest to rest, think, or just count his money
- Gonk power droid storage bay
- Arched portal into junkyard
- Dome-stabilizer reinforcer ring
- Surplus coolth conduit
- Repair and maintenance pod of unknown origin
- Corellian freighter cargo containers
- Qui-Gon Jinn and Watto haggle over the price of a T-14 hyperdrive
- Welding droid
- Landspeeder turbine engine

JUNKYARD

Watto stores the bulk of his merchandise in the yard behind his shop. Many of his (so-called) bargains are the result of insider trading information received from Jawas who owe him large gambling debts. Security is provided by two customized agricultural droids wielding motion detectors and blasters.

- Unopened gift from anonymous admirer
- Durasteel double wall
- Jar Jar Binks meddles with a pit droid
- Illegal alta-wave calibration device
- Main brace from a Corellian drop ship
- Rock infill wall
- Useless parts left out for Jawas to scavenge
- Exclusive private casino that fronts as an arms dealership to keep out uninvited guests
- Burned-out podracer engine plating

35

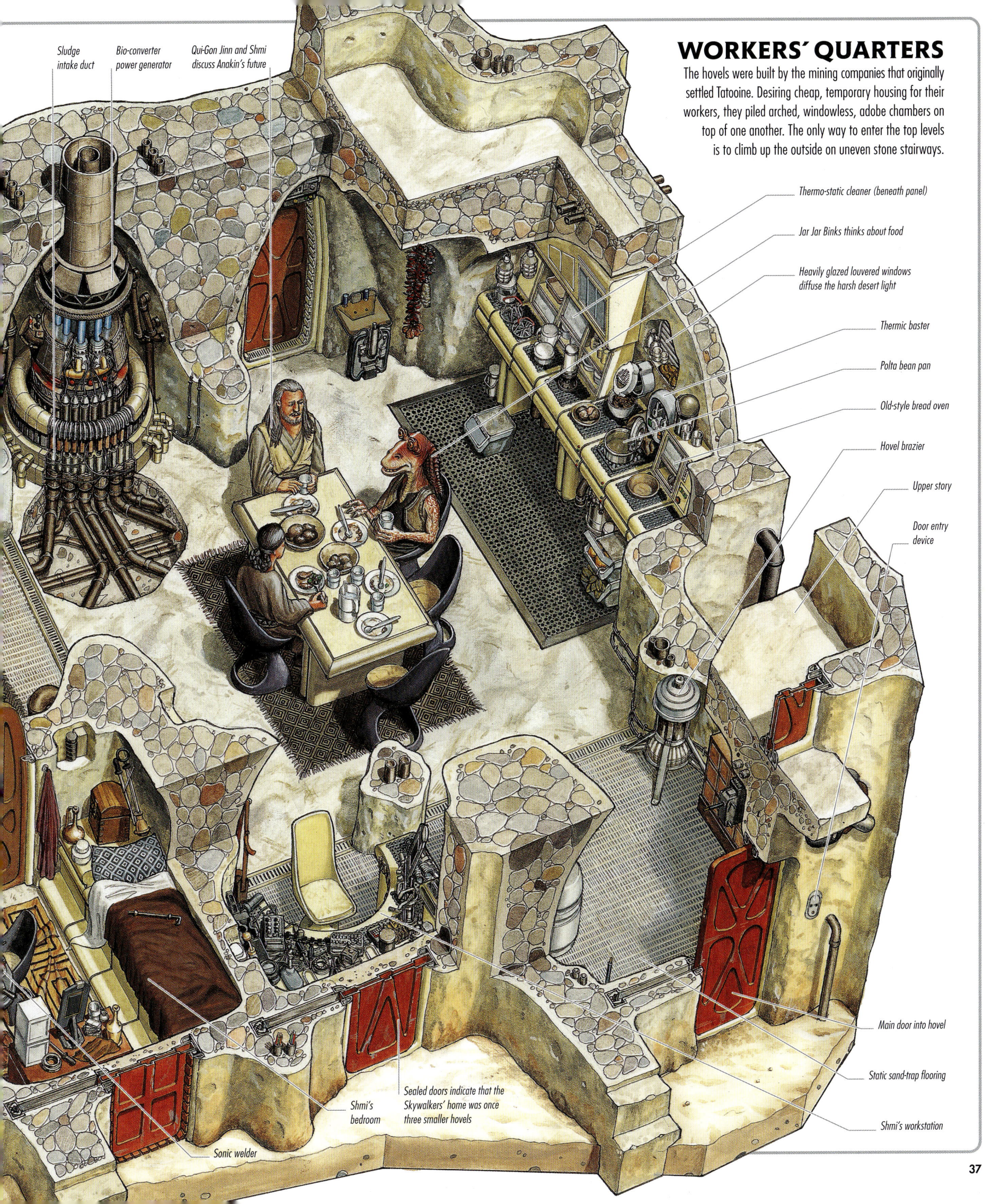

WORKERS' QUARTERS

The hovels were built by the mining companies that originally settled Tatooine. Desiring cheap, temporary housing for their workers, they piled arched, windowless, adobe chambers on top of one another. The only way to enter the top levels is to climb up the outside on uneven stone stairways.

- Sludge intake duct
- Bio-converter power generator
- Qui-Gon Jinn and Shmi discuss Anakin's future
- Thermo-static cleaner (beneath panel)
- Jar Jar Binks thinks about food
- Heavily glazed louvered windows diffuse the harsh desert light
- Thermic baster
- Polta bean pan
- Old-style bread oven
- Hovel brazier
- Upper story
- Door entry device
- Main door into hovel
- Static sand-trap flooring
- Shmi's workstation
- Sealed doors indicate that the Skywalkers' home was once three smaller hovels
- Shmi's bedroom
- Sonic welder

37

MOS ESPA CIRCUIT

HOST TO THE EAGERLY AWAITED Boonta Eve Classic and countless other races, Mos Espa podrace circuit weaves around a broad, flat-topped mountain called Ben's Mesa. Its cliff-like sides help ensure that scheming racers stick to the official course. Nevertheless, pilots continue to experiment with new shortcuts through the desert wilderness—no pilot or fan has ever agreed which route guarantees a spectacular win.

BEGGAR'S CANYON

On non-race days, Tatooine youngsters sneak into the section of the course known as Beggar's Canyon. Here, in the winding channels of this dry river bed, they push their souped-up landspeeders and super-fast skyhoppers to the limit, dreaming that one day they might be hometown heroes.

Seasoned racers have come to believe that the faces that can be discerned in the stones of Mushroom Mesa change expressions when viewed from different angles

MUSHROOM MESA

EBE CRATER VALLEY

Dead Man's Turn

Diablo Cut

Stone Needle

The Notch

BEGGAR'S CANYON

Ben's Mesa, named after Ben Neluent, the first great Tatooine-born racer, who lost his life in a spectacular attempt to scale the central mesa

BEN'S MESA

The sudden drop into Ebe Crater Valley causes many crashes; in the third lap, Sebulba bumps the ground but quickly regains control

LAGUNA CAVES

JAG CRAG GORGE

THE WHIP

DESERT PLAIN

DUNE SEA

Service ramps provide race personnel with access to valley floors when they need to scavenge for parts or make occasional repairs to cam droids

The small houses in Beggar's Canyon are inhabited by hermits who were chased out of Mos Espa (and bounty hunters on the run)

Lesser races than the Boonta Eve avoid the perilous Arch Canyon, routing pilots over the Dune Sea instead

2 Ben Quadinaros is one of many pilots who stall on the starting grid. Usually, they are moved quickly to avoid collision with pilots returning at the end of lap one. In Ben's case, however, his podracer explodes before pit droids can get to him.

3 Total concentration is needed in Mushroom Mesa, where shadows and harsh sunlight play tricks on pilots' depth perception. Mawhonic's dreams of winning are dashed when he focuses on his competitors rather than the course in lap one.

4 No pilot has yet managed to race up the steep gradient of a service ramp, control the machine as it flips beyond its maximum repulsorlift altitude, and descend safely further along the circuit. Yet Anakin Skywalker makes podrace history by doing just this.

5 For Jawas, podraces are fabulous scavenging opportunities. These cloaked Tatooine natives work in teams to cover as much of the circuit as possible, competing with P-100 salvage droids to pick up scrap engine parts from crash sites.

6 Sebulba treats the long, flat Desert Plain as light relief from the more demanding and difficult sections of the circuit. Inevitably, it is here that his vile mind turns to dirty tricks—and here that he brings down Mars Guo in the second lap.

7 In lap one, Ratts Tyerell crashes into a stalactite in Laguna Caves. Even if he had survived, he could have expected no help from rescue teams, who avoid the caves from fear of the krayt dragon that inhabits them.

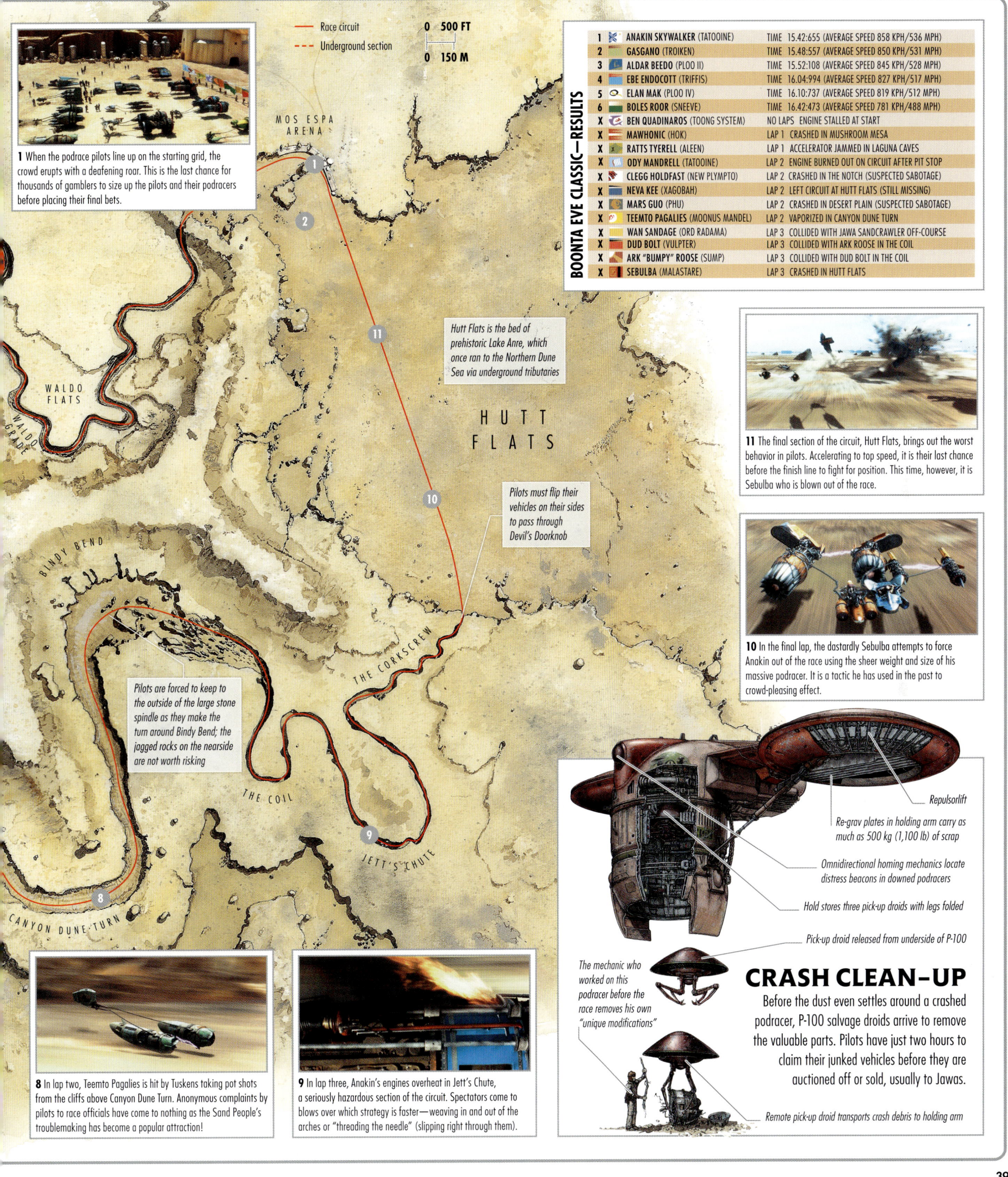

MOS ESPA ARENA

THE IMMENSE GRANDSTANDS of Mos Espa Arena are cradled within a natural canyon amphitheater on the edge of the Northern Dune Sea. Constructed of sandrock and ditanium over durasteel supports, the arena seats more than 100,000 fans—though many more squeeze in for major events like the Boonta Eve Classic. While high-priced tickets for podraces are widely sold to gullible offworlders, Tatooine's regulars simply turn up on speeders and push their way into the barely regulated stands.

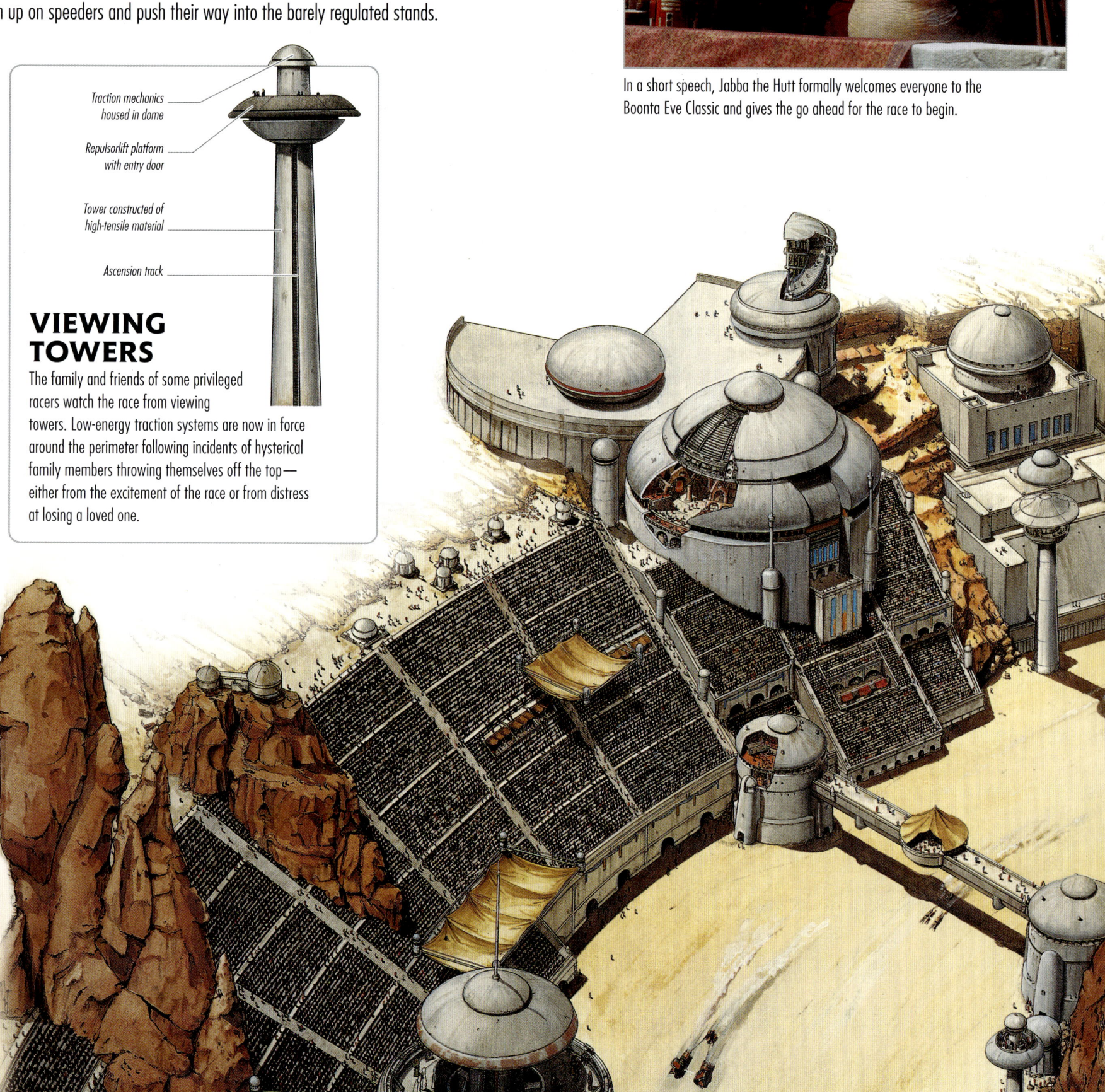

In a short speech, Jabba the Hutt formally welcomes everyone to the Boonta Eve Classic and gives the go ahead for the race to begin.

Traction mechanics housed in dome

Repulsorlift platform with entry door

Tower constructed of high-tensile material

Ascension track

VIEWING TOWERS

The family and friends of some privileged racers watch the race from viewing towers. Low-energy traction systems are now in force around the perimeter following incidents of hysterical family members throwing themselves off the top—either from the excitement of the race or from distress at losing a loved one.

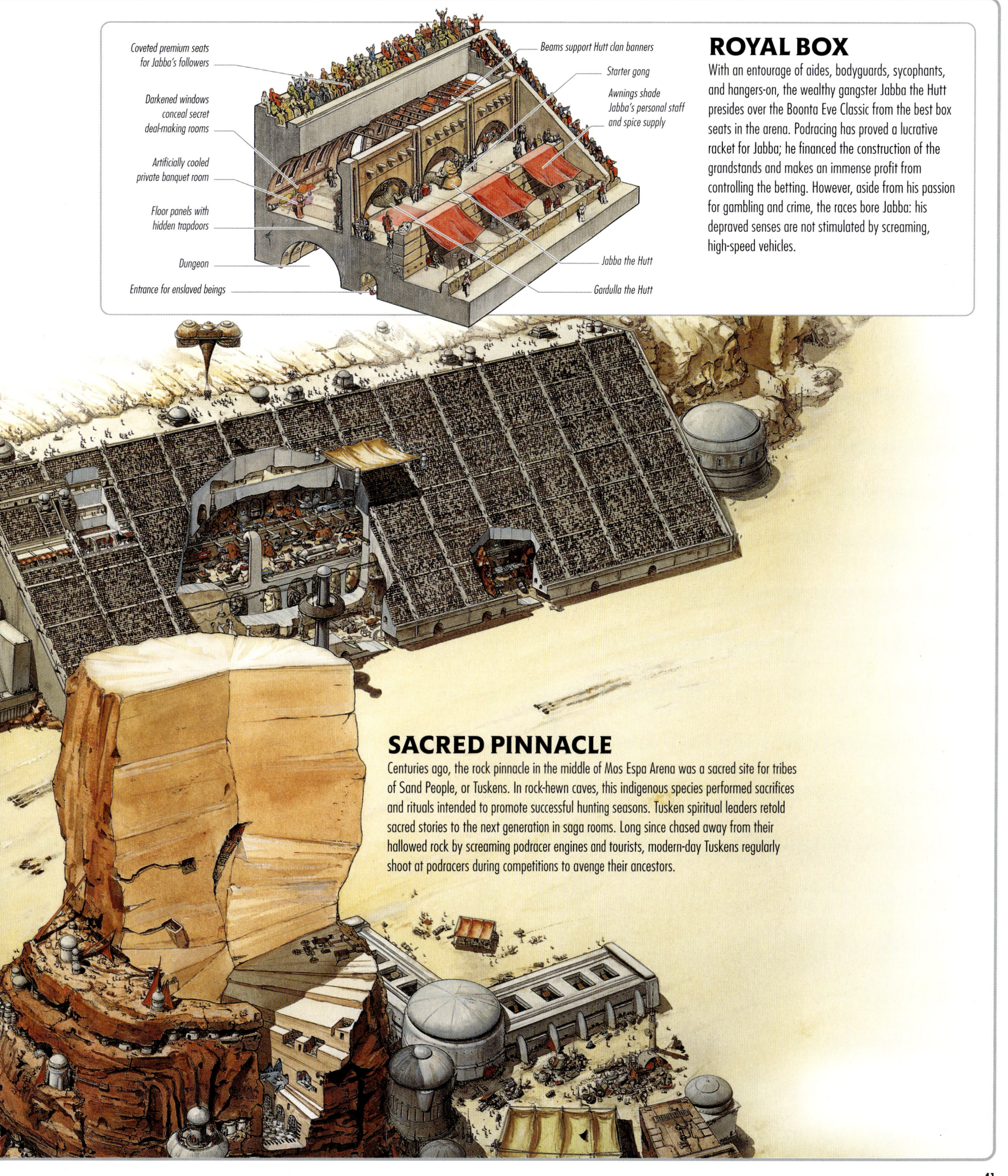

ROYAL BOX

With an entourage of aides, bodyguards, sycophants, and hangers-on, the wealthy gangster Jabba the Hutt presides over the Boonta Eve Classic from the best box seats in the arena. Podracing has proved a lucrative racket for Jabba; he financed the construction of the grandstands and makes an immense profit from controlling the betting. However, aside from his passion for gambling and crime, the races bore Jabba: his depraved senses are not stimulated by screaming, high-speed vehicles.

- Coveted premium seats for Jabba's followers
- Darkened windows conceal secret deal-making rooms
- Artificially cooled private banquet room
- Floor panels with hidden trapdoors
- Dungeon
- Entrance for enslaved beings
- Beams support Hutt clan banners
- Starter gong
- Awnings shade Jabba's personal staff and spice supply
- Jabba the Hutt
- Gardulla the Hutt

SACRED PINNACLE

Centuries ago, the rock pinnacle in the middle of Mos Espa Arena was a sacred site for tribes of Sand People, or Tuskens. In rock-hewn caves, this indigenous species performed sacrifices and rituals intended to promote successful hunting seasons. Tusken spiritual leaders retold sacred stories to the next generation in saga rooms. Long since chased away from their hallowed rock by screaming podracer engines and tourists, modern-day Tuskens regularly shoot at podracers during competitions to avenge their ancestors.

MOS ESPA ARENA CONTINUED

CONCESSIONS CONCOURSES

Once fans are safely inside the arena, armed Hutt-controlled managers "urge" them to visit the various concessions concourses. Here, they can place bets, purchase souvenirs, visit exhibits, and test-drive scaled-down podracers. Many would-be podrace pilots get their first taste for the sport here—often smashing up stalls and exhibits in the process.

FROM LOCAL CULT TO GRAND SPECTACLE

For a long time before the arena was built, Tatooine's thrill-seekers held free-for-all, no-holds-barred races here, first on animal-drawn carts, then on hanno speeders (a precursor to the landspeeder), and, finally, on podracers. The era of modern podracing was instigated on Malastare by a fearless alien racer called Gustab Wenbus, who entered himself on a virtually untested, super-fast prototype podracer that had been designed for him by a rogue mechanic called Phoebos. As use of these death-defying podracers became standard, podracing on Tatooine quickly began to draw fans from far across the space lanes.

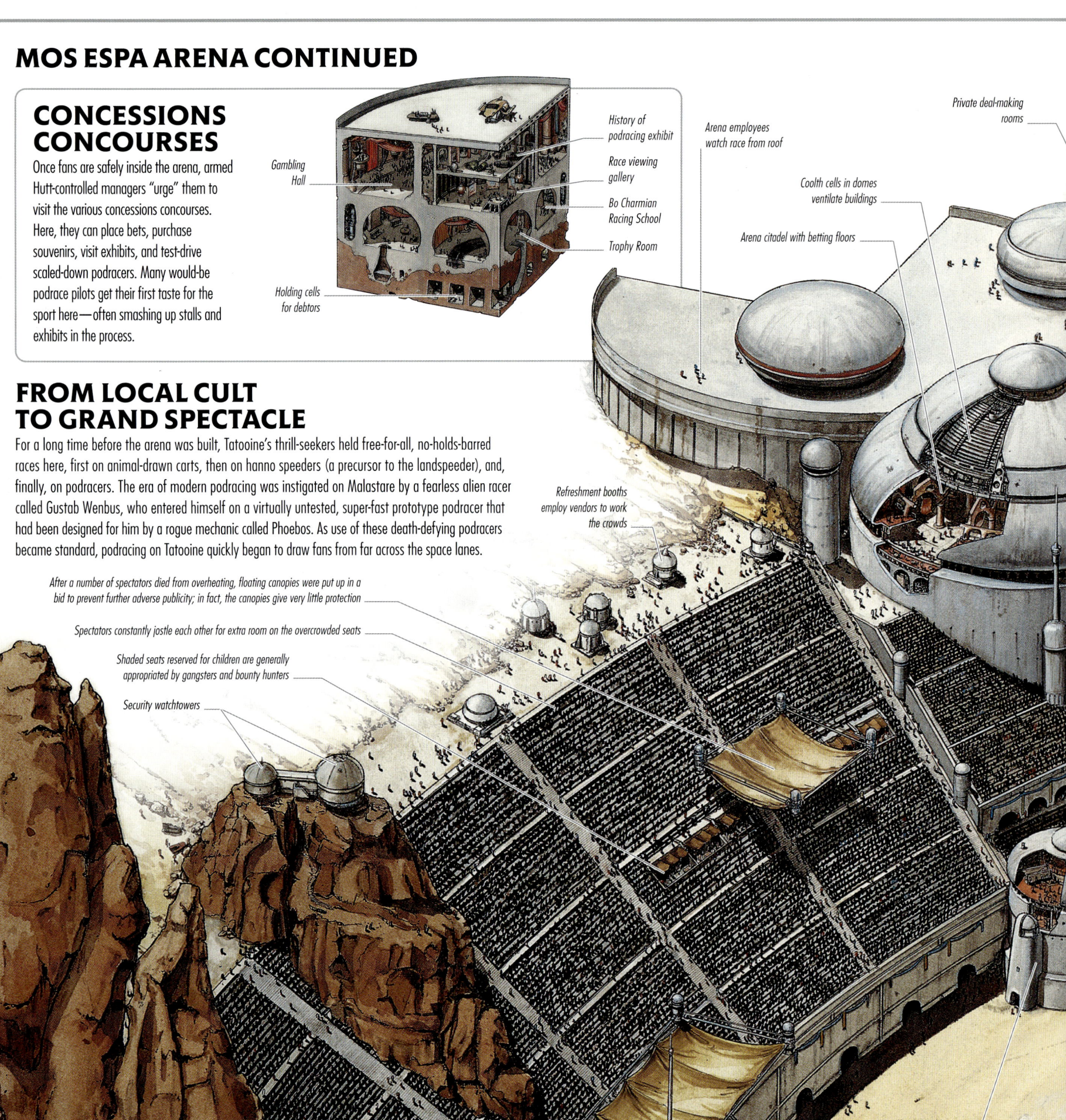

Gambling Hall
History of podracing exhibit
Race viewing gallery
Bo Charmian Racing School
Trophy Room
Holding cells for debtors
Private deal-making rooms
Arena employees watch race from roof
Coolth cells in domes ventilate buildings
Arena citadel with betting floors
Refreshment booths employ vendors to work the crowds
After a number of spectators died from overheating, floating canopies were put up in a bid to prevent further adverse publicity; in fact, the canopies give very little protection
Spectators constantly jostle each other for extra room on the overcrowded seats
Shaded seats reserved for children are generally appropriated by gangsters and bounty hunters
Security watchtowers
Race officials' building
Sebulba in first place

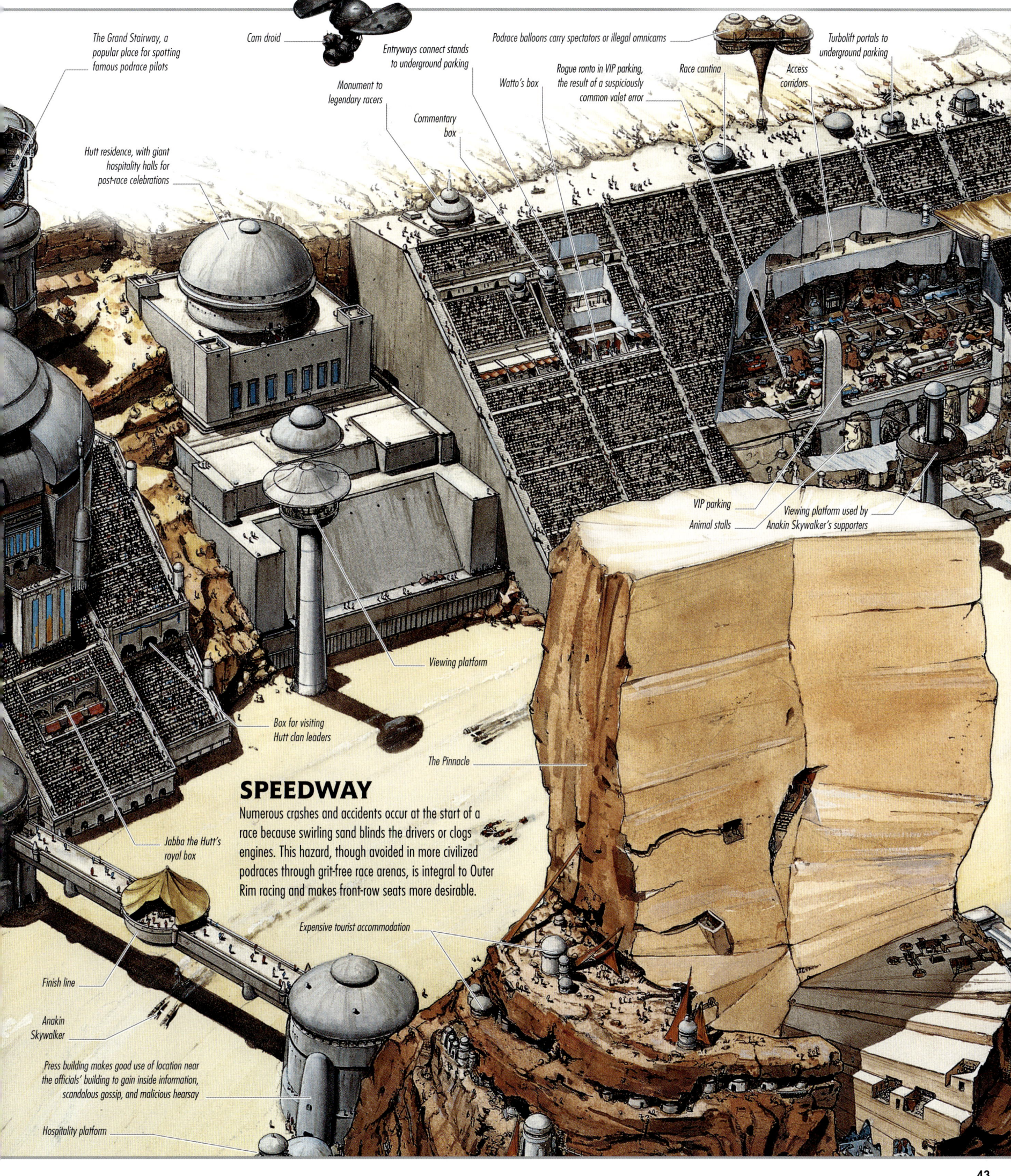

SPEEDWAY

Numerous crashes and accidents occur at the start of a race because swirling sand blinds the drivers or clogs engines. This hazard, though avoided in more civilized podraces through grit-free race arenas, is integral to Outer Rim racing and makes front-row seats more desirable.

- The Grand Stairway, a popular place for spotting famous podrace pilots
- Cam droid
- Entryways connect stands to underground parking
- Podrace balloons carry spectators or illegal omnicams
- Turbolift portals to underground parking
- Hutt residence, with giant hospitality halls for post-race celebrations
- Monument to legendary racers
- Watto's box
- Rogue ronto in VIP parking, the result of a suspiciously common valet error
- Race cantina
- Access corridors
- Commentary box
- VIP parking
- Animal stalls
- Viewing platform used by Anakin Skywalker's supporters
- Viewing platform
- Box for visiting Hutt clan leaders
- The Pinnacle
- Jabba the Hutt's royal box
- Expensive tourist accommodation
- Finish line
- Anakin Skywalker
- Press building makes good use of location near the officials' building to gain inside information, scandalous gossip, and malicious hearsay
- Hospitality platform

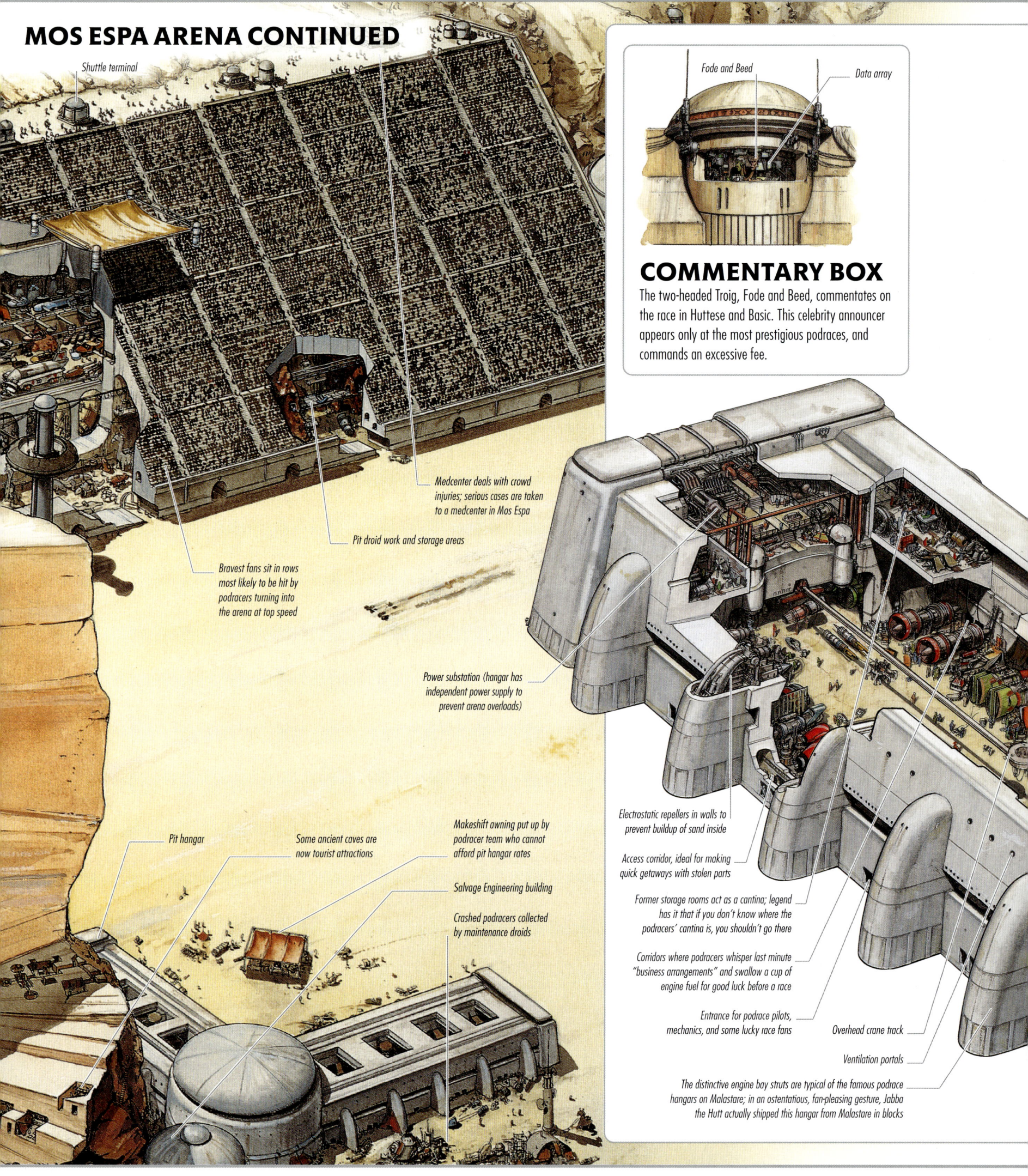

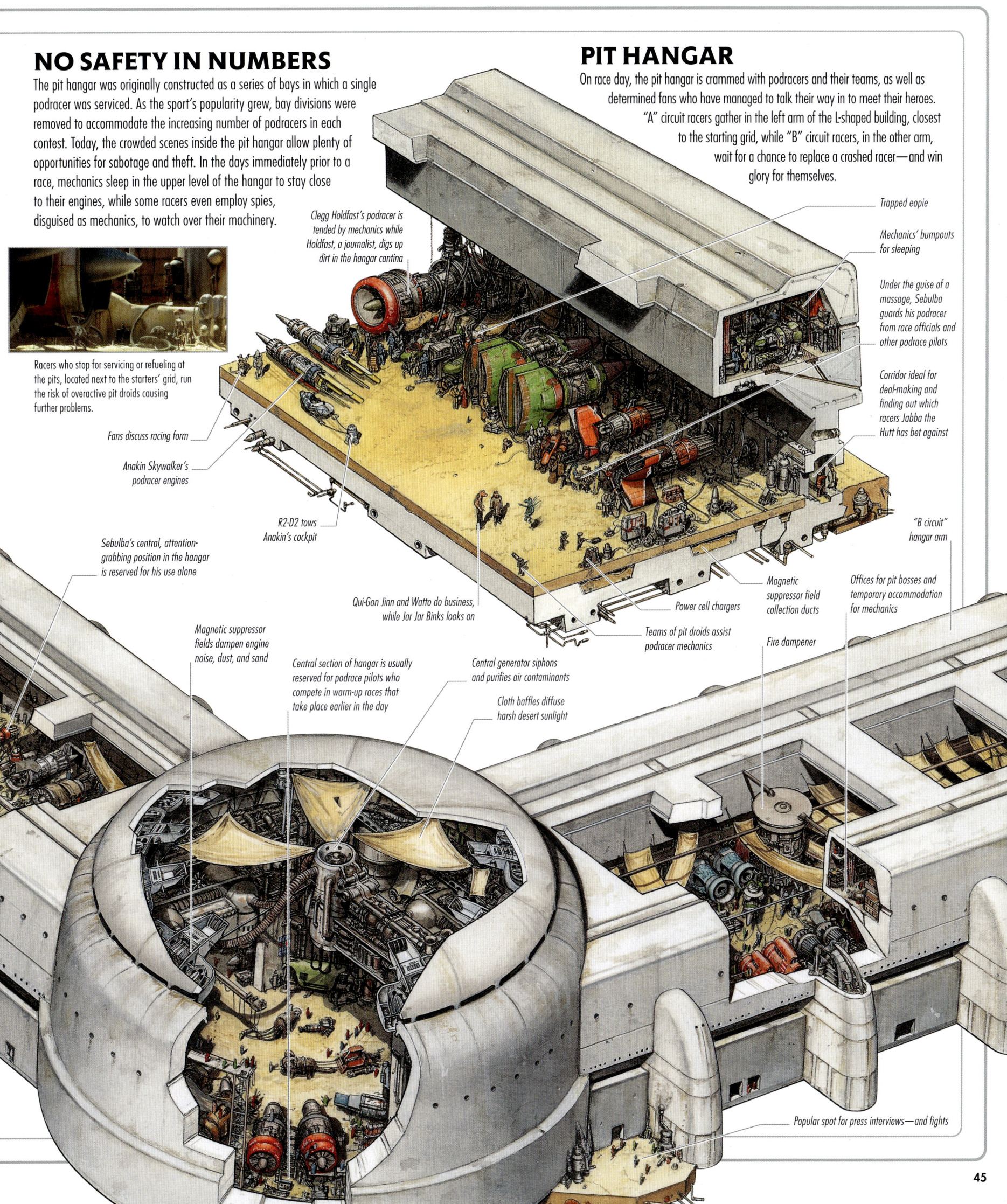

CORUSCANT

CAPITAL OF THE REPUBLIC, seat of government, and home of the powerful Jedi Order, Coruscant is the most important planet in the galaxy. One of the original Core Worlds that grouped together at the birth of the Republic, Coruscant outmaneuvered its early rivals to become the economic and cultural engine of the interplanetary community as it expanded along newly charted hyperspace lanes. As these grew into well-traveled trade routes, and scouts explored increasingly far-flung planets, large numbers of alien species made the return trip to Coruscant, swelling its population. Though not located at the geographic center of the galaxy, Coruscant's status as the effective center of the Republic led to it being awarded the coordinates 0-0-0 on standard navigation charts. Many born on Outer Rim worlds dream of reaching the galaxy's brilliant heart and proving themselves here, for whoever rules Coruscant is truly in control of the galaxy.

CITY SKYLINE

Coruscant's dazzling skyline is a potent symbol of the power and authority concentrated in the city. Many of its buildings reach 6,000 meters (20,000 feet) into the atmosphere, with sleek, transparisteel edifices standing next to older duracrete structures. Negotiating a landing path through these towering skyscrapers is not a task for the fainthearted. Tour operator pilots demand high fees for taking wide-eyed offworlders on breathtaking cruises over the planet's surface. Coruscant's air traffic is constant and busy, with large passenger ships traveling along autonavigated skylanes and smaller air taxis crisscrossing these routes to take high-paying passengers directly to their destinations.

JEDI TEMPLE

Below the towers of the Jedi Temple, the surface of Coruscant is a dense sprawl sliced through with deep, canyon-like thoroughfares. The Temple itself is reached via a long, broad promenade, which provides a symbolic and physical transition from urban tumult to Jedi tranquility. The Temple's serene exterior hides a more pragmatic interior, with many hundreds of rooms where the Jedi train, practice, meditate, and debate the problems of the Republic.

GALACTIC SENATE

The Galactic Senate stands out at the heart of Coruscant's densely packed Federal District. Here, more than a thousand senators represent their worlds in a vast, arena-like chamber. Statues adorning the entrance concourse depict the Republic's Core World founders. As the Senate swelled over time with representatives of a bewildering variety of intelligent life, the point is occasionally raised that the Core Worlds' humanoid statues are no longer characteristic of the present-day, multi-species Republic.

FEDERAL DISTRICT

MORE THAN A TRILLION INDIVIDUALS of diverse species live on Coruscant, the most overpopulated, multifarious megatropolis in the galaxy. Most of them aspire to work for the institutions of galactic government located in the Federal District. Yet for many, life on Coruscant is a room in a low-level sector with artificial light and air, anonymous neighbors of unknown species, and a data-input job in a government sub-office. In this fast-paced, artificial world, few focus on anything outside their own ambitions. Now the institutions of government are in decline, with corruption, nepotism, and negligence decaying the Republic's ideals.

Seen from space, Coruscant's brilliance is only slightly dimmed by the planet's hazy cloud cover. Weather patterns are affected by the troposphere-piercing buildings that cover the planet's surface. Inside the tallest buildings, enormous differences of temperature and air pressure from bottom to top produce unusual and unpredictable microclimates.

SENATE APARTMENTS

Senator Palpatine resides in Coruscant's prestigious Federal District. Inhabited by citizens of incredible wealth (and some fame) who demand and receive complete privacy, *500 Republica* offers private turbolifts and clandestine security armaments. The building's stepped design incorporates 53 skydocks and can accommodate even the largest air taxis as well as private vessels.

SENATE LANDING PLATFORMS

Private repulsorlift landing platforms can be reserved for the thousands of sectorial representatives, aides, and visiting dignitaries who arrive and depart daily on Coruscant. Other visitors must make do with municipal landing platforms, which are many kilometers wide and usually severely overcrowded. Vehicles are routinely forced to maintain a holding pattern for several hours until a landing spot becomes available.

MULTILEVELED CITY

The skyscrapers of Coruscant cover the entire planet surface, dwarfing almost all of the original natural features, including mountains and (now dry) seas, which lie somewhere in the depths. The only exception is the peak of Umate, the tallest Coruscanti mountain, which is visible at the center of Monument Plaza on Level 5127. Lower levels have been largely abandoned to fearsome scavengers.

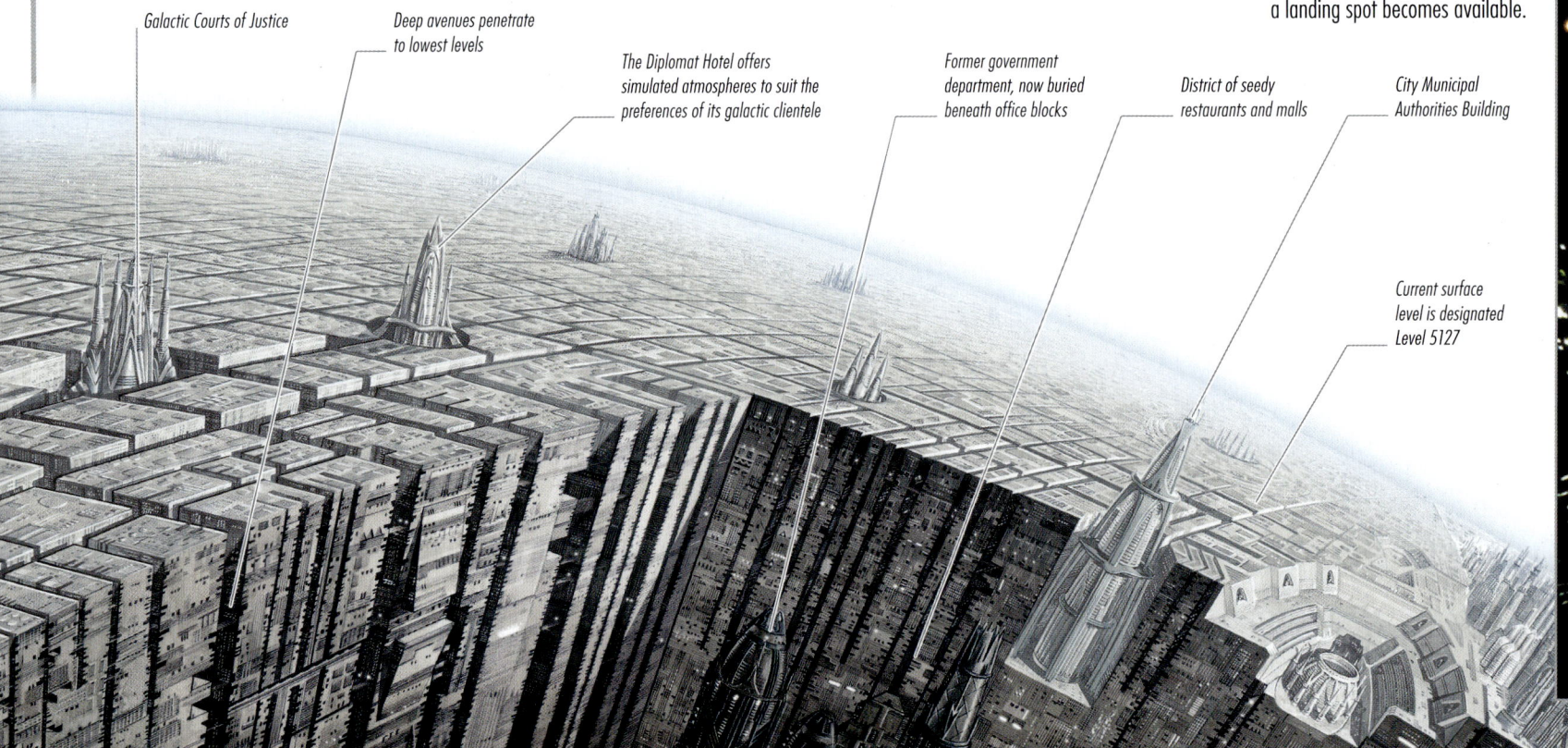

- Galactic Courts of Justice
- Deep avenues penetrate to lowest levels
- The Diplomat Hotel offers simulated atmospheres to suit the preferences of its galactic clientele
- Former government department, now buried beneath office blocks
- District of seedy restaurants and malls
- City Municipal Authorities Building
- Current surface level is designated Level 5127

ATMOSPHERES

In the top levels of Coruscant, the richest citizens breathe their preferred choice of gas in high-grade, purified form. Their buildings are routinely scanned for impurities, and problems are dealt with by teams of quality-control droids. In the dirty underworld of tunnels and corridors at the base of the massive buildings, inhabitants struggle to exist on barely breathable combinations of waste gases. Many regular visitors to Coruscant choose to bring their own air supply to last the length of their stay.

PALPATINE'S GUEST APARTMENTS

When Queen Amidala travels to Coruscant, Senator Palpatine insists that she and her retinue stay in apartments in his own building. The expansive suite of rooms is thoughtfully decorated in Palpatine's preferred colors and fitted with remote bugging devices to ensure the complete safety of its regal guest during her stay. Armed guards at the door have been instructed to keep Palpatine fully informed of the queen's every move.

CLANDESTINE MEETINGS

The architecture of the Federal District is ideally suited to the duplicitous machinations of the political classes that inhabit it. Hidden in the shadows and winding corridors of the megastructures are innumerable balconies, secret rooms, and abandoned buildings, many of which are used by clandestine organizations. In the anonymity afforded by this immense labyrinth, Darth Maul meets with his shadowy mentor, Darth Sidious, on a balcony, unnoticed by the teeming metropolis around them.

GALACTIC SENATE

THE GALACTIC SENATE BUILDING replaces a smaller, more intimate debating chamber instituted in the earliest days of the Republic. Reflecting the success of the expanding Republic, the enormous domed exterior of the modern structure is two kilometers (1.25 miles) in diameter. Inside, the debating rotunda accommodates platforms for more than 1,000 senators who represent the member worlds. The building's internal dynamics are designed to aid efficiency and the speed of decision-making. In fact, the convoluted network of private turbolifts and secret inner sanctums invites misuse, serving to facilitate underhanded dealmaking and avoidance of public accountability.

Receiving no natural light or air, the artificial atmosphere and illumination of the Senate's Great Rotunda is regulated to diminish senators' sense of time. This is intended to allow important debates to continue without being affected by nightfall.

SUPREME CHANCELLOR'S PODIUM

As the focus of the entire Senate rotunda, the supreme chancellor's 30 meter (100 feet)-tall podium is symbolic of authority and, increasingly, vulnerability. The podium itself retracts into the chancellor's office, which lies beneath the rotunda. Here, Supreme Chancellor Finis Valorum and his staff prepare before they are lifted into the debates raging above.

SENATORIAL BUSINESS

The Senate is responsible for creating laws, regulating commerce, mediating disputes, and making treaties. Decision-making is increasingly affected by powerful business interests such as the Trade Federation.

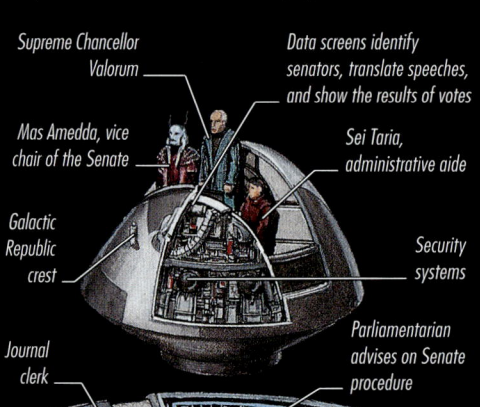

- Supreme Chancellor Valorum
- Mas Amedda, vice chair of the Senate
- Galactic Republic crest
- Journal clerk
- Data screens identify senators, translate speeches, and show the results of votes
- Sei Taria, administrative aide
- Security systems
- Parliamentarian advises on Senate procedure
- Sergeant at arms supervises message droids, pages, and other Senate workers
- Official reporter records the verbatim proceedings of the Senate
- Laser transmitters control information flow between podium and senatorial platforms

- Quarren senator
- Alarmed anti-saboteur mesh between floors
- Blast doors illustrate Neimoidian distrust of others
- Control room for senatorial platforms
- Mechno-chair used by high-ranking Neimoidians
- Intelligent mollusk keeps records
- Atmosphere-regulated meeting rooms allow Kel Dor to move about freely without their breathing equipment
- Heavy water pools mimic deep water habitat
- Imported luminescent and aromatic coral vegetation
- Artificial atmosphere generator
- Hologram of Neimoidian Trade Monarch
- Bubble-enclosed Kel Dor conference room
- Platform used by senator for Kashyyyk
- Turbolift transports senatorial guards to area behind senatorial platform (guards never enter a senator's chamber)
- Specially constructed wall cavities in Neimoidian offices are filled with covert listening and recording devices
- Wroshyr-wood cones imported from Kashyyyk
- In-wall climate control
- Venerated Wookiee elders take meetings while seated on cushions in wroshyr-paneled antechamber
- Napping rooms promote longevity and strength
- While drones take care of nearly all the Neimoidian delegation's work, aides and employees spend their work hours attending to the senator's needs
- Neimoidian-style senatorial throne with mechno-chair

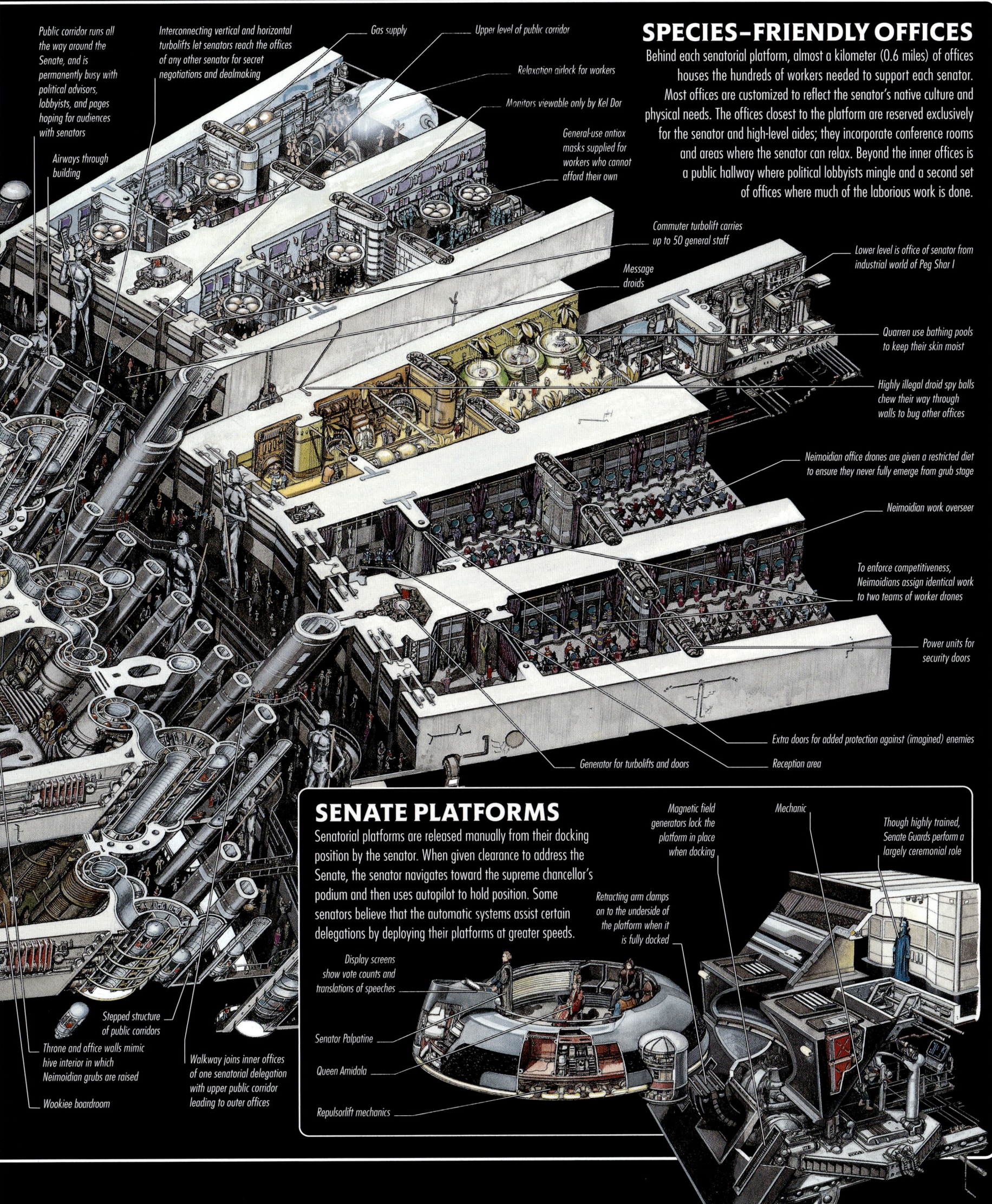

JEDI TEMPLE

TOWERING ABOVE A LOW-RISE SECTOR of the Federal
District to a height of a kilometer (0.6 miles), the Jedi Temple is the focus of Jedi life, the place where Jedi Knights are trained and housed. Centuries ago, it was more common for temples to be occupied throughout the galaxy; however, Coruscant's Temple has always been the primary hub for the Jedi Order—it is where the High Council often deliberates, and sometimes where prospective younglings are tested. Powerful reception/transmission antennas, using a wide range of broadcast systems, sprout from the top of the five towers. The communications array maintains contact with Jedi on far-flung missions in times when outpost temples are not used.

CONTEMPLATION STATIONS

Around the circumference of the High Council holomap room, a spacious, graceful balcony with three stations provides a place for calm contemplation and reflection. High-ranking Jedi are briefed in the holomap room before being sent on missions, and are encouraged to walk the balcony to focus their Force energies before leaving. It is also used by Jedi awaiting a sitting with the High Council.

HOLOMAP ROOMS

Central to the organization of Jedi activities throughout the galaxy is a pyramid system of holomaps. At the lowest level, 12 teams monitor in detail specific galactic areas. Potential problems are transferred to larger-scale holomaps for the attention of more senior Jedi. In this way, only the most serious issues reach the Jedi High Council and are plotted on their galaxy holomap.

Crowded lanes of air traffic carry Coruscant's ever-moving population around the planet

Each antenna transmits and receives data at different frequencies and with varying coverage

Door security panel

Turbolift utilizes Force-inspired internal dynamics to transport Jedi of vastly different sizes and shapes

Anakin Skywalker is tested by the Jedi High Council

Depa Billaba

Natural and circular motifs in floor mosaic symbolize harmony and balance

Eeth Koth

Yarael Poof

Adi Gallia

Internal corridor

Qui-Gon Jinn and Obi-Wan Kenobi wait on one of the tower's three Contemplation Stations

Topmast is a powerful transmitter incorporating a multi-frequency eradicator/scrambler

Plo Koon

Mace Windu

Yoda

Ki-Adi-Mundi

Masonry construction supported by high-tensile magnite

Saesee Tiin

Even Piell

Yaddle

Permern in windows helps balance gravity effects and maintain artificial air supply

Multi-field receiver assembly feeds multiple signals into holomap array

Oppo Rancisis

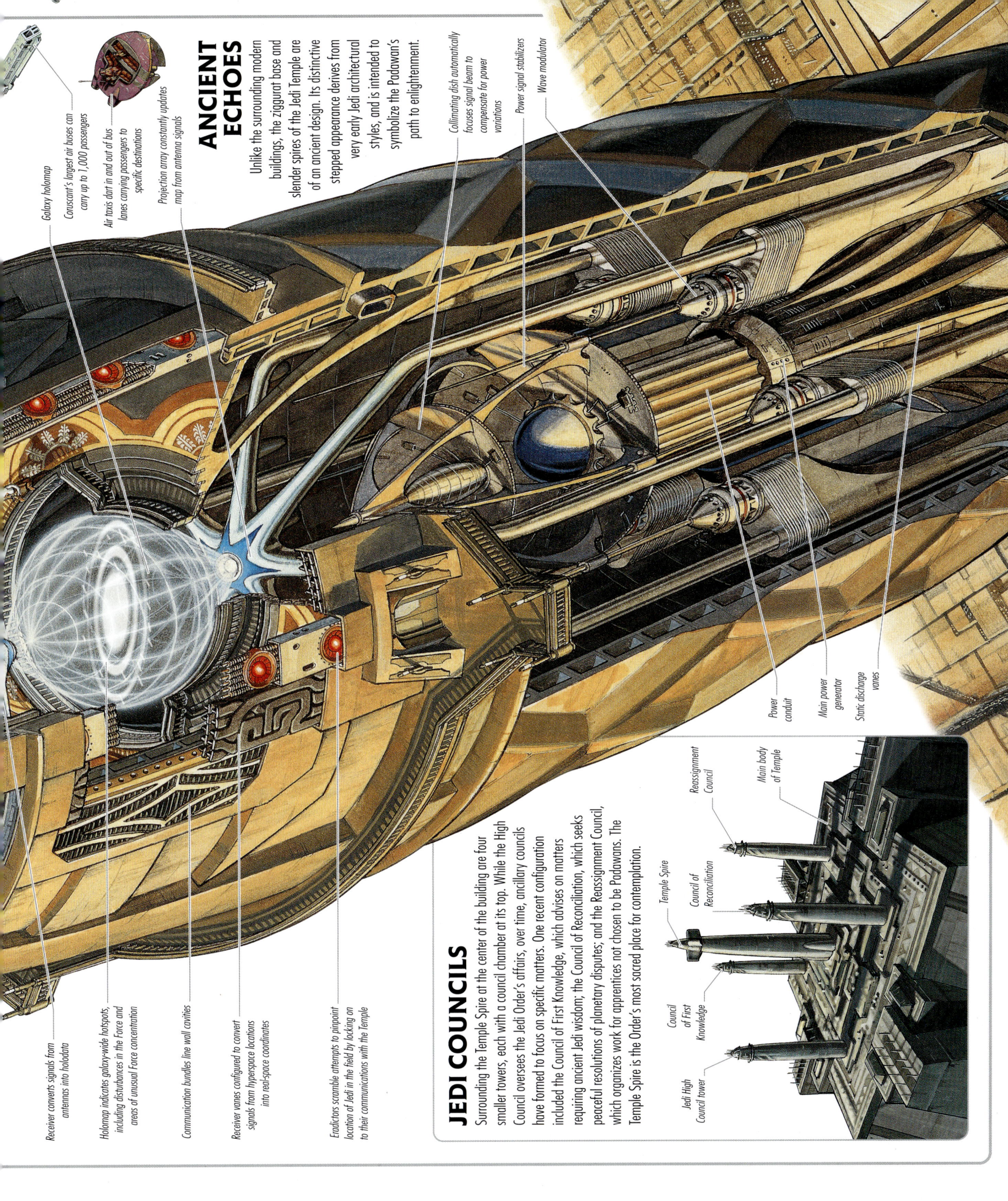

ANCIENT ECHOES

Unlike the surrounding modern buildings, the ziggurat base and slender spires of the Jedi Temple are of an ancient design. Its distinctive stepped appearance derives from very early Jedi architectural styles, and is intended to symbolize the Padawan's path to enlightenment.

- Galaxy holomap
- Coruscant's largest air buses can carry up to 1,000 passengers
- Air taxis dart in and out of bus lanes carrying passengers to specific destinations
- Projection array constantly updates map from antenna signals
- Collimating dish automatically focuses signal beam to compensate for power variations
- Power signal stabilizers
- Wave modulator
- Power conduit
- Main power generator
- Static discharge vanes
- Receiver converts signals from antennas into holodata
- Holomap indicates galaxy-wide hotspots, including disturbances in the Force and areas of unusual Force concentration
- Communication bundles line wall cavities
- Receiver vanes configured to convert signals from hyperspace locations into real-space coordinates
- Eradictors scramble attempts to pinpoint location of Jedi in the field by locking on to their communications with the Temple

JEDI COUNCILS

Surrounding the Temple Spire at the center of the building are four smaller towers, each with a council chamber at its top. While the High Council oversees the Jedi Order's affairs, over time, ancillary councils have formed to focus on specific matters. One recent configuration included the Council of First Knowledge, which advises on matters requiring ancient Jedi wisdom; the Council of Reconciliation, which seeks peaceful resolutions of planetary disputes; and the Reassignment Council, which organizes work for apprentices not chosen to be Padawans. The Temple Spire is the Order's most sacred place for contemplation.

- Reassignment Council
- Main body of Temple
- Temple Spire
- Council of Reconciliation
- Council of First Knowledge
- Jedi High Council tower

THE INVASION OF NABOO

EVEN WHILE THE TRADE FEDERATION BLOCKADES NABOO with a fleet of war freighters, its leaders finalize invasion plans with their shadowy Sith mentor. The Neimoidians do not share Darth Sidious' sinister interest in this small, relatively insignificant planet. However, they are persuaded that their victory will be easy—and ultimately profitable. On Sidious' orders, the invasion army has two primary objectives. The first is to sever Naboo's communication with the Senate. The second is to capture Queen Amidala and force her to sign a capitulation treaty. Sleek landing ships descend upon the planet, avoiding public commotion by sticking to remote areas. Under cover of darkness, the army mobilizes and takes up strategic positions. The next morning, the citizens of Theed are caught unaware by a devastating surprise attack.

LANDING SHIPS

Formations of massive C-9979 landing ships descend like vultures through Naboo's atmosphere. An elite group lands in the north of the planet, where Theed and the largest cities are found, while other groups target cities in the south and east. Each landing ship carries 11 MTTs (Multi-Troop Transports), 114 AATs (Armored Assault Tanks), and legions of droid troops. First to be deployed are droids on armed STAPs (Single Trooper Aerial Platforms), who act as scouts for the main army, seeking out any signs of resistance—including two Jedi who have evaded capture.

ENTER THE NEIMOIDIANS

Only once Theed is under battle droid control do the invasion's perpetrators show their faces. Nute Gunray and his attaché, Rune Haako, affect the air of conquerors as they make the short walk from their shuttle to Theed Palace to personally oversee the arrest of Queen Amidala and her government. Being naturally cautious and lazy, the Neimoidians rarely leave their ships, relying on droids to meet customers. But in this instance, they are keen to visit the palace for themselves, having been advised that its staterooms are full of priceless treasures.

THE FALL OF THEED

With its citizens rounded up into detention camps and its streets sealed, Theed becomes a ghost town, echoing only with the sounds of tanks rumbling and troops marching. The city's long era of peace and serenity has ended in a matter of hours. Queen Amidala and her staff are escorted from the palace by droid captors, to be taken to a camp. Even in her darkest hour, the queen refuses to abandon hope, but she knows she will need some extraordinary help from somewhere if her beloved home is to be saved.

ADVANCE OF EVIL

The invasion force that advances upon Theed in the sharp light of a Naboo early morning comprises 33 large transports, each carrying 112 battle droids, and 342 battle tanks, as well as droid starfighters and infantry. Each vehicle and battle droid is pre-programmed with a ground map of the city, with specific instructions for key objectives.

DEFENSE OF NABOO

WHEN THE TRADE FEDERATION INVADES NABOO, it expects little resistance from the planet's peace-loving inhabitants. But the invaders underestimate the courage and determination of its principal species, the Naboo and the Gungans, who overcome their traditional antipathy to form an unlikely alliance in the face of the emergency. The chief advantage the allies have is knowledge of the terrain. The Gungans amass a huge army in the swamps to lure the droid forces away from Theed, while the Naboo utilize hidden passages to infiltrate the palace and hangar, enabling them to mount attacks on multiple fronts.

While the inhabitants of Naboo struggle to rescue their planet from Trade Federation control, Qui-Gon Jinn and Obi-Wan Kenobi battle for their lives against a Sith warrior who appears to have an agenda all of his own.

SYMBOLIC MEETING PLACE

Naboo and Gungan leaders plan their battle strategy on the dividing line between Naboo and Gungan lands. Long considered a no-man's-land, a refuge for outcasts like Jar Jar Binks, the swamp edges will play host to regular Freedom of Naboo celebrations in years to come.

SEARCH FOR THE GUNGANS

Traversing through dense swampland along nearly impenetrable paths known only to Gungans, Jar Jar Binks guides the Naboo and Jedi to the Gungan sacred place. When they near the hidden entrance, Jar Jar is unsure of the protocol for allowing outsiders into such a restricted zone and uses a Gungan call to alert scouts to his presence. The path threads its way beneath a thick canopy of ancient trees until the party emerges in a dry clearing filled with Gungan refugees. The Gungans gather at their sacred place in times of anxiety and apparent danger. These evacuations prove to be valuable practice when the time comes for a genuine emergency.

SECRET OPERATIONS

On Captain Panaka's instructions, Theed's underground resistance movement infiltrates the hangar in advance of its liberation. Secretly, officers and guards have checked that their fighters have not been disabled by battle droids. They have also restored access to the hangar computer system in order to program battle flight-path coordinates.

GROUND WAR

Although the Naboo people are rounded up into camps en masse, the Gungans prove more difficult to reach. By the time the invading battle droids reach Otoh Gunga and the other underwater cities, they find them nearly empty and most of the Gungan populace evacuated. Convening in the swamps, the Gungans raise an army large enough to challenge Trade Federation troops on the Great Grass Plains, buying Captain Panaka's soldiers some much-needed time.

SPACE BATTLE

Naboo's pilot squadron, Bravo Flight, led by Ric Olié, is assigned the daunting task of knocking out the transmitter aboard the Droid Control Ship orbiting Naboo. Its combined firepower barely gets through the Control Ship's deflector shields. However, a reckless spin causes a split-second breach and Anakin Skywalker's craft shoots into the right-hand hangar arm toward the heart of the enemy.

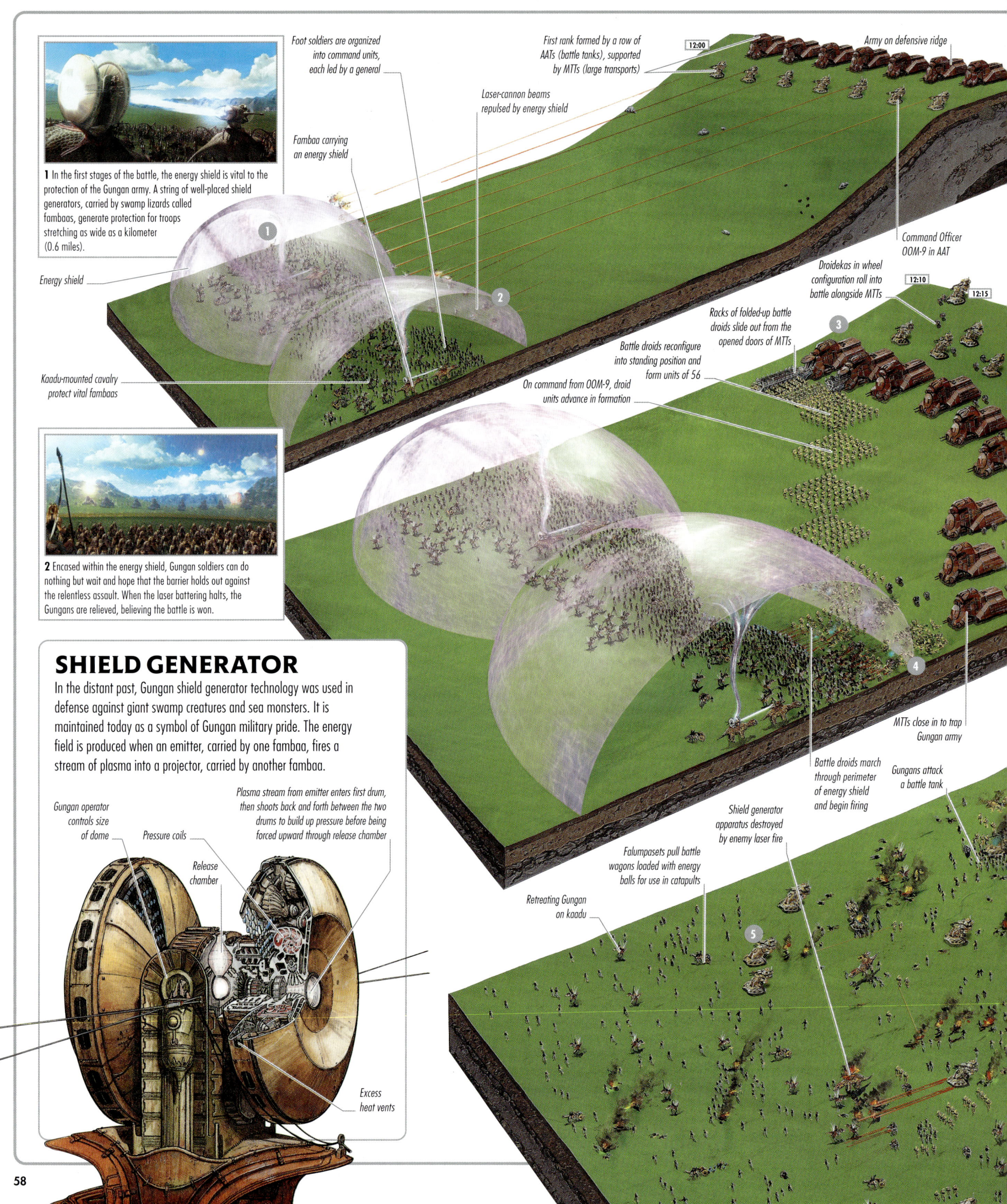

GRASS PLAINS BATTLE

THE CONFRONTATION BETWEEN Gungan troops and Trade Federation droids takes place 40 kilometers (25 miles) from Theed. On the morning of the battle, Gungan troops assemble under cover of the swamps. Soon after, the Neimoidians are alerted to the military buildup by rumors spread deliberately by Captain Panaka. The Gungan strategy is to wait until the droid army emerges from Theed to meet them on their own ground—in a spot near enough to the swamps to allow a hasty retreat if necessary. The plan works: by midday, two immense armies face each other across a shallow valley between ridges of low hills...

3 Deprived of an easy victory over the Gungans, Trade Federation battle tanks fall back. Agonizing moments of silence follow as MTTs (large transports) advance and begin unloading rack after rack of deadly battle droids.

GUNGAN BATTLE STRATEGY

Realizing that the Trade Federation's military might is far superior to their own, the Gungans plan to protect their army within a huge energy shield. The liquid energy surface repels laser bolts and large, slow-moving objects like tanks. Denied the option to wipe out the Gungans with their heavy artillery, the enemy is forced to send in individual battle droids. This gives the Gungans a fighting chance of engaging the droids long enough for the Naboo to capture the Viceroy.

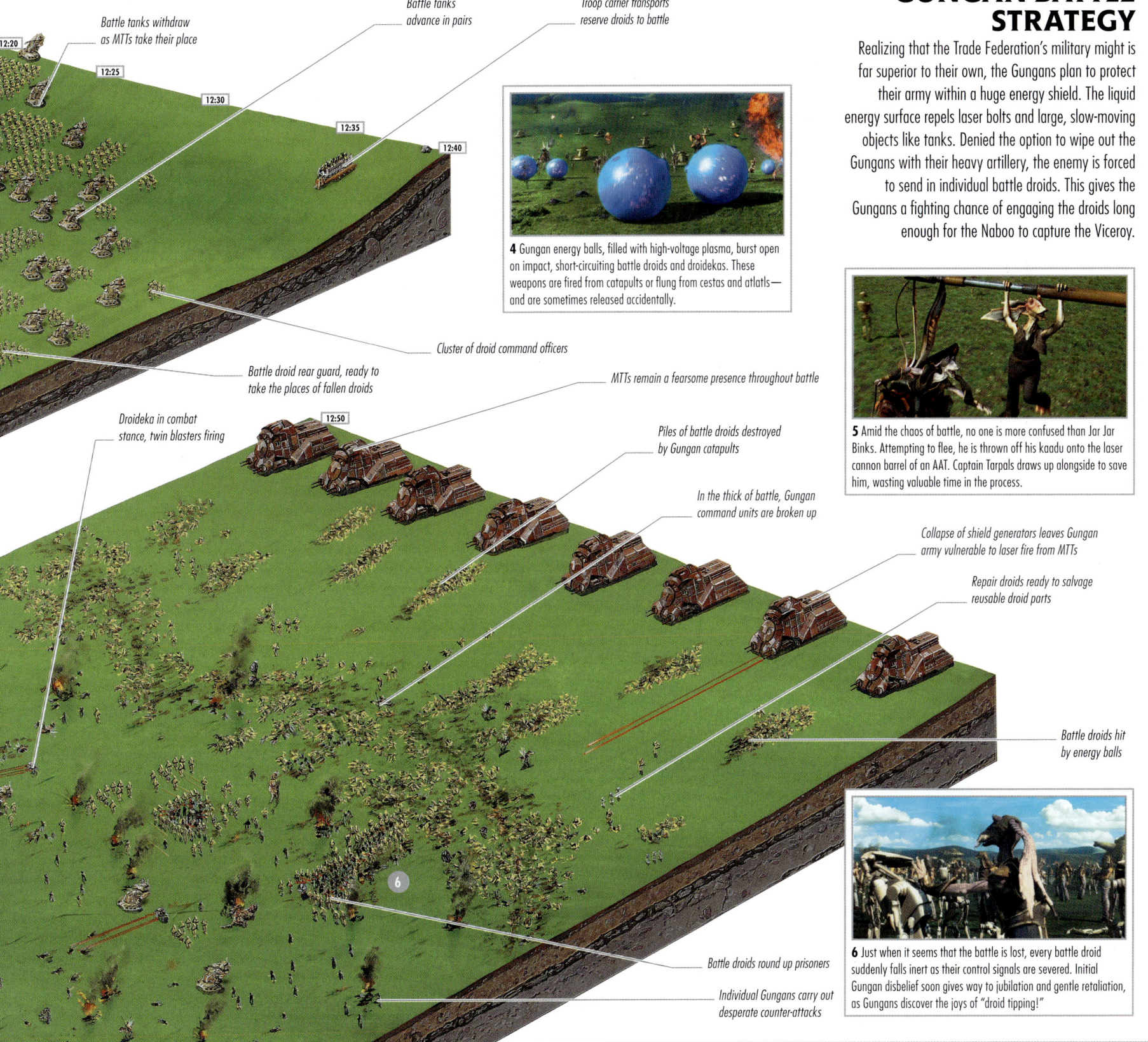

4 Gungan energy balls, filled with high-voltage plasma, burst open on impact, short-circuiting battle droids and droidekas. These weapons are fired from catapults or flung from cestas and atlatls— and are sometimes released accidentally.

5 Amid the chaos of battle, no one is more confused than Jar Jar Binks. Attempting to flee, he is thrown off his kaadu onto the laser cannon barrel of an AAT. Captain Tarpals draws up alongside to save him, wasting valuable time in the process.

6 Just when it seems that the battle is lost, every battle droid suddenly falls inert as their control signals are severed. Initial Gungan disbelief soon gives way to jubilation and gentle retaliation, as Gungans discover the joys of "droid tipping!"

Labels on diagram:
- Battle tanks withdraw as MTTs take their place
- Battle tanks advance in pairs
- Troop carrier transports reserve droids to battle
- Cluster of droid command officers
- Battle droid rear guard, ready to take the places of fallen droids
- MTTs remain a fearsome presence throughout battle
- Droideka in combat stance, twin blasters firing
- Piles of battle droids destroyed by Gungan catapults
- In the thick of battle, Gungan command units are broken up
- Collapse of shield generators leaves Gungan army vulnerable to laser fire from MTTs
- Repair droids ready to salvage reusable droid parts
- Battle droids hit by energy balls
- Battle droids round up prisoners
- Individual Gungans carry out desperate counter-attacks

GENERATOR BATTLE

WITH ITS SLEEK, MECHANISTIC INTERIOR LINES, Theed's immense power generator stands in stark contrast to the city's elegant, handcrafted aesthetic. Indeed, this ingenious feat of engineering is now a popular attraction in Theed. The gigantic machinery works day and night to mine and stabilize naturally occurring plasma from deep within the planet. The Naboo people rely on this plasmic energy, using it for trade and to power their own cities, spacecraft, and even the glowing bulbs on Queen Amidala's throne-room gown. During the Battle of Naboo, the power generator becomes the scene of a climactic battle between Darth Maul and the Jedi Qui-Gon Jinn and Obi-Wan Kenobi.

As Obi-Wan hangs on to a security beacon within the power generator's core tunnel, Darth Maul lashes out with his lightsaber.

BREAK WITH THE PAST

For centuries, Theed's energy supply was provided by small outlying mines. However, evidence of a vast plasma source below the city's cliff face led to the construction of the new generator. Its efficient machinery mines much more than the city itself needs.

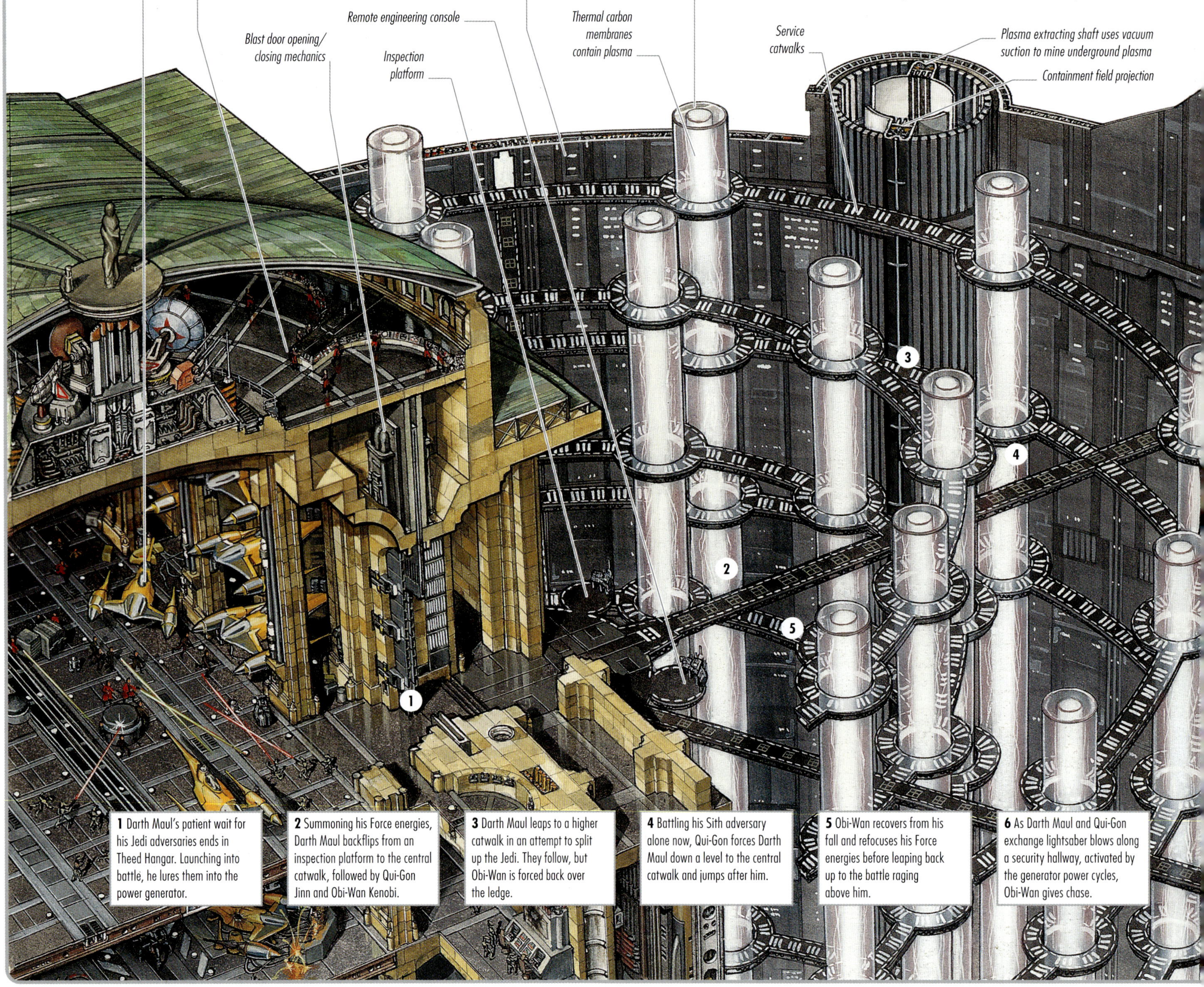

- Theed Hangar is liberated and fighter pilots take off for space battle
- Freed from battle droid control, Naboo flight controllers return to their stations
- Panels constantly monitor and compensate for pressure changes and power fluctuations
- Plasma from extracting shaft is forced through each of the acceleration shafts in turn to intensify the energy output
- Remote engineering console
- Thermal carbon membranes contain plasma
- Service catwalks
- Plasma extracting shaft uses vacuum suction to mine underground plasma
- Blast door opening/closing mechanics
- Inspection platform
- Containment field projection

1 Darth Maul's patient wait for his Jedi adversaries ends in Theed Hangar. Launching into battle, he lures them into the power generator.

2 Summoning his Force energies, Darth Maul backflips from an inspection platform to the central catwalk, followed by Qui-Gon Jinn and Obi-Wan Kenobi.

3 Darth Maul leaps to a higher catwalk in an attempt to split up the Jedi. They follow, but Obi-Wan is forced back over the ledge.

4 Battling his Sith adversary alone now, Qui-Gon forces Darth Maul down a level to the central catwalk and jumps after him.

5 Obi-Wan recovers from his fall and refocuses his Force energies before leaping back up to the battle raging above him.

6 As Darth Maul and Qui-Gon exchange lightsaber blows along a security hallway, activated by the generator power cycles, Obi-Wan gives chase.

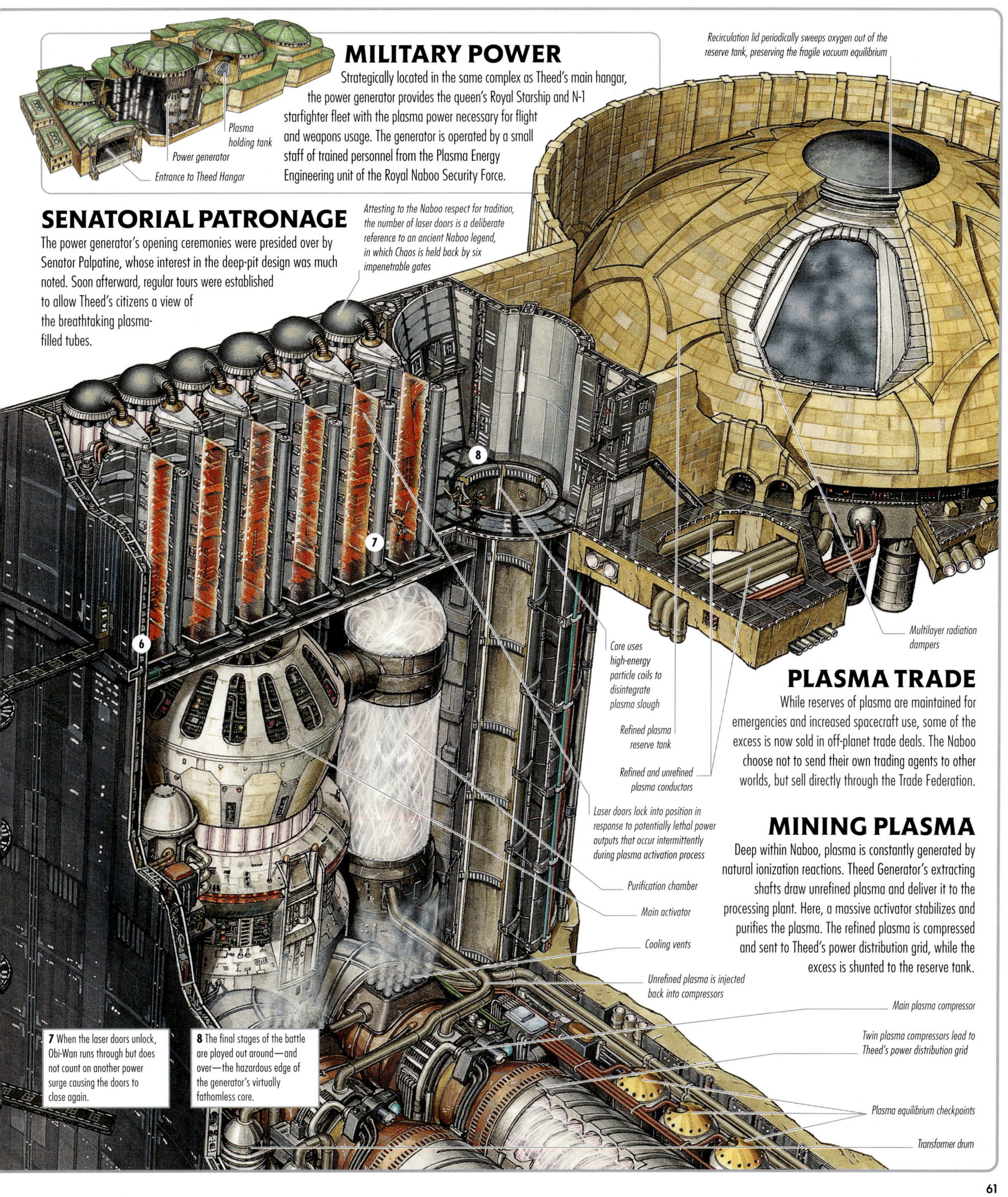

MILITARY POWER

Strategically located in the same complex as Theed's main hangar, the power generator provides the queen's Royal Starship and N-1 starfighter fleet with the plasma power necessary for flight and weapons usage. The generator is operated by a small staff of trained personnel from the Plasma Energy Engineering unit of the Royal Naboo Security Force.

Plasma holding tank
Power generator
Entrance to Theed Hangar

Recirculation lid periodically sweeps oxygen out of the reserve tank, preserving the fragile vacuum equilibrium

SENATORIAL PATRONAGE

The power generator's opening ceremonies were presided over by Senator Palpatine, whose interest in the deep-pit design was much noted. Soon afterward, regular tours were established to allow Theed's citizens a view of the breathtaking plasma-filled tubes.

Attesting to the Naboo respect for tradition, the number of laser doors is a deliberate reference to an ancient Naboo legend, in which Chaos is held back by six impenetrable gates

Core uses high-energy particle coils to disintegrate plasma slough

Refined plasma reserve tank

Refined and unrefined plasma conductors

Laser doors lock into position in response to potentially lethal power outputs that occur intermittently during plasma activation process

Purification chamber

Main activator

Cooling vents

Unrefined plasma is injected back into compressors

Multilayer radiation dampers

PLASMA TRADE

While reserves of plasma are maintained for emergencies and increased spacecraft use, some of the excess is now sold in off-planet trade deals. The Naboo choose not to send their own trading agents to other worlds, but sell directly through the Trade Federation.

MINING PLASMA

Deep within Naboo, plasma is constantly generated by natural ionization reactions. Theed Generator's extracting shafts draw unrefined plasma and deliver it to the processing plant. Here, a massive activator stabilizes and purifies the plasma. The refined plasma is compressed and sent to Theed's power distribution grid, while the excess is shunted to the reserve tank.

Main plasma compressor
Twin plasma compressors lead to Theed's power distribution grid
Plasma equilibrium checkpoints
Transformer drum

7 When the laser doors unlock, Obi-Wan runs through but does not count on another power surge causing the doors to close again.

8 The final stages of the battle are played out around—and over—the hazardous edge of the generator's virtually fathomless core.

61

THE CITY OF THEED

WITH SQUADRONS OF BATTLE DROIDS patrolling the streets, battle tanks guarding access routes, and Trade Federation rulers holding the palace, Theed is a city under occupation. Yet, as a result of the quick capitulation of its populace, its buildings and monuments have remained relatively unscathed—most structural damage was caused by battle tanks steering through narrow streets. With all entrances and exits blocked, the small band of Naboo defenders has no choice but to use a hazardous network of underground passages to infiltrate their own city.

Pergola's Bridge has become the main crossing point over the Solleu, taking some of the strain off the more fragile Bassa Bridge further downstream

Captain Panaka's private residence

Tomarian's theater

Secret access to subterranean tunnels

One of the tributaries of the Solleu River

Boathouse

Royal Naboo Security Forces headquarters

Theed Generator

Virdugo Plunge is the largest waterfall in Theed

Hangar entrance

Cliff edge is stabilized by hidden tension field generators

Ellié Arcadium

The Hall of Perri-Teeka, a monument to a legendary statesman

Officers' clubhouse

1 The defenders of Naboo use droid holoprojections to locate the secret routes into the city and the palace. These highly classified maps are stored in the Royal Starship's computers. The defenders emerge from the underground tunnels near the hangar.

2 Under Captain Panaka's command, Naboo soldiers in a Gian speeder blast at a Trade Federation tank regiment that is guarding the entrance to Theed Hangar. This courageous action diverts the droids away from the entrance.

3 Taking advantage of the diversion caused by Panaka, the Jedi, Anakin Skywalker, Padmé Amidala, and R2-D2 emerge from the corner of the hangar where they have been hiding and slip into the entrance. Panaka and his soldiers expertly dispatch the droids and join them.

UNDERGROUND TUNNELS

Like their Gungan counterparts, the Naboo have long made use of the porous qualities of their planet. The naturally forming subterranean tunnels that run underneath Theed were once made safe, extended, and mapped, but have since fallen into disrepair. As head of security, Captain Quarsh Panaka recently inspected these secret routes in and out of the city, but had no idea how useful they would become when the city was occupied.

4 With most droid squads needed at the Gungan battle, the hangar interior is not left well guarded. Yet warning signals from the droids that are hit alert the command officer to the security breach and droidekas are swiftly dispatched.

5 Pockets of battle droids guard key buildings in Theed. Nevertheless, when the Naboo defenders cross the city to reach the palace, they find they can take advantage of the city's maze of hidden passageways and connecting skywalks.

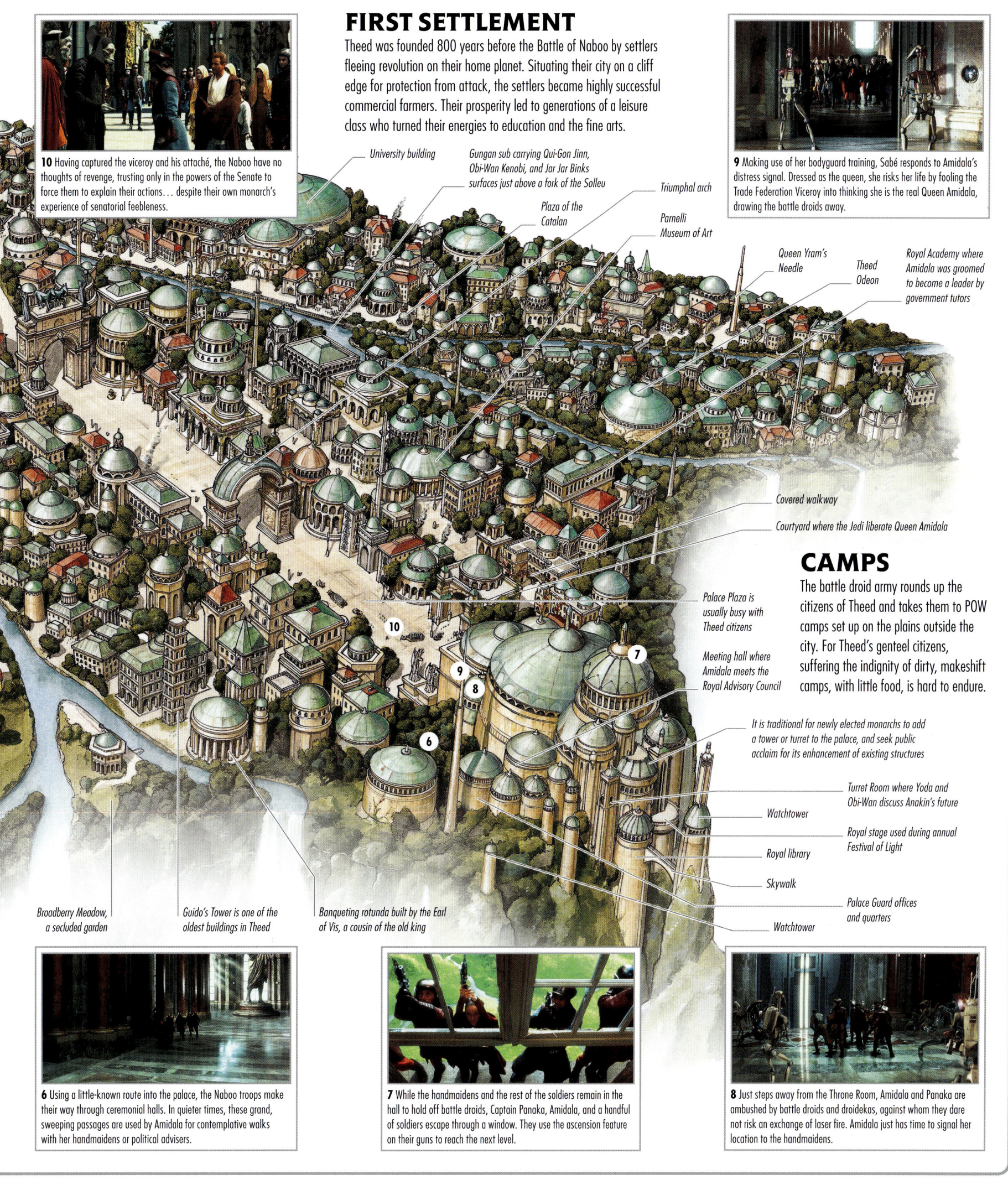

CORUSCANT UNDER CRISIS

SEEN FROM ABOVE THE CLOUDLINE, Coruscant appears still and serene, with just the tops of the tallest buildings visible. Beneath the clouds, the galactic capital planet is a heavily populated, multilayered metropolis. Its skylanes are constantly busy with traffic, from small personal speeders to air buses and larger freighters. Most skylanes on Coruscant are autonavigated, with each vehicle traveling along a preprogrammed route to minimize the risk of collisions. The fastest traffic makes use of the highest skylanes as it travels long distances across the planet. Below the elevated skylanes, traffic moves in a more disorderly way, vying for space with garbage scows, unmarked speedervans, and small private conveyances. Vehicles may change skylanes at giant spiral interchanges, where they move up or down, or switch directions.

URBAN GROWTH

The Galactic Senate stands at the heart of the Federal District. In the 10 years since the crisis on Naboo, this area has altered almost beyond recognition. New buildings and floors house the thousands of extra departments and commissions that have been formed in the name of bolstering the stability of the Republic. In addition, corpulent senators, keen to minimize their journey to the Senate, have used every form of persuasion to ensure that their offices and suites are built as close to the chamber as possible.

ENTERTAINMENT DISTRICTS

Coruscant's sprawling entertainment districts are equally alluring and unsettling for the hordes of revelers drawn to nightclubs, gaming houses, bars, and palaces of hedonism. Such districts are generally safe if slightly seedy, awash with bright lights and gaudy partygoers. Those with more daring tastes may seek out the city's underlevels, where any vice can be indulged provided one has credits and connections. But visiting these dark and dangerous levels can be a one-way trip for naïve pleasure-seekers who get in over their heads.

UPPER LEVEL DINERS

Exclusive stores and restaurants cater to the wealthy citizens who inhabit the highest levels of Coruscant. Small canteens serve maintenance crews and support staff working in these lofty heights. Many of the more fly-by-night canteens operate without trading licenses and are repulsor-fitted for easy getaway if officials come snooping. Located in Coco Town, Dex's Diner is one such mobile installation. In Coco Town (short for "collective commerce"), immigrants of diverse species have established mutually supportive manufacturing businesses.

THE WORKS

Coruscant's single planetwide metropolis is divided into several thousand regions, which are further subdivided into numbered sectors. Whereas official maps use this classification, most people refer to districts by colloquial names. One large sector is known as the Works. It is a manufacturing district, where, for hundreds of standard years, spacecraft parts, construction droids, and building materials of every kind were churned out at an astonishing rate. Now, much of this manufacturing is done more cheaply offworld, and the area has fallen into disrepair. Coruscanti stay well clear of the Works, as it has gained a reputation for the most sinister kind of criminal activity—making it ideal for a clandestine meeting between two shadowy Sith leaders.

SPEEDER CHASE

AFTER A NEAR-FATAL ASSASSINATION ATTEMPT as she arrived on Coruscant, Padmé Amidala is assigned two Jedi bodyguards, who keep watch on the senator as she sleeps in her apartment. Yet a modified ASN-121 assassin/sentry droid bypasses the window shields in a further attempt on Padmé's life—only, this time, Obi-Wan Kenobi smashes through the window and grabs onto it as it turns to flee.

Meanwhile, Anakin Skywalker "hotwires" an airspeeder from a nearby parking bay. In the ensuing chase, both Jedi hurtle through the skylanes in pursuit of bounty hunter Zam Wesell, who avoids the heavy circulation, high-lane interchanges, choosing instead to dip down into the lower lanes, where traffic is lighter but less orderly.

1 Anakin quickly spots the only open-top airspeeder in a parking bay—which happens to be the fastest, too. The speeder is later recovered and returned to its designated parkslot, effectively cutting short the official enquiry into the "theft" and leaving its owner, Senator Simon Greyshade, unable to press charges.

2 At the mercy of the droid's defensive stratagems, Obi-Wan is repeatedly scraped against the walls of buildings or dangled in the path of oncoming speeders. He narrowly escapes a collision with holodrama star Sebaca from Malastare, who is entertaining a female senator from Aleen, Boga Tyrell.

ROUTE KEY

- Assassin droid
- Anakin's speeder
- Zam's speeder
- Zam's rifle slug
- Obi-Wan's fall
- Zam's speeder
- Anakin's leap

Assassin droid supporting Obi-Wan is hit by a bolt from Zam's sniper rifle

Obi-Wan freefalls for 285 m (950 ft) before landing in Anakin's speeder

Zam throws her speeder into a daring nose-dive

Zam waits on an upper balcony of a Trade Federation office tower

Trade Federation advertising screens

3 Obi-wan struggles to hold on to the speeding assassin droid as it repeatedly sends defensive electrical shocks into his unprotected hands. Several skylanes below him, Anakin pilots his airspeeder, using the Force to seek his master and hoping that the droid will lead him to the unknown assassin.

Obi-Wan nearly collides with Magaloof, who is joyriding in a stolen speeder

Bonadan Embassy

Office occupied by regulatory body for mobile communication droids

Anakin in the speeder trails Obi-Wan, who hangs from the assassin droid

Obi-Wan is thrown against the side of the Champalan Embassy

Nicandra Counterrevolutionary Signalmen's Memorial Building

Anakin takes an airspeeder from a parking balcony several floors beneath Padmé's apartment

Only the wealthiest senators dine in the 1,000 m (3,280 ft)-high revolving Skysitter Restaurant

Padmé's rooms are in a high-security Senate apartment complex

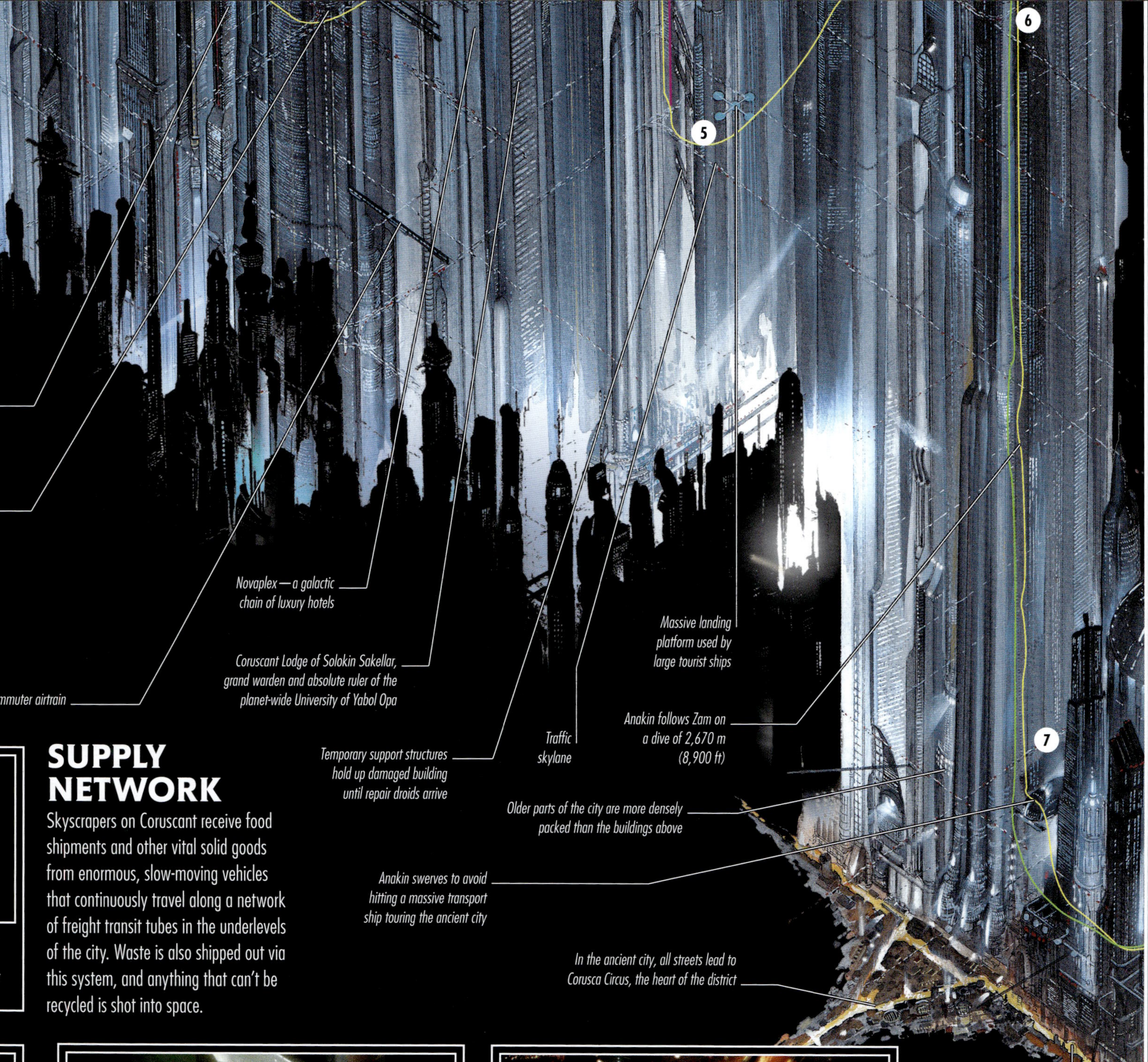

Brightly lit older city is hundreds of meters deep

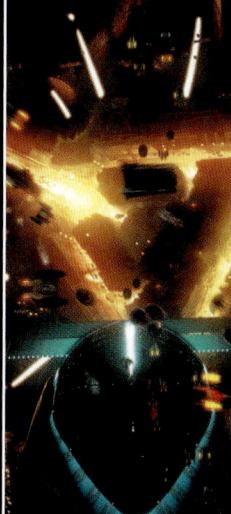

7 As the Jedi follow Zam toward a giant blue transport, the lights of the lower metropolitan canyons shine brightly. Three main canyons intersect here, passing around an accumulation of public buildings known as Corusca Circus that has been expanding haphazardly for centuries.

In the ancient city, all streets lead to Corusca Circus, the heart of the district

Anakin swerves to avoid hitting a massive transport ship touring the ancient city

Older parts of the city are more densely packed than the buildings above

Anakin follows Zam on a dive of 2,670 m (8,900 ft)

Traffic skylane

Massive landing platform used by large tourist ships

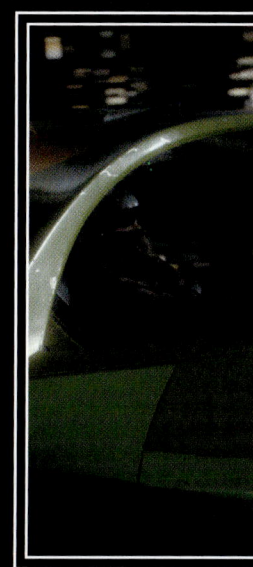

6 In an attempt to lose her pursuers, Zam performs a sudden nose-dive, which stretches the capacities of her repulsorlift balance elements to the max. She plummets from the lofty spires of the upper city to an older neighborhood in the lower levels, a journey that takes her from one class to another in seconds.

Temporary support structures hold up damaged building until repair droids arrive

Novaplex — a galactic chain of luxury hotels

Coruscant Lodge of Solokin Sakellar, grand warden and absolute ruler of the planet-wide University of Yabol Opa

SUPPLY NETWORK

Skyscrapers on Coruscant receive food shipments and other vital solid goods from enormous, slow-moving vehicles that continuously travel along a network of freight transit tubes in the underlevels of the city. Waste is also shipped out via this system, and anything that can't be recycled is shot into space.

Commuter airtrain

Skylane interchange

Top floors of building occupied by Senatorial News Agency

Many of these buildings are occupied by diplomatic staff from the millions of star systems enfranchised in the Senate

Padmé's apartment building stands in the Federal District, an upscale region located near the Senate Rotunda

WINDOW SHIELDS

Many structures on Coruscant have defensive shields to protect windows from stray or out-of-control vehicles. Zam's assassin droid uses a short-range disruptor to "burn" through the window shield of Padmé's suite.

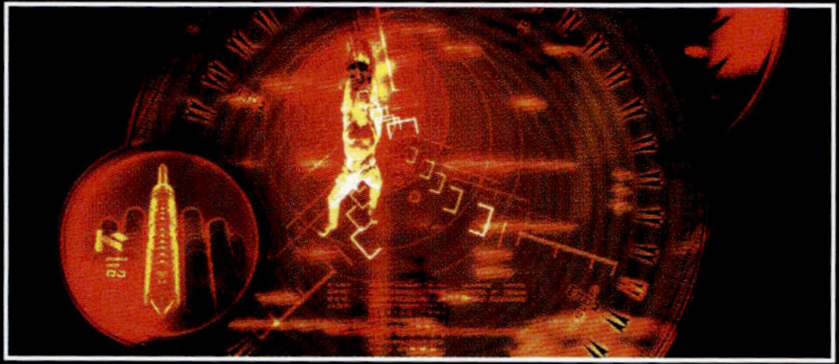

4 When bounty hunter Zam Wesell spots an intruder hanging from her droid, she reaches for her projectile rifle. With Obi-Wan in her scopes, she fires at the droid rather than the Jedi—knowing that a Jedi who plunges to his death leaves fewer clues than one who dies with a traceable slug in him.

5 After his ride is blown to bits, Obi-Wan plummets for hundreds of meters before Anakin's timely appearance in his yellow speeder narrowly averts his imminent death. With Anakin in the driver's seat, Obi-Wan has no choice but to control his frustration at this reversal in their roles of master and Padawan.

RISKY PURSUIT

The pursuit continues through the lower levels of Coruscant. These are the areas the upper classes rarely see: the industrial plants that supply Coruscant with power and fuel, and the warehouse zones where essential supplies from offworld are readied for distribution around the planet. In all, the Jedi chase Zam Wesell through the skies for more than 100 kilometers (62 miles), until Anakin Skywalker forces Zam to crash-land in a busy entertainment district.

10 Zam flies past a HoloNet News display beacon, which provides clearly illuminated, up-to-the-minute news flashes on galactic events in a variety of common languages. On Coruscant and on many other urbanized planets, these displays can be seen wherever there are busy skylanes.

11 Zam enters a skytunnel that takes her over the Huosnoughow Foundation — a powerful financial think tank with close links to myriad Senate budgeting offices. Zam hits 400 kph (248 mph) in a strict 200 kph (124 mph) flyzone, trusting in her superb piloting skills to win out over her pursuers.

SKYTUNNELS

Certain neighborhoods of Coruscant are accessible only via skytunnels, such as the one Zam soars into. Some skytunnels serve as shortcuts through structures built by powerful but uncaring official bodies that end up blocking established skyways. Other tunnels allow civilian traffic to pass through private airspace, such as high-security banking or governmental zones.

9 Bounty hunter Wesell fires a blaster bolt at the couplings of an on-surface power refinery, activating massive electrical bolts between the prongs. As the Jedi have no time to avoid them, they are enveloped in nerve-jarring lightning. The powerful shock would induce a heart attack in those not trained in the Force.

MAPPING CORUSCANT

Coruscant is divided into sectors with official coordinates, which often receive unofficial names. For example, sector H-46 is more colloquially known as Sah'c Town (named after a wealthy family that owns much of it). Sectors are further subdivided into zones: for instance, the senatorial, financial, and industrial zones through which Skywalker and Obi-Wan Kenobi pursue Padmé Amidala's would-be assassin.

8 Zam, in her sealed vehicle, deliberately leads her pursuers through the flaming exhaust vents of a recycling plant, knowing their open-top speeder will leave them dangerously exposed. These vents burn toxic waste gas into less harmful forms (atmospheric carbon dioxide and water vapor).

GHOST SHIP

The *Gigar*-class transport ship *Ultimo Vista* that Anakin and Obi-Wan narrowly avoid hitting is one of Coruscant's most bizarre sights. Established decades ago as a leisure cruise ship, it is now a separate, contained world in which its elderly passengers are full-time residents. Almost entirely self-sufficient, the slow-moving craft endlessly circles Coruscant on its original route to nowhere.

- Storage
- Sports fields
- Apartment blocks house a population of several thousand residents
- Habitation areas include forests, rivers, and seas, with a controlled climate

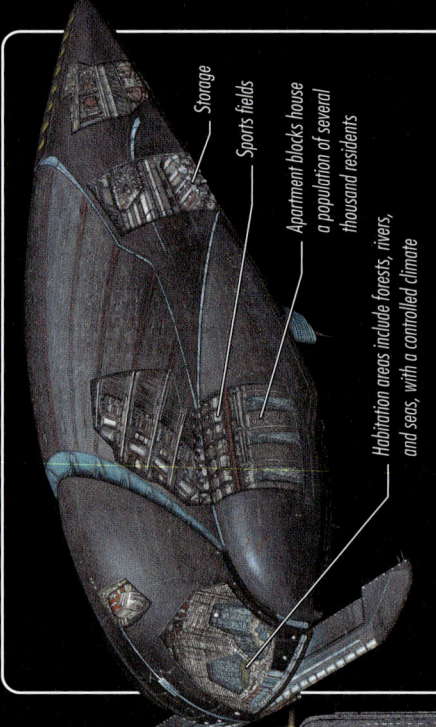

- Obi-Wan catches Anakin's lightsaber
- Half-finished buildings, supported by cranes and girders
- Giant conveyors continuously move goods to unloading bays in the lower levels for distribution around the planet
- Warehouse zone entrance portal employs massive electrostatic dampers to keep dust clouds from spreading
- Loading docks use framework of girders to support varying sizes of container
- Steam from drying silos and heating generators
- Warehouses receive imported goods and foods from all around the galaxy
- Financial zone covers an area of about 30 square kilometers (12 square miles)
- Anakin spots Zam's speeder passing through a droid research institute
- The largest, tallest buildings accommodate populations in the millions

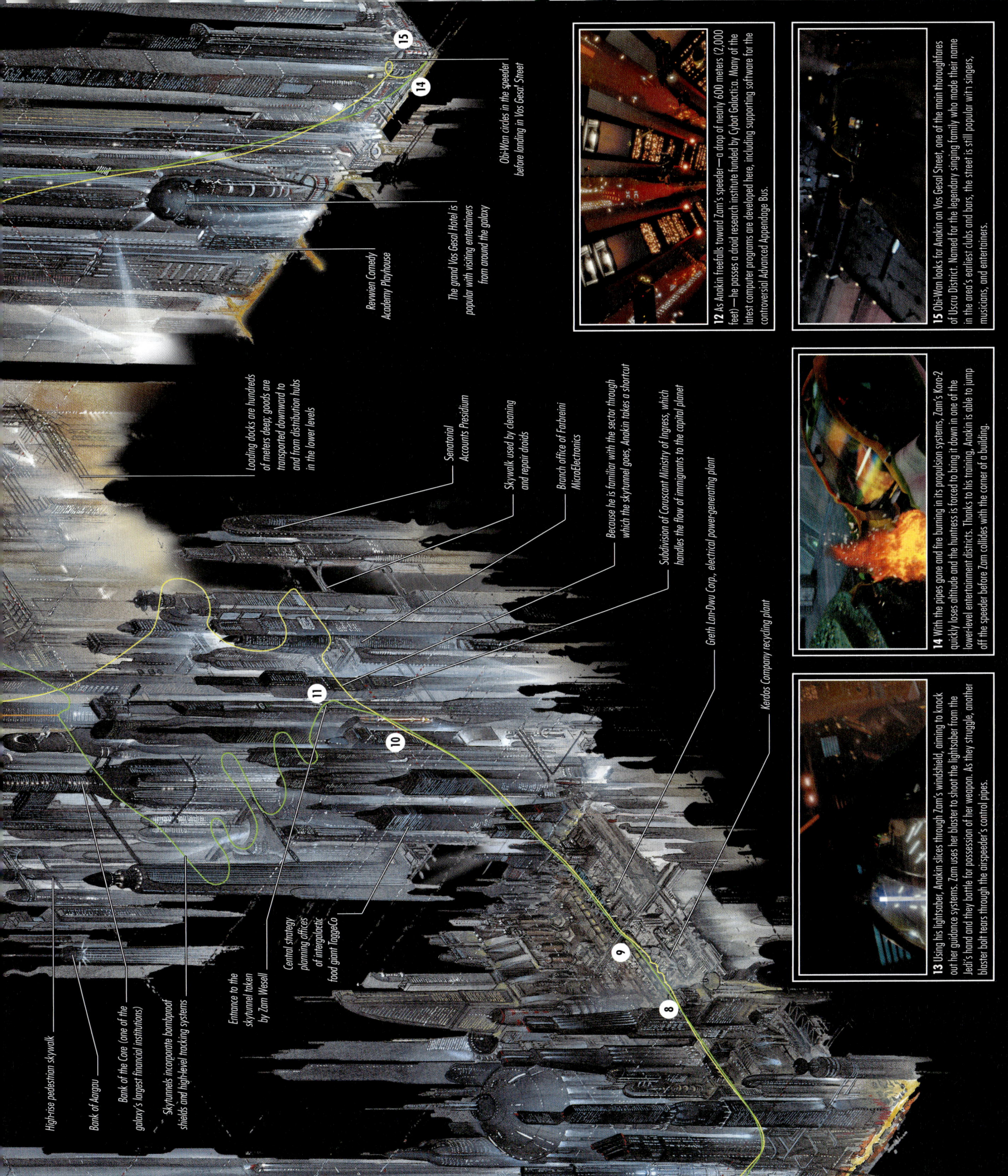

OUTLANDER CLUB

THE OUTLANDER CLUB is located in Coruscant's Uscru entertainment district. The locale is a labyrinth of bars and gaming rooms, where Coruscanti revelers, underworld characters, and wide-eyed offworlders jostle one another while staking what wealth they have on sporting events and on-site games of chance. The club stays open day and night, with some hardened gamblers spending days at a time here. When Zam slips inside, she aims to lose the pursuing Jedi in the crowded, dimly lit interior—or finish them off for good.

Some sports events shown at the Outlander are officially illegal in the Republic, such as podracing (live here from the ice-covered planet of Ando Prime). Other popular games are only barely tolerated—including nuna-ball (a violent ball-game for souped-up droids) and odupiendo-racing.

Highly exclusive suite in which visiting crime lords, gang bosses, and top-ranking politicians are entertained

Four-armed kiughfid dealers on main gambling floor are fast and efficient at taking people's money

Visiting princess from Soun IV

The Outlander offers its own version of sabacc with house rules

Betting kiosk

Holographic gamescreens offer inexpensive but highly addictive gambling

The Rodian Tyyx makes his living selling tips on podraces

Anj Rujj is one of the infamous Thugs of Thule, a gang of highly educated mercenaries

Lower level denizens are escorted by a tour guide to Digisee Gaming Floor

Side entrance to alleyway

Anakin Skywalker and Obi-Wan Kenobi escort out wounded Zam Wesell

Chadra-Fan looking for a strong juri juice

Ayy Vida stalls those seeking business with crime boss Hat Lo

Automixer enables users to select their species to ensure non-toxic drink

Gamblers in underlevel bet on illegal fights

Deathfinger monks plot revenge against Greez Dritus

ILLEGAL GAMING

Because it is tucked away in one of the less developed areas of the entertainment district, which is rarely patrolled by law enforcement crews, the club makes little secret of its policy to accept bids on just about any game in the galaxy—even the ever-popular Galactic Games, on which betting is highly illegal.

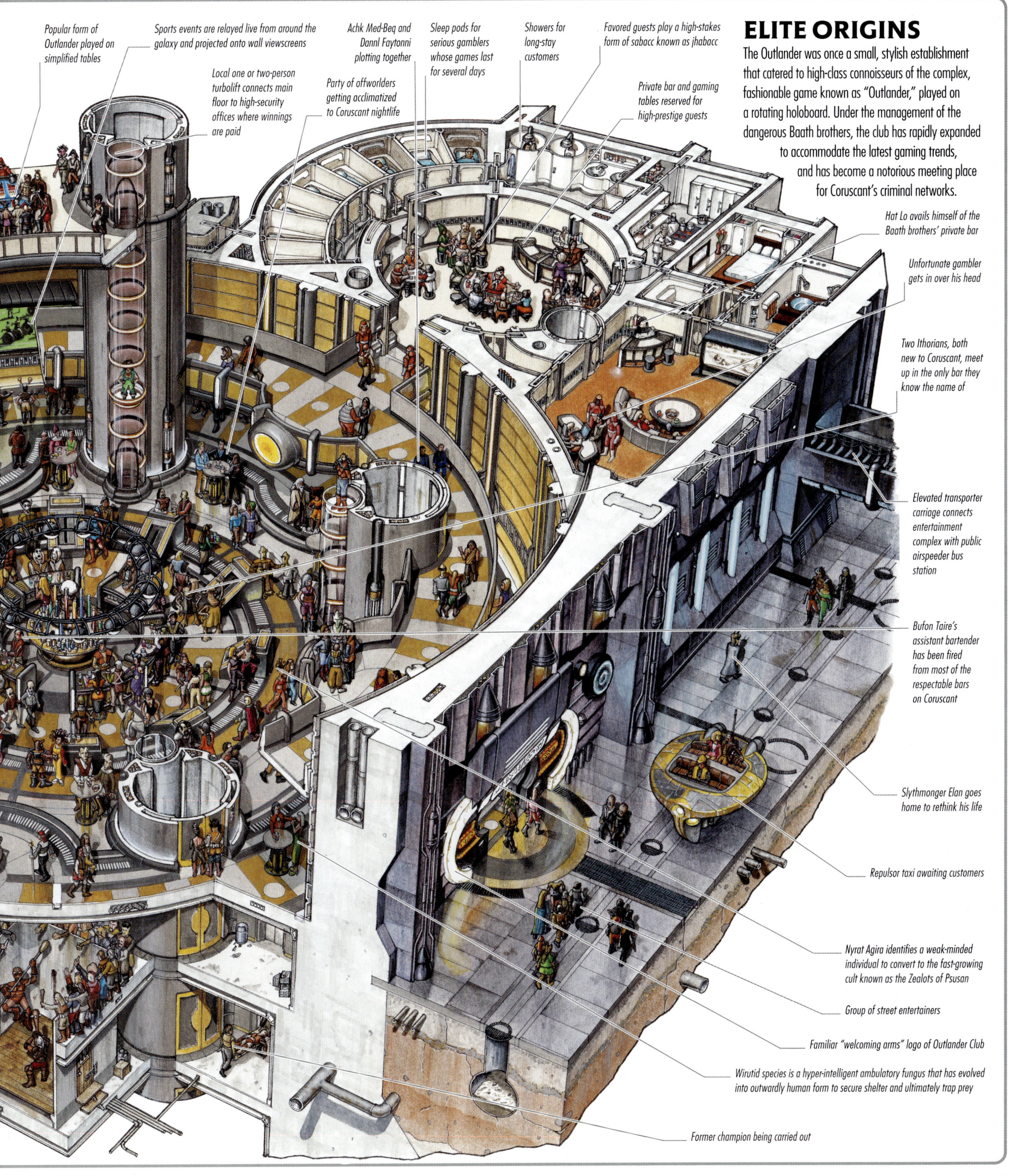

JEDI TEMPLE OPERATIONS

FOR THE LAST 100 YEARS or so, Jedi activity in the galaxy has been centered at the Jedi Temple on Coruscant, with lesser Jedi sanctuaries, libraries, and outposts dotted throughout the Republic. Not long ago, during the High Republic, some Jedi even studied aboard starships and space stations, like the *Star Hopper* and Starlight Beacon. The Coruscant Temple is home to some 10,000 Jedi in the waning years of the Republic, providing all the means necessary for them to thrive, from younglings to grand masters.

Coleman Trebor's seat

TEMPLE HANGAR
Jedi have to depart for any sector of the galaxy at a moment's notice in response to some imminent trouble or crisis. The Temple's hangars store a fleet of Delta-7 starfighters with specially adapted versions for non-humanoid Knights and a number of shuttles for less perilous missions. These ships are launched from an extendible platform.

COUNCIL CHAMBER DATABANK
Temple databanks show the latest seating plan of the Jedi High Council, with information on the current location and status of its 12 members. Only Jedi with appropriate access privileges are able to view such information. Coleman Trebor, one of the latest appointees to the Council, perishes in the First Battle of Geonosis, which marked the start of the Clone Wars.

Temple tracking system operational

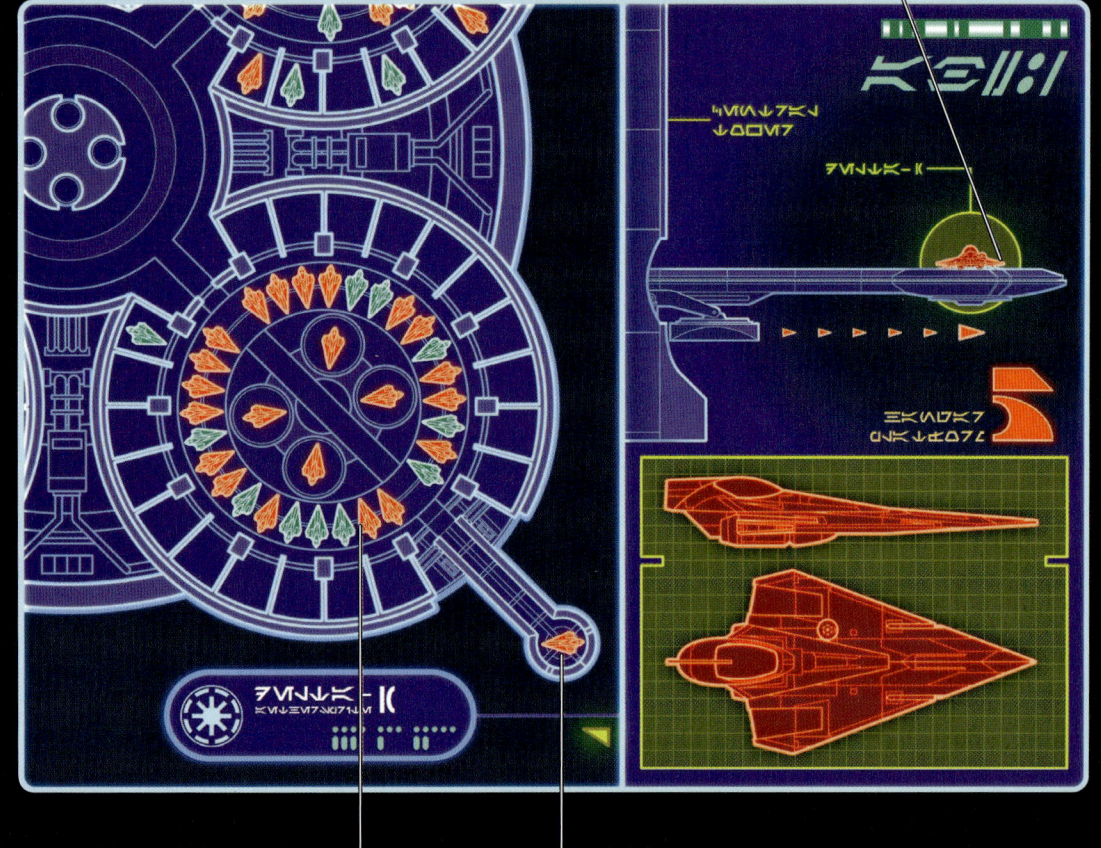

Starfighters coded red are for use by particular Jedi; green-coded ships are for general use

Launch platform in use

MEDITATION AND EDUCATION
The Jedi Temple dominates the landscape for kilometers around, its noble spires seeming almost to pierce the sky. The Temple is the heart of the ancient Jedi Order, its many serene, spacious chambers and walkways—including its room of a thousand fountains—facilitating deep contemplation of the Force. High-ranking Jedi Masters, such as lightsaber virtuoso Soara Antana, hold prestige classes for Padawans in specialized halls and instruction rooms, although much of their training takes place in the standard accommodations of the Temple Precinct.

ANALYSIS ROOMS

Analysis spaces fall under the overall jurisdiction of the Temple Archives and chief librarian Jocasta Nu. They are used by Jedi for many tasks, including locating the provenance of alien objects, either organic or inorganic. SP-4 and JN-66 analysis droids that staff the facility can access the computer systems of the Jedi Archives to match identification indices. Their multispectral readers and polysensitive graspers detect even the slightest odor traces. The room is therefore hermetically sealed to humans or aliens, so no contamination can occur that would cause false readings from the highly sensitive equipment.

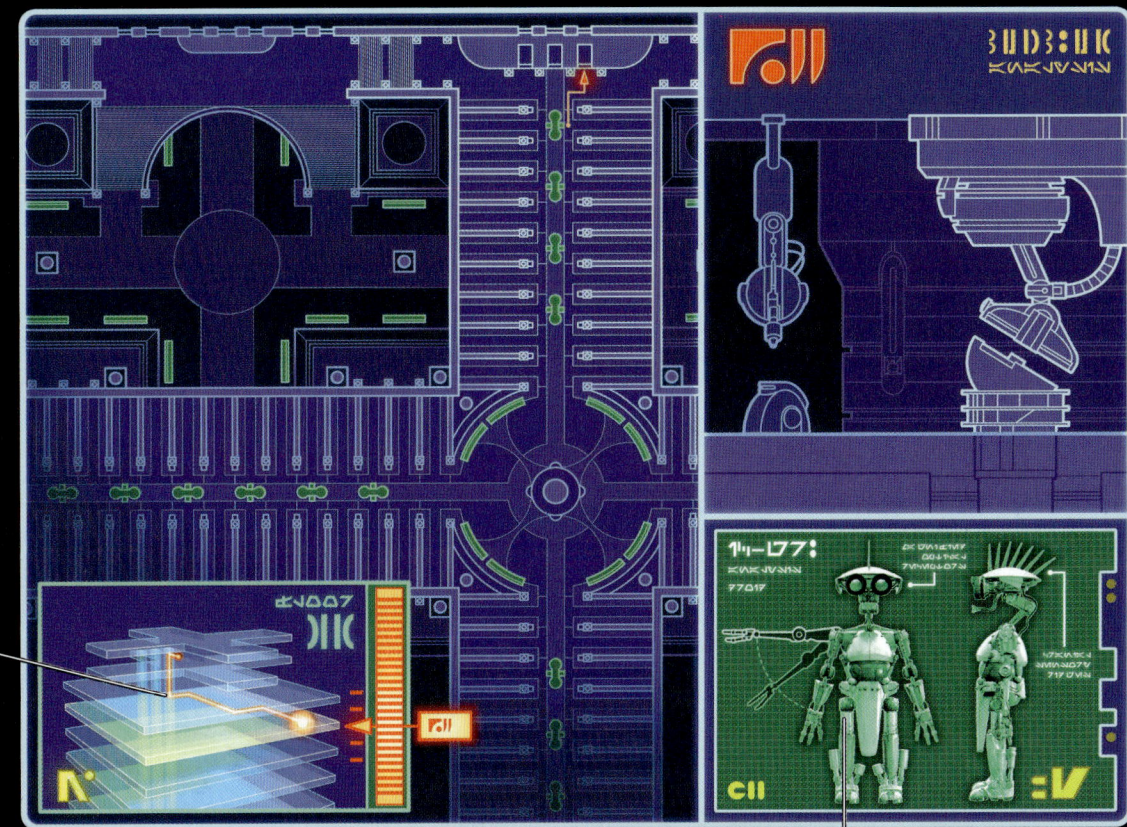

Temple data screen shows route from Archives to Analysis Rooms

Spaceport tower allows larger spaceships to dock in the Jedi Temple complex

Buildings added after initial construction are contained in the extensive Temple Precinct

Central spire of Jedi Temple

Specifications of SP-4 analysis droid

73

NABOO RETREATS

SINCE THE TRADE FEDERATION INVASION, Naboo has undergone a period of adjustment. New building works in the capital, Theed, have repaired the damage done by the invasion force, and Queen Jamillia has accepted the necessity of increased security for her people. A well-equipped new spaceport is a bold symbol of the people's expanded outlook. When Anakin Skywalker accompanies Padmé Amidala to Naboo as her bodyguard, he visits the planet's most remote region, the Lake Country.

Like many of the rooms in the grand house, the rotunda in which Padmé and Anakin dine has associations with its former celebrated resident Omar Berenko. In this Room of Morning Mists, Berenko wrote some of his most famous works, including the disturbing and visionary epic poem *Defense of Naboo*.

VARYKINO

The Lake Country is sealed off from Naboo's underground waterways and caverns, making the lakes safe from sea monsters. The sparse population is made up mostly of farmers and craftspeople famed for their almost mystically bewitching glassworks. Padmé and Anakin stay at Varykino, a large villa that stands on the lake's most distant island. The house was occupied centuries earlier by the tragic Naboo poet Omar Berenko, who lived in an unconventional community of Naboo—and even Gungan—outsiders. Varykino is now owned by the Naberrie family, who see themselves as caretakers of the villa's beauty and traditions.

TRANQUIL OASIS

The Lake Country boasts some of the most idyllic water meadows on Naboo, with dramatic waterfalls and flocks of peacefully grazing shaak. The fertile land is regularly flooded by its rivers, but is pleasantly dry in summer. The communally owned meadows are maintained by the Pastoral Collective. In springtime, the festival of Glad Arrival is held here, when, for several days, the meadows are transformed by colorful pageants and music-making.

CLANDESTINE CEREMONY

Following the First Battle of Geonosis, Anakin escorts Padmé back to Naboo, where they marry in secret—an act forbidden to Jedi. The simple ritual takes place on a shaded balcony at Varykino. The marriage rites are pronounced by a holy man from the region. Unknown to either bride or groom, it was on this very spot that the controversial poet Berenko was kidnapped by unknown assailants, never to be seen again.

PUBLIC SPLENDOR

Traveling by public airbus, Anakin and Padmé arrive in Theed's new Palace Courtyard. Built over a part of the city that was severely damaged by Trade Federation tanks 10 years earlier, the new enclosure is designed to foster and encourage principles of enlightened thought and practice. Theed's inhabitants wander through the courtyard's graceful walkways and sit in the shade of the circular colonnade, within which a holographic frieze depicts great philosophers and artists from the planet's history. Naboo is not entirely free from trouble, however: in recent months, migrant workers have staged protests about their work conditions, only to be forcibly removed by Theed police. Naboo's leaders are largely sheltered from these events by their security advisors in order to preserve—for the time being at least—the utopian outlook of which the planet is so proud.

KAMINO

KAMINO IS A REMOTE AND INHOSPITABLE WORLD covered in one unending ocean. Located in a dwarf satellite galaxy beyond the Outer Rim, the planet receives very little traffic and only as much trade as is necessary to supply the basic needs of its inhabitants, the amphibious Kaminoans. This highly intelligent species has specialized in the high-skill, value-added industry of human, alien, and creature cloning, supplying a select client base with workers, private security forces, and a range of unusual, one-off requests. The Kaminoans live in stilt-cities scattered across the planet's watery surface, the majority of which are devoted to cloning projects. The Kaminoans only rarely receive visitors: the remoteness of the planet and its extensive rainy season deter all but the occasional representative of a clone-purchasing authority.

CAPITAL CITY

When Obi-Wan Kenobi enters Kaminoan airspace, he is cleared to land at the planet's capital, Tipoca City, where the first shipments of the Republic's clone army are being readied. The giant domes house Kamino's largest and most prestigious military complex, although many other cloning facilities exist at other sites across the planet. The center at Tipoca extends throughout the domes, and includes hatcheries, growth pods, and learning and training facilities, as well as dormitories and dining halls. In addition to creating clones, the Kaminoans produce a range of specialized, high-tech weapons and missiles for a number of clients: for example, interrogation devices and an array of saberdarts, mainly for use by professional bounty hunters and security specialists. The cloners subcontract the manufacturing of larger weapons and vehicles to offworld suppliers such as Rothana Heavy Engineering.

A network of suboceanic tubes carries spherical passenger transports. This little-known system allows for discreet travel between Tipoca City locales.

LANDING PLATFORMS

The bounty hunter Jango Fett makes use of one of Tipoca City's landing platforms for his *Firespray*-class patrol craft. Despite the severity of weather conditions on Kamino, landing platforms on the planet are generally uncovered. A shield generator array on the underside, however, can be activated to protect the ship from power overloads during electrical storms. Sensor masts provide electronic surveillance and warn of any accidental intrusions.

AIR-TO-SEA TRANSPORT

The amphibious Kaminoans often travel between their stilt-cities on cloned aiwhas, animals that can both fly and swim. For much of the year, severe electrical storms rage across the planet. At these times, Kaminoan aiwha-riders tend to travel underwater to escape the lashing tempests, surfacing as they near their destination. Another, more unusual imperative drives the Kaminoans under the waves—pilgrimages to the sunken cities on the seabed, relics of the ancient land-based Kaminoan civilization that existed before the entire planet was flooded. These sacred journeys are made purely to honor their ancestors, rather than for scientific or archaeological research, and seem highly inconsistent with the Kaminoans' more characteristic scientific rationalism.

CLONERS' SECRETS

For centuries, Kamino's cloners have tailored the living beings they create to meet the specifications of their clients, reshaping both bodies and brains according to altered genetic blueprints. The clones created from Jango Fett's genetic material age on an accelerated timetable and are hardy and disciplined, yet also less independent and volatile than Jango. Additionally, all are implanted with inhibitor chips designed to ensure they follow orders, a contingency measure kept secret from the Jedi Order and the leadership of the Republic. It's not the only secret kept by the Kaminoans: Chief Medical Scientist Nala Se maintains a private lab connected to an undersea landing platform by a network of transport tubes left off Tipoca City schematics. Here, she pursues secret research into enhanced and aberrant clones, both to satisfy her own scientific curiosity and to explore promising research avenues that might prove profitable in future cloning projects.

TIPOCA CITY

THE KAMINOAN CAPITAL stands above the ferocious waves on massive legs anchored in the seabed, its gently sloping roof-domes shedding the driving rains that fall almost continuously. The city is actually a network of stilt structures distributed over 150 kilometers (93 miles) at the planet's equator. The central hub houses extensive cloning facilities and administrative offices occupied by the planet's Ruling Council. Because all the millions of Kaminoans who live and work in Tipoca are involved in either the cloning industry or governmental business—the two are closely interlinked—there is no public space within the central domes. Satellite cities ranged around Tipoca provide homes and recreation for the highly skilled workers.

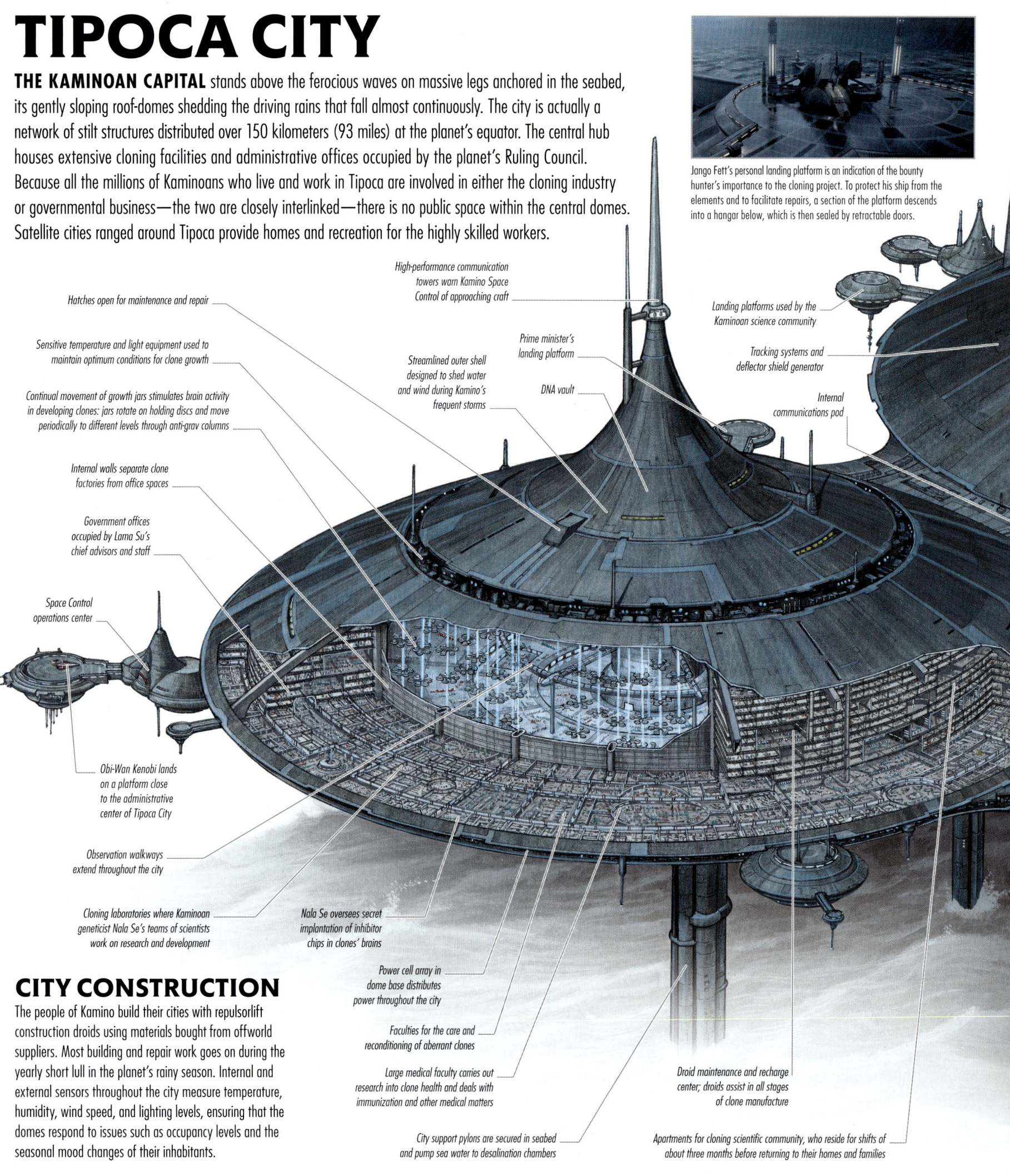

Jango Fett's personal landing platform is an indication of the bounty hunter's importance to the cloning project. To protect his ship from the elements and to facilitate repairs, a section of the platform descends into a hangar below, which is then sealed by retractable doors.

- Hatches open for maintenance and repair
- Sensitive temperature and light equipment used to maintain optimum conditions for clone growth
- Continual movement of growth jars stimulates brain activity in developing clones: jars rotate on holding discs and move periodically to different levels through anti-grav columns
- Internal walls separate clone factories from office spaces
- Government offices occupied by Lama Su's chief advisors and staff
- Space Control operations center
- Obi-Wan Kenobi lands on a platform close to the administrative center of Tipoca City
- Observation walkways extend throughout the city
- Cloning laboratories where Kaminoan geneticist Nala Se's teams of scientists work on research and development
- High-performance communication towers warn Kamino Space Control of approaching craft
- Prime minister's landing platform
- Streamlined outer shell designed to shed water and wind during Kamino's frequent storms
- DNA vault
- Nala Se oversees secret implantation of inhibitor chips in clones' brains
- Power cell array in dome base distributes power throughout the city
- Faculties for the care and reconditioning of aberrant clones
- Large medical faculty carries out research into clone health and deals with immunization and other medical matters
- City support pylons are secured in seabed and pump sea water to desalination chambers
- Landing platforms used by the Kaminoan science community
- Tracking systems and deflector shield generator
- Internal communications pod
- Droid maintenance and recharge center; droids assist in all stages of clone manufacture
- Apartments for cloning scientific community, who reside for shifts of about three months before returning to their homes and families

CITY CONSTRUCTION

The people of Kamino build their cities with repulsorlift construction droids using materials bought from offworld suppliers. Most building and repair work goes on during the yearly short lull in the planet's rainy season. Internal and external sensors throughout the city measure temperature, humidity, wind speed, and lighting levels, ensuring that the domes respond to issues such as occupancy levels and the seasonal mood changes of their inhabitants.

SELF-RELIANT CULTURE

Architecture on Kamino has long been characterized by domed buildings. Before the planet flooded, the Kaminoans lived in dome-shaped wattle-and-daub houses on land. As the floodwaters rose, they migrated to increasingly higher land until forced to raise their houses on stilts. Modern high-tech cities feature heavy military capabilities and high-security systems, which reflect a characteristic Kaminoan attitude of self-reliance and suspicion of others.

LIVING ON KAMINO

Domestic apartments on Kamino are sparsely furnished. Certain furniture is designed to descend from the ceiling on stalks, connecting with electromagnetic floor markings. Jango Fett's apartment is typically modest, but has some concessions to human comfort in the replacement of luminous surfaces with stable furniture.

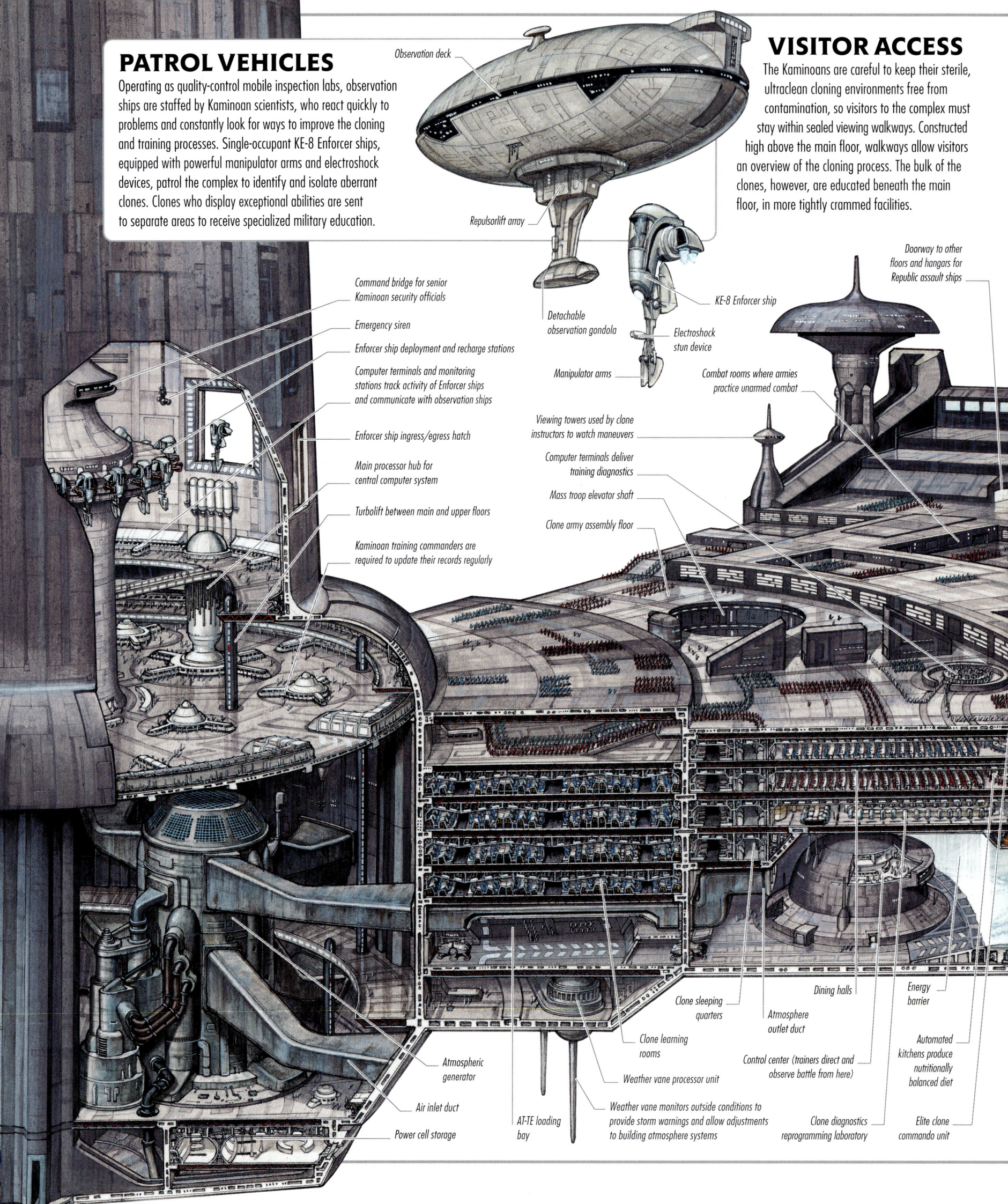

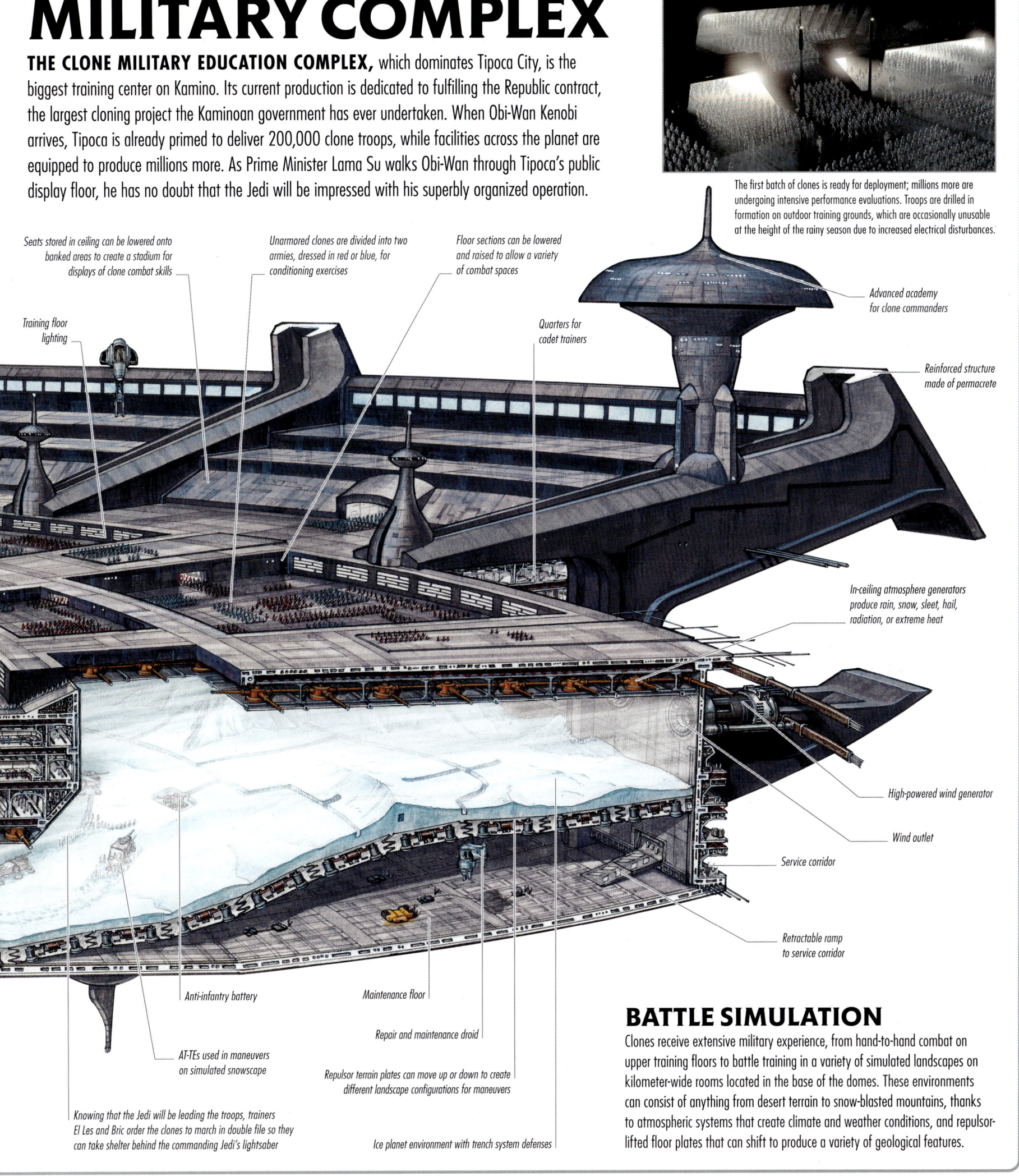

MILITARY COMPLEX

THE CLONE MILITARY EDUCATION COMPLEX, which dominates Tipoca City, is the biggest training center on Kamino. Its current production is dedicated to fulfilling the Republic contract, the largest cloning project the Kaminoan government has ever undertaken. When Obi-Wan Kenobi arrives, Tipoca is already primed to deliver 200,000 clone troops, while facilities across the planet are equipped to produce millions more. As Prime Minister Lama Su walks Obi-Wan through Tipoca's public display floor, he has no doubt that the Jedi will be impressed with his superbly organized operation.

The first batch of clones is ready for deployment; millions more are undergoing intensive performance evaluations. Troops are drilled in formation on outdoor training grounds, which are occasionally unusable at the height of the rainy season due to increased electrical disturbances.

- Seats stored in ceiling can be lowered onto banked areas to create a stadium for displays of clone combat skills
- Unarmored clones are divided into two armies, dressed in red or blue, for conditioning exercises
- Floor sections can be lowered and raised to allow a variety of combat spaces
- Training floor lighting
- Quarters for cadet trainers
- Advanced academy for clone commanders
- Reinforced structure made of permacrete
- In-ceiling atmosphere generators produce rain, snow, sleet, hail, radiation, or extreme heat
- High-powered wind generator
- Wind outlet
- Service corridor
- Retractable ramp to service corridor
- Anti-infantry battery
- Maintenance floor
- Repair and maintenance droid
- AT-TEs used in maneuvers on simulated snowscape
- Repulsor terrain plates can move up or down to create different landscape configurations for maneuvers
- Knowing that the Jedi will be leading the troops, trainers El Les and Bric order the clones to march in double file so they can take shelter behind the commanding Jedi's lightsaber
- Ice planet environment with trench system defenses

BATTLE SIMULATION

Clones receive extensive military experience, from hand-to-hand combat on upper training floors to battle training in a variety of simulated landscapes on kilometer-wide rooms located in the base of the domes. These environments can consist of anything from desert terrain to snow-blasted mountains, thanks to atmospheric systems that create climate and weather conditions, and repulsor-lifted floor plates that can shift to produce a variety of geological features.

RETURN TO TATOOINE

WHEN ANAKIN SKYWALKER returns to Tatooine, he finds a world unchanged from 10 years earlier. Slavery still exists in the lawless Outer Rim, and the threat of danger hangs in the air. Yet Tatooine functions with a kind of rough order: droid taxis navigate the spaceports, where merchants sell their wares; podraces and cantinas provide entertainment; and harsh justice is administered by Hutt crime lords. Out in the wastelands, moisture farmers eke out a living, raising their families to have a sense of community and morality. The slow turning of the galaxy's political fortunes has yet to impinge on this inward-looking world.

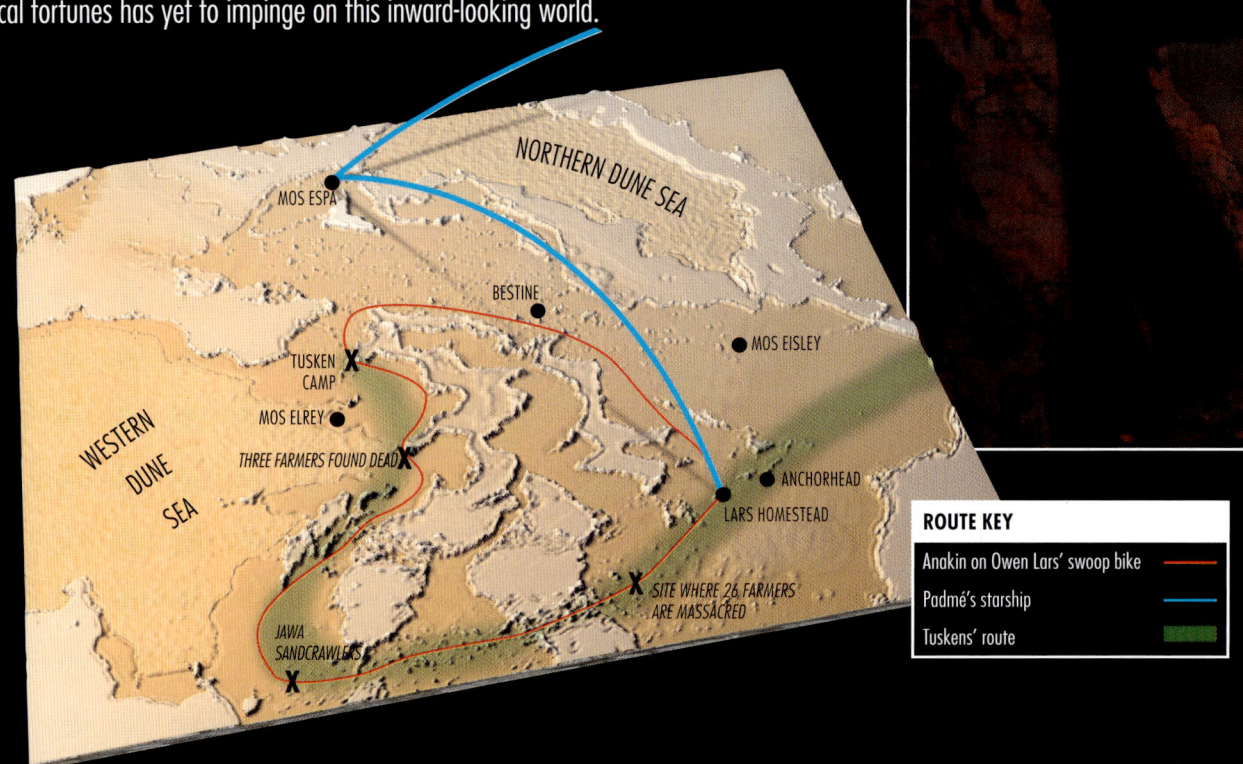

ANAKIN'S JOURNEY

Tuskens abducted Shmi Lars as they skirted the Lars homestead on their nomadic wanderings that had lately included numerous conflicts with settlers. In search of her, Anakin sets off in the direction of the Tuskens' last sighting—the massacre of Cliegg Lars' posse of farmers. He picks up the trail from Jawas and other isolated settlers. Finally, he comes upon a camp, deep in the barren wastes.

WATTO'S JUNKSHOP

In the 10 years since Anakin said farewell to his former enslaver, Watto has remained wedded to his used-parts dealership in a Mos Espa backstreet. Despite purchasing parts of the adjoining buildings in order to enlarge his premises, Watto's business future is uncertain thanks to numerous gambling losses. His locales are also severely understaffed, with Watto doing most of the work himself. Spoiled by Anakin's surprising skills, Watto can no longer find enslaved beings with enough technical knowledge. The hovering junk dealer now lives in constant fear of thieves and customers who default on payment.

JAWA SANDCRAWLERS

About 150 kilometers (93 miles) from the Lars homestead, on the edge of the Western Dune Sea, just beyond the giant rock canyons of the Jundland Wastes, Anakin encounters a fleet of sandcrawlers that belong to Jawas, who are working with their portable smelter beneath a tent. He questions these tiny, cloaked scrap dealers about the nomadic Tuskens. For only a few small items from his bike pannier—a multitool and a portable scanner—they point Anakin toward the east, advising him to stick to the high ground in order to gain a vantage point from which to descend on the Tuskens, who travel and set up camps in the valleys.

B'THAZOSHE BRIDGE

The Jundland Wastes are dotted with unusual rock forms, many of which have significance to the Tusken tribes who have inhabited this area for thousands of years. Anakin passes under the 90 meter (300 feet)-high B'Thazoshe Bridge (which translates into basic as "bantha horn turned to stone"). Formed by ancient drainage channels, it is the largest natural bridge on Tatooine, and is considered a sacred site by the Sand People. The bridge also marks the boundary of the Tuskens' ancient hunting territory. Sand People have a tradition of letting off rounds of blaster fire before passing through—failure to do so is said to bring bad luck on the tribe.

TUSKEN CAMP

Tusken settlements are scattered across Tatooine's deserts. Because the Tuskens are a nomadic species, they keep few possessions beyond weapons and food stores, although they set great store on the spoils of raids on Jawas or human settlers. These raids are not entirely mercenary, but are intrinsic to Tusken culture, which demands that males prove their skill in battle to maintain their standing in the tribe. Prisoners taken in such raids are usually subjected to harsh rituals.

BURIAL SITE

Cliegg buries his beloved wife, Shmi, alongside the graves of his parents, Gredda and Lef, and his brother Edern, who died aged 14 when he lost control of the family V-35 speeder. For most Tatooine farmers, the untimely death of family members and friends is a common experience that is borne stoically. Burial is a private matter for these isolated communities. Utility droids dig plots, which are marked by plain headstones. During a simple ceremony, surviving family members usually speak a few poignant last words while the body is placed beneath the hot sand.

SPACEPORTS

THE FLOW OF INTERGALACTIC TRADE makes spaceports common on most inhabited worlds. They range from the cosmopolitan, bustling megaports on Coruscant to tiny docking bays on outworld planets such as Tatooine. Most spaceports are noisy, polluted places populated by an entire community of pilots, mechanics, inspectors, parts dealers, and smugglers. These professionals talk the complex language of galactic spacecraft, while spacers discuss little-known, high-risk space routes and tell tales of encounters with pirates. Working alongside the spaceports is space traffic control, which receives landing requests from incoming craft and assigns docking coordinates, allowing them to land safely.

TATOOINE DOCKING BAYS

Mos Espa is dotted with dozens of small to mid-size docking bays, equipped for refueling and general repairs. Many bays are rented by spacers running missions ranging from simple cargo and passenger delivery to smuggling of contraband. Arrivals are usually greeted with a flood of mechanics-for-hire, droid taxis, con-artists, and courtesans.

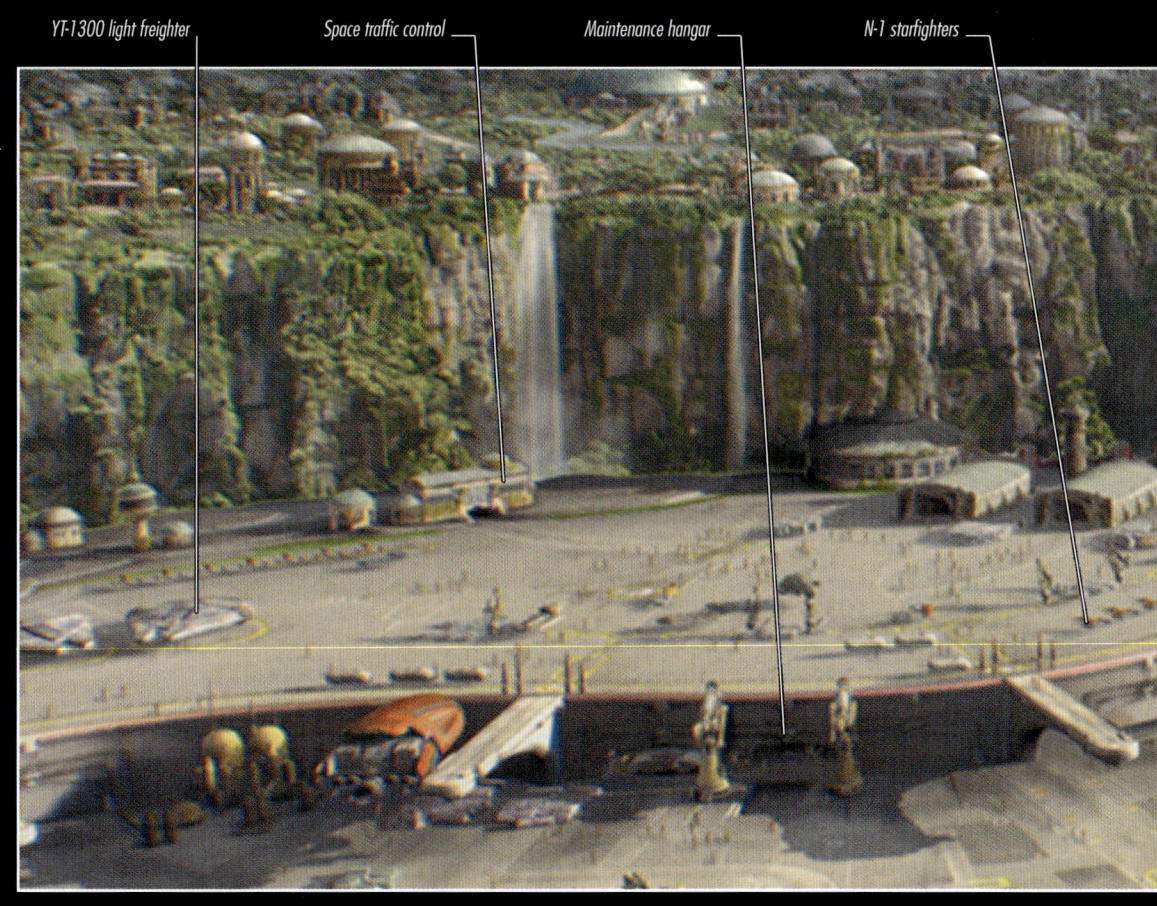

YT-1300 light freighter — *Space traffic control* — *Maintenance hangar* — *N-1 starfighters*

THEED SPACEPORT

Dominating the land below the great cliffs, Theed Spaceport is an unprecedented development in the Naboo's tradition-bound culture. Its unadorned, functional construction is testament to the speed and urgency with which it was built. The only nod to the Naboo design aesthetic is its elegantly curved docking platform, which mimics the natural sweep of the cliffs. Built with reparation money from the Republic after the Trade Federation invasion, the spaceport accommodates the increased space traffic resulting from Senator Amidala's high-profile tenure. The spaceport also receives immigrants seeking mining work on Naboo's spice-rich moons.

CORUSCANT SPACEPORT

When Anakin Skywalker accompanies Senator Padmé Amidala into hiding off-planet, he is advised that the least noticeable way to leave is via a freighter spaceport. The huge craft that dock here are cargo carriers, transporting luxury goods from Coruscant to every corner of the galaxy, and returning with raw materials not available on the urbanized capital planet. These craft are not passenger ships, although many impoverished emigrants obtain steerage on them. Passenger areas are made and furnished with makeshift components, with unreliable air and life-support. As well as migrants, the spaceport is busy with loading droids and overseers ensuring that each ship receives its correct load of cargo.

CORONET SPACEPORT

The sprawling Coronet Spaceport serves the capital city of Corellia, a bustling Core World that's been famous for millennia for its shipbuilding prowess. The profits from Corellia's industrial might never seem to reach Coronet City's legions of impoverished citizens, and so spaceport security is heavy, with local authorities acting aggressively to keep the capital's downtrodden out of the sight of visiting tourists, government officials, and magnates from the galaxy's megacorps.

- Cargo loading droid
- Refueling droid
- Auxiliary power generator
- Cargo modules
- Action VI bulk freighter

GEONOSIS

THE RED, OUTER RIM PLANET of Geonosis is ringed by asteroids that were created by the decimation of a local moonlet by a 2 km (1.25 mile)-wide comet. The planet's surface is scarred from falling meteors and episodic radiation storms, which have caused several mass extinctions. The semi-insectoid Geonosians—the planet's higher life-forms—were consequently driven underground, where they now inhabit hives and manufacture battle droids. The planet's barren exterior is dominated by huge insectoids called merdeths, and various other animals, including savage massiffs.

SECRET HANGAR

In his Delta-7 Jedi starfighter, Obi-Wan Kenobi follows Jango and Boba Fett in their spaceship from Kamino to Geonosis. The bounty hunters descend toward small shutter doors located beside the docked Trade Federation core ships. Jango uses a clearance code signal to enter a hangar inside the underground droid-loading bays. These small hangars dot the perimeter of the droid-loading fields, and are equipped with Geonosian fighters ready to make lightning strikes against the occasional marauding merdeth or other uninvited visitors. The Geonosians are particularly vigilant when clients are taking receipt of their droid units.

CORE SHIPS

The Geonosians have begun to fulfill their battle droid order for the Separatist Alliance, and the first fleet of battleships has arrived to take delivery of the units. Core ships detach from the orbiting Trade Federation battleships and land in docking bays that connect to the droid factory loading hangars wherever fissures in the ground make excavation possible. The ships lower in stages into the docking bays to facilitate transferral of the droids into storage holds on various levels. The core ships also undergo maintenance and are upgraded with hardware for the semi-autonomous droids.

HIVE GALLERIES

The Archduke of the ruling Stalgasin hive colony, Poggle the Lesser, takes his business clients, the Neimoidians, around one of the galleries inside the hive entrance tower, toward the suite of meeting rooms provided for esteemed guests. Geonosian hives are connected to each other by kilometers of populated tunnels that extend underneath much of the planet; each hive guards its own tunnels with vigilance. Periodically, great wars are fought for control of the major hives, with battles taking place throughout the tunnel networks. Few outsiders know that Geonosian nobles like Poggle are themselves servants of ruling queens, who dwell deep below their colonies or in secret redoubts, sending emissaries to issue orders to their underlings.

ENTRANCE TOWER

The factory entrance tower that Obi-Wan encounters after he lands on Geonosis is an impressive piece of Geonosian hive architecture. Every major factory has a grand entrance like this, through which Geonosians receive visiting clients. Meeting rooms and board rooms are located along nearby corridors, which means that customers are afforded only the briefest of glimpses into the turmoil of the factory before signing the all-important contract. The Geonosis landscape is dotted with similar rock towers, constructed from solidified rock paste strengthened with a laminasteel framework. Most towers act as cooling chimneys for the heavily populated hives below, letting out hot air through side vents. The factories typically lie just beneath the surface, with living areas for the drones alongside; beneath this are the more opulent nests and public spaces occupied by the ruling caste. Deeper still are enormous caverns fed by underground streams in which an edible fungus is cultivated. The queen's egg chamber occupies the deepest level, though the Stalgasin matriarch, Karina the Great, has abandoned her chamber for more secure quarters.

DROID FACTORY

GEONOSIS' GIGANTIC FACTORIES mass-produce droids, vehicles, weapons, and military parts for a select range of shadowy clients. The underground factories are grimy, noisy, foul-smelling places cut from the rock of the planet and maintained by an industrious workforce of flightless Geonosian drones. The Geonosians tinker relentlessly with their manufacturing processes until they achieve peak efficiency, with maimed and crushed drones an unavoidable price of achieving such gains. Speed and reliability are the hives' main concerns, an attitude that appeals to the Separatist Alliance's ruthless commercial instincts. It is in this hostile environment that Anakin Skywalker and Padmé Amidala find themselves battling for their lives against the machinery's inhuman might.

Droid manufacturing is virtually automated, utilizing a network of conveyor belts to turn molten metal into an army of fighting machines.

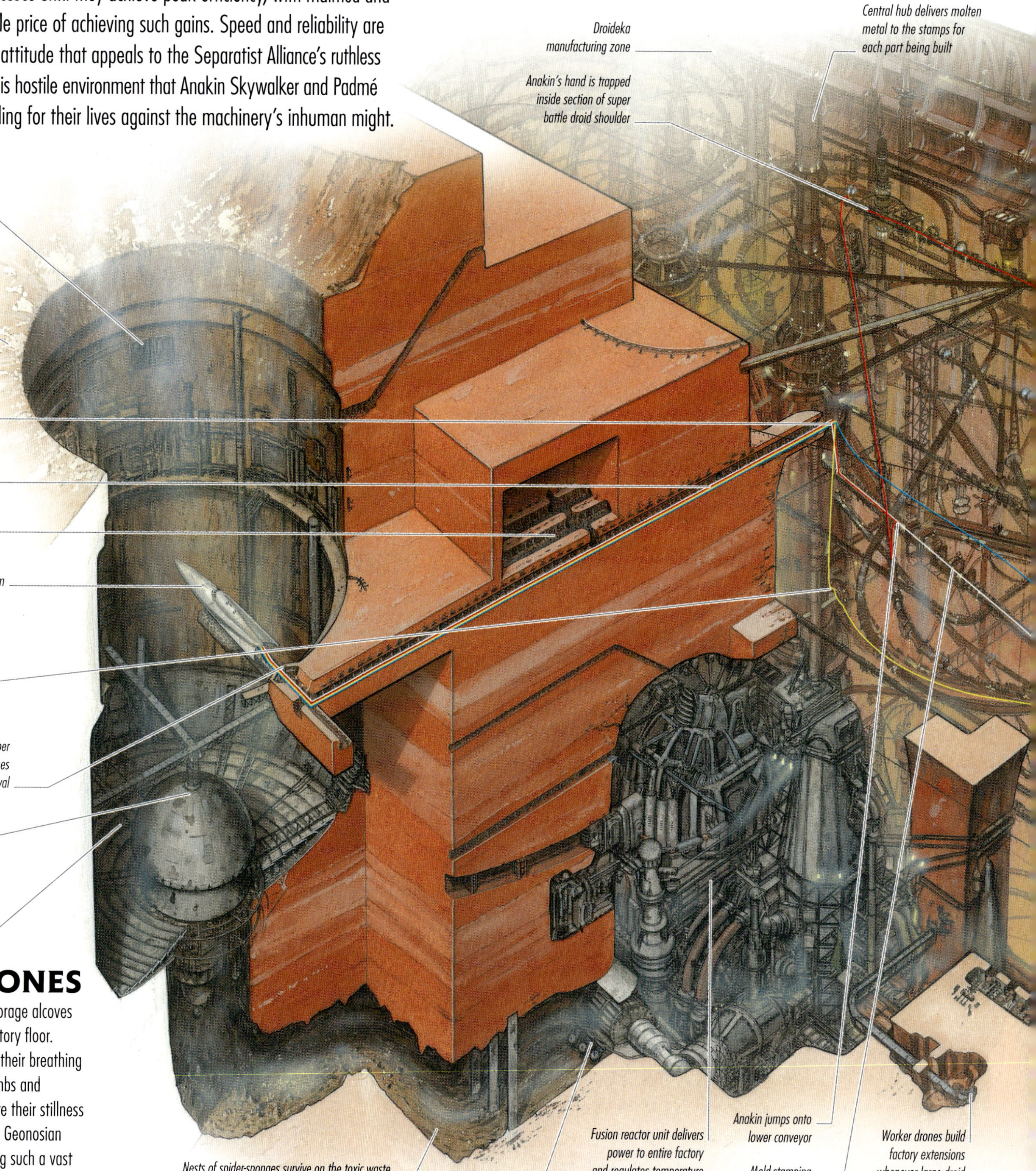

- Vent shaft
- White mineral deposits from vaporizing gases
- Retractable ledge used by winged Geonosian overseers
- Geonosian drones attack Anakin and Padmé
- Surplus workers in storage alcoves
- Padmé's starship lands on an inspection platform
- SRT (Short-Range Transport) droid picks up C-3PO
- Airlock doors to small maintenance antechamber with security consoles, used by Geonosian drones to raise the alarm at Anakin and Padmé's arrival
- Power-generator hub
- Cooling plates extract water and usable gases from exhaust fumes for use in the factory
- Droideka manufacturing zone
- Anakin's hand is trapped inside section of super battle droid shoulder
- Central hub delivers molten metal to the stamps for each part being built
- Nests of spider-sponges survive on the toxic waste gases produced by the factory
- Air vent
- Fusion reactor unit delivers power to entire factory and regulates temperature of molten metal
- Anakin jumps onto lower conveyor
- Mold-stamping equipment
- Worker drones build factory extensions whenever large droid orders require extra space

SLEEPING DRONES

In between shifts, workers rest in storage alcoves located in warm corridors off the factory floor. They do not actually sleep, but slow their breathing and reduce the circulation to their limbs and extremities. They remain alert despite their stillness and it takes little to rouse them. The Geonosian rulers realize the usefulness of having such a vast number of watchful (but disposable) eyes.

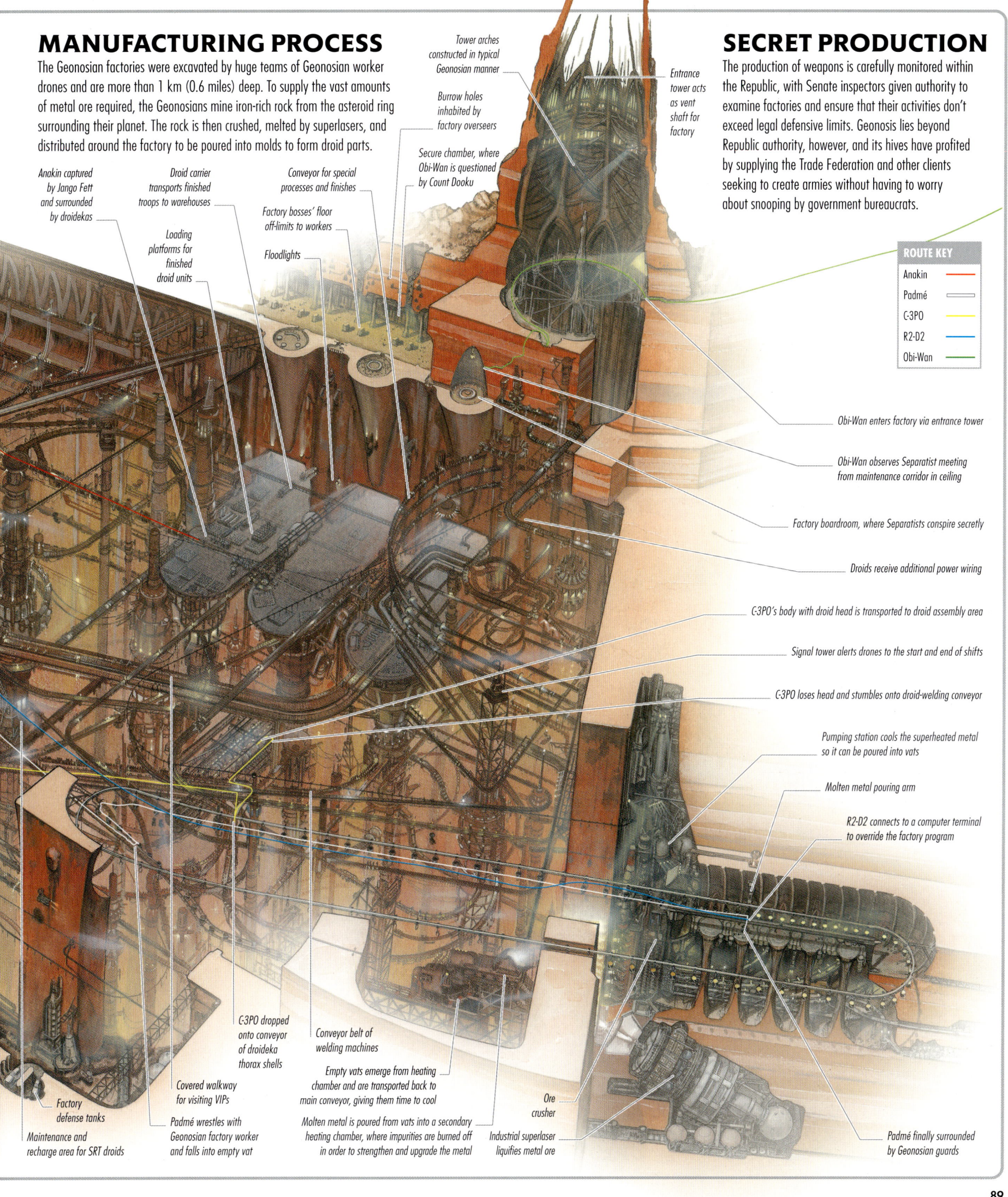

MANUFACTURING PROCESS

The Geonosian factories were excavated by huge teams of Geonosian worker drones and are more than 1 km (0.6 miles) deep. To supply the vast amounts of metal ore required, the Geonosians mine iron-rich rock from the asteroid ring surrounding their planet. The rock is then crushed, melted by superlasers, and distributed around the factory to be poured into molds to form droid parts.

SECRET PRODUCTION

The production of weapons is carefully monitored within the Republic, with Senate inspectors given authority to examine factories and ensure that their activities don't exceed legal defensive limits. Geonosis lies beyond Republic authority, however, and its hives have profited by supplying the Trade Federation and other clients seeking to create armies without having to worry about snooping by government bureaucrats.

ROUTE KEY
- Anakin
- Padmé
- C-3PO
- R2-D2
- Obi-Wan

- Anakin captured by Jango Fett and surrounded by droidekas
- Droid carrier transports finished troops to warehouses
- Loading platforms for finished droid units
- Conveyor for special processes and finishes
- Factory bosses' floor off-limits to workers
- Floodlights
- Tower arches constructed in typical Geonosian manner
- Burrow holes inhabited by factory overseers
- Secure chamber, where Obi-Wan is questioned by Count Dooku
- Entrance tower acts as vent shaft for factory
- Obi-Wan enters factory via entrance tower
- Obi-Wan observes Separatist meeting from maintenance corridor in ceiling
- Factory boardroom, where Separatists conspire secretly
- Droids receive additional power wiring
- C-3PO's body with droid head is transported to droid assembly area
- Signal tower alerts drones to the start and end of shifts
- C-3PO loses head and stumbles onto droid-welding conveyor
- Pumping station cools the superheated metal so it can be poured into vats
- Molten metal pouring arm
- R2-D2 connects to a computer terminal to override the factory program
- Factory defense tanks
- Maintenance and recharge area for SRT droids
- Padmé wrestles with Geonosian factory worker and falls into empty vat
- C-3PO dropped onto conveyor of droideka thorax shells
- Covered walkway for visiting VIPs
- Conveyor belt of welding machines
- Empty vats emerge from heating chamber and are transported back to main conveyor, giving them time to cool
- Molten metal is poured from vats into a secondary heating chamber, where impurities are burned off in order to strengthen and upgrade the metal
- Ore crusher
- Industrial superlaser liquifies metal ore
- Padmé finally surrounded by Geonosian guards

89

EXECUTION ARENA

FOR THE GEONOSIAN MASSES, who live most of their lives underground, a visit to the execution arena is a dramatic and festive occasion. As the surface of the planet is dominated by fierce predatory insects, the risk of the arena being attacked is an added thrill. As the ruling archduke watches imperiously, drones and aristocrats crack their forelimbs together in appreciation of staged events: public executions, unarmed prisoner combat, and choreographed battles that demonstrate the military skills of new droid prototypes or Geonosian soldier hatchlings.

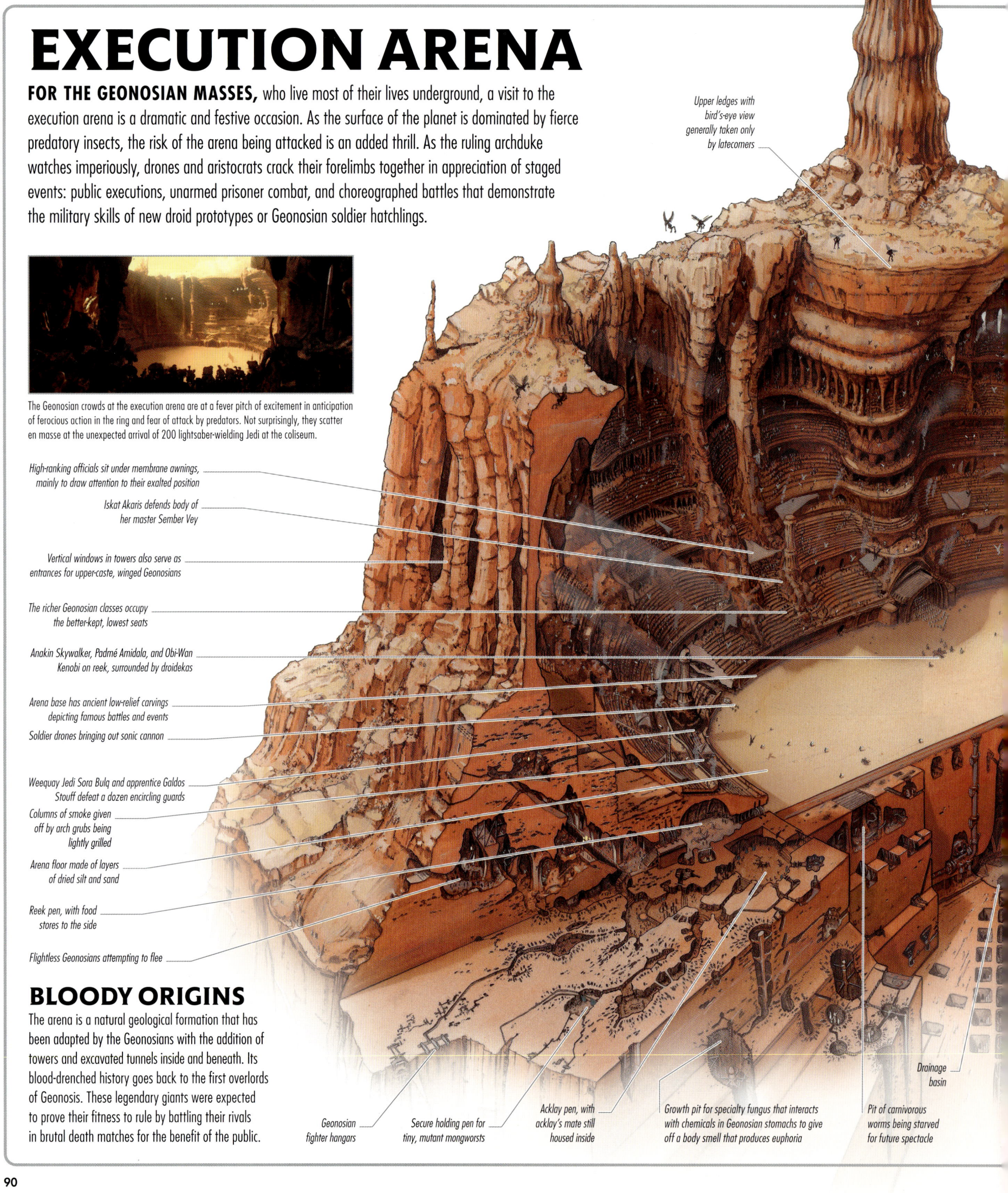

The Geonosian crowds at the execution arena are at a fever pitch of excitement in anticipation of ferocious action in the ring and fear of attack by predators. Not surprisingly, they scatter en masse at the unexpected arrival of 200 lightsaber-wielding Jedi at the coliseum.

- High-ranking officials sit under membrane awnings, mainly to draw attention to their exalted position
- Iskat Akaris defends body of her master Sember Vey
- Vertical windows in towers also serve as entrances for upper-caste, winged Geonosians
- The richer Geonosian classes occupy the better-kept, lowest seats
- Anakin Skywalker, Padmé Amidala, and Obi-Wan Kenobi on reek, surrounded by droidekas
- Arena base has ancient low-relief carvings depicting famous battles and events
- Soldier drones bringing out sonic cannon
- Weequay Jedi Sora Bulq and apprentice Galdos Stouff defeat a dozen encircling guards
- Columns of smoke given off by arch grubs being lightly grilled
- Arena floor made of layers of dried silt and sand
- Reek pen, with food stores to the side
- Flightless Geonosians attempting to flee

- Upper ledges with bird's-eye view generally taken only by latecomers
- Geonosian fighter hangars
- Secure holding pen for tiny, mutant mongworsts
- Acklay pen, with acklay's mate still housed inside
- Growth pit for specialty fungus that interacts with chemicals in Geonosian stomachs to give off a body smell that produces euphoria
- Pit of carnivorous worms being starved for future spectacle
- Drainage basin

BLOODY ORIGINS

The arena is a natural geological formation that has been adapted by the Geonosians with the addition of towers and excavated tunnels inside and beneath. Its blood-drenched history goes back to the first overlords of Geonosis. These legendary giants were expected to prove their fitness to rule by battling their rivals in brutal death matches for the benefit of the public.

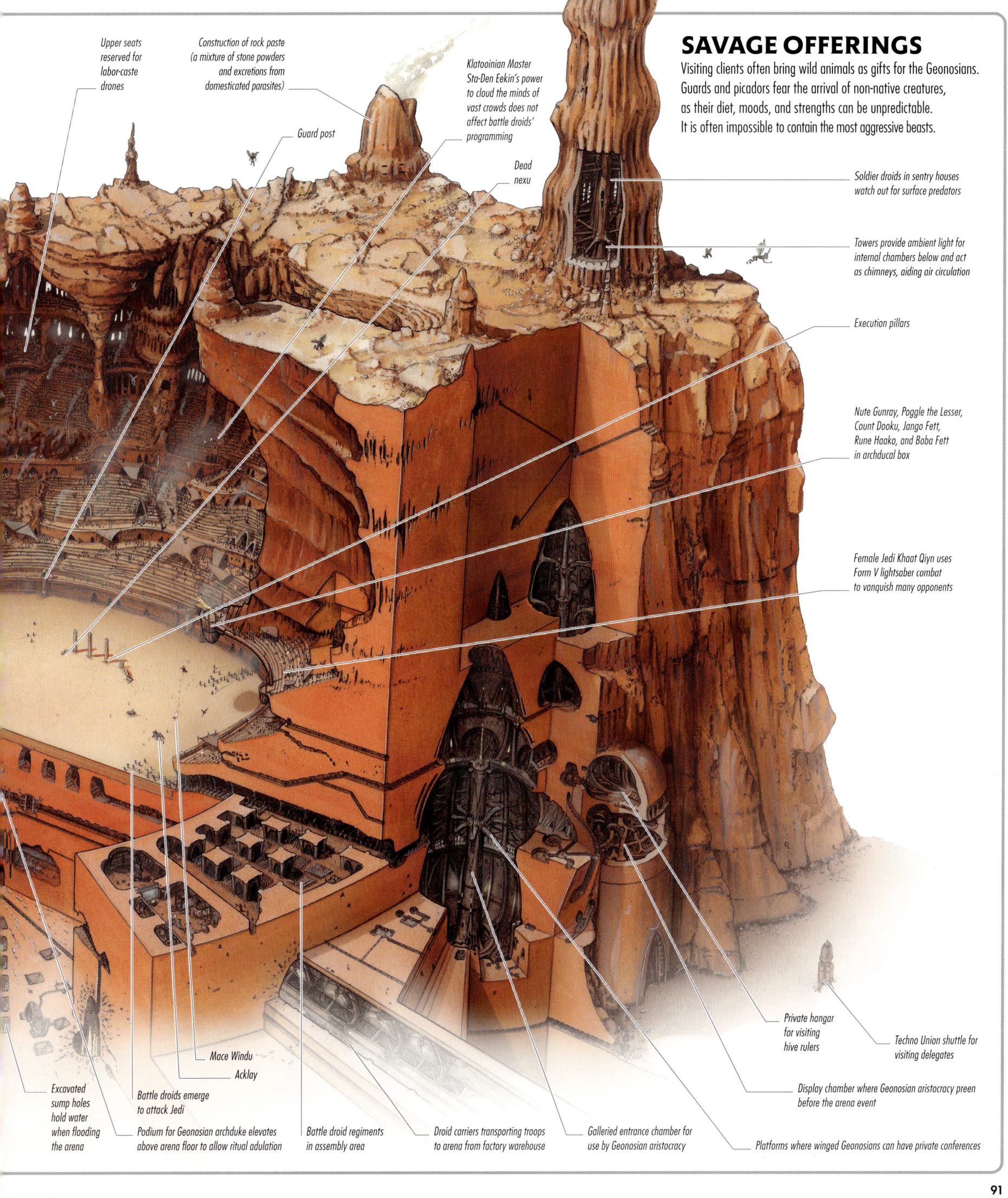

SAVAGE OFFERINGS

Visiting clients often bring wild animals as gifts for the Geonosians. Guards and picadors fear the arrival of non-native creatures, as their diet, moods, and strengths can be unpredictable. It is often impossible to contain the most aggressive beasts.

- Upper seats reserved for labor-caste drones
- Construction of rock paste (a mixture of stone powders and excretions from domesticated parasites)
- Guard post
- Klatooinian Master Sta-Den Eekin's power to cloud the minds of vast crowds does not affect battle droids' programming
- Dead nexu
- Soldier droids in sentry houses watch out for surface predators
- Towers provide ambient light for internal chambers below and act as chimneys, aiding air circulation
- Execution pillars
- Nute Gunray, Poggle the Lesser, Count Dooku, Jango Fett, Rune Haako, and Boba Fett in archducal box
- Female Jedi Khaat Qiyn uses Form V lightsaber combat to vanquish many opponents
- Private hangar for visiting hive rulers
- Techno Union shuttle for visiting delegates
- Display chamber where Geonosian aristocracy preen before the arena event
- Platforms where winged Geonosians can have private conferences
- Galleried entrance chamber for use by Geonosian aristocracy
- Droid carriers transporting troops to arena from factory warehouse
- Battle droid regiments in assembly area
- Podium for Geonosian archduke elevates above arena floor to allow ritual adulation
- Battle droids emerge to attack Jedi
- Mace Windu
- Acklay
- Excavated sump holes hold water when flooding the arena

91

REPUBLIC ARMY

FACING THE OMINOUS REALITY of a Separatist war machine poised for an all-out attack on the great Galactic Republic, the Senate has no choice but to respond quickly and decisively. The risks are great: the Republic must deploy an army it has neither amassed nor trained, and whose battle effectiveness is as yet unproven. The Jedi Council's skillful command, however, ensures that the Republic's bold, pre-emptive strike on the Separatist forces is effective, by utilizing a full complement of battle vehicles to achieve air and ground supremacy against formidable odds in the unfamiliar landscape of Geonosis.

With high-ranking Jedi acting as de facto generals, more than 80 regiments of clone troopers are deployed on Geonosis. The clones use imaging systems in their helmet visors to see through dense smoke on the battlefield, allowing an unbroken advance on the Trade Federation battle droids.

REPUBLIC TROOPERS

On Geonosis, the Republic deploys two full battle armies, with Yoda and Mace Windu commanding one each and other veteran Jedi Knights in charge of eight corps of 36,864 troops each. All other divisions are led by specially trained clones: commanders head regiments of 2,304 individuals; clone captains lead companies of 144 troops; lieutenants head platoons of 36 soldiers, and sergeants command squads, each made up of nine clone troopers. Separate ranks of specialized clones operate gunships, drop ships, AT-TEs, and SPHA-Ts.

LAAT/C

LAAT/c (Low-Altitude Assault Transport/carrier) are used to airlift military hardware right into the thick of battle, such as AT-TEs, portable power generators and shield projectors, observation posts, field medical centers, supplies, and fixed artillery. They also ensure the heavy-strike SPHA-Ts are well defended by AT-TEs and infantry on foot to a distance of several kilometers. Magnetic clamps hold payloads in place and can be disengaged instantly, allowing the payloads to be dropped speedily. A wide wingspan allows maximum distribution of repulsorlift vanes when carrying heavy weights.

       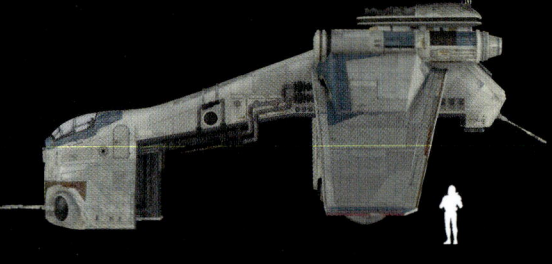

TROOPER | **SERGEANT** | **LIEUTENANT** | **CAPTAIN** | **COMMANDER**
192,000 DEPLOYED IN BATTLE

LAAT/I GUNSHIP
1,600 DEPLOYED

LAAT/C (AT-TE CARRIER)
400 DEPLOYED

GUNSHIPS

Fast and maneuverable LAAT/i gunships make repeated passes over the entire battlefield, responding to situations and opportunities wherever needed. They rain fire on enemy vehicles, clearing a path for the advancing clone infantry, and drop squads of clone trooper commandos at the battlefront. Commandos are specially trained for high-risk covert work and wear a higher grade armor with additional weapons capacity. Despite their strengths, gunships prove vulnerable to Separatist antiair batteries positioned in rough terrain below.

DEADLY JUGGERNAUT

Deployed in squads of four at the rear of advancing AT-TEs, SPHA-Ts combine the devastating firepower of a permanent laser-cannon emplacement with the ability to literally walk into battle on powerful articulated legs. SPHA-Ts are deployed in key positions on several battlefronts, proving particularly effective on the battlefield commanded by Yoda. They also provide an impregnable line of defense for the fleet of assault ships that land immediately outside the arena.

ASSAULT SHIPS

Acclamator-class assault ships land outside the smoking arena, unloading military vehicles and troops, and providing an assembly point for SPHA-Ts. Disembarked troops initially prevail on the flat ground of the canyon floor, where their beam weapons are most effective, while Separatist artillery persists in the rougher lands. Earlier, assault ships made preemptive strikes against Geonosian beak-wing facilities, leaving the fighters that remained unable to make headway against the Republic's orbital blockade.

AT-TE
2,160 DEPLOYED

SPHA-T
100 DEPLOYED

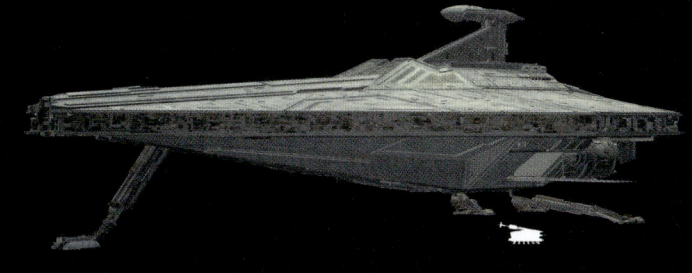

ASSAULT SHIP
12 DEPLOYED

SEPARATIST FORCES

ALTHOUGH THE REPUBLIC FORBIDS the existence of mass armies, many private interests maintain small armies in local territories. The most powerful armies are those owned by the wealthy commerce organizations, who use a number of attack droids for purposes of debt collection and revenue enforcement. However, these trade bodies have now illegally pooled their armies to create a single, truly sinister force that threatens the hegemony of the Republic. Geonosis' barren rock landscapes are the backdrop to its clone army's first encounter with the combined ranks of the commerce organizations' droid armies.

In the command room behind Separatist lines, Geonosian rulers observe and direct the battle on a live-feed holomap provided by at-site camdroids. The Separatists are able to reassign battle objectives and targets to their droid forces via radio signals to their processors. In the past, the Geonosians staged large-scale training and exhibition battles from the command room.

SEPARATIST HARDWARE

Surprised by the Republic's assault, the Separatists mobilize all forces not already loaded onto their starships, supplementing droid contingents with battle droids direct from the factories. They have no airborne vehicles, although spider droids and hailfire droids carry ground-to-air weapons, which prove effective against Republic gunships. Techno Union starships and Trade Federation core ships carry no weapons, and rely on the defense of the droids. Droidekas were preferentially loaded into the escaping starships, and are mostly absent from the battle.

DWARF SPIDER DROIDS

Dwarf spider droids advance in front of a platoon of battle droids, closely followed by homing spider droids, and after that another infantry formation. Their low height allows the larger homing spider droids to fire over them, providing a formidable advance attack. Much of the dwarf spider droid's head space is devoted to power cells for two blasters, one mounted on the head and one underneath. Designed for use in narrow mine shafts, these droids are slow to react to fast-moving targets above or to the side because they cannot swivel their blasters independently of their heads.

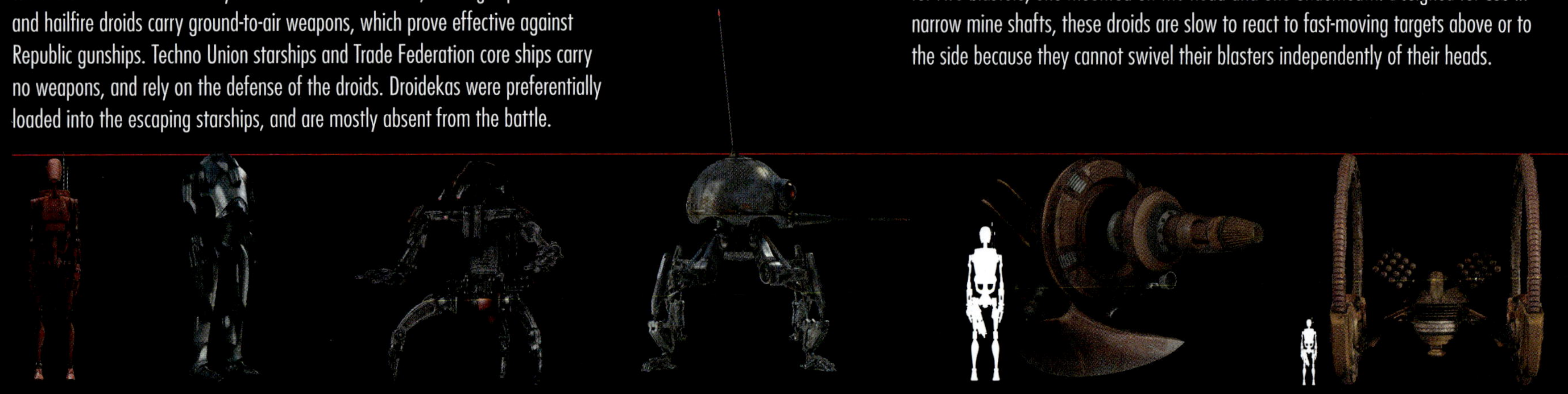

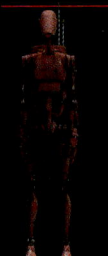
BATTLE DROID
1,000,000 DEPLOYED

SUPER BATTLE DROID
100,000 DEPLOYED

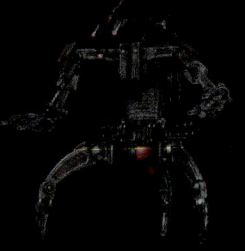
DROIDEKA
3,000 DEPLOYED

DWARF SPIDER DROID
15,000 DEPLOYED

SONIC CANNON
4 DEPLOYED (IN ARENA)

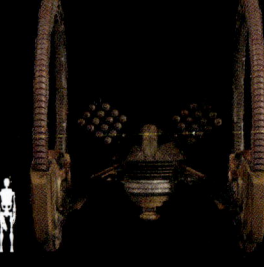
HAILFIRE DROID
4,100 DEPLOYED

HOMING SPIDER DROIDS

Commerce Guild homing spider droids are effective against ground-based and airborne targets, covering wide expanses of battlefield at great speed on their all-terrain legs. Sensor equipment locks onto and keeps track of enemy targets, while their dish-shaped laser cannons supply sustained fire. Providing effective ground cover for the Trade Federation core ships, as well as their own smaller spaceships, homing spider droids manage to decimate whole contingents of Republic AT-TEs although they are eventually subdued by daring gunship assaults.

SONIC CANNON

A Geonosian soldier drone operates a sonic cannon, which fires balls of high-impact concussion energy. The Geonosians house an arsenal of these weapons at the execution arena for use in the event of outbreaks by particularly violent creatures or disturbances in the audience. Geonosians also use sonic weapons in inter-hive conflicts. Sonic cannons have an advantage in that they can be set to varying degrees of force, so they smash bones but leave rock tunnels undamaged.

HAILFIRE DROIDS

The InterGalactic Banking Clan's hailfire droids are a powerful presence on the battlefield, although their use is short-lived because they carry a limited number of missiles. They make fast, concerted charges on Republic AT-TEs, using twin chin-mounted blasters once their missiles are depleted. Missiles are effective against stationary or slow-moving targets on terrain where blaster weapons are unusable due to a lack of clear lines of sight.

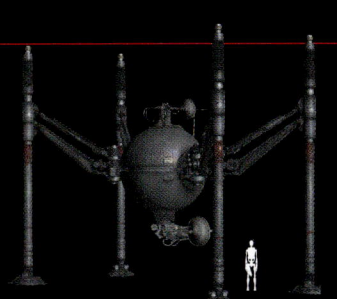  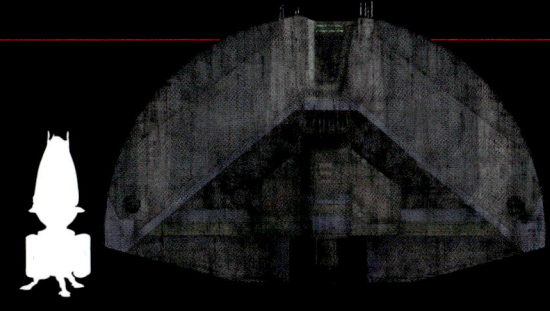 

HOMING SPIDER DROID
7,500 DEPLOYED

TECHNO UNION STARSHIP
286 ON BATTLEFIELD (169 ESCAPE)

COMMERCE GUILD STARSHIP
41 IN BATTLE (36 ESCAPE)

TRADE FEDERATION CORE SHIP
60 ON BATTLEFIELD (46 ESCAPE)

6 On the battlefield that Mace Windu commands, the Separatists deploy a large number of homing spider droids and dwarf spider droids, followed by battle droid infantry formations. With clear lines of sight across the flat canyon floor, these large droids are able to make terrifyingly effective use of their blaster weapons.

7 Jedi Master Kit Fisto leads a charge of clone troopers, using his Force senses to deflect blaster bolts and protect his men. The Republic army in this part of the battle heads off an attempt by the droid forces to break through a canyon and into the clone ranks.

8 Yoda lands at the forward command center beside a concentration of mighty SPHA-T guns—the Republic's heaviest artillery. Airlifted in by LAAT/c, the mobile command center is a fully equipped tactical communications station, receiving signal feeds from clone commanders across the battlefield.

5 Mace and Yoda's gunship lands in a large assembly area protected from rear attack by hills behind. While clone commanders oversee the unloading of clone troops and AT-TEs from assault ships, Mace takes control of clone commando units and Yoda departs for the forward command center.

4 Mace Windu, Yoda, Ki-Adi-Mundi, and Kit Fisto witness a direct hit on one of the six gunships used to evacuate Jedi from the arena. These gunships carry few clone troopers in order to allow more room for Jedi passengers. Yoda silently mourns the addition of more names to the ranks of Jedi lost in the battle.

3 Separatist leaders travel by underground route from the arena to the command center. Already unsettled by the sudden appearance of a Republic army, they are now experiencing jammed communication signals and are unable to send in their entire droid armies, many of which are already loaded onto ships.

2 Well-armored and self-shielded Trade Federation core ships attempt to finish loading their huge cargoes rather than launching half-empty at the first sight of danger. Smaller, more vulnerable Techno Union ships attempt to escape with their payloads of droid artillery, but gunship fire prevents many from doing so.

1 Republic gunships make the first assault on Techno Union starships docked outside the arena. The Geonosians build their docking facilities and warehouses primarily in the valleys of their planet, where permanent habitation is undesirable; Geonosian cities are situated mostly on cliff faces and highlands.

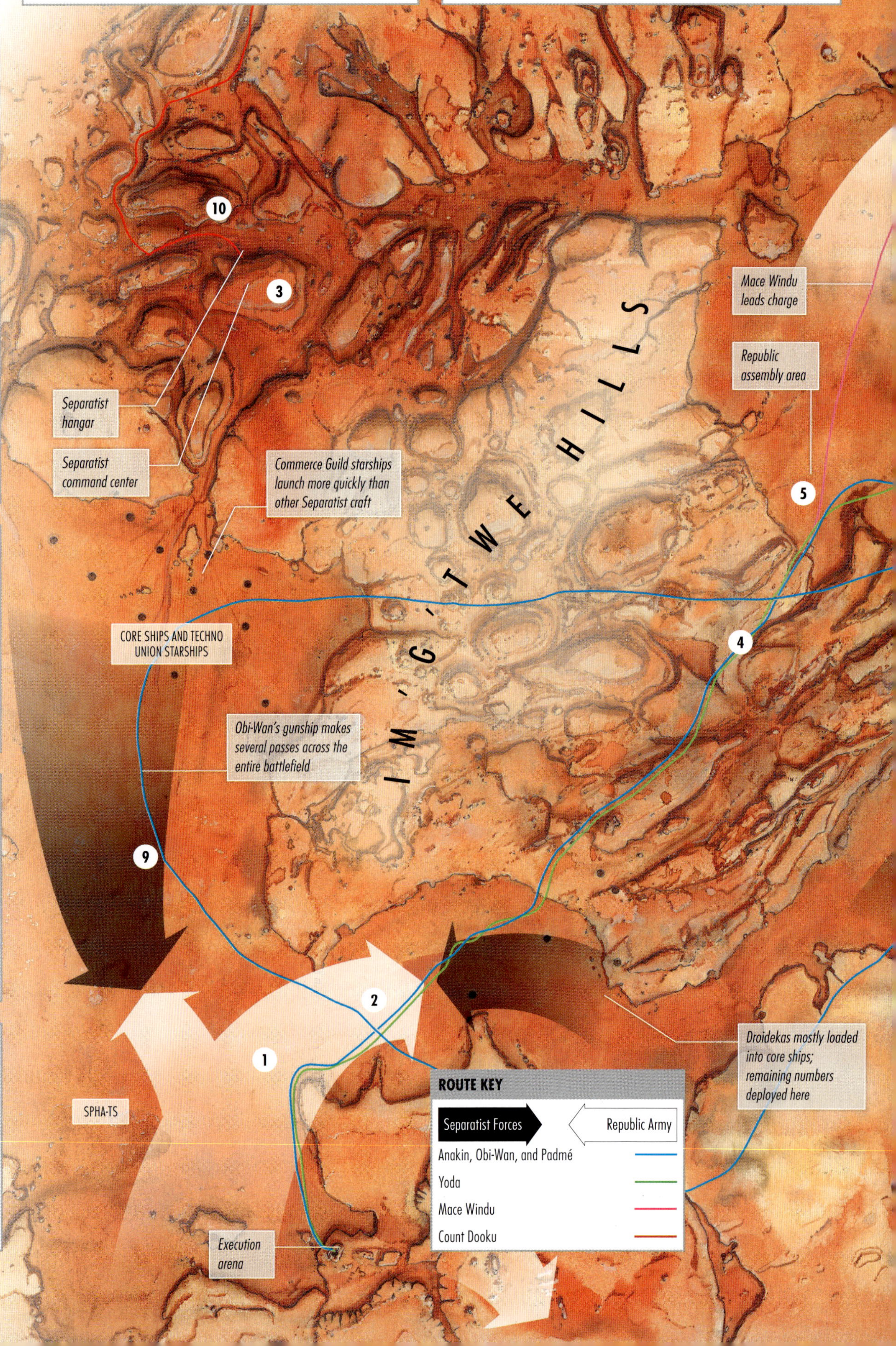

IM-G'TWE HILLS

Mace Windu leads charge

Republic assembly area

Separatist hangar

Separatist command center

Commerce Guild starships launch more quickly than other Separatist craft

CORE SHIPS AND TECHNO UNION STARSHIPS

Obi-Wan's gunship makes several passes across the entire battlefield

Droidekas mostly loaded into core ships; remaining numbers deployed here

SPHA-Ts

Execution arena

ROUTE KEY

Separatist Forces → ← Republic Army

Anakin, Obi-Wan, and Padmé
Yoda
Mace Windu
Count Dooku

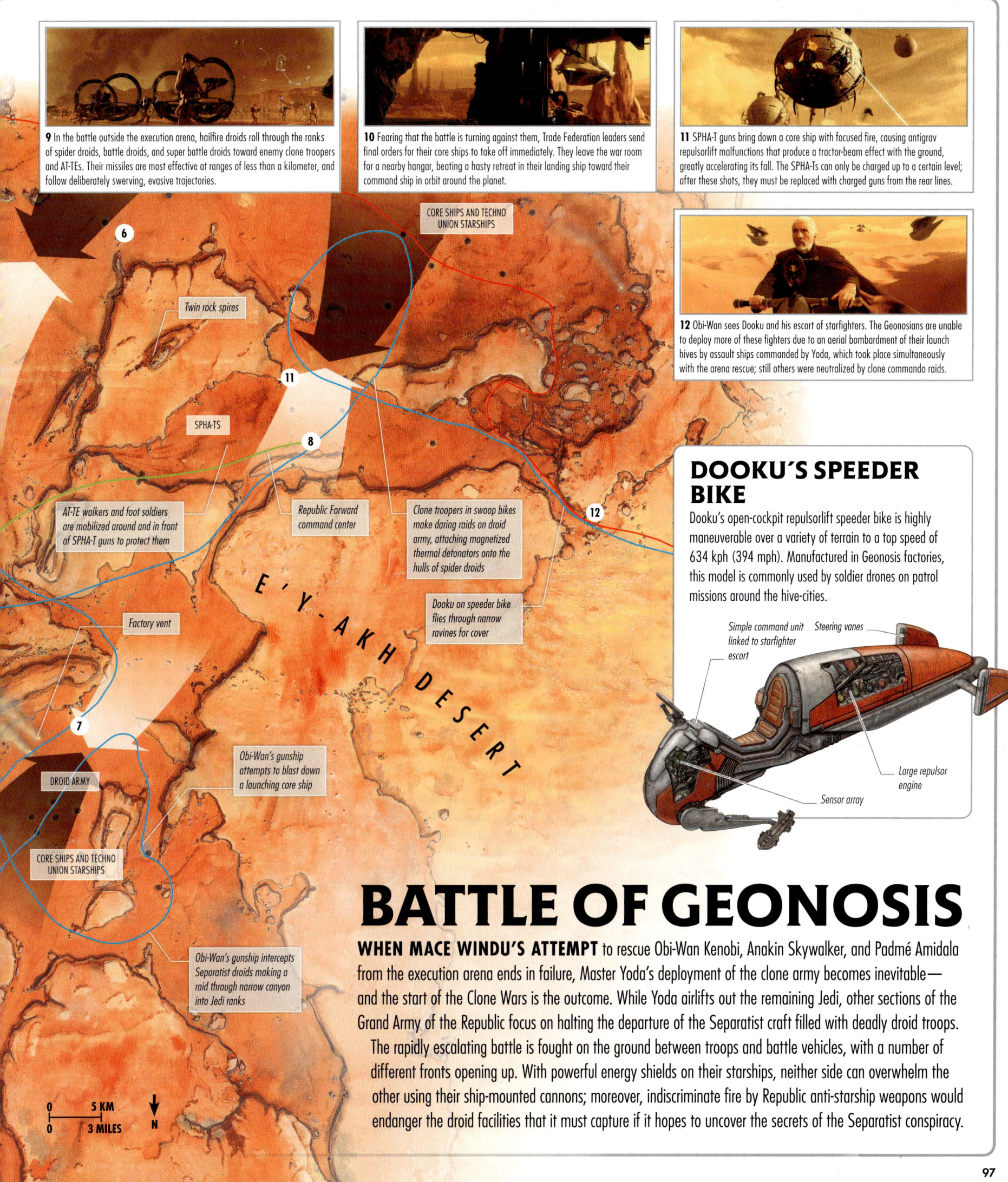

HANGAR DUELS

IN HIS DEALINGS WITH THE GEONOSIANS, Count Dooku avails himself of a dedicated hangar removed from the war room and those hangars used by financial and industrial cartel officials. Dooku's hangar lies northward of the main battlefield, in an abandoned factory outpost, where his getaway vessel is manned by an FA-4 pilot droid and stands ready for takeoff. The remoteness of the building suits Dooku's hidden agenda, but the long journey to his ship is almost his undoing: carrying the Geonosians' secret plans for their ultimate weapon, he is soon sighted by Obi-Wan Kenobi…

DOOKU'S FLIGHT

Leaving the Separatist command center, Dooku flies to his hangar by speeder bike, located many kilometers away across the E'Y-Akh Desert. He skirts around the edge of the battlefield behind Separatist lines, passing close by the gunship in which Obi-Wan travels with Anakin Skywalker and Padmé Amidala.

BATTLE OF WILLS

Alerted by his Force sensitivity, Yoda comes to the aid of Obi-Wan and Anakin. Dooku hurls chunks of the ceiling at Yoda, which risks bringing the entire structure down on both of them. Yoda intercepts and redirects each piece with ease.

LIGHTSABER COMBAT

Yoda knows only too well that if Count Dooku is not stopped from leaving Geonosis, he will rally more planets to his cause. In the half-light of the renegade leader's secret hangar, Yoda wields the lightsaber he so reluctantly uses in combat, attempting to block Dooku's path to his ship.

SEALING THE HANGAR

On Padmé's arrival, contingents of clone troopers seal all the entrances from potential intervention by Separatist troops. Once the battle is over, Republic technicians and intelligence analysts will inspect the building for clues to Dooku's whereabouts.

ABANDONED FACTORY

Dooku's hangar is situated in the pinnacle of a tower above an abandoned factory that once supplied highly specialized, aquatic sonic weapons to both sides during a short-lived civil war on the swamp planet of Derenzil. The risk of the project made a security hangar for Geonosian fighters necessary. The Geonosians build or expand their factories when they receive big orders; afterward, once the project is completed, they relocate the surplus workers or consign them to dormancy.

- Vent
- Docking clamp for starfighters
- Flight entrance
- Geonosian wall construction absorbs shocks from docking spaceships
- Maintenance floor used by Dooku's Geonosian fighter escort
- Yoda uses the Force to prevent gas-release trunking from crushing Obi-Wan and Anakin
- Obi-Wan and Anakin, lying wounded
- Inspection walkway
- Power feeds and systems diagnostics
- Yoda
- Dooku escapes into his starship
- Launch chute designed for Geonosian fighter-class ships
- Padmé's gunship
- Southwest entrance
- Stylized floor mosaic recalls Geonosian egg-nest pattern
- Dooku's speeder bike
- Fuel stores
- Reactor powers hangar machinery
- Walkway to north entrance (where Obi-Wan and Anakin arrive)

GEONOSIAN CANYON

Padmé fires at Dooku's solar sailer in a forlorn attempt to stop the dastardly ex-Jedi from leaving the planet. Nevertheless, his ship shoots safely across the wide canyon expanse outside the hangar. This canyon is a former industrial region now totally uninhabited by Geonosians. Like many of the planet's valleys, the flat plain is occasionally flooded by sudden storms or vast groundwater eruptions.

JEDI TO THE RESCUE

To rescue the supreme chancellor before the Separatist Alliance holds the Republic to ransom, the Jedi prepare a special assault squadron led by Anakin Skywalker and Obi-Wan Kenobi with clone force backup. Anakin's boldness and audacity drive the mission to success, and he is lauded as a hero for saving Palpatine. But his cold execution of Count Dooku aboard *Invisible Hand* pushes him closer to the dark side of the Force.

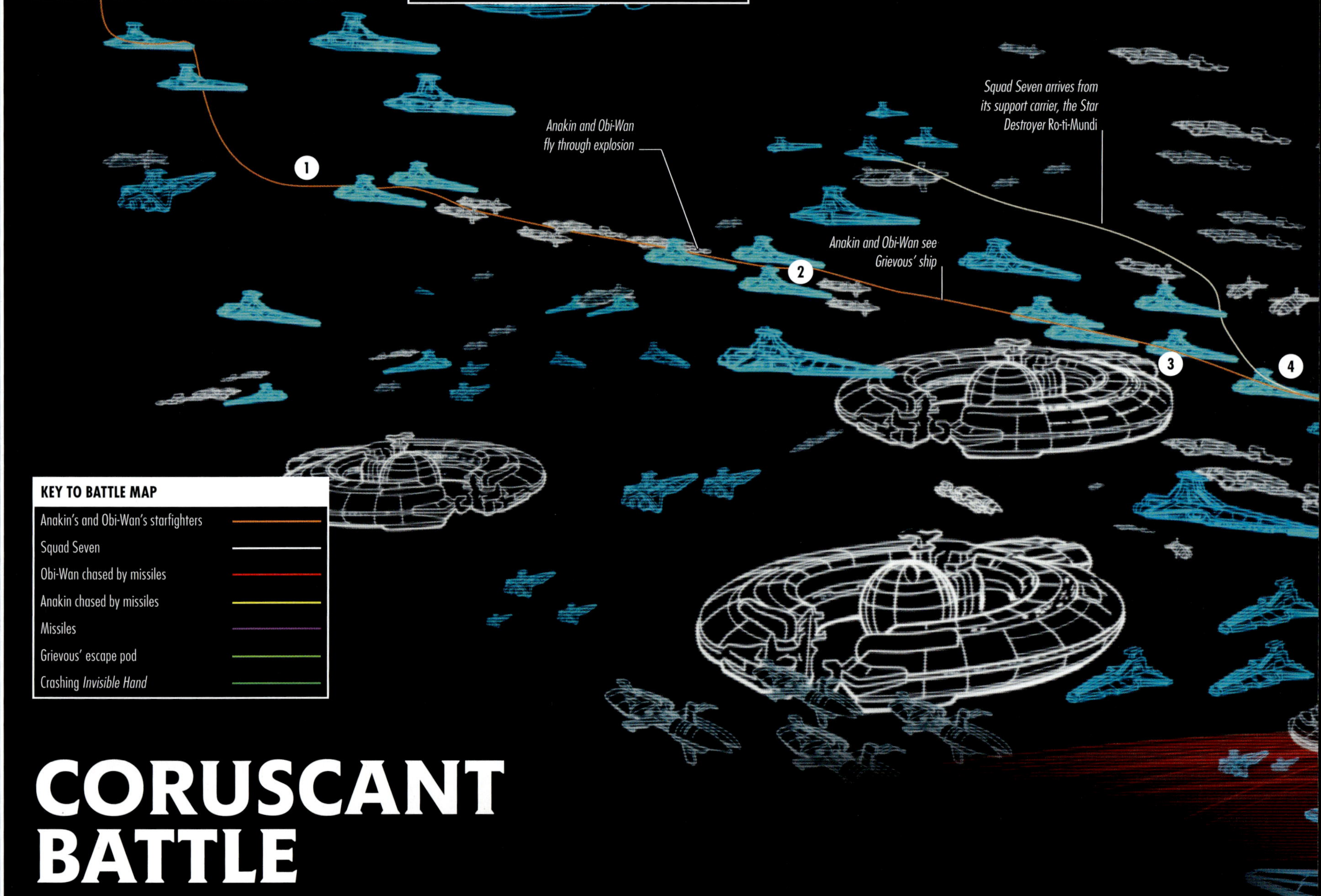

1 Newly returned from the Outer Rim Sieges, Obi-Wan and Anakin are dispatched to rescue Supreme Chancellor Palpatine. They must recover him alive, as his death from any cause would be a severe blow to the Republic.

2 In their agile Eta-2 *Actis* Interceptors, the Jedi weave between the larger craft slugging out a set-piece engagement. They make their passage through the fighting fleets count, striking at Separatist targets as they go.

Anakin and Obi-Wan fly through explosion

Squad Seven arrives from its support carrier, the Star Destroyer Ro-ti-Mundi

Anakin and Obi-Wan see Grievous' ship

KEY TO BATTLE MAP
- Anakin's and Obi-Wan's starfighters
- Squad Seven
- Obi-Wan chased by missiles
- Anakin chased by missiles
- Missiles
- Grievous' escape pod
- Crashing *Invisible Hand*

CORUSCANT BATTLE

IN A CUNNING AND AUDACIOUS MOVE, the Separatist Alliance brings the Clone Wars to Coruscant, raining death and destruction upon the helpless citizens of the galactic capital. The fierce attack on the planet is a cover for General Grievous' daring foray to kidnap Supreme Chancellor Palpatine, aiming to bring a swift end to the conflict. While the main battle between Separatist and Republic forces rages on the fringe of space, the Jedi High Council determines that the best way to rescue the chancellor is to make a lightning raid on the Separatist command ship, *Invisible Hand*, where Palpatine is being held.

SPACE ARMADAS

Both the Separatist Alliance and the Republic have invested heavily in new ships for their space navies, though the former keeps most of its fleet in the Outer Rim. During the Battle of Coruscant, the Republic fields a far greater number of heavy craft, such as the *Venator*-class Star Destroyers. The Separatists counter by deploying tens of thousands of vulture droids to supplement their adversary's crewed starfighters.

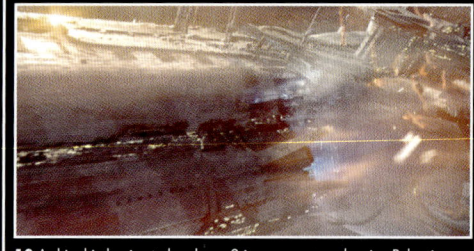

10 As his ship begins to break up, Grievous escapes, leaving Palpatine and the Jedi to their fate. They will survive a fiery re-entry thanks only to Anakin's piloting skills and the efforts of Coruscant's emergency teams.

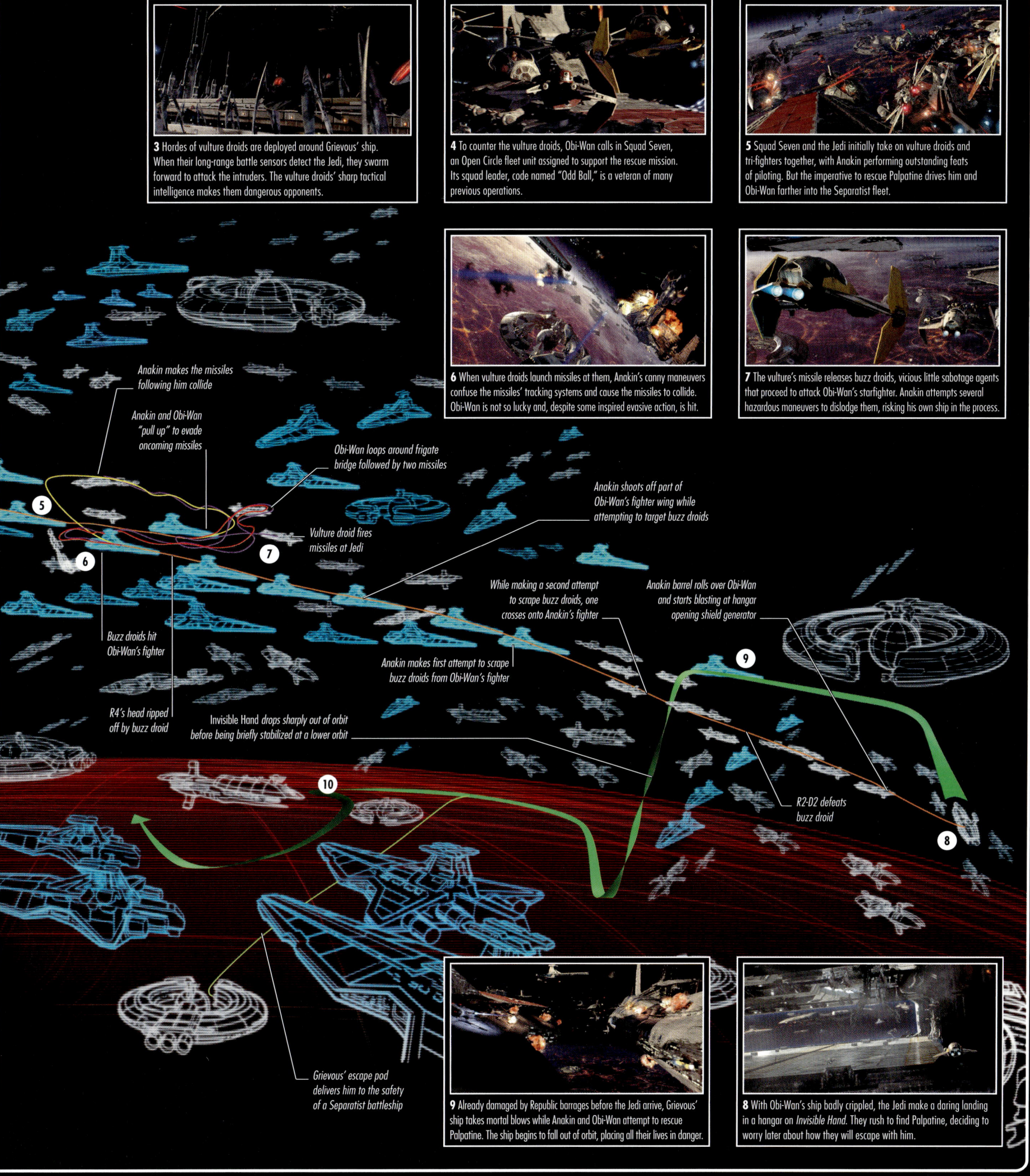

JEDI TEMPLE COMPLEX

THE HEART AND HOME of the Jedi Order, the Jedi Temple has millennia's worth of scars from more turbulent years. The ancient edifice, built and rebuilt over the centuries, fulfills several roles. It is a place of spiritual growth—a center for contemplation, meditation, and the study of the Force. It serves as a martial-arts academy, training potential Jedi and honing their physical skills to perfection. It is the Order's administrative center and headquarters for Jedi operations during the Clone Wars. And it is a repository of knowledge—open and forbidden, light and dark—that has been safeguarded and studied by generations of Jedi.

A REPOSITORY OF THE FORCE

Jedi scholars disagree on the location of the Order's first temple, making cases for Coruscant, Jedha, and Ossus as well as worlds shrouded in myth, such as Tython and Ahch-To. But all agree Coruscant's temple was built around and within a natural spire considered sacred by local Coruscanti as a locus of power, which drew Force-wielders of numerous traditions. The roots of this now-hidden mountain conceal forgotten grottos and lost shrines that remain rich wellsprings of the Force.

Pinnacle room of the Temple Spire, the most sacred Jedi site, containing the oldest-known surviving Jedi texts, in a carefully controlled environment

Hall of Knighthood. Padawans are raised to the status of Jedi Knight here in a ceremony of deep spiritual significance. The status of Master is also formally conferred here

Jedi Reassignment Council Tower houses Chamber of Judgment

Memorial statues of most revered Jedi, suspended in tower by repulsorlift pads

Chamber of Conclave, where representatives of the Jedi Order from across the galaxy meet once a year to hear reports from the Jedi Council

The sacred spire in its natural state, with ancient meditation balconies and access points to the original cave chapels

Mosaic floor salvaged from the ancient Jedi temple of Ossus

Meditation chambers where Padawans awaiting Knighthood spend the night before the ceremony, communing with the Force

Peak of the original sacred spire around which the earliest incarnation of this Jedi Temple was constructed

Meditation balcony surrounding original peak

Lower balcony around peak presents a series of holodepictions of the history of the Jedi. The smallest younglings are brought here for their education

Main vehicle/spacecraft maintenance hangar

Garages for surface utility vehicles

The massacre at the Jedi Temple not only rips out the Order's heart but also destroys its future by eliminating the younglings and Padawans—an irreplaceable loss.

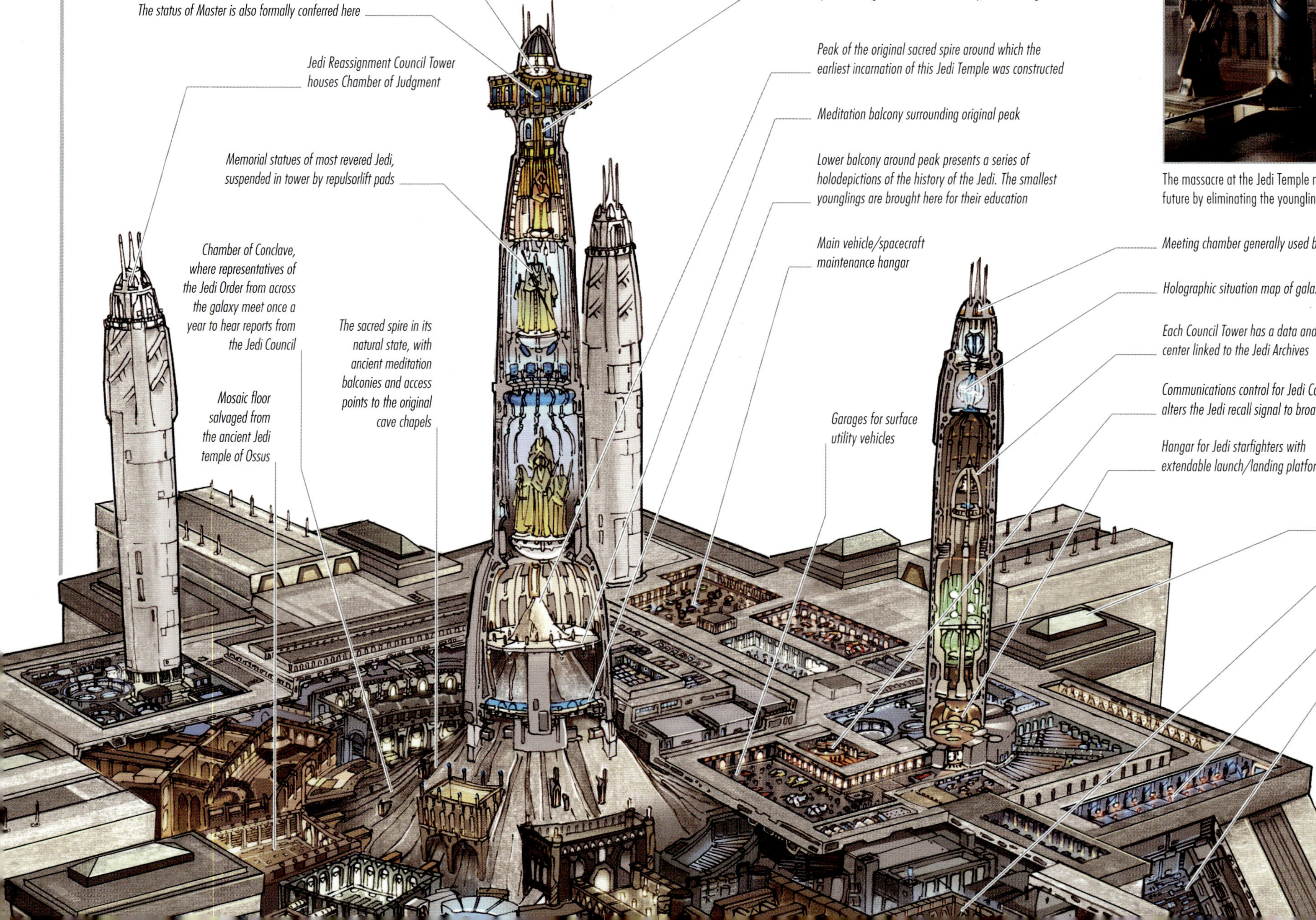

Meeting chamber generally used by Jedi High Council

Holographic situation map of galaxy

Each Council Tower has a data and planning center linked to the Jedi Archives

Communications control for Jedi Council Tower, where Obi-Wan alters the Jedi recall signal to broadcast instead a warning

Hangar for Jedi starfighters with extendable launch/landing platform

Clerestories allow light into contemplation gardens

Offices of the Jedi Exploration Corps

Lightsaber crafting facility, with lightsaber practice gallery behind

Workshops, storerooms, and maintenance facilities, as well as control and switch rooms

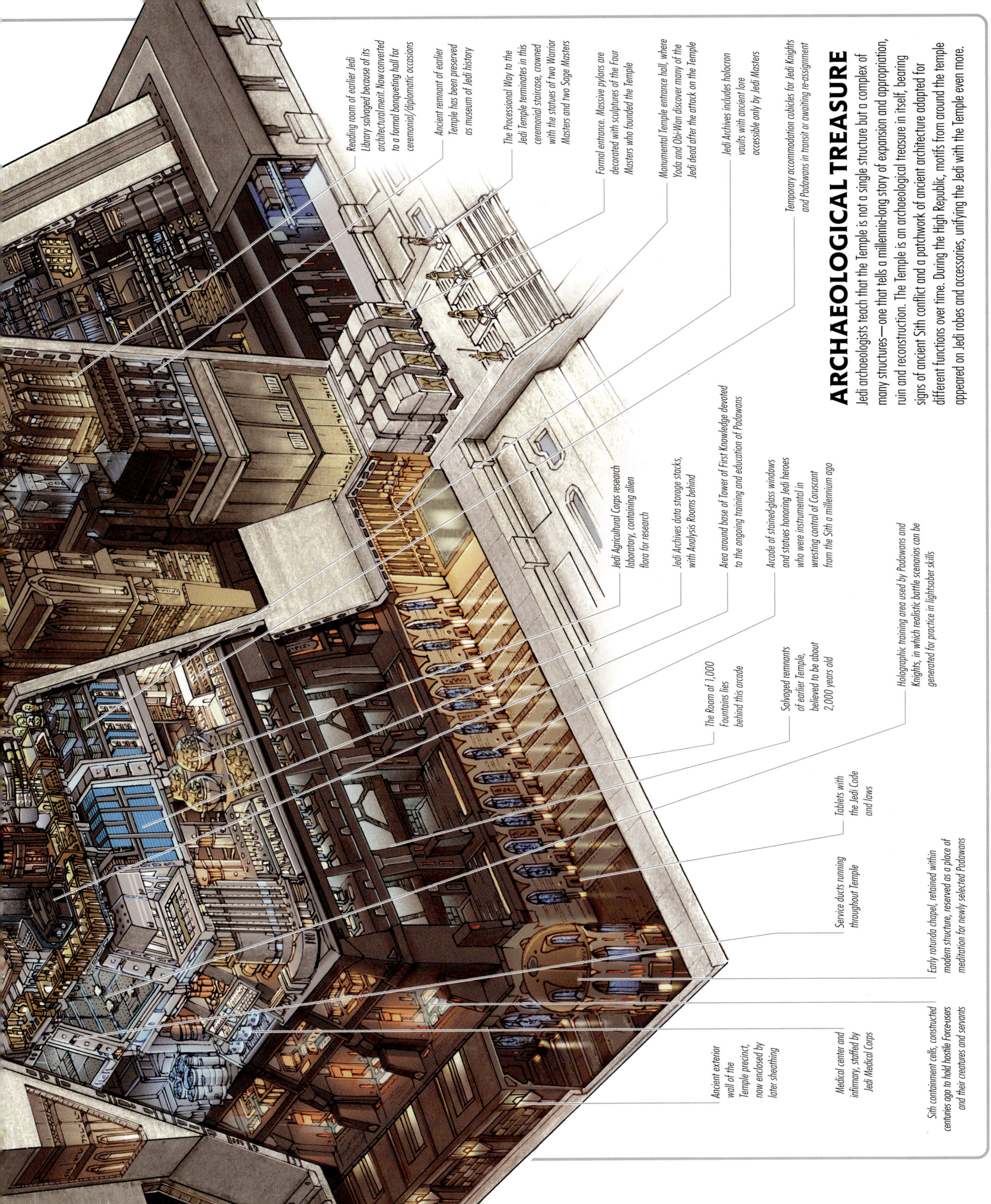

ARCHAEOLOGICAL TREASURE

Jedi archaeologists teach that the Temple is not a single structure but a complex of many structures—one that tells a millennia-long story of expansion and appropriation, ruin and reconstruction. The Temple is an archaeological treasure in itself, bearing signs of ancient Sith conflict and a patchwork of ancient architecture adapted for different functions over time. During the High Republic, motifs from around the temple appeared on Jedi robes and accessories, unifying the Jedi with the Temple even more.

- Reading room of earlier Jedi Library salvaged because of its architectural merit. Now converted to a formal banqueting hall for ceremonial/diplomatic occasions
- Ancient remnant of earlier Temple has been preserved as museum of Jedi history
- The Processional Way to the Jedi Temple terminates in this ceremonial staircase, crowned with the statues of two Warrior Masters and two Sage Masters
- Formal entrance. Massive pylons are decorated with sculptures of the Four Masters who founded the Temple
- Monumental Temple entrance hall, where Yoda and Obi-Wan discover many of the Jedi dead after the attack on the Temple
- Jedi Archives includes holocron vaults with ancient lore accessible only by Jedi Masters
- Temporary accommodation cubicles for Jedi Knights and Padawans in transit or awaiting re-assignment
- Jedi Agricultural Corps research laboratory, containing alien flora for research
- Jedi Archives data storage stacks, with Analysis Rooms behind
- Area around base of Tower of First Knowledge devoted to the ongoing training and education of Padawans
- Arcade of stained-glass windows and statues honoring Jedi heroes who were instrumental in wresting control of Coruscant from the Sith a millennium ago
- Holographic training area used by Padawans and Knights, in which realistic battle scenarios can be generated for practice in lightsaber skills
- The Room of 1,000 Fountains lies behind this arcade
- Salvaged remnants of earlier Temple, believed to be about 2,000 years old
- Tablets with the Jedi Code and laws
- Service ducts running throughout Temple
- Early rotunda chapel, retained within modern structure, reserved as a place of meditation for newly selected Padawans
- Medical center and infirmary, staffed by Jedi Medical Corps
- Ancient exterior wall of the Temple precinct, now enclosed by later sheathing
- Sith containment cells, constructed centuries ago to hold hostile Forceusers and their creatures and servants

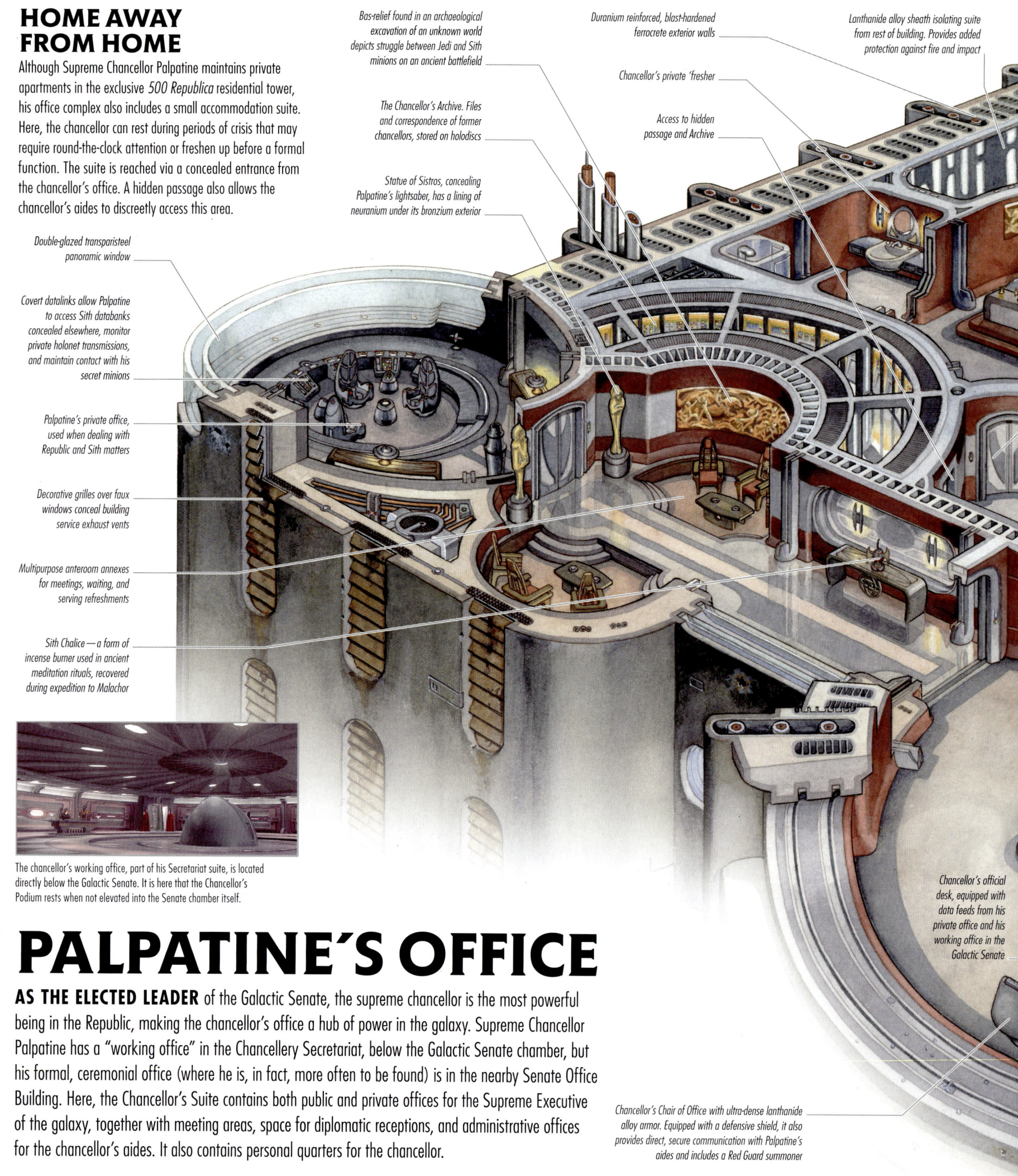

HOME AWAY FROM HOME

Although Supreme Chancellor Palpatine maintains private apartments in the exclusive *500 Republica* residential tower, his office complex also includes a small accommodation suite. Here, the chancellor can rest during periods of crisis that may require round-the-clock attention or freshen up before a formal function. The suite is reached via a concealed entrance from the chancellor's office. A hidden passage also allows the chancellor's aides to discreetly access this area.

Double-glazed transparisteel panoramic window

Covert datalinks allow Palpatine to access Sith databanks concealed elsewhere, monitor private holonet transmissions, and maintain contact with his secret minions

Palpatine's private office, used when dealing with Republic and Sith matters

Decorative grilles over faux windows conceal building service exhaust vents

Multipurpose anteroom annexes for meetings, waiting, and serving refreshments

Sith Chalice — a form of incense burner used in ancient meditation rituals, recovered during expedition to Malachor

Bas-relief found in an archaeological excavation of an unknown world depicts struggle between Jedi and Sith minions on an ancient battlefield

The Chancellor's Archive. Files and correspondence of former chancellors, stored on holodiscs

Statue of Sistros, concealing Palpatine's lightsaber, has a lining of neuranium under its bronzium exterior

Duranium reinforced, blast-hardened ferrocrete exterior walls

Chancellor's private 'fresher

Access to hidden passage and Archive

Lanthanide alloy sheath isolating suite from rest of building. Provides added protection against fire and impact

Chancellor's official desk, equipped with data feeds from his private office and his working office in the Galactic Senate

Chancellor's Chair of Office with ultra-dense lanthanide alloy armor. Equipped with a defensive shield, it also provides direct, secure communication with Palpatine's aides and includes a Red Guard summoner

The chancellor's working office, part of his Secretariat suite, is located directly below the Galactic Senate. It is here that the Chancellor's Podium rests when not elevated into the Senate chamber itself.

PALPATINE'S OFFICE

AS THE ELECTED LEADER of the Galactic Senate, the supreme chancellor is the most powerful being in the Republic, making the chancellor's office a hub of power in the galaxy. Supreme Chancellor Palpatine has a "working office" in the Chancellery Secretariat, below the Galactic Senate chamber, but his formal, ceremonial office (where he is, in fact, more often to be found) is in the nearby Senate Office Building. Here, the Chancellor's Suite contains both public and private offices for the Supreme Executive of the galaxy, together with meeting areas, space for diplomatic receptions, and administrative offices for the chancellor's aides. It also contains personal quarters for the chancellor.

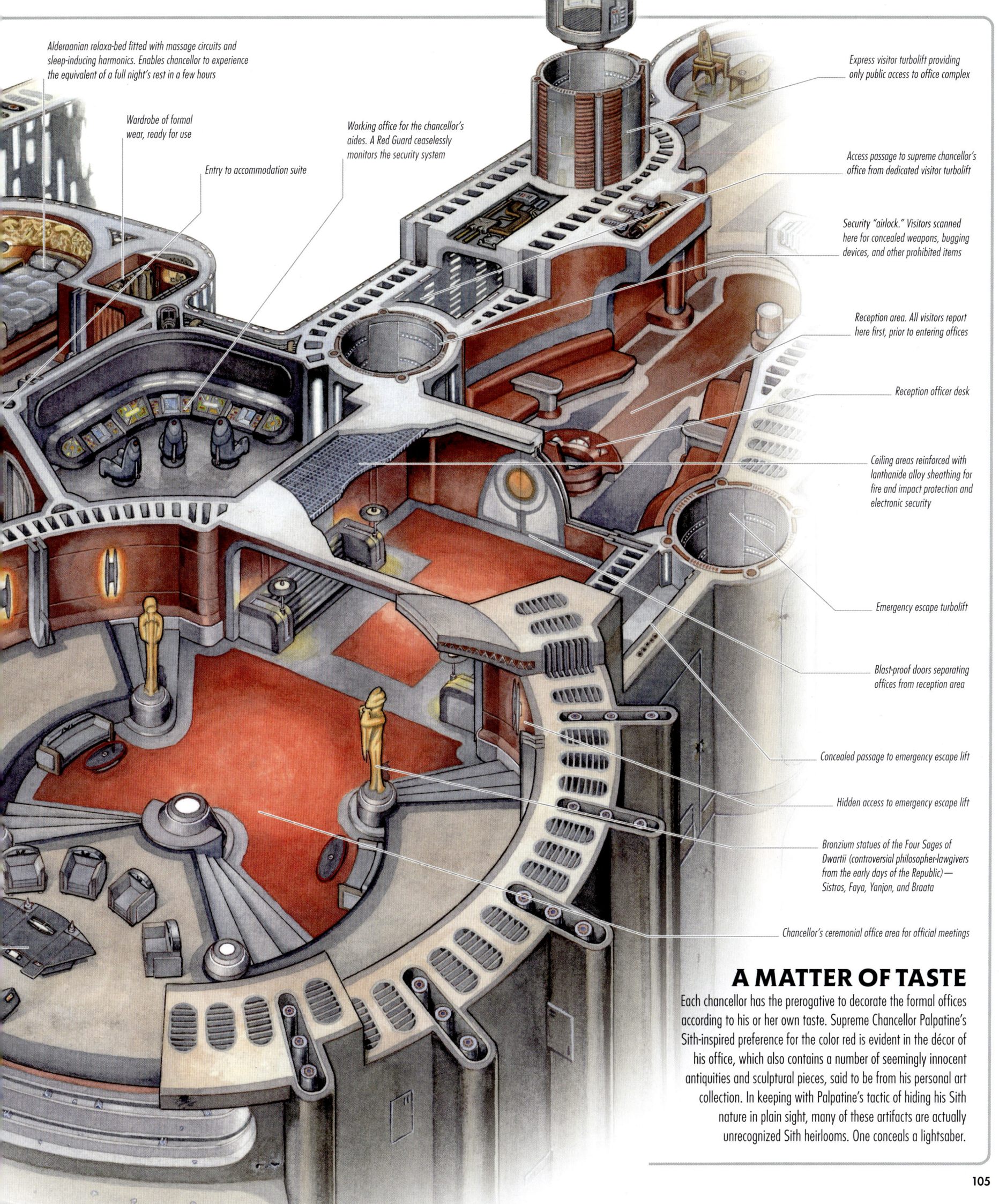

Alderaanian relaxa-bed fitted with massage circuits and sleep-inducing harmonics. Enables chancellor to experience the equivalent of a full night's rest in a few hours

Wardrobe of formal wear, ready for use

Entry to accommodation suite

Working office for the chancellor's aides. A Red Guard ceaselessly monitors the security system

Express visitor turbolift providing only public access to office complex

Access passage to supreme chancellor's office from dedicated visitor turbolift

Security "airlock." Visitors scanned here for concealed weapons, bugging devices, and other prohibited items

Reception area. All visitors report here first, prior to entering offices

Reception officer desk

Ceiling areas reinforced with lanthanide alloy sheathing for fire and impact protection and electronic security

Emergency escape turbolift

Blast-proof doors separating offices from reception area

Concealed passage to emergency escape lift

Hidden access to emergency escape lift

Bronzium statues of the Four Sages of Dwartii (controversial philosopher-lawgivers from the early days of the Republic)— Sistros, Faya, Yanjon, and Braata

Chancellor's ceremonial office area for official meetings

A MATTER OF TASTE

Each chancellor has the prerogative to decorate the formal offices according to his or her own taste. Supreme Chancellor Palpatine's Sith-inspired preference for the color red is evident in the décor of his office, which also contains a number of seemingly innocent antiquities and sculptural pieces, said to be from his personal art collection. In keeping with Palpatine's tactic of hiding his Sith nature in plain sight, many of these artifacts are actually unrecognized Sith heirlooms. One conceals a lightsaber.

UTAPAU

A REMOTE PLANET in the Outer Rim's Tarabba sector, many-mooned Utapau is a quiet, neutral backwater largely ignored by the rest of the galaxy. Its windswept surface, riven with chasms and ridged by fossilized dunes, gives little hint that its sinkholes house vertical cities that harvest minerals from the waters of the planet's subterranean world-ocean. Utapau was settled eons ago, with the original colonists evolving into two separate species: the tall, long-lived Pau'ans and the diminutive Utai. In a bond forged by the necessities of taming Utapau's harsh environment, these two peoples have established a symbiotic relationship, filling complementary niches.

STOLEN NEUTRALITY

Due to its remote location, Utapau is initially able to maintain its neutrality as turmoil engulfs the galaxy, joining neither the Republic nor any other faction. That changes when General Grievous selects Utapau as a hiding place for the Separatist Council in the final days of the war. Republic forces led by Obi-Wan Kenobi subsequently invade the planet, killing Grievous. After the Clone Wars, a steady stream of refugees leaves Utapau, seeking sanctuary on new worlds.

OSSIC ARCHITECTURE

In a world with few trees, bone has replaced timber as a structural material on Utapau. Used raw, seasoned, processed or fossilized, the bones of almost all Utapau's animals are used in construction, creating a unique form of architecture known as "Ossic." The skeletons of the great creatures that roam the lower caves and world-ocean provide bones massive enough to become load-bearing beams, while heavy fossil bone is mined in the sinkholes and caves.

TRADING PORT

Utapau's thinly populated surface and general lack of natural resources meant that the planet had little to offer off-world trade until the value of the minerals, salts, and chemicals derived from the enriched waters of the world-ocean were discovered. To connect Utapau to the interstellar economy, Pau City has developed as the main port for offworld trade, with massive docking bays lining its upper levels, capable of handling ships up to the size of a Trade Federation core ship.

SINKHOLE SANCTUARIES

Pau'ans and Utai are rare sights on Utapau's stormy surface, though recent Amanin colonists have moved out across its plains. Complex tidal forces created by Utapau's nine moons cause massive currents in the world-ocean that erode the underside of its outer crust. These currents also generate groundquakes that cause sections to collapse, creating sinkholes and yawning stress-fracture chasms. Inside these sanctuaries, the Pau'ans and Utai have built underground communities. Most Utapauan settlements are clustered on a lone "continent," the most stable of its surface plates.

PAU CITY

CAPITAL OF UTAPAU

Pau City boasts almost a million inhabitants, making it by far the largest of Utapau's sinkhole communities. Built underground, in mostly natural caves, Pau City's external access points and spacecraft docking facilities are constructed within the Pau Sinkhole, sheltered from the winds of the planet's surface. The city has 11 levels, which extend around the entire circumference of the sinkhole. To facilitate movement between its levels and to support its role as a tradeport, the city's cliff-face exterior is dotted with large and small landing platforms for craft ranging from bulk carriers to tiny inter-level flitters and dactillions. Subterranean passageways link Pau City with nearby secondary access sinkholes and settlements.

Despite his ability to wield multiple lightsabers, General Grievous' planned ambush for Obi-Wan Kenobi is unsuccessful. The resourceful Jedi Master ultimately defeats the Separatist general using a conventional weapon.

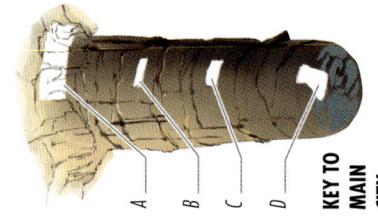

KEY TO MAIN CITY LEVELS
- A
- B
- C
- D

A. CIVIC LEVEL

Pau City's highest level is occupied by the government and bureaucracy, including the Port Administration. The city's major civic and ceremonial buildings are located on this level, together with cultural and recreational facilities and the residences of the Pau'an elite, who manage the planet's civic affairs and trade. In the twilight world of Pau City, being close to natural light from the surface is a status symbol.

- Pau City's Grand Hall of the Traders' Guild, now converted by the Techno Union to a factory building Mankvim-814 interceptors
- Many tall buildings in Pau City act as cavern roof supports, with flat-topped, shock-absorbing "pads" on top of the structure helping to stabilize the rock ceiling in case of groundquakes
- Vent holes providing natural light
- Elite residential towers for the wealthy and powerful
- Pahnum Cultural Center, Pau City's main performance and exhibition venue
- The Promenade of Seven Guilds, the main thoroughfare and ceremonial avenue
- Wind turbine. Pau City harnesses energy from the surface windstorms to help power the city
- Timon Medon Plaza, named after the Unifier of Utapau. To left of plaza is the Utapau Council Chambers
- Utapau Offworld Trade Commission, which regulates and controls the offworld mineral trade
- Port facilities, including main commercial and diplomatic landing stages for offworld craft
- Examples of Ossic architecture. Landing platform structures made from the bones of ruhar-whales
- Passenger reception facilities and port control buildings
- Obi-Wan's landing stage on arrival at Utapau
- Varactyl stables and dactillion landing point
- Dactillion roost, where they rest and sleep between flights while "on duty"
- Sinkhole air traffic control

General Grievous' ship at Level 10 docking bay

Factories manufacturing domestic appliances and light technology

Seawater extraction and mineral processing plant

Pumping station bringing water from the world-ocean to processing plants for mineral extraction

High-speed turbolift connecting to lower levels

C. PRODUCE LEVEL

Functional facilities, city services, and some heavy industries are located toward the bottom of the sinkhole. The Produce Level is where Pau City's main food supplies are produced. Plants, such as ocean-kelps, are grown hydroponically in vast "greenhouse" buildings, and small animals are raised for food. Utapauns prefer their meat uncooked, and freshly butchered meat is delivered every day throughout the city. The dactillions and varactyls used as transport within Pau City are also bred and trained on this level. The city's lower levels are where the Utai mostly make their homes.

Landing stage for meat and other produce to be transported

Bone mine. Source of fossilized bone for building construction

Caverns where the fierce resputi-seals make their lairs. Mine workers are often attacked by breeding resputi if they enter their territory

Grottoes and pools of Coranth. The water is colored blue-green due to calcium minerals absorbed through the crustal rocks

B. WEALTH LEVEL

Pau'ans place great importance on those industries and trade interests that drive the planet's economy. Consequently, the seawater processing plants and other important industries are located high up in the city, with easy access to the landing stages and port facilities for cargo loading. Middle-class Pau'ans and the few wealthy Utai also live on this level.

Ossic architecture warehouses

Landing stages for bulk carriers shipping extracted minerals and other manufactured goods

Freight elevator for transporting heavy goods and materials between levels

Freight elevator

Utai workers' accommodation

Hydroponic food facilities cultivating ocean-kelps and cave-molds, as well as small food plants high in nutrition

Pens where small livestock are raised

D. MINING LEVEL

Pau City's lowest level is where waste disposal and mining takes place. Bone mines provide fossilized bone for use in city construction, while building stone and some other ores are also mined here. Although miners may encounter giant resputi and other ferocious creatures in the darkness of the deep caves, the beautiful grottoes and settling ponds of the sinkhole floor are popular places to relax.

KASHYYYK

THE PLANET KASHYYYK is home to the Wookiees, fierce warriors and clever craftspeople, who share the Kashyyyk system with the reptilian Trandoshans. Located in the Mid Rim's Mytaranor sector, this verdant world sits at the intersection of four well-traveled hyperspace routes and houses an important HoloNet relay station—which makes it a crucial prize during the Clone Wars. Much of the planet is covered with lush forests, dominated by the mighty wroshyr trees in which the Wookiees make their homes. Kashyyyk's trees reach vertiginous heights, the apex of a complex ecosystem that becomes more dangerous the deeper one goes, reaching lightless levels prowled by katarns, wyrm-weavers, and strange, savage creatures spoken of in fireside tales delivered by grizzled Wookiee elders.

DEFENDER OF THE HOME TREE

Yoda modestly claims to have good relations with the Wookiees. He has, in fact, been honored with the ancient title "Defender of the Home Tree" for his role as a Jedi negotiator in several previous incidents involving the Wookiees and their system neighbors, the Trandoshans. For this, and other assistance to the Wookiees, Yoda is also considered a member of the honor families of many Wookiee leaders, as well as all the inhabitants of Kachirho.

ISLAND ASSAULT

Corporate Alliance tank droids and droid gunships launch a massive attack on Kachirho, intending to overrun the settlement and capture the Claatuvac archives before securing the nearby relay station complex. Wookiee warriors flock to Kachirho to help defend the region. Oevvaor catamarans and fluttercraft are thrown into the battle alongside Republic forces in an attempt to repel the invaders and prevent the capture of the town.

SECRETS OF THE GUILD

Besides a strategic location, Kashyyyk offers another valuable prize of war: the lagoons and fjords of the tropical Wawaatt Archipelago shelter the settlements of the ancient Claatuvac Guild, Wookiee cartographers and navigators legendary for their knowledge of secret hyperspace routes crisscrossing the galaxy. The Guild's chief settlement at Kachirho houses its data, which could help the Separatists reverse their declining fortunes in the Clone Wars.

TREACHEROUS ALLIES

Without warning, the clone troopers of the Republic attack the Jedi and Wookiees in response to Supreme Chancellor Palpatine's Order 66 command. In the midst of the pitched battle at Kachirho, former allies become foes, creating confusion and sowing death and destruction. Kashyyyk will become an enslaved world, stripped even of its name and designated Imperial territory G5-623. This dark period sees many Wookiees worked to death as enslaved laborers, but years later the world will be liberated by the forces of the New Republic.

WOOKIEE TREE

THE GIANT WROSHYR TREES OF KASHYYYK dominate the landscape and environment of the planet, with over 1,000 different varieties that have adapted to growing everywhere except at its poles. Living up to 50,000 years, wroshyr trees grow to massive size, reaching several kilometers in height in the deep forests. They form the backbone of a complex multilayered vertical ecosystem, extending from the roots to the crown of the tree. Wroshyr trees are an integral part of the lives of the Wookiees, who inhabit them and refer to themselves as "The People of the Trees." They form the foundation of the material, social, and spiritual culture of the Wookiees.

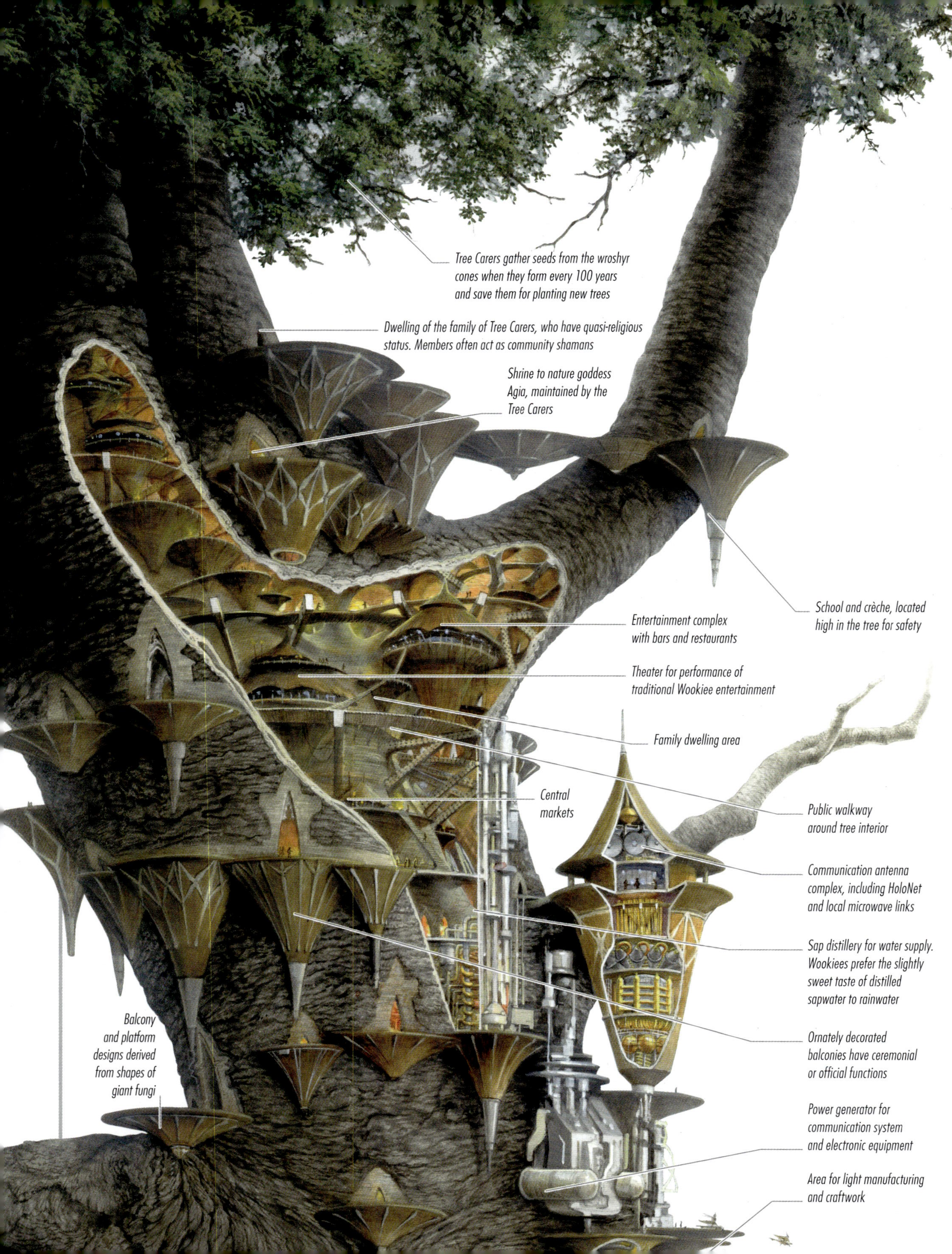

Kachirho settlement takes its name from Tarfful's home tree and includes several inhabited wroshyrs. Yoda's command post is in the Tree Kachirho, while the headquarters of the Claatuvac Guild is the Tree Vikkilynn.

HOME AND PROTECTOR

Wroshyr trees are so huge that entire communities can live within their hollowed out trunks, which, like caves, provide both shelter from the elements and defense against the many predators that roam the lower levels of Kashyyyk's forests. In the deep forest, Wookiee towns and cities expand outside the tree trunks by constructing platforms resting upon the interlocked branches of close-growing wroshyrs. In coastal environments, such as that of the lagoon-side town of Kachirho, where wroshyrs do not grow so thickly together, settlements are composed of individual tree communities. The tropical wroshyrs of Wawaatt Archipelago are much smaller than the deep forest giants, averaging 300–400 meters (1,000–1,300 feet).

- Tree Carers gather seeds from the wroshyr cones when they form every 100 years and save them for planting new trees
- Dwelling of the family of Tree Carers, who have quasi-religious status. Members often act as community shamans
- Shrine to nature goddess Aqria, maintained by the Tree Carers
- School and crèche, located high in the tree for safety
- Entertainment complex with bars and restaurants
- Theater for performance of traditional Wookiee entertainment
- Family dwelling area
- Public walkway around tree interior
- Communication antenna complex, including HoloNet and local microwave links
- Sap distillery for water supply. Wookiees prefer the slightly sweet taste of distilled sapwater to rainwater
- Ornately decorated balconies have ceremonial or official functions
- Central markets
- Power generator for communication system and electronic equipment
- Area for light manufacturing and craftwork
- Balcony and platform designs derived from shapes of giant fungi

BATTLEFRONTS

AFTER THREE YEARS OF CONFLICT, the Republic seems to be winning the Clone Wars. The Jedi are spread thinly throughout the galaxy, acting as generals in command of clone troops. Separatist leaders such as Wat Tambor and Shu Mai have already seen their homeworlds captured by Republic forces, while other Council members' homeworlds are also under siege. Victory for the Republic is in sight when Supreme Chancellor Palpatine's treacherous Order 66 turns the clone troops against their Jedi commanders.

While on patrol for signs of Separatist activity on recaptured Saleucami, Stass Allie is murdered by her clone troopers, who fire on her Aratech 74-Z speeder bike.

FUNGUS-WORLD TREACHERY

Strategically located near the Perlemian Trade Route, Felucia is the site of many hard-fought battles during the Clone Wars. The planet is dominated by forests of fungi in hallucinatory colors, and is a valuable source of medicinal spice. Native Felucians share the world with Gossam colonists, among them Shu Mai, Presidente of the Separatist-allied Commerce Guild. Jedi Master Aayla Secura leads an assault on Felucia during the Outer Rim Sieges, where she is assassinated as part of Order 66.

BATTLEFRONT KASHYYYK

The Jedi are determined to assist the Wookiees in defending the planet against a major Separatist assault, and Yoda commits his battalion to the strategically important tree-city of Kachirho. Republic and Wookiee forces prepare to repel the invaders along Kachirho's relatively narrow lagoon frontage, the only viable approach for a seaborne assault on the settlement due to the rugged terrain of the Wawaatt islands.

STRATEGIC TARGET

Kashyyyk's strategic importance is such that, although Jedi Luminara Unduli is already on the planet, additional clone troops under generals Yoda and Vos are dispatched to reinforce Kashyyyk's defenses. While Separatist Alliance forces are repulsed at several landing points on the planet, a massive attack is mounted against the lagoon-city of Kachirho. When the Jedi's clone forces turn against them, Luminara is captured and later executed, though Yoda escapes with the help of Chewbacca and Tarfful.

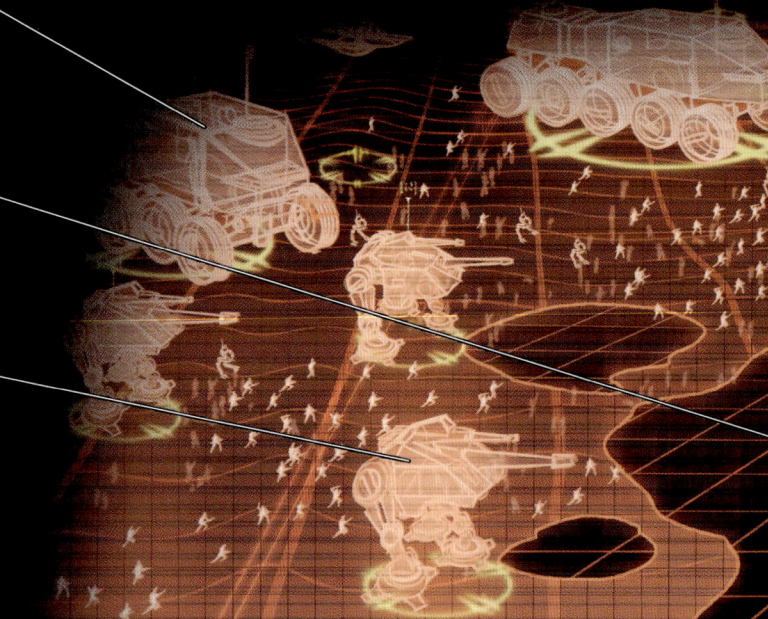

HAVw A6 Juggernauts are the Republic's answer to the tank droids

This designation indicates an active Republic/Wookiee attack craft

AT-AP "pod walkers" are also deployed in force to support the Republic ground troops and counter the Separatist Alliance spider droids

BRIDGES OF NEIMOIDIA

Homeworld of Separatist Council member Nute Gunray, Cato Neimoidia is famous for its "aerial cities" constructed on vast bridges across the planet's abyssal canyons. A Neimoidian colonial purse-world, Cato Neimoidia's capitulation is a prime strategic goal that would help to end the war. Its bridge cities are under aerial attack from a force led by Jedi Master Plo Koon when he is shot down by his own squadron.

CRYSTAL TRAP

Mygeeto's natural crystal towers, originally home to Lurmen inhabitants, are a stronghold of the InterGalactic Banking Clan. On a mission to wipe out entrenched Clan forces on the planet, Jedi Master Ki-Adi-Mundi meets his fate at the hands of the Galactic Marines under the command of Commander Bacara.

Separatist droid gunships rule the skies at the Battle of Kachirho, while Republic air support concentrates on attacking ground forces

Corporate Alliance tank droids, best suited to frontal assaults, form the backbone of the Separatist ground force at Kachirho

A contingent of Commerce Guild spider droids is deployed in the attack on Kachirho to counter the Republic AT-APs

Separatist Alliance landing ships deliver thousands of droid troops and vehicles to invasion points across Kashyyyk

This designation indicates an active Separatist attack craft

Wookiee Oevvaor catamarans join the heavier Republic units to help repulse the attack. Their agile maneuverability makes them extremely effective against Separatist droid forces

MUSTAFAR

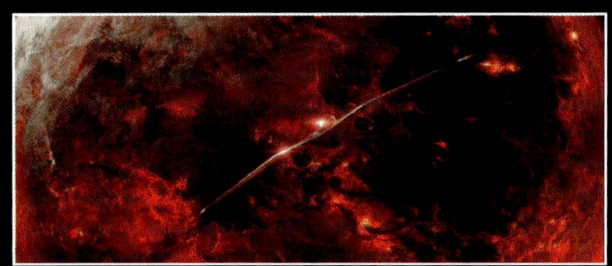

VIOLENTLY VOLCANIC MUSTAFAR is a remote Outer Rim planet that plays a pivotal role in the rise of the Galactic Empire. Though a world in its own right, Mustafar is dwarfed by the great gas giant Jestefad, with which it is twinned. A hellish world of intense heat, savage obsidian mountain ranges, lava rivers, and continuously erupting volcanoes, Mustafar is owned by the Techno Union, which mines the molten precious metals found in the planet's incessant lava flows. Used by the Separatist Council as a hideout during the Clone Wars, Mustafar becomes infamous as the site of the Council's massacre, which clears the way for the rise of the Galactic Empire.

RISE TO POWER

Mustafar was once the site of a Sith temple, a fact well-known to Darth Sidious. During the Clone Wars, Sidious maintains a secret outpost here in a former mining complex—which attracts little attention on a planet dotted with Techno Union operations, mining towns, and bolt-holes belonging to the Black Sun crime syndicate. Sidious later chooses Mustafar as the site of the Separatists' final redoubt and Darth Vader's massacre of their leaders, with the planet's dark heritage amplifying the power of this key moment in the rise of the Sith.

HELLFIRE PLANET

Mustafar is a terrifying planet where surface temperatures scorch any unshielded structure or being. Buildings, mining platforms, and robots are all protected by repulsor screens that deflect the heat and suppress the constant eruptions within the lava flows. The Mustafarians swathe themselves in insulating fabrics to survive. Yet, at 800°C (1500°F), Mustafar's lava is "cooler" than normal lava due to unusual mineral allotropes that are molten at lower temperatures.

A FIERY RELATIONSHIP

Twin planets Mustafar and Jestefad orbit so close that the massive gravitational field of the gas giant subjects its tiny neighbor to immense tidal forces. These heat Mustafar's interior, melting it and producing its constant volcanic activity. Jestefad's huge electromagnetic field also swamps Mustafar, generating wild electrical storms. Only the counter-balancing gravitational pull from another, more distant gas giant neighbor, Lefrani, prevents Mustafar from being permanently captured as Jestefad's moon.

INTELLIGENT ARTHROPODS

Though Mustafar's environment is harsh, hardy life-forms still make the planet their home. Two species now occupy the planet, evolved from extremophile arthropods that developed in insulated caves deep in the mountains. With their chitinous exoskeletons and low-water biology, Mustafarians are able to withstand their world's unforgiving elements but still require insulating clothes and breathing apparatus to work on its surface.

UNFRIENDLY SKIES

The volcanic breath of Mustafar's volcanoes and the influence of Jestefad's massive magnetic field create a turbulent atmosphere filled with ash, cyclonic-force updrafts and thermal currents, and titanic lightning storms. Electromagnetic interference renders scanners useless and interferes with navigation equipment and control systems. Landing on Mustafar is therefore an extremely hazardous operation without the aid of the specially shielded landing-support equipment at the mining complex. This includes guidance and tractor beams designed to safely lead authorized ships to and from orbit.

- Mining droid control and local communications antenna
- Separatist Council conference room, where Anakin traps and kills the Council
- Separatist Council war room, where the leaders of the Separatist Alliance monitor events during the last stages of the Clone Wars
- Balcony area where Anakin Skywalker and Obi-Wan Kenobi battle during their fateful duel
- Air-traffic control antenna. Incorporates a high-intensity guide beam to assist incoming spacecraft to overcome scanner and equipment difficulties
- Landing control room oversees landings on the "visitors" pad
- Padmé Amidala's Naboo star skiff
- Landing pad for non-cargo spacecraft, where Anakin and Padmé have their last confrontation
- Control room for droid mining operations
- Secret command facility built onto the mining complex by the Separatist Council to act as a final redoubt
- Electromagnetic/tractor-beam metal extractor heads
- Ingot foundry for electromagnetically extracted metals
- Collector arms also carry repulsor units that generate fields suppressing the constant eruptions of the lava rivers
- Electromagnetic generator powering extractor heads
- Geothermal power generators providing main power supply for mining complex
- Lava run-off is channeled back into the lava river for further mining by droids and Mustafarians

MUSTAFAR MINES

IF NOT FOR THE VALUABLE METALS dissolved in its lava flows, Mustafar would be ignored by galactic civilization. But the planet's tortured interior continually spews forth lava rich in rare heavy elements and precious ores. This molten wealth prompted the Techno Union to establish a lava mining operation, using electromagnetic extraction technologies, as well as manual mining by the Mustafarians, to remove the valuable materials from the molten rock matrix of the lava. Mustafar has been a literal gold mine for the Techno Union for almost 300 standard years.

In addition to the secret Separatist hideout, Mustafar's mining complex conceals the Techno Union's droid production operation, located inside the mountain on which the mine sits.

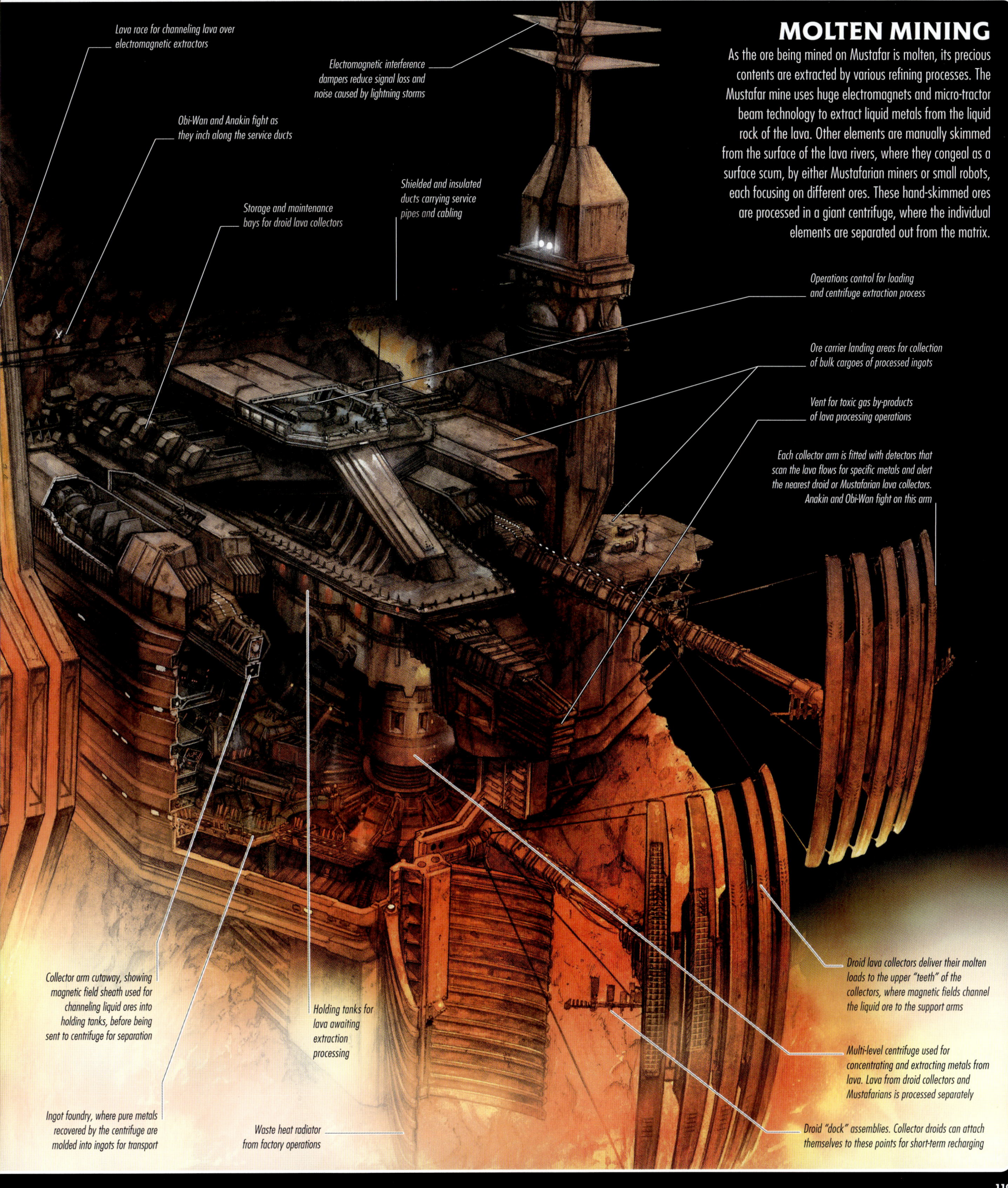

MOLTEN MINING

As the ore being mined on Mustafar is molten, its precious contents are extracted by various refining processes. The Mustafar mine uses huge electromagnets and micro-tractor beam technology to extract liquid metals from the liquid rock of the lava. Other elements are manually skimmed from the surface of the lava rivers, where they congeal as a surface scum, by either Mustafarian miners or small robots, each focusing on different ores. These hand-skimmed ores are processed in a giant centrifuge, where the individual elements are separated out from the matrix.

- Lava race for channeling lava over electromagnetic extractors
- Electromagnetic interference dampers reduce signal loss and noise caused by lightning storms
- Obi-Wan and Anakin fight as they inch along the service ducts
- Storage and maintenance bays for droid lava collectors
- Shielded and insulated ducts carrying service pipes and cabling
- Operations control for loading and centrifuge extraction process
- Ore carrier landing areas for collection of bulk cargoes of processed ingots
- Vent for toxic gas by-products of lava processing operations
- Each collector arm is fitted with detectors that scan the lava flows for specific metals and alert the nearest droid or Mustafarian lava collectors. Anakin and Obi-Wan fight on this arm
- Collector arm cutaway, showing magnetic field sheath used for channeling liquid ores into holding tanks, before being sent to centrifuge for separation
- Holding tanks for lava awaiting extraction processing
- Droid lava collectors deliver their molten loads to the upper "teeth" of the collectors, where magnetic fields channel the liquid ore to the support arms
- Multi-level centrifuge used for concentrating and extracting metals from lava. Lava from droid collectors and Mustafarians is processed separately
- Ingot foundry, where pure metals recovered by the centrifuge are molded into ingots for transport
- Waste heat radiator from factory operations
- Droid "dock" assemblies. Collector droids can attach themselves to these points for short-term recharging

MIRROR OF THE SOUL

As Anakin Skywalker's soul surrenders fully to the dark side, violent Mustafar seems to mirror his turmoil. Lefrani eclipses Mustafar's sun, just as Anakin's massacre of the Separatist Council eclipses the light of the Force within him. The violent eruptions of the lava rivers, when the repulsor fields are shut down during his duel with Obi-Wan Kenobi, seem almost driven by Anakin's own rising hatred of everyone that he believes has conspired against him and thwarted his desires. Only in the deepest core of his being does he still treasure his love for Padmé Amidala.

2 Anakin forces Obi-Wan back into the mining complex, and their battle rages through the Separatist headquarters, where the evidence of Anakin's treacherous massacre of the Council is all around them.

3 The flailing lightsabers of the Jedi and Sith smash fittings and equipment in the mining complex. This wanton damage deactivates the repulsor fields protecting the mining complex, allowing the lava rivers to erupt.

1 Obi-Wan's appearance in the door of Padmé's ship drives Anakin into a fury. Believing himself betrayed by both the woman he loves and his friend, he attacks, leaving Padmé critically injured and forcing Obi-Wan into a duel.

Fralideja is one of the few remaining Mustafarian settlements. The local population was almost destroyed by a cataclysmic eruption centuries ago

A Mustafarian rite of passage requires youths to leap across the lavafall on a lava flea without wearing any protective clothing

Residence for Techno Union mine management staff and technicians. The building's dome conceals a small landing pad. Palpatine lands here when he comes to rescue Anakin

MUSTAFAR DUEL

MUSTAFAR BECOMES THE LOCATION of the fateful duel between Anakin Skywalker and Obi-Wan Kenobi after the Jedi Master follows his friend to the remote outpost. Corrupted by Palpatine, Anakin is sinking more deeply into his Sith persona, massacring the Separatist Council and choking Padmé Amidala when he believes she has betrayed him to his Master. In his rage and self-doubt, Anakin gives himself over to Sith fury and focuses all his hatred on Obi-Wan, attempting to murder his mentor in a lightsaber battle.

10 After easily defeating Anakin's ill-judged attack, leaving him maimed, burned, and helpless, Obi-Wan is unable to kill the friend he has loved as a brother. He turns away from Anakin's torment, leaving him to his fate.

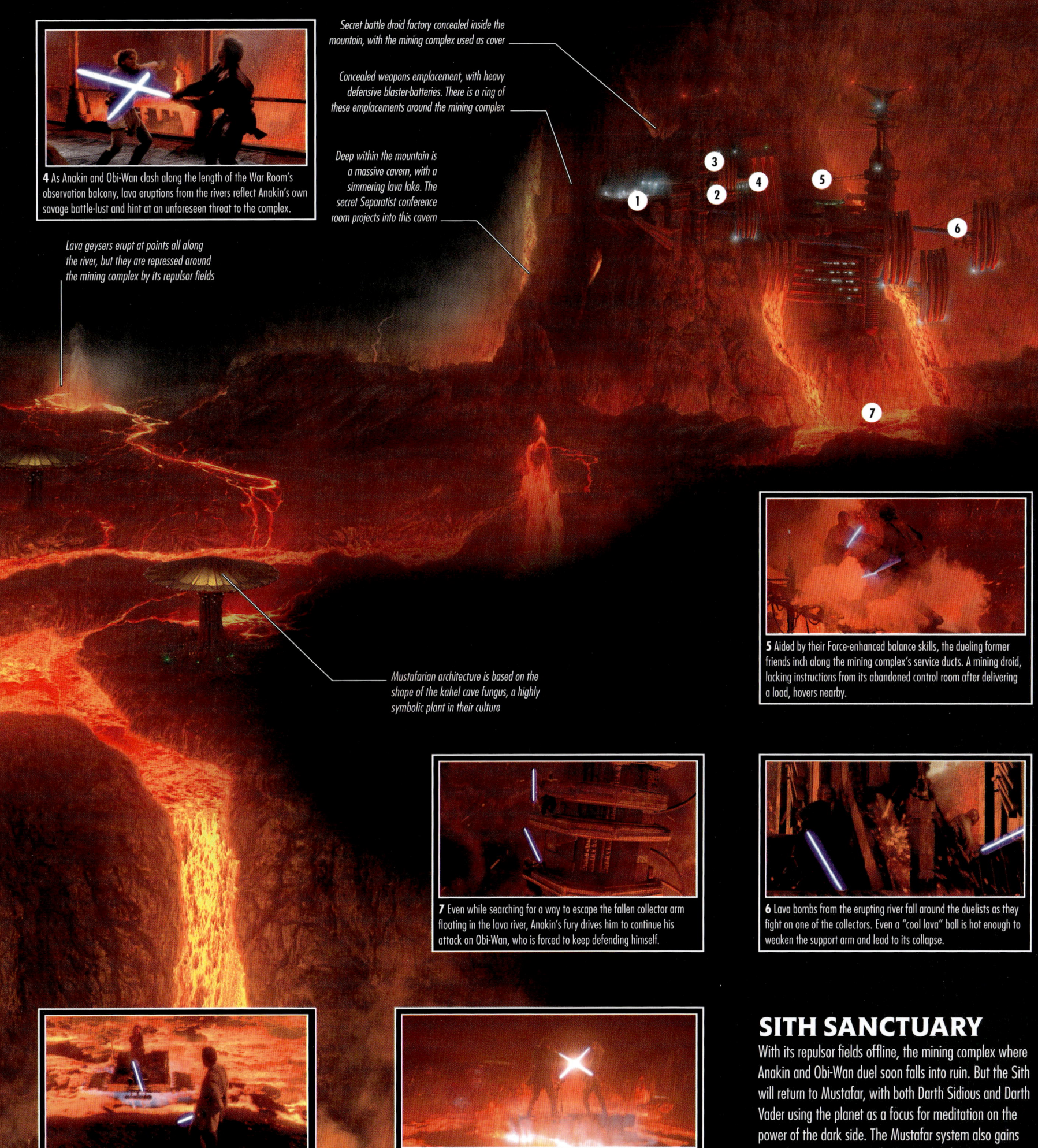

4 As Anakin and Obi-Wan clash along the length of the War Room's observation balcony, lava eruptions from the rivers reflect Anakin's own savage battle-lust and hint at an unforeseen threat to the complex.

Lava geysers erupt at points all along the river, but they are repressed around the mining complex by its repulsor fields

Secret battle droid factory concealed inside the mountain, with the mining complex used as cover

Concealed weapons emplacement, with heavy defensive blaster-batteries. There is a ring of these emplacements around the mining complex

Deep within the mountain is a massive cavern, with a simmering lava lake. The secret Separatist conference room projects into this cavern

Mustafarian architecture is based on the shape of the kahel cave fungus, a highly symbolic plant in their culture

5 Aided by their Force-enhanced balance skills, the dueling former friends inch along the mining complex's service ducts. A mining droid, lacking instructions from its abandoned control room after delivering a load, hovers nearby.

7 Even while searching for a way to escape the fallen collector arm floating in the lava river, Anakin's fury drives him to continue his attack on Obi-Wan, who is forced to keep defending himself.

6 Lava bombs from the erupting river fall around the duelists as they fight on one of the collectors. Even a "cool lava" ball is hot enough to weaken the support arm and lead to its collapse.

9 Driven by the dark side to greed and overweening arrogance, Anakin refuses to accept that Obi-Wan has the advantage when his Master occupies the high ground on the bank of the lava river.

8 Abandoning the collector arm by leaping onto mining equipment, the duelists continue their fight. Anakin pursues Obi-Wan, who has commandeered a mining platform. He boards the platform, and the two clash again.

SITH SANCTUARY

With its repulsor fields offline, the mining complex where Anakin and Obi-Wan duel soon falls into ruin. But the Sith will return to Mustafar, with both Darth Sidious and Darth Vader using the planet as a focus for meditation on the power of the dark side. The Mustafar system also gains an evil reputation among fugitive Jedi as a place where exiles from the all-but-extinct Order are brought for interrogation, torment, and death.

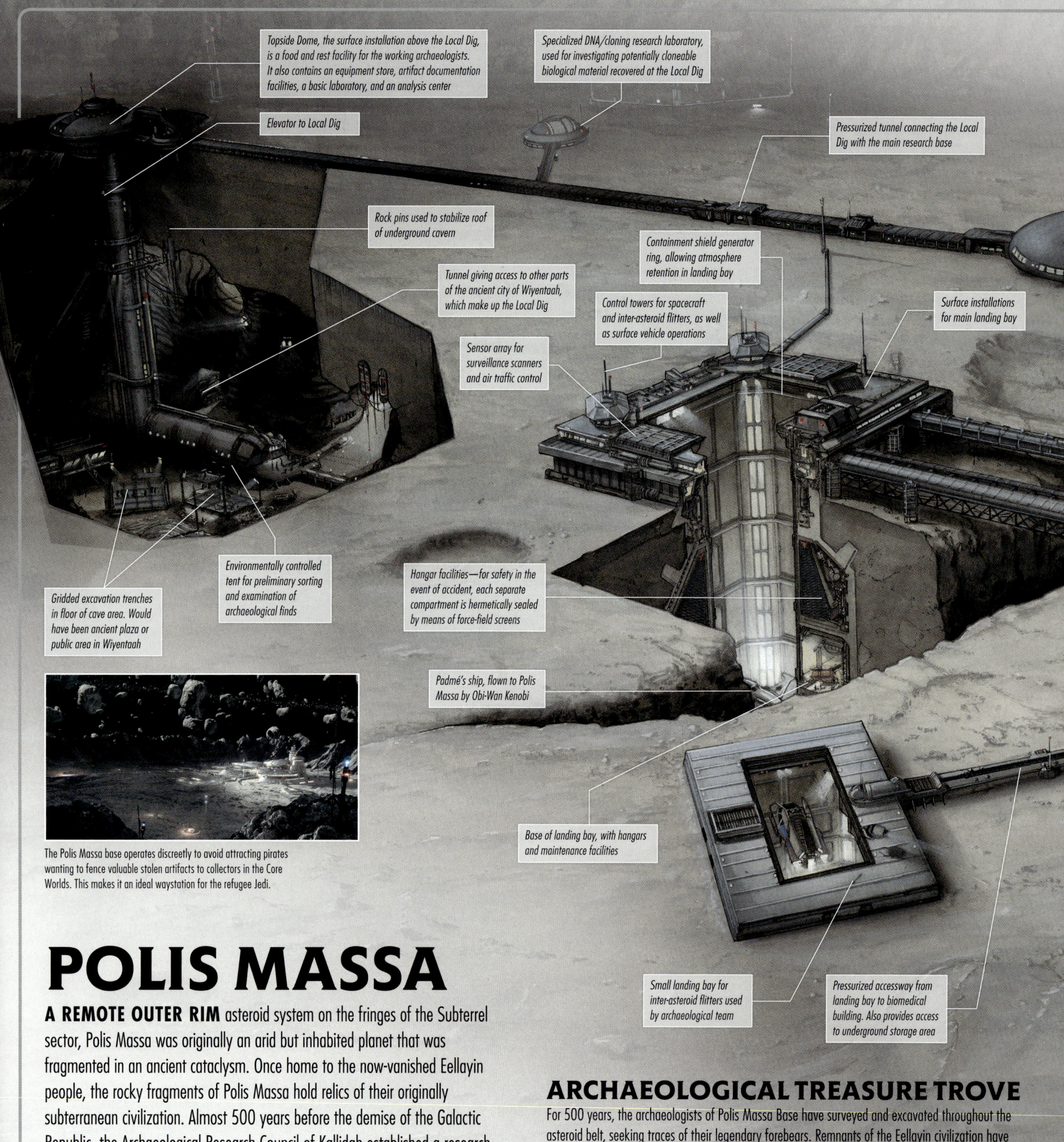

POLIS MASSA

A REMOTE OUTER RIM asteroid system on the fringes of the Subterrel sector, Polis Massa was originally an arid but inhabited planet that was fragmented in an ancient cataclysm. Once home to the now-vanished Eellayin people, the rocky fragments of Polis Massa hold relics of their originally subterranean civilization. Almost 500 years before the demise of the Galactic Republic, the Archaeological Research Council of Kallidah established a research base on one of the largest asteroid remnants of ancient Polis Massa because the Kallidahin believed themselves to be descendants of the Eellayin.

ARCHAEOLOGICAL TREASURE TROVE

For 500 years, the archaeologists of Polis Massa Base have surveyed and excavated throughout the asteroid belt, seeking traces of their legendary forebears. Remnants of the Eellayin civilization have been scant. However, 50 standard-years ago, on their very doorstep, researchers uncovered the ruins of Wiyentaah, an underground city of the ancient Polis Massans. Since that time, the Local Dig, as it is called, has been progressively excavated and its finds cataloged.

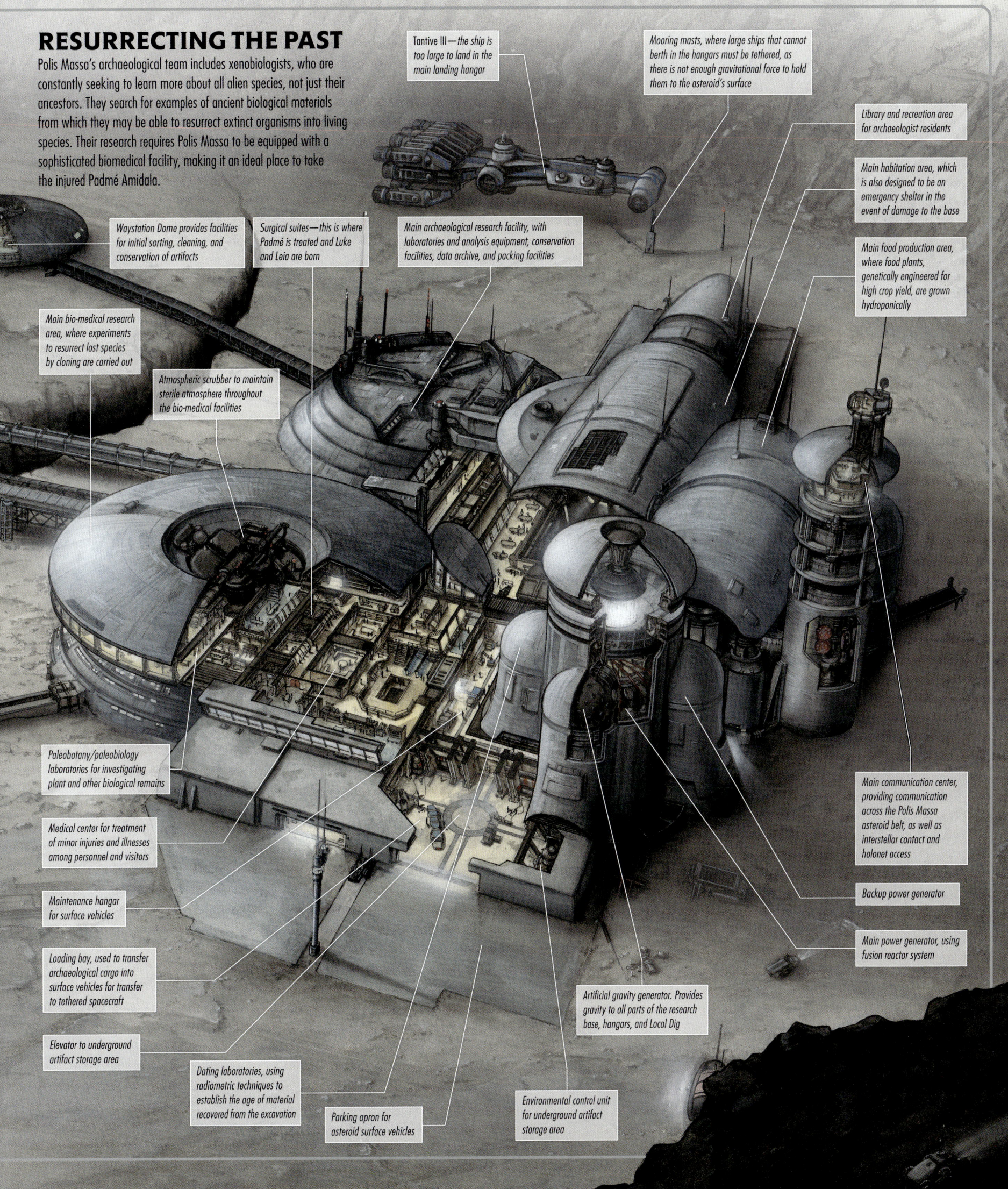

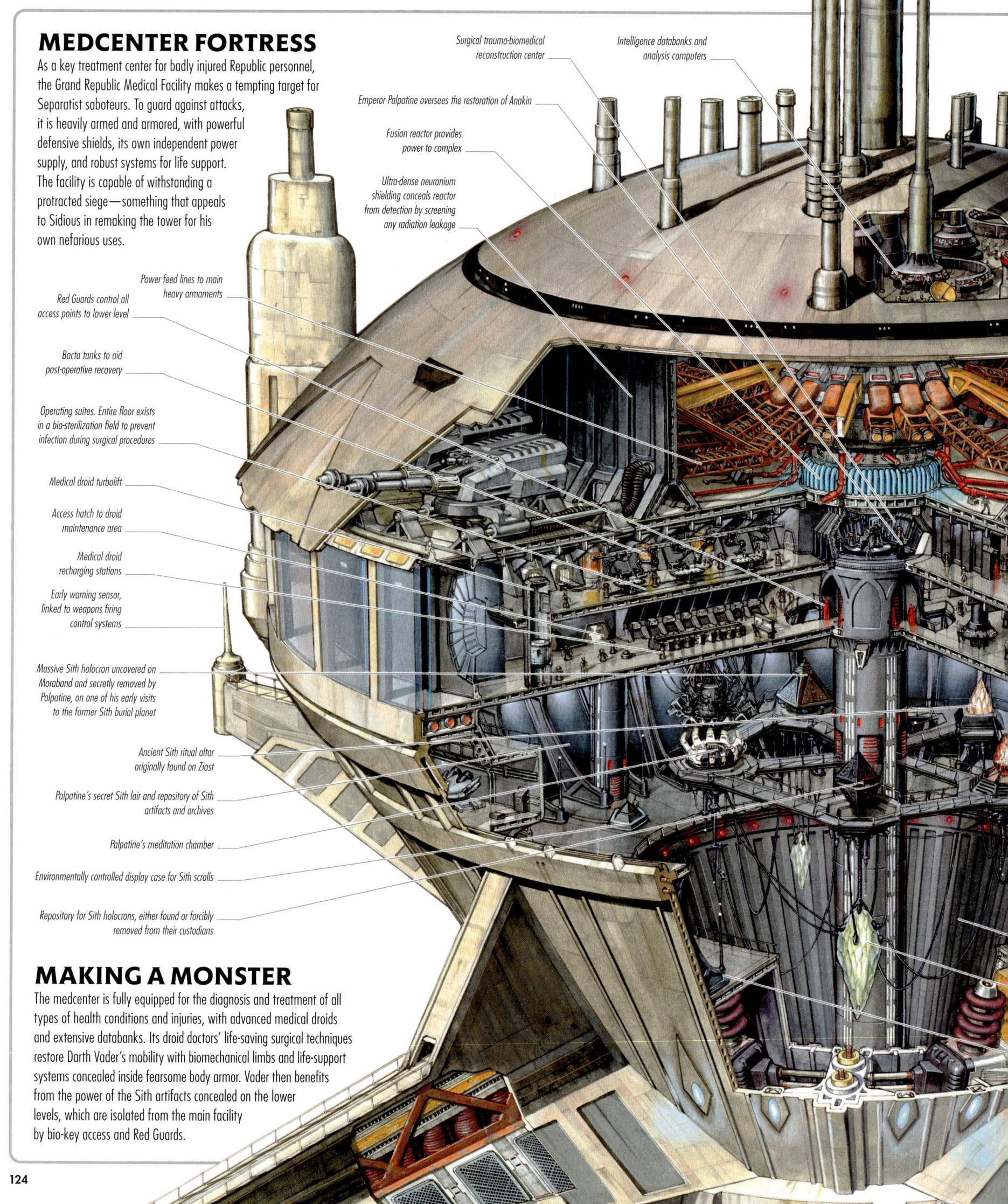

MEDCENTER FORTRESS

As a key treatment center for badly injured Republic personnel, the Grand Republic Medical Facility makes a tempting target for Separatist saboteurs. To guard against attacks, it is heavily armed and armored, with powerful defensive shields, its own independent power supply, and robust systems for life support. The facility is capable of withstanding a protracted siege—something that appeals to Sidious in remaking the tower for his own nefarious uses.

- Surgical trauma-biomedical reconstruction center
- Intelligence databanks and analysis computers
- Emperor Palpatine oversees the restoration of Anakin
- Fusion reactor provides power to complex
- Ultra-dense neuranium shielding conceals reactor from detection by screening any radiation leakage
- Power feed lines to main heavy armaments
- Red Guards control all access points to lower level
- Bacta tanks to aid post-operative recovery
- Operating suites. Entire floor exists in a bio-sterilization field to prevent infection during surgical procedures
- Medical droid turbolift
- Access hatch to droid maintenance area
- Medical droid recharging stations
- Early warning sensor, linked to weapons firing control systems
- Massive Sith holocron uncovered on Moraband and secretly removed by Palpatine, on one of his early visits to the former Sith burial planet
- Ancient Sith ritual altar originally found on Ziost
- Palpatine's secret Sith lair and repository of Sith artifacts and archives
- Palpatine's meditation chamber
- Environmentally controlled display case for Sith scrolls
- Repository for Sith holocrons, either found or forcibly removed from their custodians

MAKING A MONSTER

The medcenter is fully equipped for the diagnosis and treatment of all types of health conditions and injuries, with advanced medical droids and extensive databanks. Its droid doctors' life-saving surgical techniques restore Darth Vader's mobility with biomechanical limbs and life-support systems concealed inside fearsome body armor. Vader then benefits from the power of the Sith artifacts concealed on the lower levels, which are isolated from the main facility by bio-key access and Red Guards.

MEDCENTER

THE CITIZENS OF CORUSCANT know the Grand Republic Medical Facility as a specialist hospital that treats cases from all over the galaxy requiring leading-edge surgical techniques and biomechanical reconstruction. And for much of the Clone Wars, the medcenter is exactly that. But late in the conflict, the facility gains a new, secret purpose, with its benevolent face concealing a dark heart. The lower levels of the medcenter become Darth Sidious' Sith retreat, a focus for meditation and a repository for his collection of secret Sith artifacts and lore. It is within these walls that the fallen Anakin Skywalker is treated and transformed after his battle with Obi-Wan Kenobi.

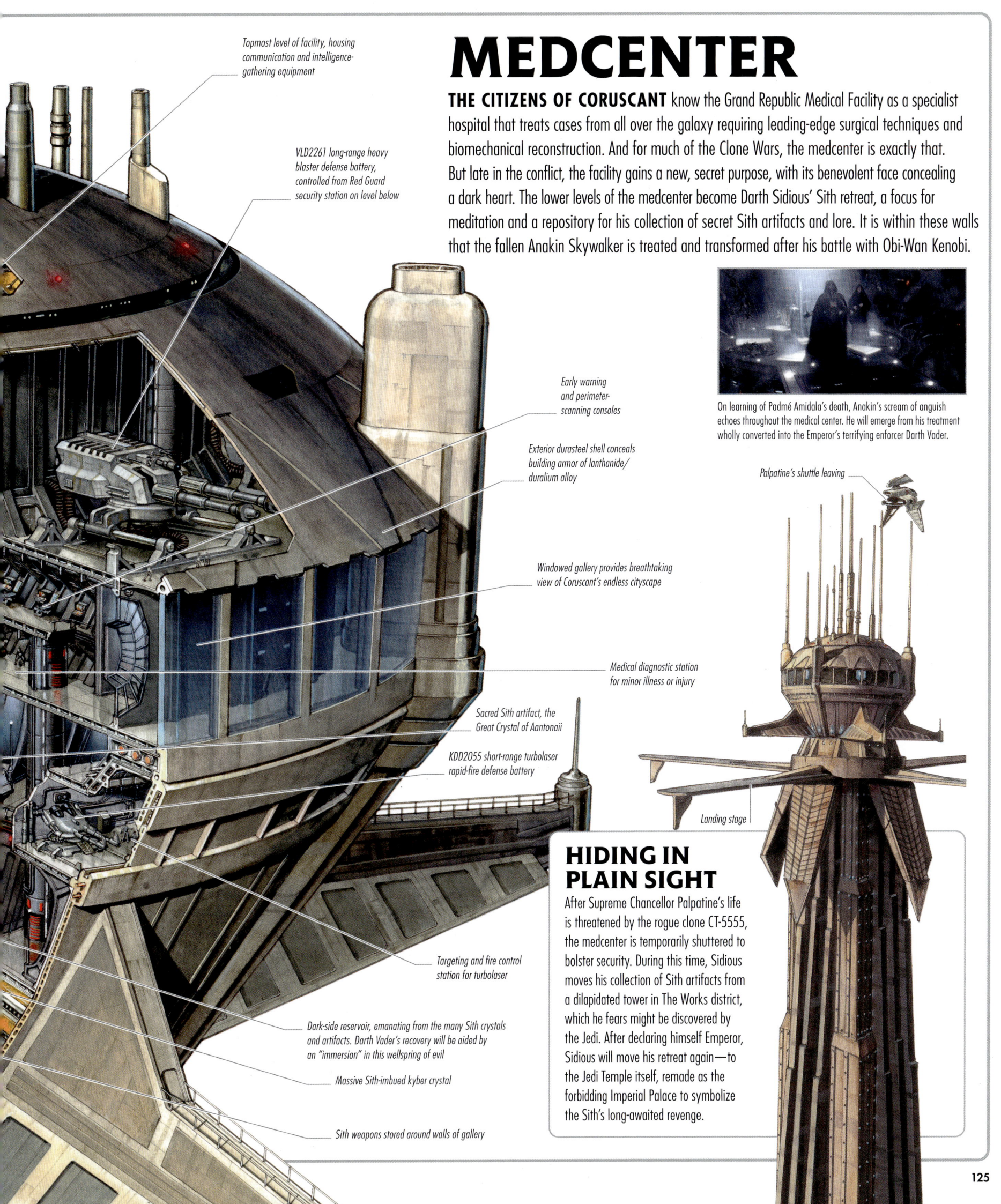

Topmost level of facility, housing communication and intelligence-gathering equipment

VLD2261 long-range heavy blaster defense battery, controlled from Red Guard security station on level below

Early warning and perimeter-scanning consoles

Exterior durasteel shell conceals building armor of lanthanide/duralium alloy

On learning of Padmé Amidala's death, Anakin's scream of anguish echoes throughout the medical center. He will emerge from his treatment wholly converted into the Emperor's terrifying enforcer Darth Vader.

Palpatine's shuttle leaving

Windowed gallery provides breathtaking view of Coruscant's endless cityscape

Medical diagnostic station for minor illness or injury

Sacred Sith artifact, the Great Crystal of Aantonaii

KDD2055 short-range turbolaser rapid-fire defense battery

Landing stage

Targeting and fire control station for turbolaser

Dark-side reservoir, emanating from the many Sith crystals and artifacts. Darth Vader's recovery will be aided by an "immersion" in this wellspring of evil

Massive Sith-imbued kyber crystal

Sith weapons stored around walls of gallery

HIDING IN PLAIN SIGHT

After Supreme Chancellor Palpatine's life is threatened by the rogue clone CT-5555, the medcenter is temporarily shuttered to bolster security. During this time, Sidious moves his collection of Sith artifacts from a dilapidated tower in The Works district, which he fears might be discovered by the Jedi. After declaring himself Emperor, Sidious will move his retreat again—to the Jedi Temple itself, remade as the forbidding Imperial Palace to symbolize the Sith's long-awaited revenge.

THE IMPERIAL ERA

Galactic citizens refer to this era as the "Dark Times," marked by subjugation and occupation by the newly founded Empire. In the early years of this regime, many worlds fall victim to the government's powerful propaganda machine, which claims to promote peace and encourages citizens to enlist in Imperial roles, from military to bureaucratic. For over a decade the Empire reigns supreme, absorbing more and more worlds into its fold. While some places like Morlana One and Corellia feed off the Empire's authority, others like Ferrix and Lothal resist. These pockets of resistance become inspirational to a larger, growing movement dubbed the Alliance to Restore the Republic, or the Rebellion, which takes shape in the waning years of the Dark Times. However, the Empire has bigger machinations at play than just promoting propaganda and occupying planets. Across the galaxy at top secret Imperial sites like Ilum, resources are mined to build its ultimate weapon—the Death Star—which will be capable of obliterating an entire planet with a single blast from its kyber-powered cannon.

It takes countless laborers to construct the Death Star, many of whom have no idea what they're working on, but when a scientist learns the true purpose of his research, he makes it his mission to expose the Empire. This one act of bravery creates a cascading effect that leads rogue rebels to defy their own leadership, stealing the plans for the Death Star so that they may have a fighting chance against the Empire. After the battle station displays its full destructive power by blowing up Alderaan, the Battle of Yavin ensues, wherein the superweapon prepares to fire on the rebel base while the Rebellion makes a desperate attack run on the Death Star. Among the rebels are Leia Organa, who so bravely ferried the stolen plans back to the organization, and Luke Skywalker, a recent recruit destined to be crucial to the cause. Using the stolen plans, the rebels successfully destroy the Death Star before any more planets can fall victim to its destructive power. This victory is a tipping point for the galaxy, ushering in an age of Rebellion that sees many hard-fought battles, such as on Hoth, where the rebels are forced to disperse their fleet after the Empire discovers their latest base, and later at Endor, when the rebels take on a second Death Star and the Emperor himself. The Galactic Civil War finally comes to an end at Jakku, where the remainder of the Empire's fleet is defeated and most outstanding Imperials either surrender or flee.

3 Moloch catches up with the M-68 in his truckspeeder, trying to force Han and Qi'ra to stop. A near-collision with an industrial cargo speeder forces Han to make a hasty detour onto the Shug Drabor Causeway.

4 Forced to take the long way, Han races past a Santhe/Sienar TIE fighter assembly plant, only to find a gate blocking his path south. The M-68 smashes through the gate, to the consternation of an RA-7 droid.

5 The M-68 speeds past the huge Kuat Drive Yards factory Coronet-KDY-14, which builds Imperial Star Destroyers from components brought in on barges and crane walkers.

2 Han and Qi'ra race down Narro Sienar Boulevard, named after the legendary shipbuilder. The spaceport is a straight shot across the shallow Antonian Lagoon, and they can see starliners lifting off into Corellia's skies ahead.

1 ESCAPING THE DEN

The White Worms' Den is a long-abandoned water processing plant, with Lady Proxima holding court in its central cistern. Once shuttered, Coronet City's industrial sites are never empty for long—scavengers strip them of equipment and machinery, and squatters move in. Han, Qi'ra, and the other scrumrats dwell in the Den's tunnels, venturing out to scavenge and steal for Proxima. After Han steals a powerful M-68 speeder and a vial of coaxium, he and Qi'ra flee the Den, hoping to barter the coaxium for passage offworld.

Han knew about the M-68's speed and performance, but even he is surprised by the speeder's acceleration.

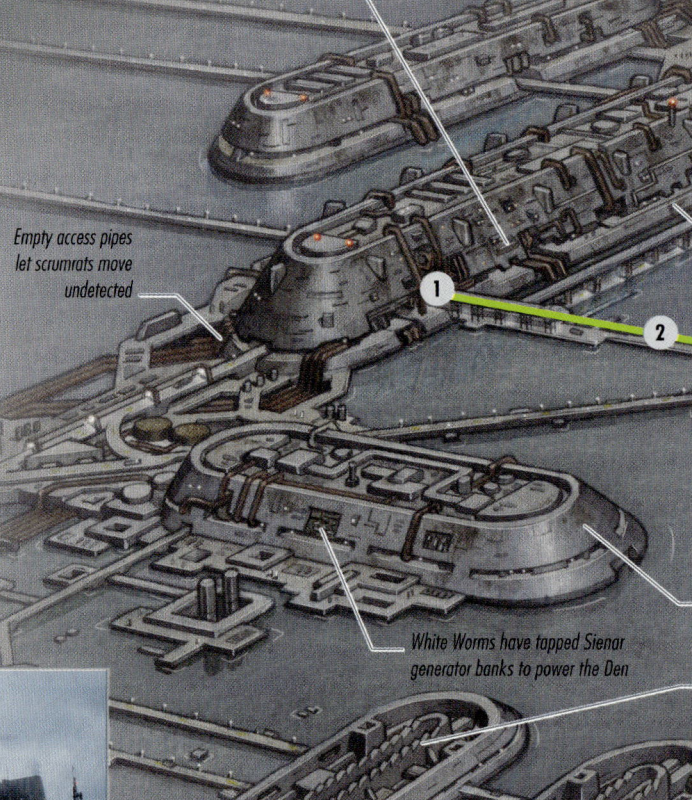

CORELLIA

CORELLIA'S CAPITAL OF CORONET CITY began as a seaport with houses and shops built on islands joined by bridges. Millennia later, this architectural plan still underpins Coronet City—the islands have largely vanished beneath modern structures, forming "pills" linked by causeways crossing the water. Factories and shipyards dominate many pills, and sit alongside housing blocks, markets, and public spaces. In making their bid for freedom, scrumrats Han and Qi'ra flee the pill hiding the White Worms' lair and race through the Santhe shipyards and an ancient fish market to reach Coronet Spaceport.

ROUTE KEY
Han and Qi'ra's route

6 Moloch chases Han and Qi'ra through the assembly yards, smashing equipment and scattering organic and droid workers. A hapless Imperial patrol trooper gives chase before a collision sends his C-PH bike airborne.

7 CLOSE QUARTERS

The eastern half of the pill housing Coronet-KDY-14 is the site of the Otlair fish market, one of Corellia's oldest. Han hopes to outrun Moloch's truckspeeder on the long straightaway hugging the factory's southern edge, then gun the M-68 around the fish market's periphery and cross the causeway to the spaceport and safety. But Moloch's stinger proves too fast; to Qi'ra's dismay, Han is forced to improvise, making a hard left and racing into the heart of the Santhe/Sienar factory.

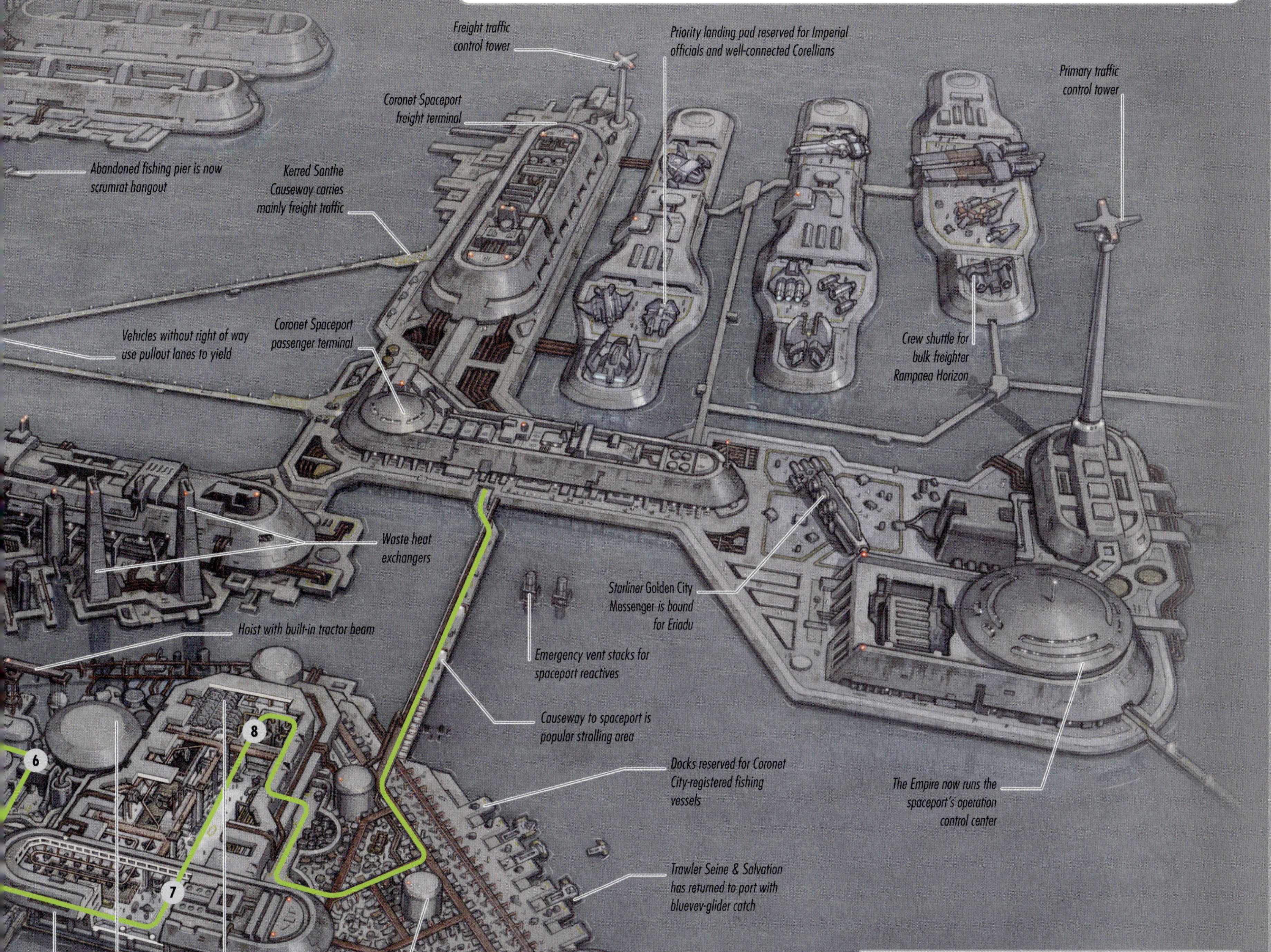

- Abandoned fishing pier is now scrumrat hangout
- Kerred Santhe Causeway carries mainly freight traffic
- Freight traffic control tower
- Coronet Spaceport freight terminal
- Priority landing pad reserved for Imperial officials and well-connected Corellians
- Primary traffic control tower
- Vehicles without right of way use pullout lanes to yield
- Coronet Spaceport passenger terminal
- Crew shuttle for bulk freighter Rampaea Horizon
- Waste heat exchangers
- Hoist with built-in tractor beam
- Starliner Golden City Messenger is bound for Eriadu
- Emergency vent stacks for spaceport reactives
- Causeway to spaceport is popular strolling area
- Docks reserved for Coronet City-registered fishing vessels
- The Empire now runs the spaceport's operation control center
- Trawler Seine & Salvation has returned to port with bluevev-glider catch
- Shipyard central office now houses Imperial garrison
- TIE fighter wings awaiting assembly
- Maritime operations center and CorSec coast guard station
- Terminus of tunnel-rail transport system
- Refrigerated silos for fish market
- Coast guard waveskimmer ready to respond to emergencies

8 Han spots an alley that's too narrow for Moloch's truckspeeder to navigate. Unfortunately, it also proves slightly too narrow for the M-68, forcing Han and Qi'ra to flee through the fish market on foot.

1 THE HEIST BEGINS

Everything goes well at first. After the conveyex train leaves the Imperial depository with its cargo, Rio drops Beckett, Han, and Chewie from the AT-hauler and keeps pace with the train. They're 9.6 kilometers (6 miles) from the bridge where Val is setting explosives, and time is tight. The three swiftly locate the target container and verify it's full of coaxium.

2 Range troopers emerge from the rear of the train, firing at the thieves, but Han and Chewie decouple the last seven cars and the caboose, leaving the helpless Imperials behind.

3 Beckett, Han, and Chewie attach the cables, but there's a new complication: Val spots Enfys Nest and the Cloud-Riders speeding by on an intercept course with the conveyex train.

CONVEYEX HEIST

YEARS AFTER HAN SOLO'S ESCAPE from Corellia, Tobias Beckett's gang plans to steal a container full of coaxium from an Imperial conveyex train on Vandor. Rio Durant will drop Beckett, Han Solo, and Chewbacca onto the train from a stolen AT-hauler. They'll find the coaxium container and attach it to the hauler. After Val blows up a bridge along the route, the others will decouple the container and fly off with their prize as the rest of the train plunges into an abyss. It's a fine plan—until everything goes wrong.

ROUTE KEY
Coaxium container route ———

4 The Cloud-Riders attack, and Rio is mortally wounded. Han takes over flying the AT-hauler but clips a sensor on the track, alerting Imperial viper droids to the attempted heist.

5 With the train perilously close, Val is pinned down by vipers and unarmed. She sacrifices herself to save Beckett, blowing up the bridge as the Imperial droids close in.

6 The Cloud-Riders and Beckett battle for the coaxium as the conveyex hurtles along. Chewie manages to uncouple the container just before the cars plummet into the void.

The gang camps in trenchworks dug for frontier skirmishes against Spinnaker Raiders

Beckett, Han, and Val observe the conveyex route from this ridge

IRIDIUM MOUNTAINS

Viper droids deploy from the Imperial watch tower overlooking the bridge end and tunnel entrance

Bridge wreckage

Scar left by coaxium detonation

Beckett creates monuments for Rio and Val where the damaged AT-hauler crash lands.

7 TUG OF WAR
The container lurches back and forth above the peaks of the Iridium Mountains, cabled to both Han's hauler and the Cloud-Riders' swoops. Unable to maintain control, Han ignores Beckett's protests and releases the container, with Chewie and Beckett clinging to a cable as the victors fly off with the coaxium in tow.

8 NOBODY'S PRIZE
But Enfys Nest has only moments to enjoy this triumph. The Cloud-Riders are also forced to release their prize and the coaxium explodes, with the massive detonation turning Luftgriff Peak into pea-sized gravel. The heist has been a costly disaster, claiming the lives of Val and Rio, and Beckett reveals more bad news: he was working for Crimson Dawn, so now owes its ruthless leader Dryden Vos 100 k-grams of refined coaxium.

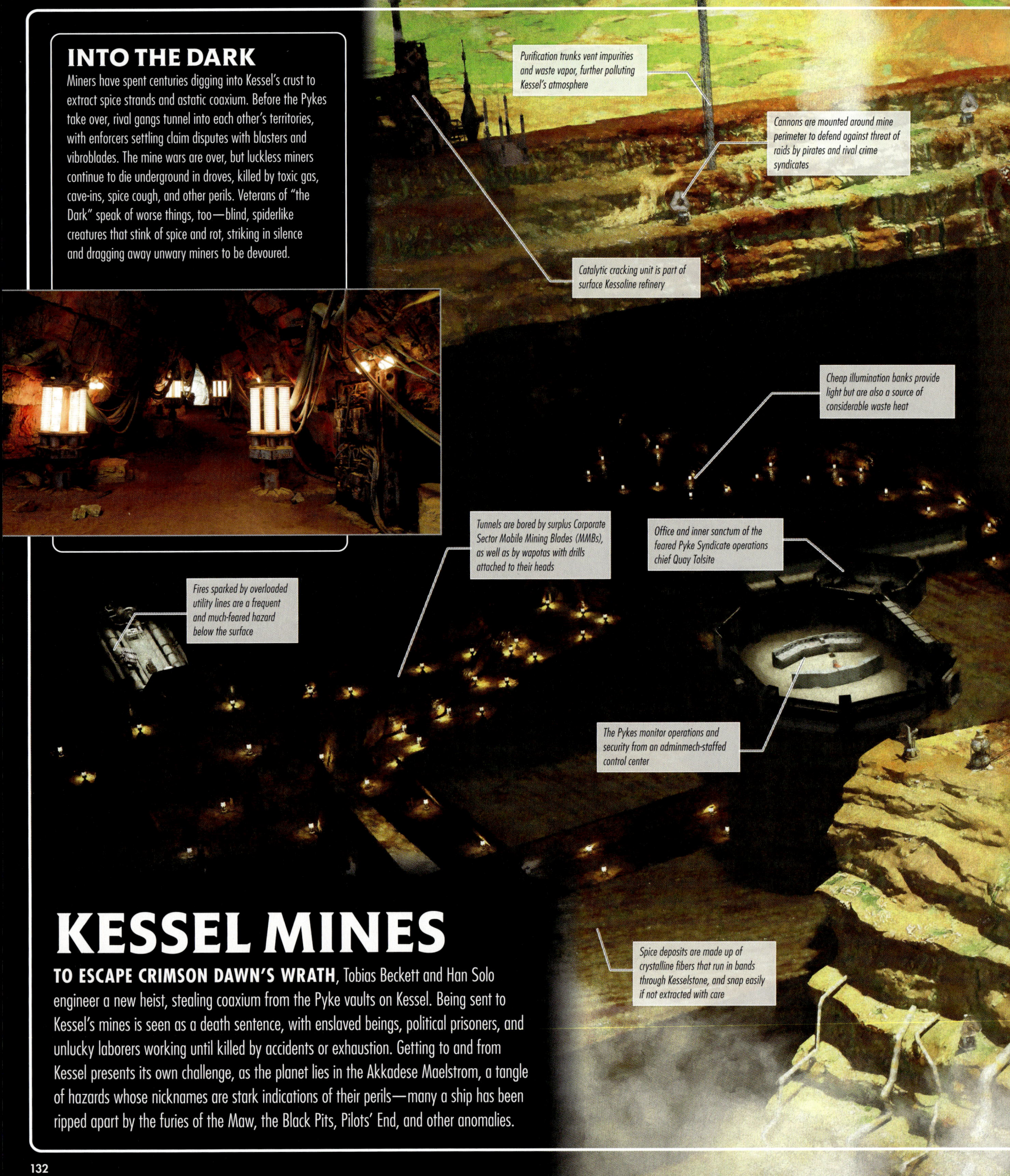

INTO THE DARK

Miners have spent centuries digging into Kessel's crust to extract spice strands and astatic coaxium. Before the Pykes take over, rival gangs tunnel into each other's territories, with enforcers settling claim disputes with blasters and vibroblades. The mine wars are over, but luckless miners continue to die underground in droves, killed by toxic gas, cave-ins, spice cough, and other perils. Veterans of "the Dark" speak of worse things, too—blind, spiderlike creatures that stink of spice and rot, striking in silence and dragging away unwary miners to be devoured.

Purification trunks vent impurities and waste vapor, further polluting Kessel's atmosphere

Cannons are mounted around mine perimeter to defend against threat of raids by pirates and rival crime syndicates

Catalytic cracking unit is part of surface Kessoline refinery

Cheap illumination banks provide light but are also a source of considerable waste heat

Tunnels are bored by surplus Corporate Sector Mobile Mining Blades (MMBs), as well as by wapotas with drills attached to their heads

Office and inner sanctum of the feared Pyke Syndicate operations chief Quay Tolsite

Fires sparked by overloaded utility lines are a frequent and much-feared hazard below the surface

The Pykes monitor operations and security from an adminmech-staffed control center

Spice deposits are made up of crystalline fibers that run in bands through Kesselstone, and snap easily if not extracted with care

KESSEL MINES

TO ESCAPE CRIMSON DAWN'S WRATH, Tobias Beckett and Han Solo engineer a new heist, stealing coaxium from the Pyke vaults on Kessel. Being sent to Kessel's mines is seen as a death sentence, with enslaved beings, political prisoners, and unlucky laborers working until killed by accidents or exhaustion. Getting to and from Kessel presents its own challenge, as the planet lies in the Akkadese Maelstrom, a tangle of hazards whose nicknames are stark indications of their perils—many a ship has been ripped apart by the furies of the Maw, the Black Pits, Pilots' End, and other anomalies.

Terraces dug out by generations of luckless pit miners

Vapor vented from mine operations will cool and rain back down as acidic precipitate

Landing platform services both cargo speeders and low-altitude industrial load lifters

Gantries and lifts frequently break down in the corrosive atmosphere

Distillation columns refine Kessoline and store it for later collection and distribution

Kessel's corrosive atmosphere is discoloring and pitting the Millennium Falcon's hull plating, much to Lando Calrissian's consternation

Kessoline waste pools impede movement of workers and are a health hazard

POLLUTED PARADISE

Along with spice, mining Kesselstone produces a toxic by-product known as Kessoline, which collects in noxious green pools in and around the mines and leaks into Kessel's aquifers, further damaging the planet's fragile ecosystem. Miners have discovered Kessoline can be used as fuel for machinery. It's not a good power source, producing smoke that irritates both eyes and skin, and corrodes machines. But that matters little on a world where both equipment and lives are seen as disposable.

FERRIX

FROM SPACE, FERRIX IS MOSTLY covered in amber-colored terrain and blue oceans. The people of this world are called Ferrixians and are known for their loyalty to their community. The surface of Ferrix is a combination of farmland and wasteland that features mountain ranges and scattered urban areas. At Ferrix City, one of the most densely populated areas on the planet, laborers work in salvage yards breaking down starships and other machinery left over from wars past. Ferrixians pride themselves on their work ethic, but if there's anything they're more devoted to, it's each other.

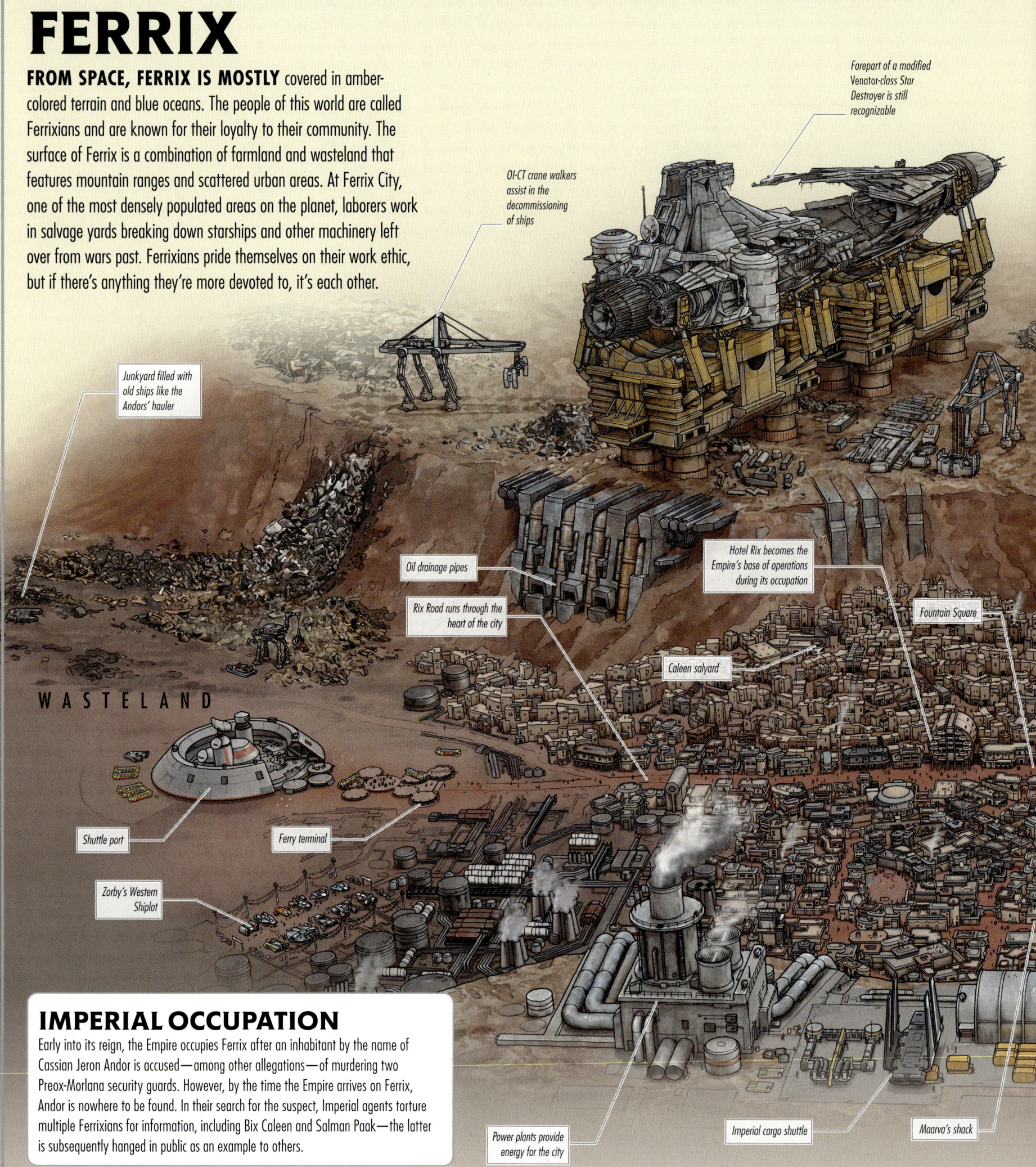

Forepart of a modified Venator-class Star Destroyer is still recognizable

OI-CT crane walkers assist in the decommissioning of ships

Junkyard filled with old ships like the Andors' hauler

Hotel Rix becomes the Empire's base of operations during its occupation

Fountain Square

Oil drainage pipes

Rix Road runs through the heart of the city

Caleen salyard

WASTELAND

Shuttle port

Ferry terminal

Zorby's Western Shiplot

Power plants provide energy for the city

Imperial cargo shuttle

Maarva's shack

IMPERIAL OCCUPATION

Early into its reign, the Empire occupies Ferrix after an inhabitant by the name of Cassian Jeron Andor is accused—among other allegations—of murdering two Preox-Morlana security guards. However, by the time the Empire arrives on Ferrix, Andor is nowhere to be found. In their search for the suspect, Imperial agents torture multiple Ferrixians for information, including Bix Caleen and Salman Paak—the latter is subsequently hanged in public as an example to others.

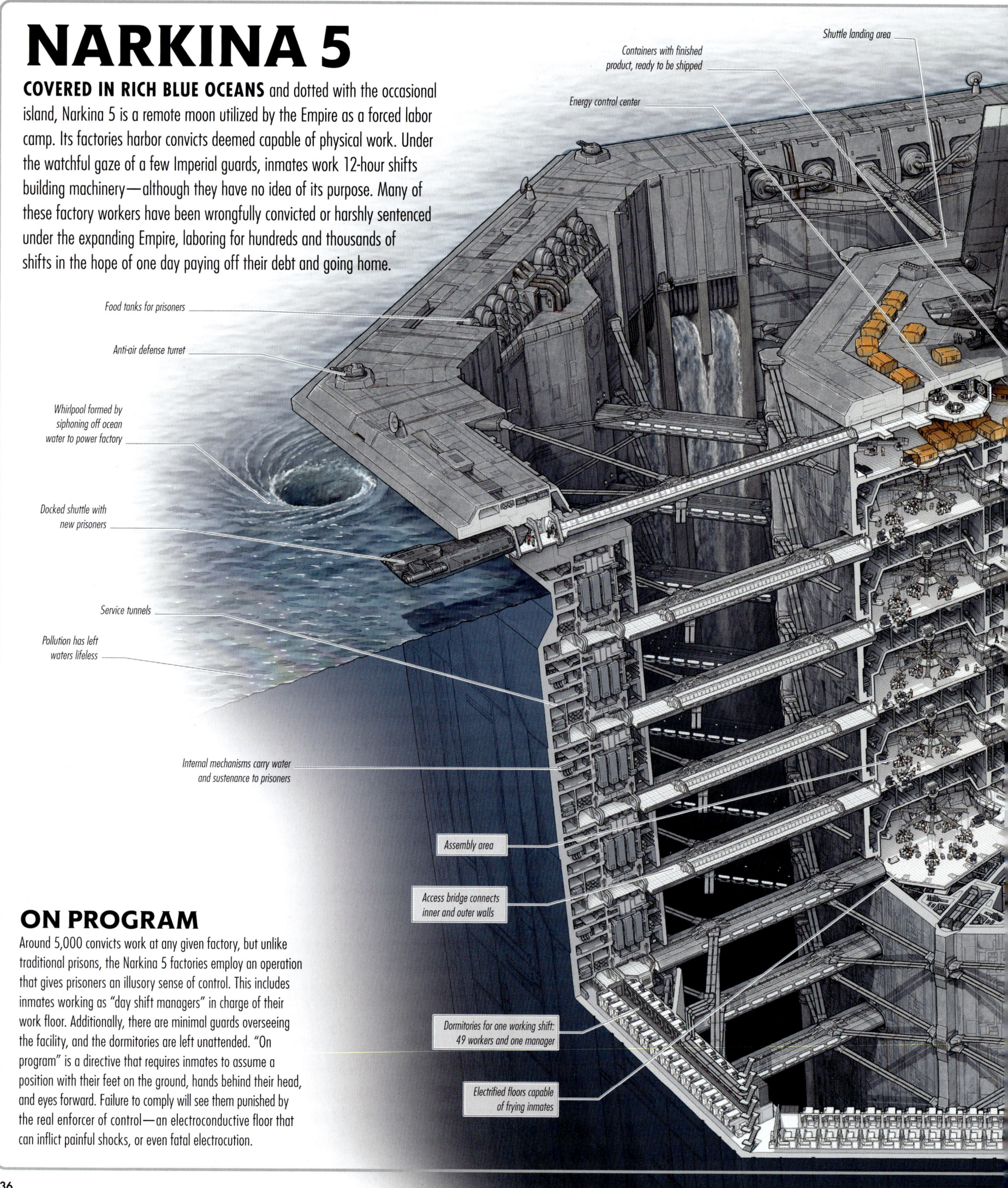

NARKINA 5

COVERED IN RICH BLUE OCEANS and dotted with the occasional island, Narkina 5 is a remote moon utilized by the Empire as a forced labor camp. Its factories harbor convicts deemed capable of physical work. Under the watchful gaze of a few Imperial guards, inmates work 12-hour shifts building machinery—although they have no idea of its purpose. Many of these factory workers have been wrongfully convicted or harshly sentenced under the expanding Empire, laboring for hundreds and thousands of shifts in the hope of one day paying off their debt and going home.

- Food tanks for prisoners
- Anti-air defense turret
- Whirlpool formed by siphoning off ocean water to power factory
- Docked shuttle with new prisoners
- Service tunnels
- Pollution has left waters lifeless
- Internal mechanisms carry water and sustenance to prisoners
- Assembly area
- Access bridge connects inner and outer walls
- Dormitories for one working shift: 49 workers and one manager
- Electrified floors capable of frying inmates
- Containers with finished product, ready to be shipped
- Energy control center
- Shuttle landing area

ON PROGRAM

Around 5,000 convicts work at any given factory, but unlike traditional prisons, the Narkina 5 factories employ an operation that gives prisoners an illusory sense of control. This includes inmates working as "day shift managers" in charge of their work floor. Additionally, there are minimal guards overseeing the facility, and the dormitories are left unattended. "On program" is a directive that requires inmates to assume a position with their feet on the ground, hands behind their head, and eyes forward. Failure to comply will see them punished by the real enforcer of control—an electroconductive floor that can inflict painful shocks, or even fatal electrocution.

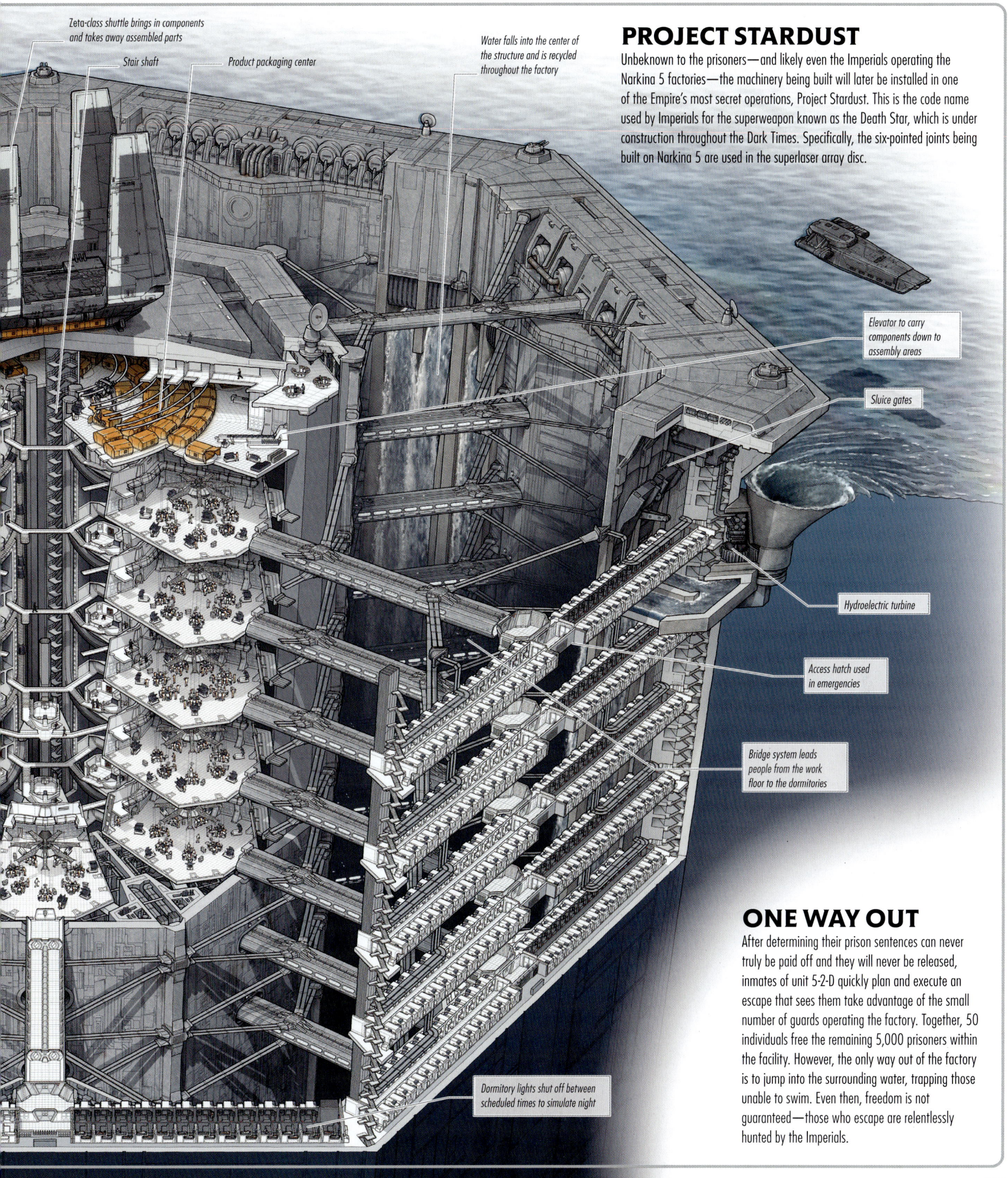

PROJECT STARDUST

Unbeknown to the prisoners—and likely even the Imperials operating the Narkina 5 factories—the machinery being built will later be installed in one of the Empire's most secret operations, Project Stardust. This is the code name used by Imperials for the superweapon known as the Death Star, which is under construction throughout the Dark Times. Specifically, the six-pointed joints being built on Narkina 5 are used in the superlaser array disc.

ONE WAY OUT

After determining their prison sentences can never truly be paid off and they will never be released, inmates of unit 5-2-D quickly plan and execute an escape that sees them take advantage of the small number of guards operating the factory. Together, 50 individuals free the remaining 5,000 prisoners within the facility. However, the only way out of the factory is to jump into the surrounding water, trapping those unable to swim. Even then, freedom is not guaranteed—those who escape are relentlessly hunted by the Imperials.

THE IMPERIAL SENATE

LONG THE HOME of the Republic Senate, following the rise of the Empire this vast building on Coruscant becomes the center of its Imperial successor. In fact, the transition from Galactic Republic to Empire happens within its walls, when Sheev Palpatine declares his own transformation from supreme chancellor to Emperor. Much like its predecessor, the Imperial Senate features delegates from virtually every sector in the known galaxy and is host to much political intrigue. Over the course of the Empire's reign, more and more power is siphoned to the Emperor, hindering the Imperial Senate's efficacy.

DARK TIMES

Not only does the Emperor sap power from the Senate, he and his administration also pit Imperial worlds against each other by constantly manipulating narratives in the media and preaching harmful propaganda. By the later years of the Empire, many delegates no longer regularly attend sessions of the Senate and, as a result, refuse to even hear their opponents' positions. Others have vanished in mysterious circumstances.

Senator Mon Mothma of Chandrila advocates before the Imperial Senate for the Ghormans, who fight for their basic rights under Imperial oppression.

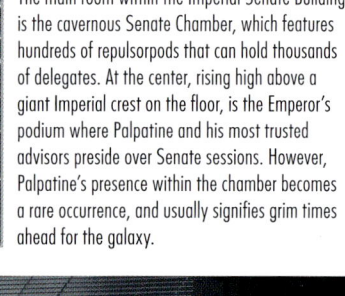

The main room within the Imperial Senate Building is the cavernous Senate Chamber, which features hundreds of repulsorpods that can hold thousands of delegates. At the center, rising high above a giant Imperial crest on the floor, is the Emperor's podium where Palpatine and his most trusted advisors preside over Senate sessions. However, Palpatine's presence within the chamber becomes a rare occurrence, and usually signifies grim times ahead for the galaxy.

Exterior lighting on senatorial repulsorpods indicate the interest a delegate may or may not have in the topic being discussed on the Senate floor. An illuminated light signifies interest while a light switched off indicates opposition. In contrast to the hectic debates of the Republic era, many orators in the Imperial Senate are faced with banks of empty pods, their unenthusiastic delegates to be found elsewhere.

SIDE ELEVATION

While Coruscant's skyline is mostly defined by its tall skyscrapers, the Senate Building is instantly recognizable for its wide, oval-shaped structure. Its sheer size is both impressive and intimidating, and has been a defining feature of the planet for centuries.

Exterior largely unchanged since Republic era, implying continuity and stability

Long-range comms antennas transmit senatorial rulings and receive petitions

Ground-level entrance archways

1+ kilometer (0.62+ miles)

2+ kilometers (1.24+ miles)

INTERIOR VIEW

In addition to the Senate Chamber, the Senate Building is honeycombed with offices for senators, advisors, representatives, and more, as well as the Emperor's working office, although he rarely ventures from the Imperial Palace. A dining commons featuring galactic cuisine is also available onsite.

Holo recording systems and lighting mounted in ceiling

Media complex and data center

Atmospheric processing

Senate Chamber

Senatorial offices

Shuttle docking bay

Emperor's podium

Rebuilt office of the Imperial Secretariat

Turbolift

Secret ISB complex in basement

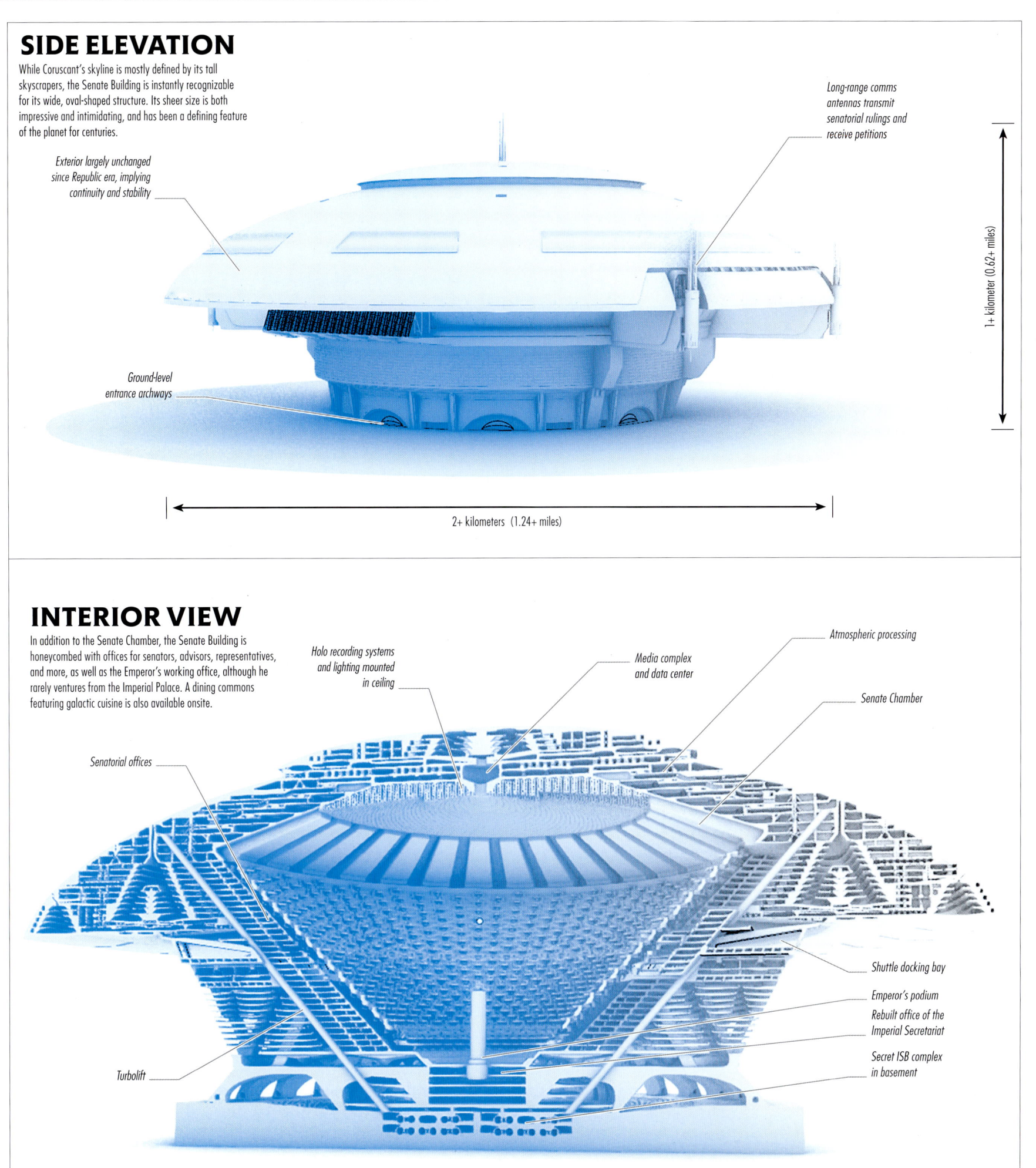

JEDHA

SITUATED IN THE MID RIM, orbiting the planet of NaJedha, Jedha is a frigid desert moon. Throughout history, Jedha has served as an epicenter for a number of religions, most of which worship the Force (whether their faith call it that or not). After the fall of the Republic, Jedha becomes a last spiritual bastion of the Jedi, who are deemed traitors by the rising Empire. In the midst of the Dark Times, Master Cere Junda organizes and operates a covert archive of Jedi knowledge on the moon before it is discovered and destroyed by the Empire. Later, as believers keep faith alive, the Empire becomes interested in Jedha's naturally occurring and sacred crystal, kyber. This results in an Imperial occupation of the moon, with Jedha turning into a war zone when local partisans interfere with the Empire's operations.

Air Cover
Flights of TIE fighters launch from the Dauntless above NiJedha for regular patrols of the city and the surrounding area.

Dome of the Anointed
The partisans establish a secondary base here to stage missions in the city. They launch their final onslaught from this location.

Checkpoint 7
Imperials maintain checkpoints in the streets to monitor the population, stopping suspicious individuals for interrogation.

Pilgrim's Gate
Visitors to Jedha City are funneled through this ancient entry point in a narrow canyon. It is the scene of fierce firefights with the Imperial garrison.

THE FINAL PROTECTOR

Located in the Dunes of Contemplation in the surrounding deserts of Jedha City, this sandstone statue of a Jedi—called the Final Protector—stood tall in eras past. It is toppled in the High Republic era during the Battle of Jedha, when a Force cult stirs chaos and protestors push over the statue.

Over the hundreds of years since it fell, the statue has been continuously buried by blowing sands.

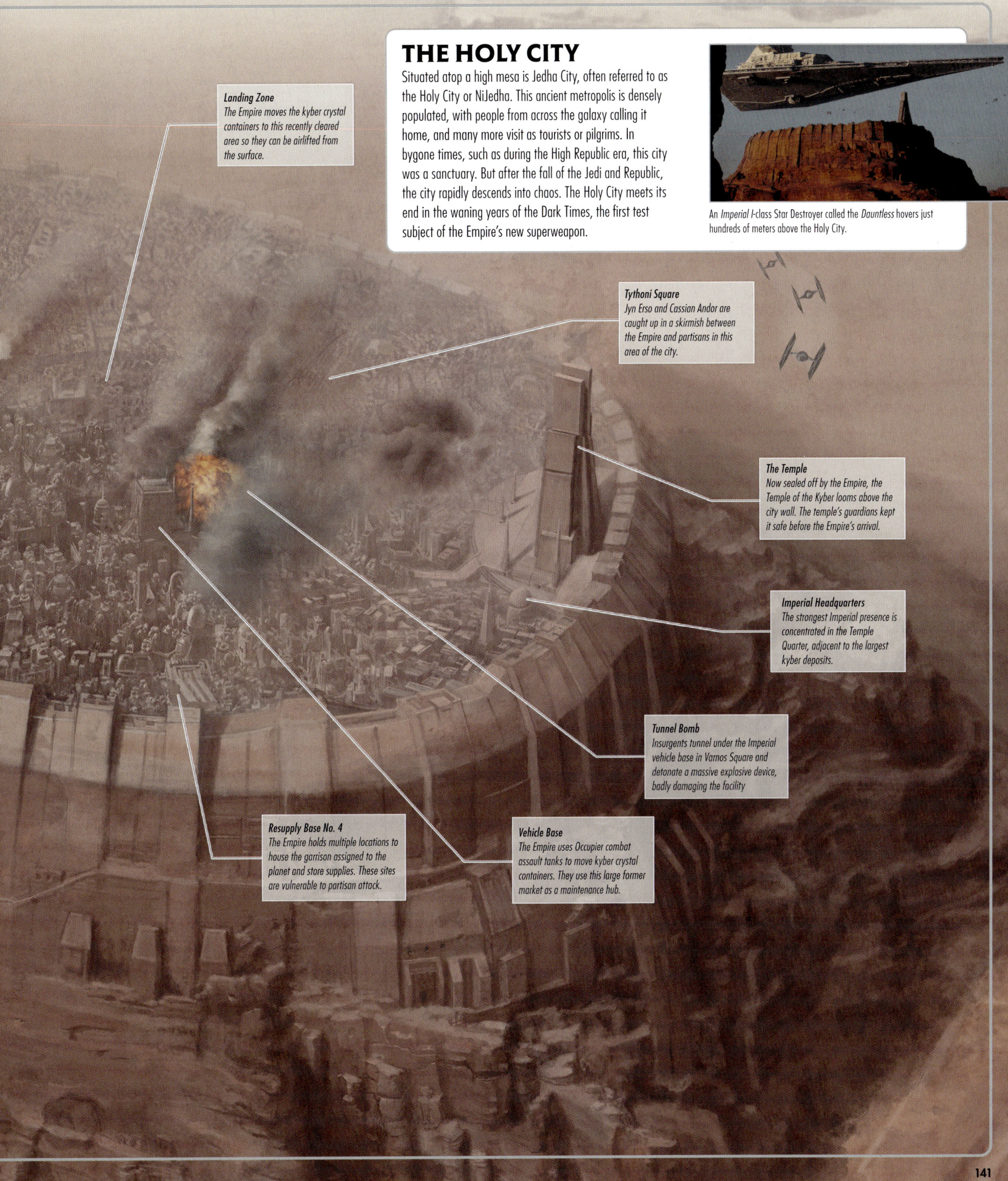

THE HOLY CITY

Situated atop a high mesa is Jedha City, often referred to as the Holy City or NiJedha. This ancient metropolis is densely populated, with people from across the galaxy calling it home, and many more visit as tourists or pilgrims. In bygone times, such as during the High Republic era, this city was a sanctuary. But after the fall of the Jedi and Republic, the city rapidly descends into chaos. The Holy City meets its end in the waning years of the Dark Times, the first test subject of the Empire's new superweapon.

An *Imperial I*-class Star Destroyer called the *Dauntless* hovers just hundreds of meters above the Holy City.

Landing Zone
The Empire moves the kyber crystal containers to this recently cleared area so they can be airlifted from the surface.

Tythoni Square
Jyn Erso and Cassian Andor are caught up in a skirmish between the Empire and partisans in this area of the city.

The Temple
Now sealed off by the Empire, the Temple of the Kyber looms above the city wall. The temple's guardians kept it safe before the Empire's arrival.

Imperial Headquarters
The strongest Imperial presence is concentrated in the Temple Quarter, adjacent to the largest kyber deposits.

Tunnel Bomb
Insurgents tunnel under the Imperial vehicle base in Vamos Square and detonate a massive explosive device, badly damaging the facility

Resupply Base No. 4
The Empire holds multiple locations to house the garrison assigned to the planet and store supplies. These sites are vulnerable to partisan attack.

Vehicle Base
The Empire uses Occupier combat assault tanks to move kyber crystal containers. They use this large former market as a maintenance hub.

VADER'S CASTLE

RISING FROM THE LAVA rivers on Mustafar is Darth Vader's inimitable castle. Defined by dual spires and lava flowing through the center of its structure, the castle's silhouette is devised by the late Darth Momin, speaking to Vader from the beyond through Momin's old helmet. This fortress is where Vader's most personal and private machinations are pursued. In particular, Vader is obsessed with the idea of resurrection and desperately searches for a way to return his beloved Padmé Amidala to him. Momin promises Vader the structure he's designed will aid him in his endeavor, allowing him to access a Force locus the castle is built upon.

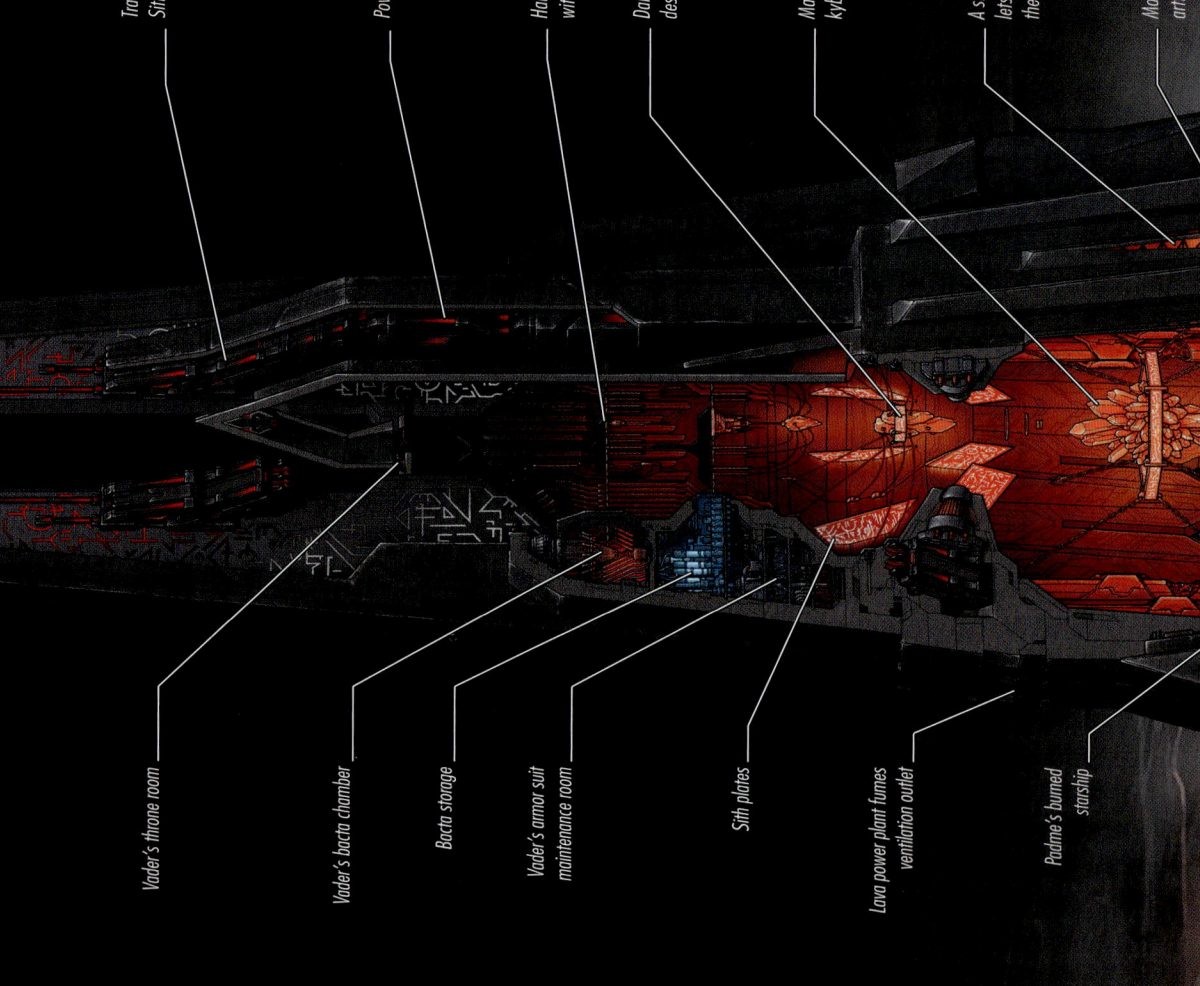

Director Orson Krennic is summoned to Vader's castle where he reports the latest on Project Stardust to the dark lord. Receiving an invitation to the fortress is something all senior Imperials fear.

- Sith plates inside "tuning fork"
- Transmission line to the Sith plate
- Power transformer
- Hall where Vader meets with Director Krennic
- Dark force multiplier system designed by Darth Momin
- Massive Sith-imbued bleeding kyber crystals
- A stained glass window lets through red light of the main hall
- Main hall with Sith artifacts
- TIE fighters returning from a mission
- Vader's throne room
- Vader's bacta chamber
- Bacta storage
- Vader's armor suit maintenance room
- Sith plates
- Lava power plant fumes ventilation outlet
- Padmé's burned starship

CENTRAL CHAMBER

Vader takes house calls and holo transmissions from two primary locations: the central chamber and his throne room. Both locations use Mustafar's hellscape to intimidate those who beckon Vader. In the central chamber, steam rises from the lava-powered station below, creating a choking atmosphere. In the throne room, behind Vader's seat is a panoramic view of the red planet's ruthless environment, complementing the dark lord's vicious style.

Labels (top to bottom along pointers):
- Stormtrooper barracks
- Gates
- Hangar
- Conductor tunnel focuses energy into dedicated chamber
- Elevator down to vehicle repair
- Lava power plant
- Lava outlet
- Power plant control center
- Main entrance
- Stairway to the main hall
- Lava dam
- The external entrance to the focusing chamber is used in the early stages of the castle's construction. It is currently sealed.
- Accumulator
- Lava flow control gates
- Lava penstock
- Generator
- Turbine
- Focusing chamber with Sith stone
- Vaneé's lava fume laboratory
- Elevators connect the castle and the excavations beneath

BACTA TANK

Scorched by the very lava flowing through his castle, Vader routinely bathes in a bacta tank to help heal his scarred skin. This procedure has been going on for years, a testament to the severity of the burns inflicted on him. Although bacta can heal flesh wounds, it cannot repair the damage done to Vader's internal organs, such as his lungs.

LAVA WATERFALL

Vader's castle doubles as a dam, impeding the natural lava flow and using it to create energy that powers the fortress. In the bowels of the castle, lava is funneled through a power station where it spins the turbines that supply the castle with electricity. Processed lava flows out the opposite end in a striking lavafall. Although lights and other fixtures adorn the walls of the castle, some chambers are illuminated by the soft, amber glow of the lava that flows through the fortress.

SCARIF

DEEP IN THE OUTER RIM lies the picturesque planet of Scarif, featuring tropical islands surrounded by warm, turquoise oceans. This small world, although idyllic, is so far out of the way that its location made it unpopular as a destination. That didn't mean it was completely uninhabited, but by the time the Empire rises, it isn't hard for Imperial forces to take over and claim the world with little to no resistance. Far from prying eyes, the Empire uses Scarif to file all their most sensitive data in a vault. A planet-wide energy shield with a single entry point encases the world, restricting access to its surface.

3 Bodhi's Ruse
To further confuse things, Bodhi Rook and Corporal Tonc mislead the Empire by reporting a rebel attack on Pads 2 and 5.

DATA VAULT

A trove of files exists within the Empire's data vault on Scarif, from experimental weapons projects to scientific research. In the later years of the Dark Times, the recently formed Rebel Alliance becomes aware of the data vault and is involved in an impromptu attack on the Imperial base in order to retrieve information vital to their cause.

CITADEL TOWER

Rising up from the waters of Scarif is the citadel tower, which houses the data vault. This tall tower is topped with a communications antenna that requires alignment to send messages offworld or beyond the shield gate. The rebel attack on Scarif sees the infiltration of the citadel tower by incognito operatives. They are successful in stealing the plans to the Death Star superweapon and send them to the rebel fleet that has amassed beyond the shield gate.

The citadel tower is the tallest construction on the planet, rising hundreds of meters above sea level.

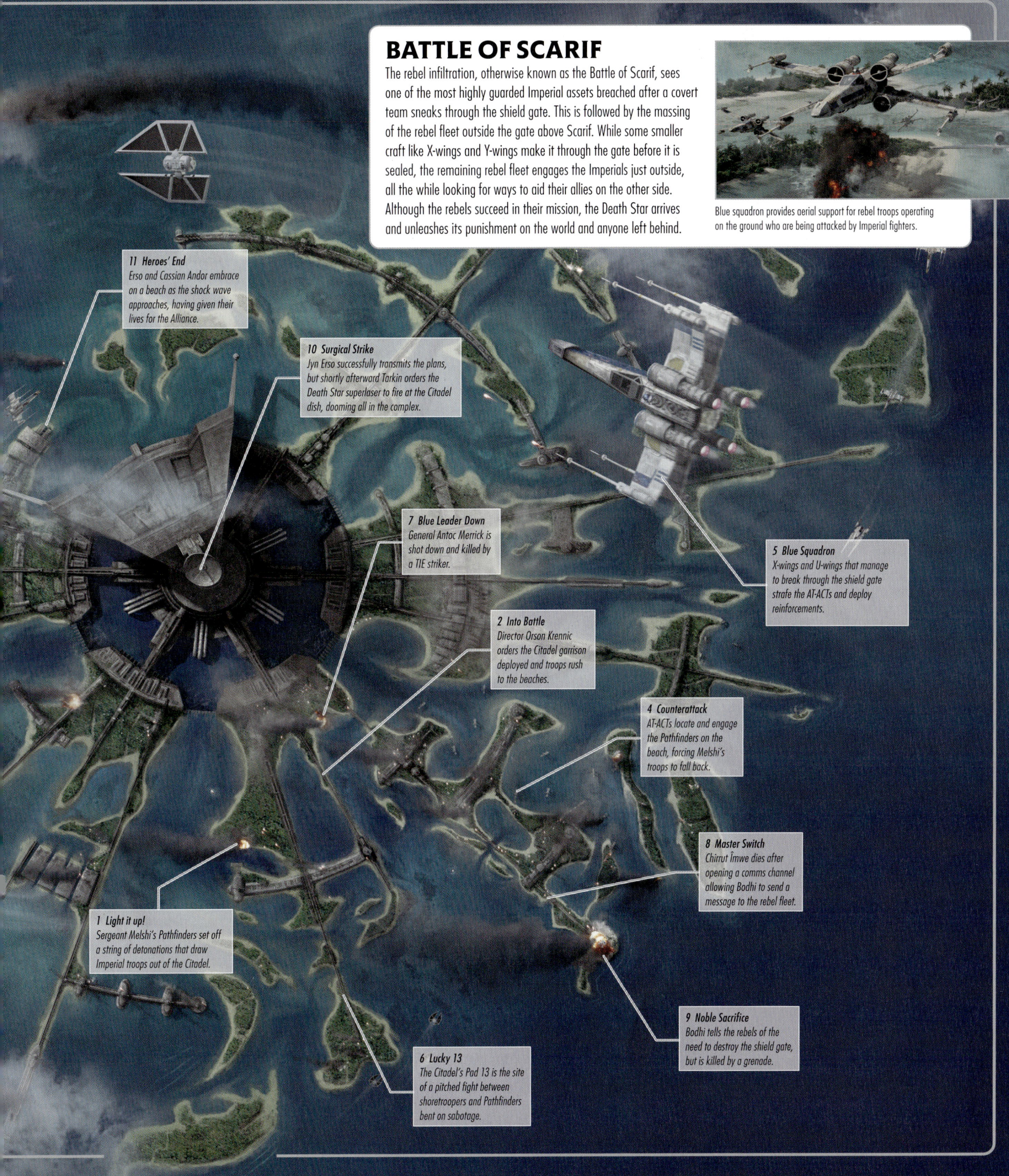

BATTLE OF SCARIF

The rebel infiltration, otherwise known as the Battle of Scarif, sees one of the most highly guarded Imperial assets breached after a covert team sneaks through the shield gate above Scarif. This is followed by the massing of the rebel fleet outside the gate above Scarif. While some smaller craft like X-wings and Y-wings make it through the gate before it is sealed, the remaining rebel fleet engages the Imperials just outside, all the while looking for ways to aid their allies on the other side. Although the rebels succeed in their mission, the Death Star arrives and unleashes its punishment on the world and anyone left behind.

Blue squadron provides aerial support for rebel troops operating on the ground who are being attacked by Imperial fighters.

11 Heroes' End
Erso and Cassian Andor embrace on a beach as the shock wave approaches, having given their lives for the Alliance.

10 Surgical Strike
Jyn Erso successfully transmits the plans, but shortly afterward Tarkin orders the Death Star superlaser to fire at the Citadel dish, dooming all in the complex.

7 Blue Leader Down
General Antoc Merrick is shot down and killed by a TIE striker.

5 Blue Squadron
X-wings and U-wings that manage to break through the shield gate strafe the AT-ACTs and deploy reinforcements.

2 Into Battle
Director Orson Krennic orders the Citadel garrison deployed and troops rush to the beaches.

4 Counterattack
AT-ACTs locate and engage the Pathfinders on the beach, forcing Melshi's troops to fall back.

8 Master Switch
Chirrut Îmwe dies after opening a comms channel allowing Bodhi to send a message to the rebel fleet.

1 Light it up!
Sergeant Melshi's Pathfinders set off a string of detonations that draw Imperial troops out of the Citadel.

9 Noble Sacrifice
Bodhi tells the rebels of the need to destroy the shield gate, but is killed by a grenade.

6 Lucky 13
The Citadel's Pad 13 is the site of a pitched fight between shoretroopers and Pathfinders bent on sabotage.

TRIALS ON TATOOINE

A YELLOW GLOBE baked by the heat of twin suns, the desert world of Tatooine is as rugged and desolate a planet as exists anywhere in the Outer Rim. Scorched by day, near frozen at night, the hardscrabble planet might never have been colonized by humans except for the fact that its long-vanished seabeds suggested mineral wealth might be found, luring a few desperate settlers from the Core to bet their lives on a lucky strike. Raids launched by indigenous Tuskens and swindles orchestrated by Jawas were the first indications that the newcomers had made a poor gamble, but still they came. Pilfering what little moisture there was from the parched air, the farmers grew more hardened with each generation, accepting the smugglers, enslavers, and outlaws who followed, finally becoming resigned to lives filled with adversity.

8 Returning to Tatooine to save Han Solo from Jabba the Hutt, Luke Skywalker, now a Jedi Knight, is captured and forced to walk the plank over the Pit of Carkoon, lair of the insatiable sarlacc. Luke prepares to catch the lightsaber R2-D2 will propel him from the deck of Jabba's sail barge.

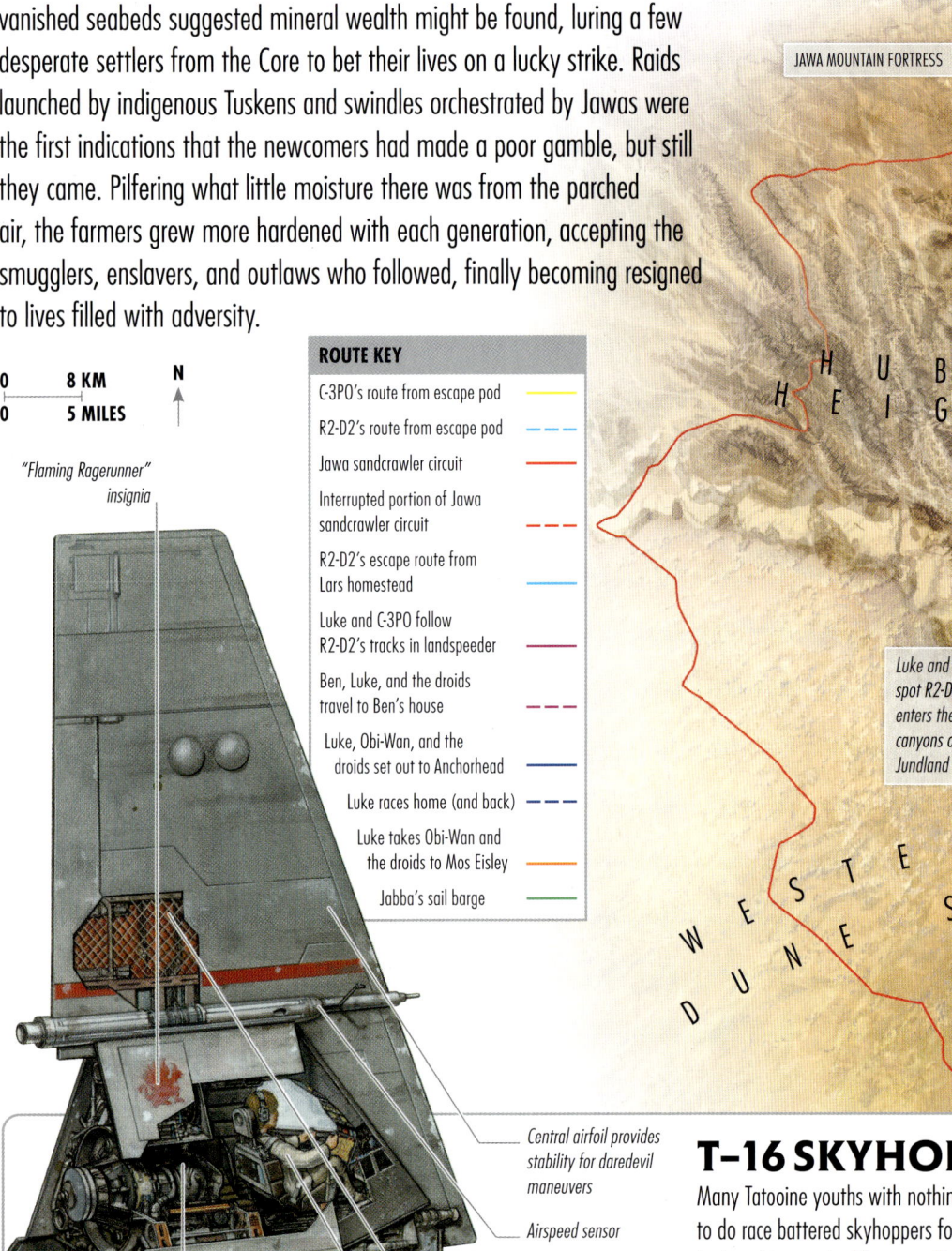

ROUTE KEY
- C-3PO's route from escape pod
- R2-D2's route from escape pod
- Jawa sandcrawler circuit
- Interrupted portion of Jawa sandcrawler circuit
- R2-D2's escape route from Lars homestead
- Luke and C-3PO follow R2-D2's tracks in landspeeder
- Ben, Luke, and the droids travel to Ben's house
- Luke, Obi-Wan, and the droids set out to Anchorhead
- Luke races home (and back)
- Luke takes Obi-Wan and the droids to Mos Eisley
- Jabba's sail barge

"Flaming Ragerunner" insignia

T-16 SKYHOPPER

Many Tatooine youths with nothing better to do race battered skyhoppers for kicks. Levitated by repulsorlifts, propelled by an ion engine, and outfitted with a pneumatic cannon package, Luke Skywalker's modified skyhopper is the perfect craft for making quick hops to Bestine or bulls-eyeing womp rats in the Jawa Heights. Luke is so fond of his skyhopper that when he damages its airfoil, he resorts to toying with a scale model he has had since his early adolescence.

- Central airfoil provides stability for daredevil maneuvers
- Airspeed sensor
- Pneumatic cannon (laser cannon removed for repairs)
- Lightweight lattice construction
- Pilot relies on computer displays and holographic terrain-following maps
- Ion engine can attain supersonic speeds
- Inertia damper coils of matched DCJ-45 repulsorlifts

1 Having bickered with R2-D2 about the best route to take, C-3PO sets out alone. Joints almost frozen, he staggers toward the summit of a towering sand dune. Typical of those that crawl slowly across Tatooine's Jundland Wastes, the dune is necklaced with the bleached bones of a greater krayt dragon.

SOROSUUB X–34 LANDSPEEDER

Landspeeders are a standard personal transport on Tatooine. Although superseded by the XP-38, SoroSuub's "Thirty-four" is still considered a classic because of its no-frills design and powerful engine. Even without modifications, the X-34 can attain top speeds of 250 kph (155 mph), and is highly maneuverable in tight quarters.

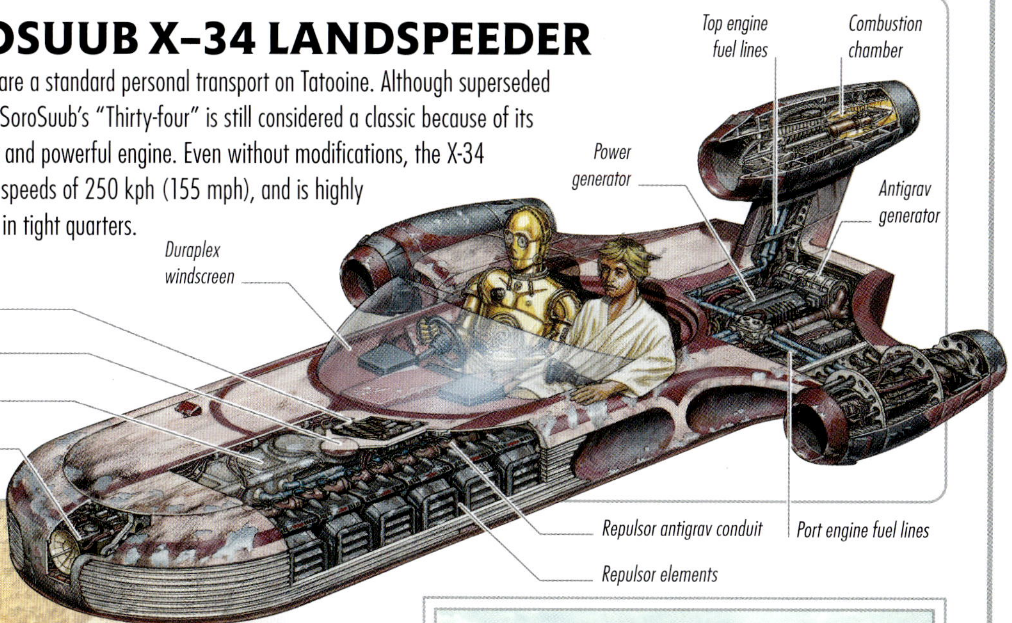

Labels: Top engine fuel lines; Combustion chamber; Power generator; Antigrav generator; Duraplex windscreen; Service access panel; Fuel filler cap; Fuel tank; Forward scanner; Repulsor antigrav conduit; Port engine fuel lines; Repulsor elements

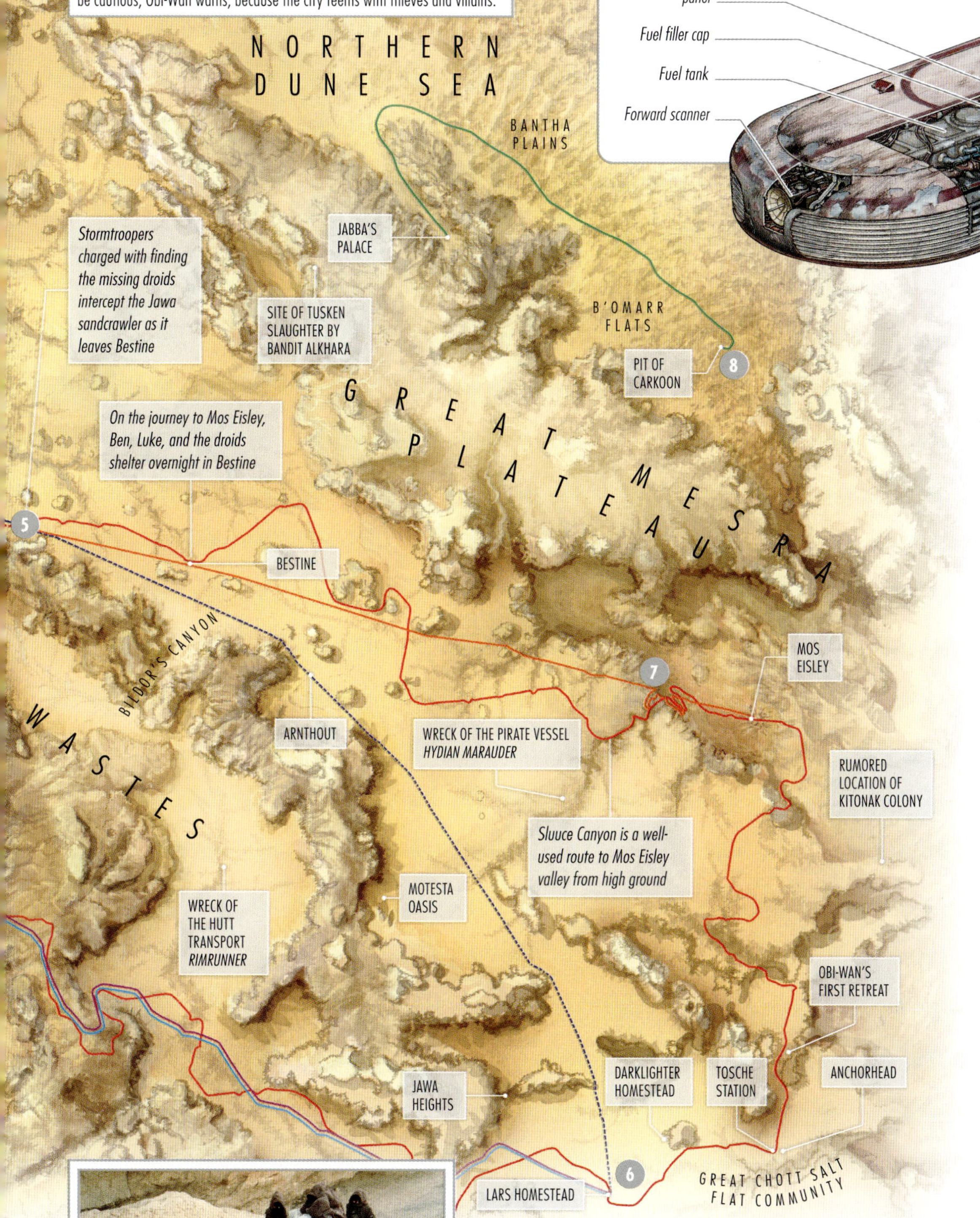

7 Rejoining Obi-Wan and the droids, Luke speeds to Mos Eisley, stopping only briefly to gaze on the spaceport from a steep-sided bluff. While Mos Eisley is the group's best chance of finding safe transport off Tatooine, they will have to be cautious, Obi-Wan warns, because the city teems with thieves and villains.

Map labels: NORTHERN DUNE SEA; BANTHA PLAINS; Stormtroopers charged with finding the missing droids intercept the Jawa sandcrawler as it leaves Bestine; JABBA'S PALACE; SITE OF TUSKEN SLAUGHTER BY BANDIT ALKHARA; B'OMARR FLATS; On the journey to Mos Eisley, Ben, Luke, and the droids shelter overnight in Bestine; PIT OF CARKOON; GREAT MESRA PLATTEAU; BESTINE; BILDOR'S CANYON; WASTES; ARNTHOUT; WRECK OF THE PIRATE VESSEL HYDIAN MARAUDER; MOS EISLEY; RUMORED LOCATION OF KITONAK COLONY; Sluuce Canyon is a well-used route to Mos Eisley valley from high ground; MOTESTA OASIS; WRECK OF THE HUTT TRANSPORT RIMRUNNER; OBI-WAN'S FIRST RETREAT; JAWA HEIGHTS; DARKLIGHTER HOMESTEAD; TOSCHE STATION; ANCHORHEAD; LARS HOMESTEAD; GREAT CHOTT SALT FLAT COMMUNITY

6 Hurrying home, Luke discovers that the Lars farm has been burned, along with the bodies of his foster parents, Uncle Owen and Aunt Beru. His own life suddenly reduced to ashes, a grief-stricken Luke resolves to learn the ways of the Force and to become a Jedi—like his father.

5 Revived by Obi-Wan from the blows of a Tusken gaffi stick, Luke offers Ben a landspeeder ride to the settlement of Anchorhead. Along the way, they chance upon a crippled sandcrawler and its Jawa crew, who have been massacred by Imperial troops, possibly in search of the droids.

4 The two droids wind up as possessions of the moisture-farming Lars family. Under cover of darkness, however, R2-D2 escapes the compound, setting out in search of Obi-Wan Kenobi. The next morning, Luke pursues with C-3PO—only to be waylaid by a band of vicious Tuskens.

DESERT DANGERS

Tatooine offers ample opportunities for personal misfortune: vast unpopulated stretches of rock and sand, primitive roads and barely marked hovertrain routes, and the unlit alleys of its principal settlements. For sentients and droids alike, safety is as scarce as water, and banditry, abduction, and hijacking have been raised to art forms. Casual travelers risk being shot at by Tusken Raiders. Moisture farmers are often robbed of their profits by gangs of outlaws. A lone droid need always be fearful of being abducted by Jawas. Tatooine's local authorities are too overwhelmed to deal with petty crime, and the troops of the Imperial garrison couldn't care less.

2 With suns-set, Tatooine's temperatures plunge, the darkened rocky canyons fill with unsettling sounds, and even R2-D2 is forced to reconsider his route. Stunned to immobility by an ionization blaster fired by a Jawa, the astromech is carried off by a group of entrepreneurial beings, led by Dathcha.

3 On the hazy horizon, reflected sunlight glints off the thick bow-plating of a massive sandcrawler. Once used by ore-prospecting colonists, then abandoned to the wastes, the steam-powered transports are now piloted by clans of tech-scavenging Jawas, ever on the alert for things they can salvage or steal.

LARS HOMESTEAD

SHADOWS SHORTEN as Tatooine's twin suns climb high above the Jundland Wastes, whose southern extreme is home to the several dozen moisture farms that make up the Great Chott salt flat community. Established by Lef and Gredda Lars, the farm now belongs to their grandson Owen and his wife Beru. The underground homestead is a warren of interconnected rooms, with vast storage areas and a marginally profitable hydroponic garden. Baked by the midday heat and scoured by gritty winds, the farm's pourstone entry dome and scattered moisture vaporators are the only exceptions to the glaring monotony of the desiccated seabed.

Luke brings up the difficult question of when he can join the Academy—unaware that his life is soon to change forever.

TYPICAL FARMSTEAD

Ringed by rudimentary weather monitors and motion-detection sensors, the farm sprawls across a bleached expanse of low ridges and hard-packed ground. Many of the homestead's sand-pitted moisture vaporators are decades old and in need of almost constant maintenance. Desperate to conserve power from solar radiation and small fusion-cell generators, the compound is shut down at nightfall—except for perimeter security sensors, which warn of roaming Tuskens and desert monsters.

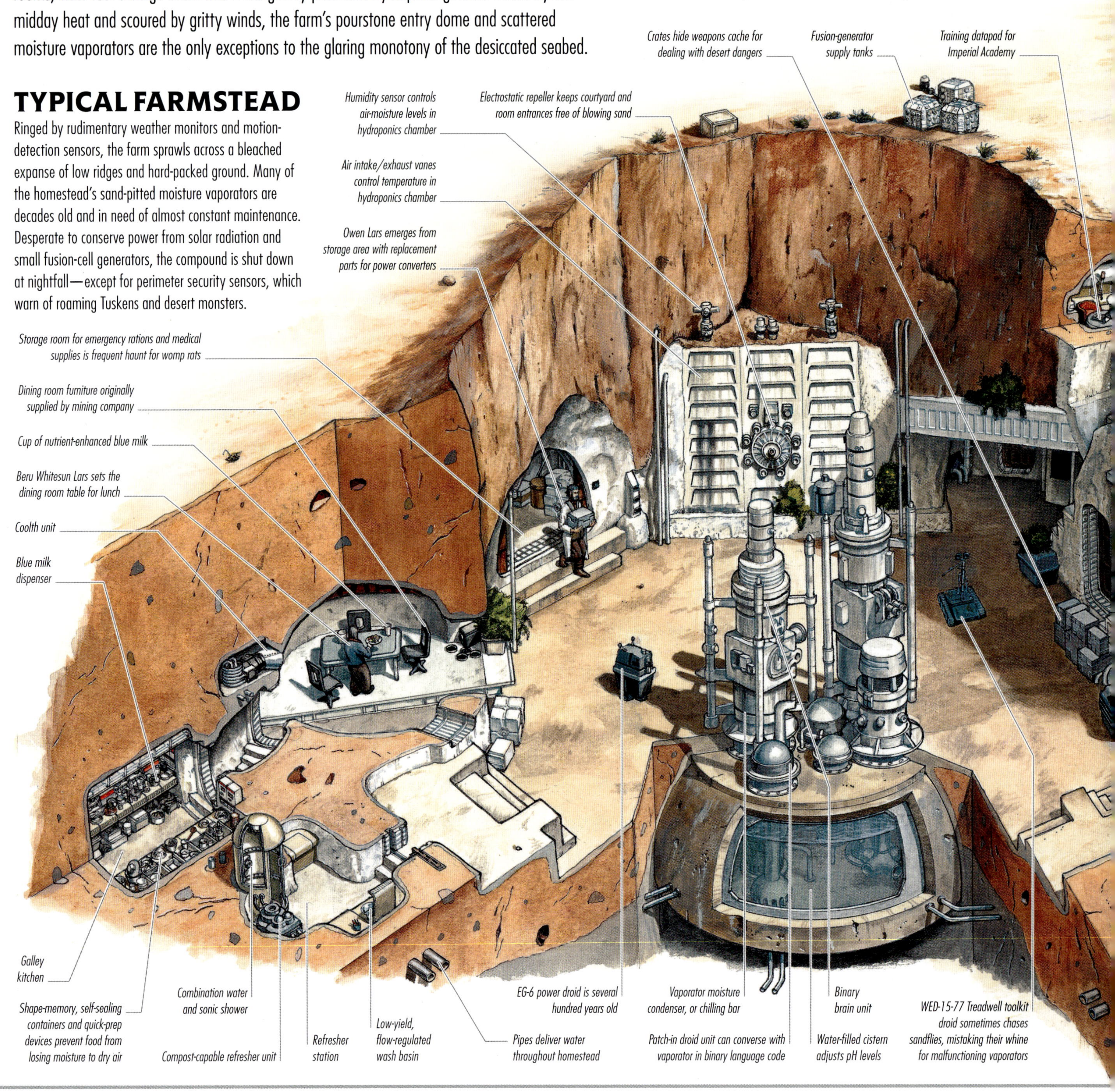

- Storage room for emergency rations and medical supplies is frequent haunt for womp rats
- Dining room furniture originally supplied by mining company
- Cup of nutrient-enhanced blue milk
- Beru Whitesun Lars sets the dining room table for lunch
- Coolth unit
- Blue milk dispenser
- Humidity sensor controls air-moisture levels in hydroponics chamber
- Air intake/exhaust vanes control temperature in hydroponics chamber
- Owen Lars emerges from storage area with replacement parts for power converters
- Crates hide weapons cache for dealing with desert dangers
- Electrostatic repeller keeps courtyard and room entrances free of blowing sand
- Fusion-generator supply tanks
- Training datapad for Imperial Academy
- Galley kitchen
- Shape-memory, self-sealing containers and quick-prep devices prevent food from losing moisture to dry air
- Combination water and sonic shower
- Compost-capable refresher unit
- Refresher station
- Low-yield, flow-regulated wash basin
- EG-6 power droid is several hundred years old
- Pipes deliver water throughout homestead
- Vaporator moisture condenser, or chilling bar
- Patch-in droid unit can converse with vaporator in binary language code
- Binary brain unit
- Water-filled cistern adjusts pH levels
- WED-15-77 Treadwell toolkit droid sometimes chases sandflies, mistaking their whine for malfunctioning vaporators

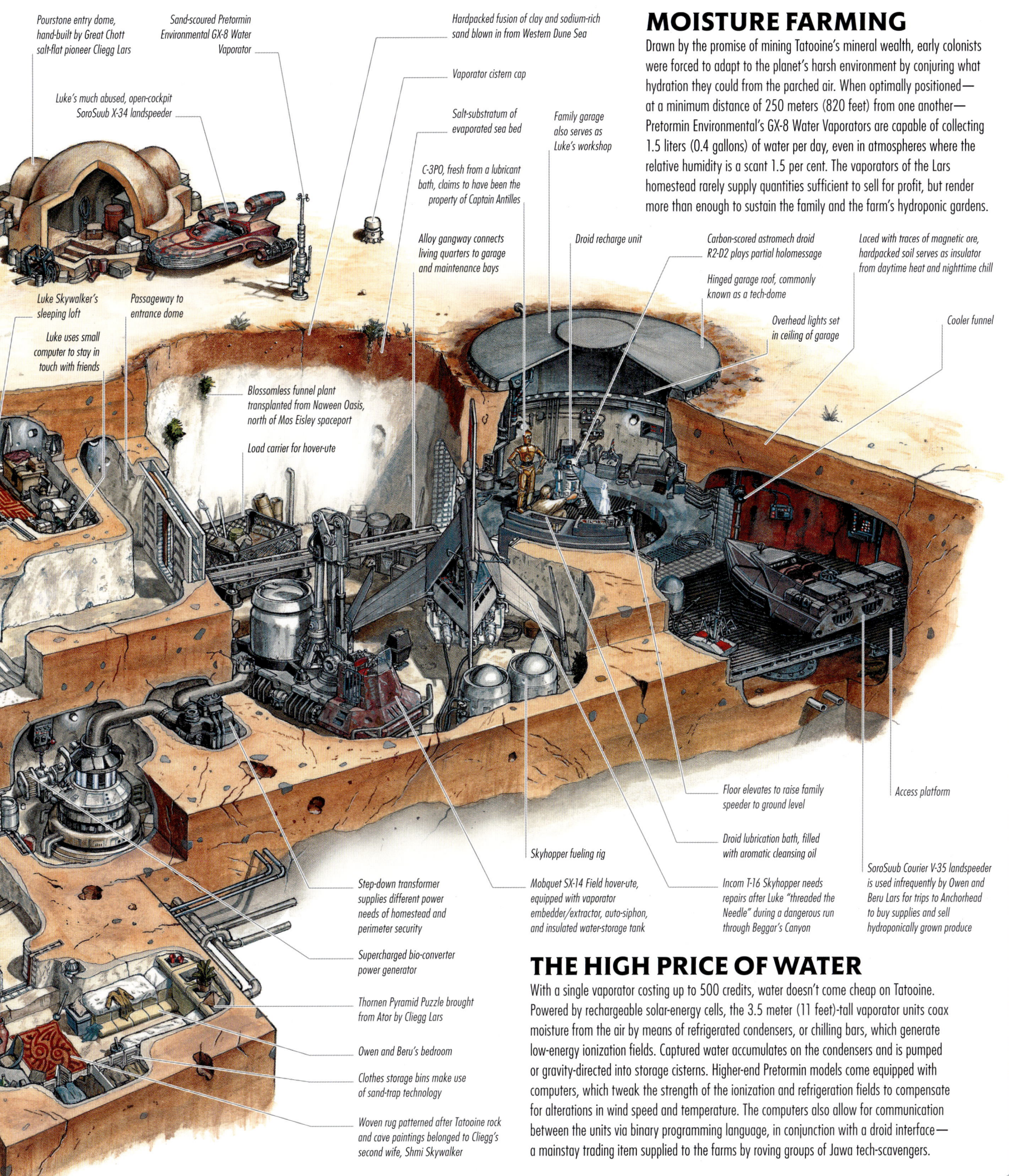

MOISTURE FARMING

Drawn by the promise of mining Tatooine's mineral wealth, early colonists were forced to adapt to the planet's harsh environment by conjuring what hydration they could from the parched air. When optimally positioned—at a minimum distance of 250 meters (820 feet) from one another—Pretormin Environmental's GX-8 Water Vaporators are capable of collecting 1.5 liters (0.4 gallons) of water per day, even in atmospheres where the relative humidity is a scant 1.5 per cent. The vaporators of the Lars homestead rarely supply quantities sufficient to sell for profit, but render more than enough to sustain the family and the farm's hydroponic gardens.

THE HIGH PRICE OF WATER

With a single vaporator costing up to 500 credits, water doesn't come cheap on Tatooine. Powered by rechargeable solar-energy cells, the 3.5 meter (11 feet)-tall vaporator units coax moisture from the air by means of refrigerated condensers, or chilling bars, which generate low-energy ionization fields. Captured water accumulates on the condensers and is pumped or gravity-directed into storage cisterns. Higher-end Pretormin models come equipped with computers, which tweak the strength of the ionization and refrigeration fields to compensate for alterations in wind speed and temperature. The computers also allow for communication between the units via binary programming language, in conjunction with a droid interface—a mainstay trading item supplied to the farms by roving groups of Jawa tech-scavengers.

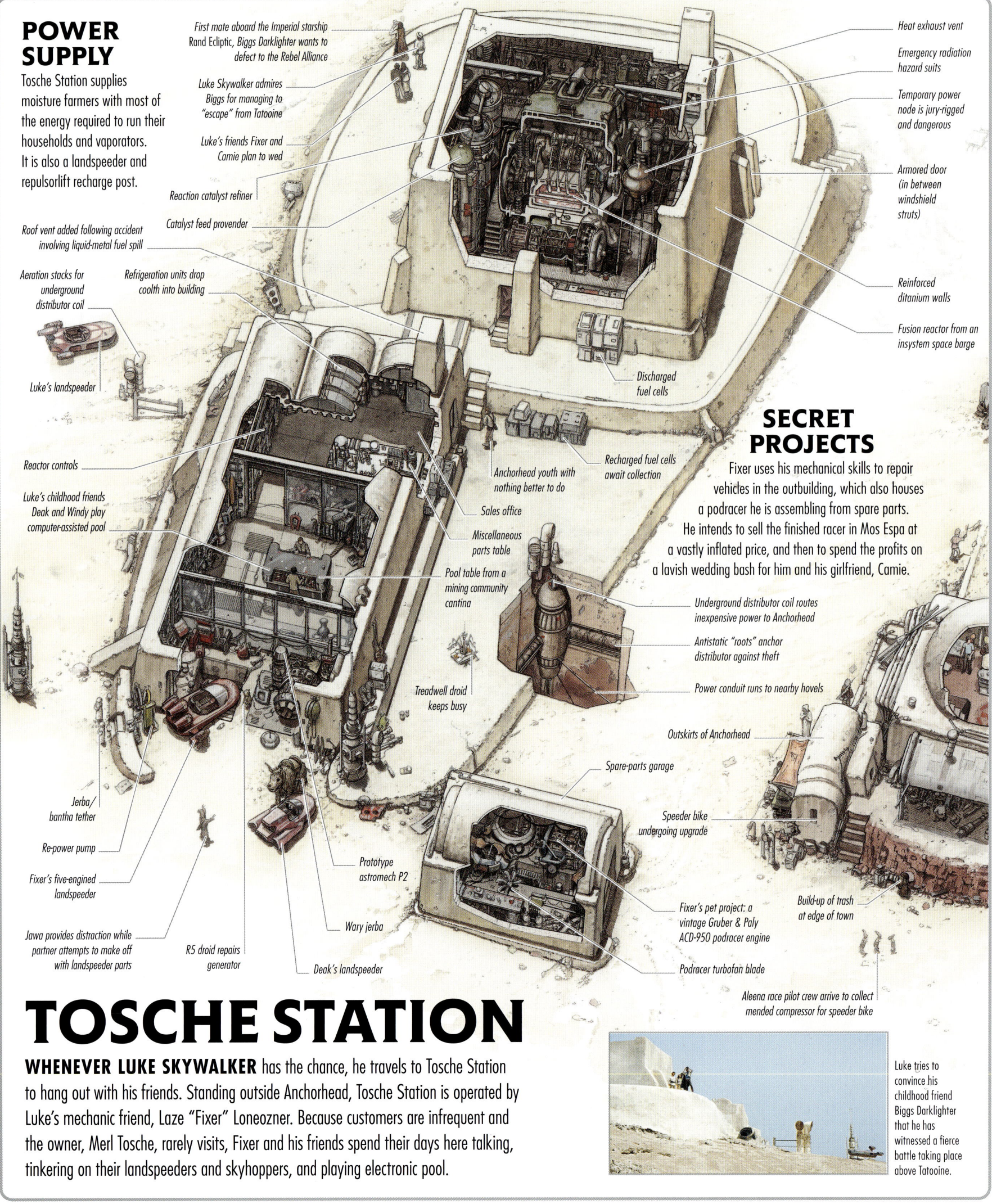

POWER SUPPLY

Tosche Station supplies moisture farmers with most of the energy required to run their households and vaporators. It is also a landspeeder and repulsorlift recharge post.

- Roof vent added following accident involving liquid-metal fuel spill
- Aeration stacks for underground distributor coil
- Luke's landspeeder
- Reactor controls
- Luke's childhood friends Deak and Windy play computer-assisted pool
- Jerba/bantha tether
- Re-power pump
- Fixer's five-engined landspeeder
- Jawa provides distraction while partner attempts to make off with landspeeder parts
- First mate aboard the Imperial starship Rand Ecliptic, Biggs Darklighter wants to defect to the Rebel Alliance
- Luke Skywalker admires Biggs for managing to "escape" from Tatooine
- Luke's friends Fixer and Camie plan to wed
- Reaction catalyst refiner
- Catalyst feed provender
- Refrigeration units drop coolth into building
- R5 droid repairs generator
- Prototype astromech P2
- Wary jerba
- Deak's landspeeder
- Anchorhead youth with nothing better to do
- Sales office
- Miscellaneous parts table
- Pool table from a mining community cantina
- Treadwell droid keeps busy
- Discharged fuel cells
- Recharged fuel cells await collection
- Heat exhaust vent
- Emergency radiation hazard suits
- Temporary power node is jury-rigged and dangerous
- Armored door (in between windshield struts)
- Reinforced ditanium walls
- Fusion reactor from an insystem space barge
- Underground distributor coil routes inexpensive power to Anchorhead
- Antistatic "roots" anchor distributor against theft
- Power conduit runs to nearby hovels
- Outskirts of Anchorhead
- Spare-parts garage
- Speeder bike undergoing upgrade
- Fixer's pet project: a vintage Gruber & Paly ACD-950 podracer engine
- Podracer turbofan blade
- Build-up of trash at edge of town
- Aleena race pilot crew arrive to collect mended compressor for speeder bike

SECRET PROJECTS

Fixer uses his mechanical skills to repair vehicles in the outbuilding, which also houses a podracer he is assembling from spare parts. He intends to sell the finished racer in Mos Espa at a vastly inflated price, and then to spend the profits on a lavish wedding bash for him and his girlfriend, Camie.

TOSCHE STATION

WHENEVER LUKE SKYWALKER has the chance, he travels to Tosche Station to hang out with his friends. Standing outside Anchorhead, Tosche Station is operated by Luke's mechanic friend, Laze "Fixer" Loneozner. Because customers are infrequent and the owner, Merl Tosche, rarely visits, Fixer and his friends spend their days here talking, tinkering on their landspeeders and skyhoppers, and playing electronic pool.

Luke tries to convince his childhood friend Biggs Darklighter that he has witnessed a fierce battle taking place above Tatooine.

BEN'S HOUSE

TATOOINE IS DOTTED with remote dwellings built by those in search of profitable areas with higher-than-average nighttime condensation. Typically, these frontier moisture farmers return to safer and more populous areas after a single harsh season. One such abandoned dwelling, constructed over a well-sheltered cave, became the home of a Jedi Knight in hiding—Obi-Wan "Ben" Kenobi.

Ben's home is located on a remote bluff in the Jundland Wastes, surrounded on all sides by the Western Dune Sea. The nearest settlement is Bestine.

BASIC HOME

Ben Kenobi's simple house consists of one main room in which he lives and sleeps. He uses the natural cellar for food and water storage, and constructs mechanical items, for trading with Jawas, on a workbench.

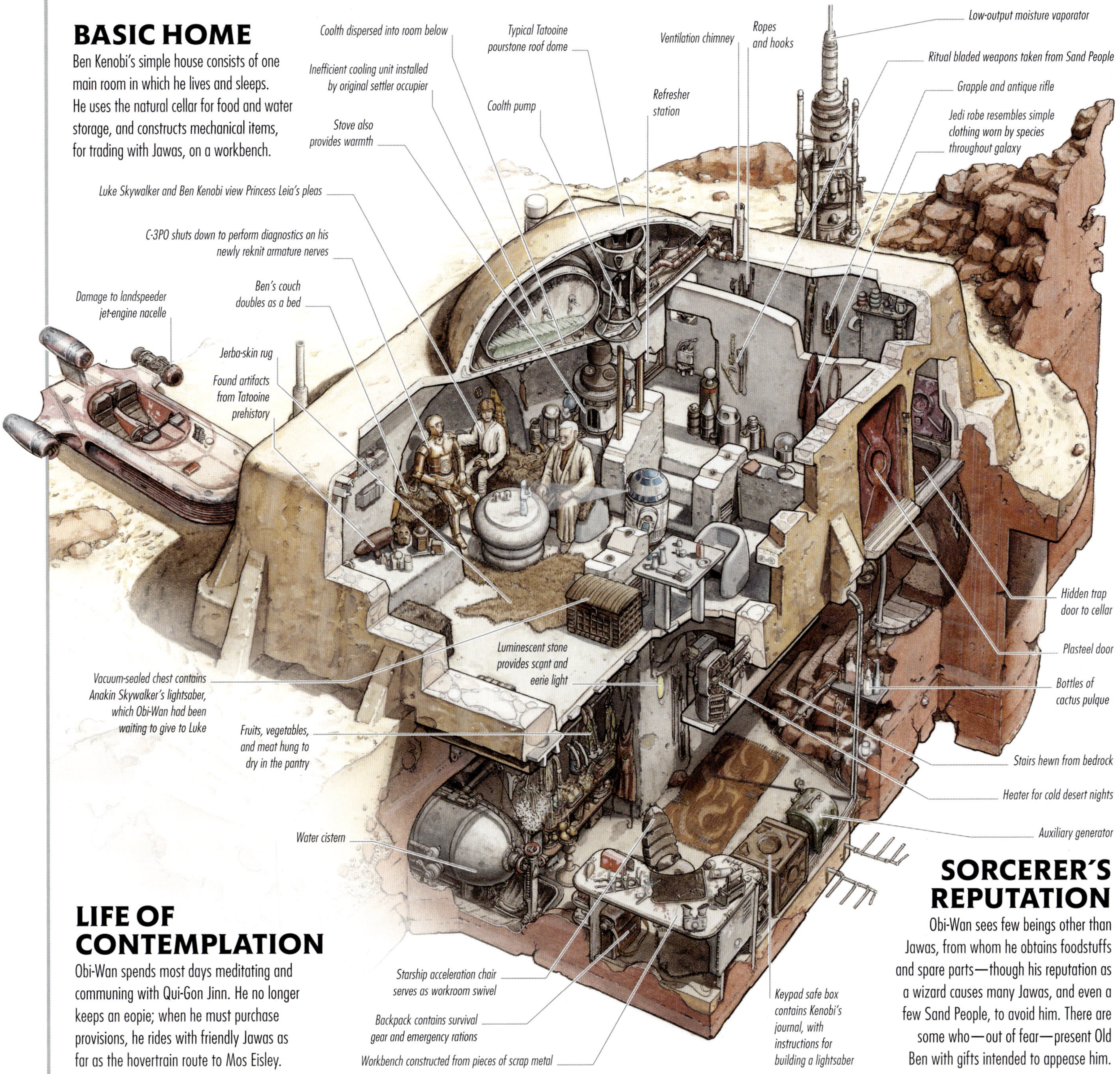

LIFE OF CONTEMPLATION

Obi-Wan spends most days meditating and communing with Qui-Gon Jinn. He no longer keeps an eopie; when he must purchase provisions, he rides with friendly Jawas as far as the hovertrain route to Mos Eisley.

SORCERER'S REPUTATION

Obi-Wan sees few beings other than Jawas, from whom he obtains foodstuffs and spare parts—though his reputation as a wizard causes many Jawas, and even a few Sand People, to avoid him. There are some who—out of fear—present Old Ben with gifts intended to appease him.

Labels:
- Coolth dispersed into room below
- Typical Tatooine pourstone roof dome
- Ventilation chimney
- Ropes and hooks
- Low-output moisture vaporator
- Inefficient cooling unit installed by original settler occupier
- Ritual bladed weapons taken from Sand People
- Coolth pump
- Refresher station
- Grapple and antique rifle
- Stove also provides warmth
- Jedi robe resembles simple clothing worn by species throughout galaxy
- Luke Skywalker and Ben Kenobi view Princess Leia's pleas
- C-3PO shuts down to perform diagnostics on his newly reknit armature nerves
- Ben's couch doubles as a bed
- Damage to landspeeder jet-engine nacelle
- Jerba-skin rug
- Found artifacts from Tatooine prehistory
- Hidden trap door to cellar
- Plasteel door
- Luminescent stone provides scant and eerie light
- Bottles of cactus pulque
- Vacuum-sealed chest contains Anakin Skywalker's lightsaber, which Obi-Wan had been waiting to give to Luke
- Fruits, vegetables, and meat hung to dry in the pantry
- Stairs hewn from bedrock
- Heater for cold desert nights
- Auxiliary generator
- Water cistern
- Starship acceleration chair serves as workroom swivel
- Backpack contains survival gear and emergency rations
- Keypad safe box contains Kenobi's journal, with instructions for building a lightsaber
- Workbench constructed from pieces of scrap metal

MOS EISLEY

THE UNRULY SPACEPORT of Mos Eisley sprawls in a broad valley south-east of Tatooine's Jundland Wastes. The old quarter was originally laid out like a wheel, with a teeming market place located adjacent to water and power distribution centers. Now, bargains on vaporators, cooling units, and hydroponic produce can be found in the bazaars and junkyards of the newer quarter, the hub of which is Chalmun's Spaceport Cantina.

CITY–WIDE TRAFFIC

With no central landing area, the whole of Mos Eisley is cratered with 362 docking bays, many of which are large enough to accommodate space freighters. All the bays are under the ostensible control of the city prefect and a handful of overworked customs agents.

1 Luke Skywalker races toward Mos Eisley with Ben Kenobi, C-3PO, and R2-D2 crammed into his landspeeder. A slum of ramshackle pourstone buildings, the area is populated by squatters, failed moisture farmers, scavengers, and those outlaws who have come to Tatooine to lose or reinvent themselves.

2 Teams of ASP-7 droids assist in the loading of a Gallofree Yards, civilian-use GR-45 medium transport. Easily programmed and equipped with magnetized feet, clawed hands, and voice synthesizers, the agile droids will have the vessel's cargo loaded by suns-set.

3 Familiar with the layout of the city from previous visits, Obi-Wan directs Luke toward Chalmun's Cantina, on the far side of the city. Where Outer Curved Street and Straight Street intersect at the new city center, the skyline is dominated by hotels, casinos, and tall complexes built by off-world corporations.

ONE CITY'S MISFORTUNE

Long a haven for spacers, thieves, smugglers, and rogues of all species and variety, Mos Eisley prides itself on being a wretched hive of scum and villainy. The spaceport's status swelled when podracing fell out of favor, and slave traders and criminals like Jabba the Hutt abandoned that sport's epicenter to the north, Mos Espa. Jabba's increased presence attracted the notice of starship design corporations Ubrikkian and Queblux, both of which constructed high-rise buildings in the gentrified heart of the old city.

11 Having struck a sweet deal with Obi-Wan and Luke for passage to Alderaan, Han Solo finds Jabba the Hutt and his gang of mercenaries and bounty hunters waiting for him in Docking Bay 94. Han bargains with the Hutt for one final chance to pay for a load of spice he was forced to jettison.

- Millennium Falcon makes a hasty exit
- Former podracer spare parts dealership
- Passenger ship belonging to Roon Tours, which offers short vacations in Tatooine for wealthy, jaded tourists seeking unusual thrills
- Hutt-owned exotic restaurant, Court of the Fountain
- Overcrowded city jail
- Illegally parked GR-45 medium transport
- Spaceport Speeders, where Luke and Ben sell the family speeder
- Docking Bay 94
- Headquarters of Quebe-Luxfause Systems, manufacturers of queblux power technology
- Water distribution plant
- Spaceport Express
- Masse Goskey's famous Arms Emporium
- Entrance dome to Jabba the Hutt's townhouse, known as the Desilijic Complex, much of which is constructed over extensive system of caves and grottos
- Jabba's private box
- Felvath Kurs Arena (named in honor of the legendary Loovrian pit-fighter) features all types of combat spectacles
- Many of Mos Eisley's citizens ride rontos, jerbas, dewbacks, and other beasts
- The sight of an insectile Neimoidian shuttle is an indication that shady dealings are afoot somewhere in Mos Eisley's criminal dens

4 Luke maneuvers the landspeeder into Straight Street toward what was once the heart of the Old City. As varied as the city's vehicles and droids, Mos Eisley's residents and transients have come to Tatooine from worlds as near as Ryloth and Piroket, and as distant as Nar Shaddaa and Ord Mantell.

5 Startled by a recklessly-piloted S-swoop, a ronto pack-beast rears up to avoid a collision, unseating his pair of Jawa riders. Animals such as rontos, banthas, dewbacks, jerbas, and eopies are as common a sight in Mos Eisley as landspeeders, skyhoppers, or arriving and departing spacecraft.

GALACTIC HOTSPOT

Moisture farmers bring their harvests to Mos Eisley only if markets in the capital of Bestine are overly busy. Notoriously open to bribes, customs officials make little attempt to curtail the smuggling of spice, illegal arms, and other proscribed goods that pass through Tatooine on their way to other worlds. Ben Kenobi makes occasional trips to Mos Eisley to learn the latest news about the Empire and the contemptible activities of his former apprentice, Anakin Skywalker—now Darth Vader.

10 Renowned in Mos Eisley for his spying aptitude, a long-snouted alien from Kubindi, named Garindan, shadows Luke and Ben as they hastily sell their speeder in order to rendezvous with starship pilots Han Solo and Chewbacca at Docking Bay 94.

9 Partnered with Mark IV repulsorlift patrol droids and armed with BlasTech E-11, DLT-19, and T-21 repeating blasters, squads of stormtroopers search for the fugitive droids, sometimes resorting to house-to-house searches. C-3PO and R2-D2 are forced to hide in the maze of narrow streets to evade capture.

- Local prefecture militia base, occupied by Imperial detachment deployed by Star Destroyer during search for droids
- Armored tank demolishes private house to make room for Imperial base
- AT-DP (All Terrain Defense Pod) walker
- Landing platform
- AT-ST scout
- Turbolaser tower
- Triple-hulled TIE Lander can deploy a stormtrooper company
- Imperial Lambda-class shuttle takes off
- Alley where C-3PO and R2-D2 evade stormtroopers
- Jawa traders
- "Community" junk yard
- Chalmun's Spaceport Cantina
- Used droid lot
- Dim-U monastery
- Safehouse owned by Boba Fett and used for Tatooine operations
- Luke turns back because street ahead is blocked by wedding ceremony for local notaries
- Stormtrooper transport
- Incoming passenger freighter
- Wreckage of the Dowager Queen
- Corellian space cruiser used by local food supplier
- Methane Fix Cantina
- Two-person shuttle owned by local playboy
- Spaceport Traffic Control
- Imperial order D6-66 requires all hangars be equipped with timelock devices
- Errant pilot crash-lands into retired spacers home
- Ubrikkian Trade Tower
- Covered market stalls
- Spaceport prefect's office
- Lup's General Store
- Customs House

STRAIGHT STREET · KERNER PLAZA · INNER CURVED STREET · CORPORATIONS ROAD · DUNE STREET

6 At a checkpoint set up by a contingent of sandtroopers, Ben employs a Jedi mind trick to persuade the weak-willed Imperial soldiers that they don't need to ascertain his or Luke's identity or establish just how long they have owned the pair of droids.

7 The early colony ship *Dowager Queen* towers above a sprawl of low domes and crater-like landing bays. The upended spaceship is one of many that have crashed on the surface of the planet and become either local landmarks or occupied structures in Mos Eisley.

8 While Luke and Obi-Wan attempt to seek out a skilled pilot with a fast ship, R2-D2 and C-3PO—having been ejected from Chalmun's Cantina—conceal themselves from a search party of stormtroopers by standing among a group of droids in a used droid lot nearby.

ROUTE KEY

Luke, Obi-Wan, and droids (in landspeeder) ⎯⎯⎯

CHALMUN'S PRIVATE STASH

Chalmun graduated from street fighter to bar owner over the course of a few years spent swindling hapless tourists in the casinos of Ord Mantell. His office in the Cantina is appointed with the barest of necessities: shisha, assorted blasters and bowcasters, and a steady supply of premium spice. Chalmun entertains Hutt-affiliated cronies and the occasional retired celebrity podracer in his private bar, while his henchmen monitor the main crowd from a surveillance room.

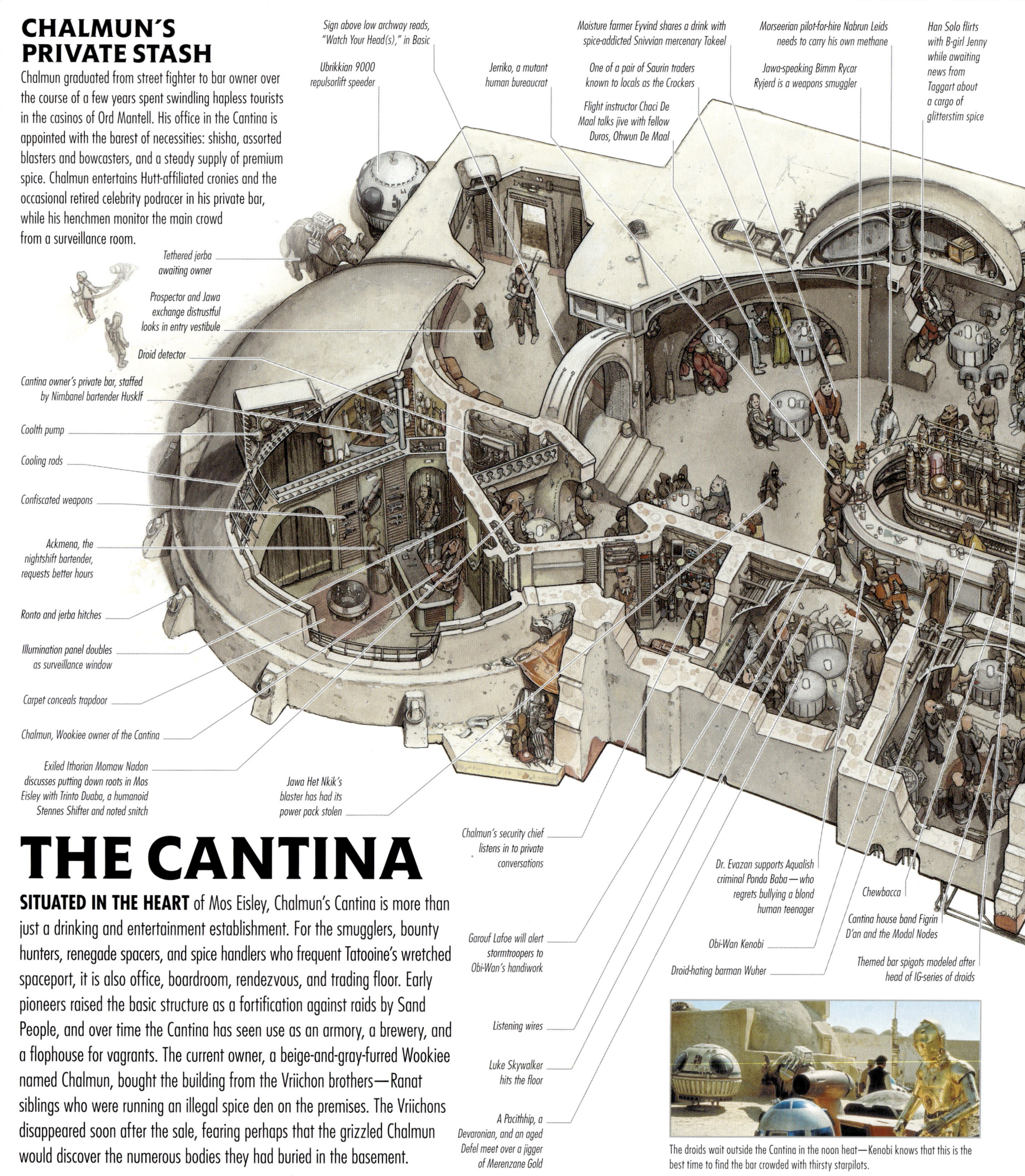

- Sign above low archway reads, "Watch Your Head(s)," in Basic
- Ubrikkian 9000 repulsorlift speeder
- Jerriko, a mutant human bureaucrat
- Moisture farmer Eyvind shares a drink with spice-addicted Snivvian mercenary Takeel
- One of a pair of Saurin traders known to locals as the Crockers
- Flight instructor Chaci De Maal talks jive with fellow Duros, Ohwun De Maal
- Morseerian pilot-for-hire Nabrun Leids needs to carry his own methane
- Jawa-speaking Bimm Rycar Ryjerd is a weapons smuggler
- Han Solo flirts with B-girl Jenny while awaiting news from Taggart about a cargo of glitterstim spice
- Tethered jerba awaiting owner
- Prospector and Jawa exchange distrustful looks in entry vestibule
- Droid detector
- Cantina owner's private bar, staffed by Nimbanel bartender Husklf
- Coolth pump
- Cooling rods
- Confiscated weapons
- Ackmena, the nightshift bartender, requests better hours
- Ronto and jerba hitches
- Illumination panel doubles as surveillance window
- Carpet conceals trapdoor
- Chalmun, Wookiee owner of the Cantina
- Exiled Ithorian Momaw Nadon discusses putting down roots in Mos Eisley with Trinto Duaba, a humanoid Stennes Shifter and noted snitch
- Jawa Het Nkik's blaster has had its power pack stolen
- Chalmun's security chief listens in to private conversations
- Dr. Evazan supports Aqualish criminal Ponda Baba—who regrets bullying a blond human teenager
- Chewbacca
- Garouf Lafoe will alert stormtroopers to Obi-Wan's handiwork
- Obi-Wan Kenobi
- Cantina house band Figrin D'an and the Modal Nodes
- Droid-hating barman Wuher
- Themed bar spigots modeled after head of IG-series of droids
- Listening wires
- Luke Skywalker hits the floor
- A Pacithhip, a Devaronian, and an aged Defel meet over a jigger of Merenzane Gold

THE CANTINA

SITUATED IN THE HEART of Mos Eisley, Chalmun's Cantina is more than just a drinking and entertainment establishment. For the smugglers, bounty hunters, renegade spacers, and spice handlers who frequent Tatooine's wretched spaceport, it is also office, boardroom, rendezvous, and trading floor. Early pioneers raised the basic structure as a fortification against raids by Sand People, and over time the Cantina has seen use as an armory, a brewery, and a flophouse for vagrants. The current owner, a beige-and-gray-furred Wookiee named Chalmun, bought the building from the Vriichon brothers—Ranat siblings who were running an illegal spice den on the premises. The Vriichons disappeared soon after the sale, fearing perhaps that the grizzled Chalmun would discover the numerous bodies they had buried in the basement.

The droids wait outside the Cantina in the noon heat—Kenobi knows that this is the best time to find the bar crowded with thirsty starpilots.

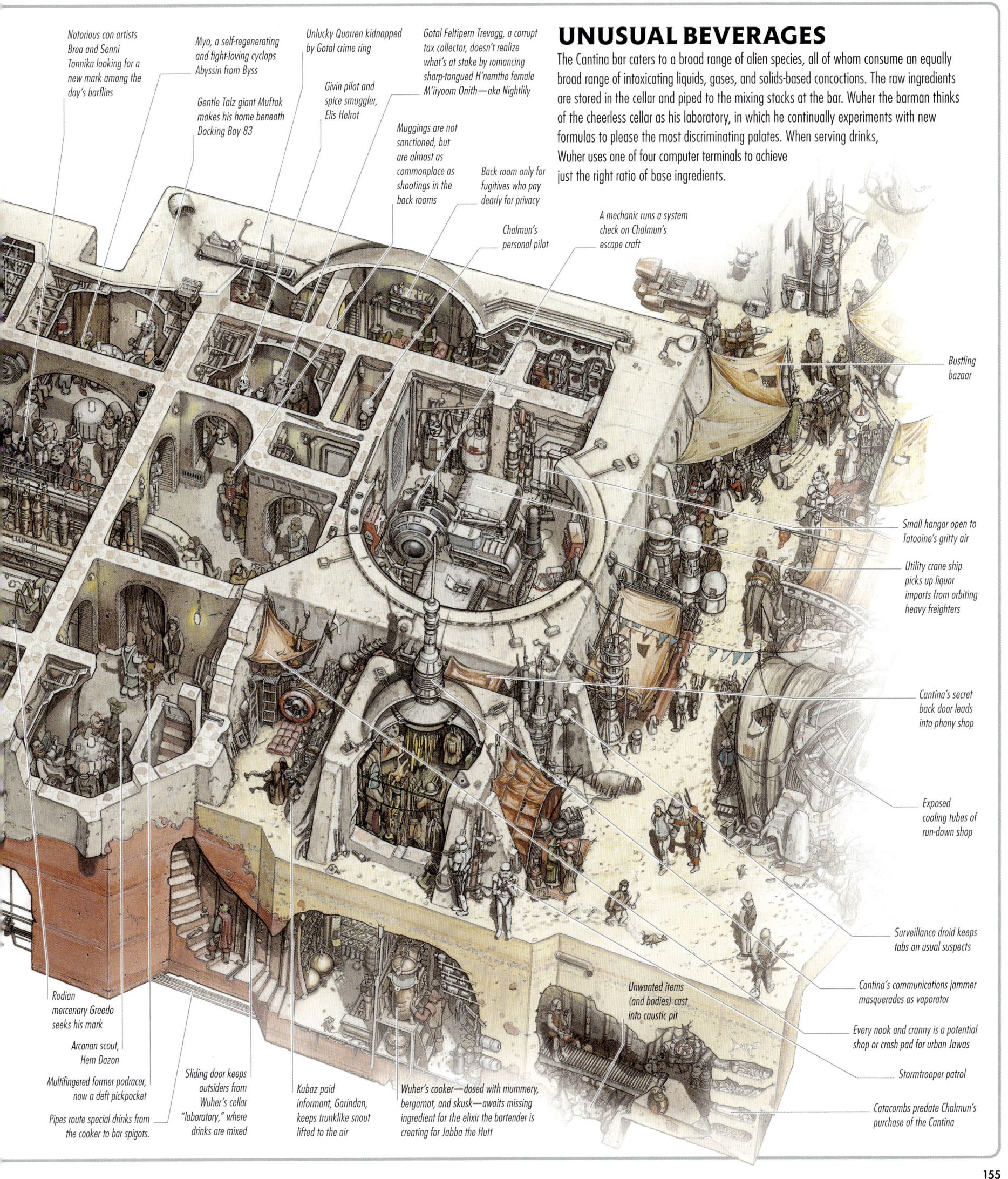

UNUSUAL BEVERAGES

The Cantina bar caters to a broad range of alien species, all of whom consume an equally broad range of intoxicating liquids, gases, and solids-based concoctions. The raw ingredients are stored in the cellar and piped to the mixing stacks at the bar. Wuher the barman thinks of the cheerless cellar as his laboratory, in which he continually experiments with new formulas to please the most discriminating palates. When serving drinks, Wuher uses one of four computer terminals to achieve just the right ratio of base ingredients.

- Notorious con artists Brea and Senni Tonnika looking for a new mark among the day's barflies
- Myo, a self-regenerating and fight-loving cyclops Abyssin from Byss
- Gentle Talz giant Muftak makes his home beneath Docking Bay 83
- Unlucky Quarren kidnapped by Gotal crime ring
- Givin pilot and spice smuggler, Elis Helrot
- Gotal Feltipern Trevagg, a corrupt tax collector, doesn't realize what's at stake by romancing sharp-tongued H'nemthe female M'iiyoom Onith—aka Nightlily
- Muggings are not sanctioned, but are almost as commonplace as shootings in the back rooms
- Back room only for fugitives who pay dearly for privacy
- Chalmun's personal pilot
- A mechanic runs a system check on Chalmun's escape craft
- Bustling bazaar
- Small hangar open to Tatooine's gritty air
- Utility crane ship picks up liquor imports from orbiting heavy freighters
- Cantina's secret back door leads into phony shop
- Exposed cooling tubes of run-down shop
- Surveillance droid keeps tabs on usual suspects
- Cantina's communications jammer masquerades as vaporator
- Every nook and cranny is a potential shop or crash pad for urban Jawas
- Stormtrooper patrol
- Catacombs predate Chalmun's purchase of the Cantina
- Unwanted items (and bodies) cast into caustic pit
- Wuher's cooker—dosed with mummery, bergamot, and skusk—awaits missing ingredient for the elixir the bartender is creating for Jabba the Hutt
- Kubaz paid informant, Garindan, keeps trunklike snout lifted to the air
- Sliding door keeps outsiders from Wuher's cellar "laboratory," where drinks are mixed
- Pipes route special drinks from the cooker to bar spigots
- Multifingered former podracer, now a deft pickpocket
- Arconan scout, Hem Dazon
- Rodian mercenary Greedo seeks his mark

ANCIENT ORIGINS

The Rebel Alliance sees the Death Star as a technological terror emblematic of the Empire's new order, but the battle station actually has an ancient pedigree: long ago, the Sith had created similar superweapons powered by massive kyber crystals. In the Empire's secret weapons labs, scientists tasked with refining the Geonosis prototype choose a new approach: vast arrays of smaller kyber crystals focus and amplify eight laser beams, combining them into a single massive beam that can destroy a planet. But turning that concept into a reality proves fiendishly complex—if the firing-chamber arrays are not precisely aligned, crystals will burn out and overload, sending dangerous levels of waste heat back into the Death Star's main reactor.

FLIGHT, NOT FIGHT

When Obi-Wan Kenobi advises Captain Han Solo that there are alternatives to fighting, he has in mind nothing more than deactivating one of the battle station's tractor-beam power couplings to allow the *Millennium Falcon* to escape the clutches of the Empire. Drawing on the Force to conceal himself from stormtroopers, the Jedi Master sets out for the most inaccessible coupling in the station. He knows that this will aid the *Falcon*'s escape by maximizing the time taken to reconnect the power.

- Han chases stormtroopers into large drill hall
- Luke and Leia swing across sub-core shaft
- Tractor-beam focusing shaft
- Tractor-beam projector
- Control room reached by Luke, Leia, Han, and Chewbacca in rescue mission
- Control room occupied by C-3PO and R2-D2
- Corridor where Obi-Wan faces Darth Vader
- Atmosphere containment projector
- *Millennium Falcon*, docked in hangar bay 327
- Cargo loading assembly area
- Buttress with radar and turbolaser turrets
- TIE fighter staging area, with 20 battle-ready ships stored in docking racks
- Life-support staging modules inhabited by workers during construction of Death Star—can still be used in an emergency
- Walkway
- High-speed, off-rotor-use shuttle system orbits the space station
- Power conduit
- Off-duty personnel walk in atrium between two housing blocks
- TIE fighter storage area
- Generator
- Officer accommodation
- Turbolift taken by Luke, Han, and Chewbacca to prison cells; turbolifts move vertically and horizontally
- Cavernous airway
- Artificial atmosphere station for this sector
- Maintenance gantry
- Abandoned crane used in Death Star construction
- Water recycling tank for creation of artificial air humidity
- Lateral transport taken by Obi-Wan to reach tractor-beam power coupling #12 located in sector six of Death Star's northern hemisphere

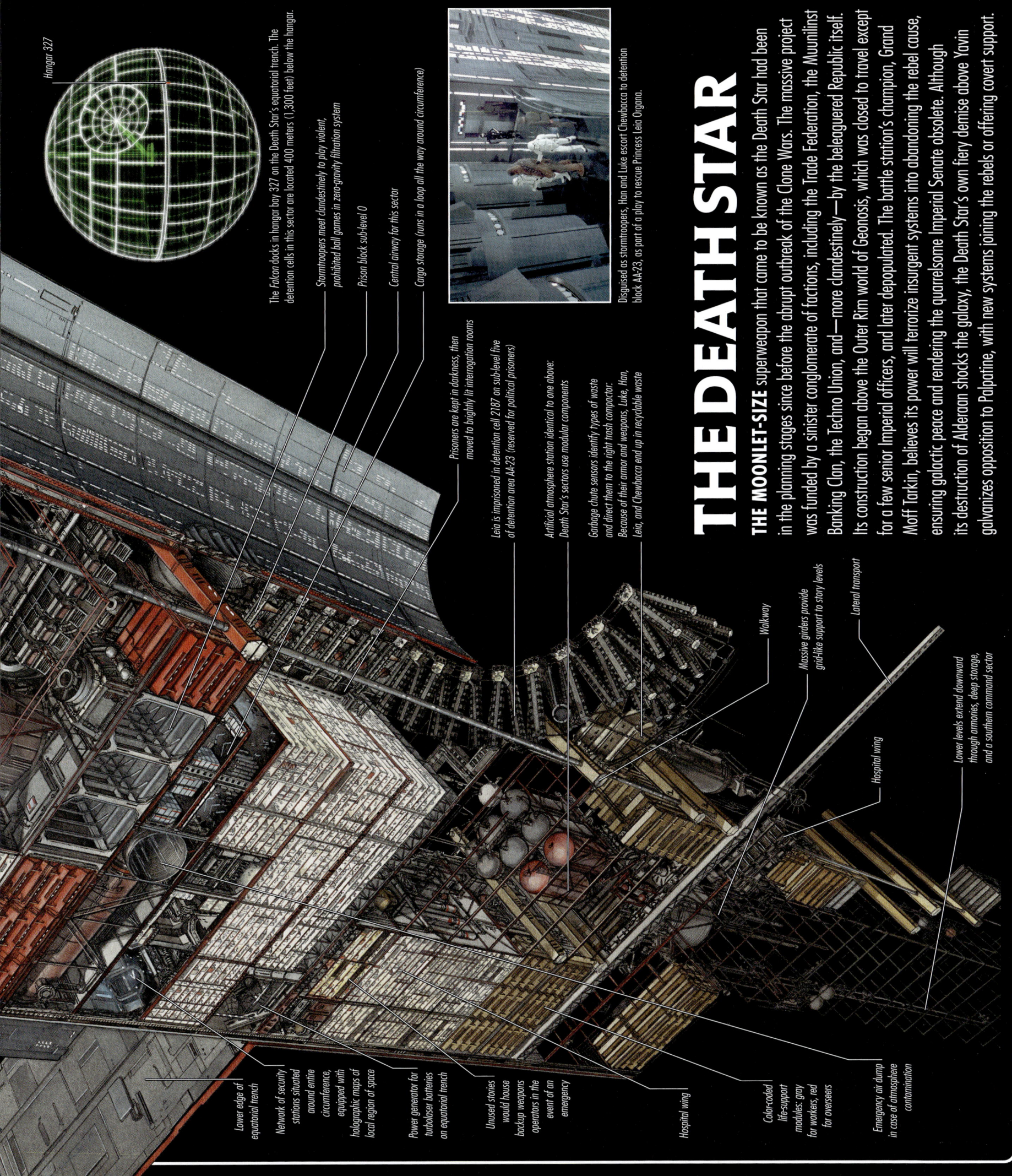

THE DEATH STAR

THE MOONLET-SIZE superweapon that came to be known as the Death Star had been in the planning stages since before the abrupt outbreak of the Clone Wars. The massive project was funded by a sinister conglomerate of factions, including the Trade Federation, the Muunilinst Banking Clan, the Techno Union, and—more clandestinely—by the beleaguered Republic itself. Its construction began above the Outer Rim world of Geonosis, which was closed to travel except for a few senior Imperial officers, and later depopulated. The battle station's champion, Grand Moff Tarkin, believes its power will terrorize insurgent systems into abandoning the rebel cause, ensuring galactic peace and rendering the quarrelsome Imperial Senate obsolete. Although its destruction of Alderaan shocks the galaxy, the Death Star's own fiery demise above Yavin galvanizes opposition to Palpatine, with new systems joining the rebels or offering covert support.

Hangar 327

The Falcon docks in hangar bay 327 on the Death Star's equatorial trench. The detention cells in this sector are located 400 meters (1,300 feet) below the hangar.

Stormtroopers meet clandestinely to play violent, prohibited ball games in zero-gravity filtration system

Prison block sub-level 0

Central airway for this sector

Cargo storage (runs in a loop all the way around circumference)

Disguised as stormtroopers, Han and Luke escort Chewbacca to detention block AA-23, as part of a ploy to rescue Princess Leia Organa.

Prisoners are kept in darkness, then moved to brightly lit interrogation rooms

Leia is imprisoned in detention cell 2187 on sub-level five of detention area AA-23 (reserved for political prisoners)

Artificial atmosphere station identical to one above: Death Star's sectors use modular components

Garbage chute sensors identify types of waste and direct them to the right trash compactor: Because of their armor and weapons, Luke, Han, Leia, and Chewbacca end up in recyclable waste

Walkway

Massive girders provide grid-like support to story levels

Lateral transport

Hospital wing

Lower levels extend downward through armories, deep storage, and a southern command sector

Hospital wing

Emergency air dump in case of atmosphere contamination

Color-coded life-support modules: gray for workers, red for overseers

Unused stories would house backup weapons operators in the event of an emergency

Power generator for turbolaser batteries on equatorial trench

Network of security stations situated around entire circumference, equipped with holographic maps of local region of space

Lower edge of equatorial trench

THE GREAT TEMPLE

BLANKETED WITH NEARLY impenetrable vegetation, Yavin 4 is home to countless unique species of plants, animals, and insects, but hosts no intelligent lifeforms. The fourth moon of an uninhabitable gas giant, the world had been of interest only to galactic archeologists, who had marveled at the ancient stone temples that rise majestically from its jungles. These towering, stepped structures are all that remain of the lost civilization of the Massassi. With no sentient population to subdue and no mineral wealth to exploit, Yavin 4 has been overlooked by the Empire and is little known within the wider galaxy. It is for precisely this reason that the resourceful leaders of the Rebel Alliance choose Yavin 4 as their base after having been forced to flee their previous command center on the planet Dantooine.

- Apex houses observation and communications room
- Ceremony commemorating destruction of Death Star takes place in audience chamber
- Tall skylights align with equinox and solstice
- Holographic memorials to those killed in Battle of Yavin will be placed outside ceremonial hall
- Massassi-built staircase to observation room at the apex
- Interior of temple clad with sheets of seamed metal
- Command center
- Entrance to command center
- Audience chamber floor tiled with translucent precious stones
- Temple built with no visible sign of advanced machinery
- Data storage and processing complex
- Anti-personnel cannons
- Briefing room
- Algae, mosses, and vines resist rebel attempts to blast original rock face clean of vegetation
- Water and fuel reservoirs and purification system
- Barracks area has space for thousands of troops (but only a limited number of bunks)
- BTL-A4 Y-wing starfighter
- Thick blast door lowers to protect hangar bay
- Mess hall
- Repair and maintenance bay
- Launch/landing apron
- Stores protected against bombardment by multiple layers of reinforced ferrocrete and sealable blast doors
- Original stone floors reinforced with ferrocrete
- Red Squadron X-wing starfighter
- Roughly cut cavities drilled by rebels into straighter sides of original Massassi interior

POWER SUPPLY

The functioning of the base is reliant on a power-generating station located two kilometers (1.2 miles) away. Pieced together from turbines and a main reactor stolen from a wrecked Imperial Star Destroyer, the station supplies sufficient power for a protective shield, ion cannons, and other defenses that could hold off an assault from a single large battleship.

Rebel pilots scramble from Yavin 4 to support the Rogue One infiltration team embattled on Scarif.

UNTAMED NATURE

The surrounding jungle of purple-barked Massassi trees resounds with the eerie cries and blood-chilling moans of unseen creatures: woolamanders, lizard crabs, stintaril rodents, and armored eels, among others. Dense thickets of thorny vegetation and unpredictable storms thwart the progress of surveyors and construction engineers. As a result, the rebels stick to the laser-cut access and patrol routes that link the Great Temple to outlying landing zones and the distant power station.

MYSTERIOUS MASONS

Shining like an emerald among the necklace of moons that encircles its gas giant host, Yavin 4 is rich with life and full of mysteries. Little is known of the now-vanished species that crafted the moon's Great Temple except its name—the Massassi. Long ago, this extinct people somehow hewed giant blocks of stone from the moon's crust and transported them many kilometers to locations deemed holy—or perhaps significant for primitive scientific purposes. The rebel pilots and soldiers who now occupy the ancient Massassi ruins can only speculate about what became of their sanctuary's lost builders.

Having docked the *Millennium Falcon* at the nearby visitor landing zone, Luke Skywalker, Han Solo, Leia Organa, and the droids are met by rebel leaders outside the base's impregnable blast door.

The T-65 X-wing's rugged construction allows rebel techs to keep these complex machines battle-ready, even in improvised hangars within the Great Temple's vine-encrusted interior.

Cassian Andor and Jyn Erso leave Yavin 4 on their fateful mission to Scarif. Though neither will return, their actions will ultimately save the Rebellion and help inflict a crushing defeat on the Empire.

BATTLE OF HOTH

HOTH IS OFTEN CITED as the worst defeat suffered by the Rebel Alliance during the Galactic Civil War, but it was not a crushing one. Admiral Kendal Ozzel unintentionally granted the rebels time to mount a holding action—and the ensuing organized retreat—by arrogantly bringing the Imperial fleet out of hyperspace too close to Hoth. Darth Vader added to the blunder by being so fixated on capturing Luke Skywalker alive that he ordered his flotilla of Star Destroyers to pursue the *Millennium Falcon* rather than hunt down the escaped rebel transports. Moreover, historians have pointed out that if not for this painful rout, the Alliance might never have risked everything at Endor a year later, where they inflicted a defeat on the Empire from which it never recovered.

1 One of thousands seeded by the Imperial Star Destroyer *Stalker*, an Arakyd Viper probe droid meanders over Hoth's snowfields and glaciers, alert for anomalous energy signatures that might point to Rebel Alliance activity. Its images of the rebel power generator are transmitted back to Imperial officers.

2 In the trenches, Beta Outpost troops commanded by Trey Callum ready their repeating blasters for in-close fighting. Precision targeting by anti-personnel batteries decimates Veers' snowtroopers, buying the rebels more time to evacuate the base and weave their transports through the Star Destroyer blockade.

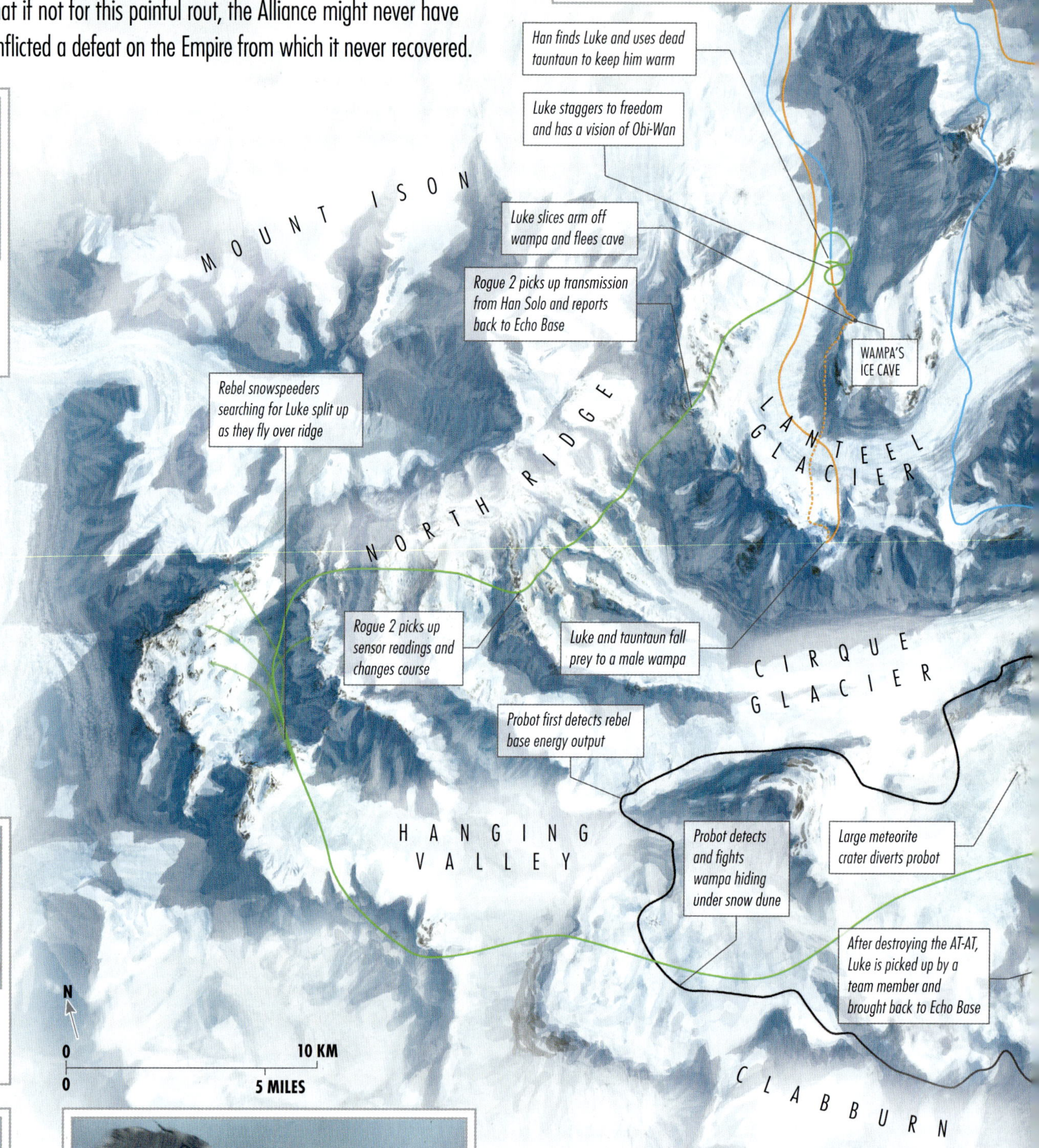

IMPERIAL GROUND ASSAULT

General Maximilian Veers is tasked with destroying the shield power generator and capturing rather than killing the rebels who survive his assault. Forced to steer clear of the shield perimeter, Imperial landing barges and troop transports set down on the precarious Moorsh Moraine, well north of the heavily fortified mountain base. Having thus surrendered the element of surprise, but augmented with legions of snowtroopers, Veers' contingent of AT-ATs (large, four-legged walkers) and AT-STs (medium bipeds)—dubbed Blizzard Force—begins its inexorable march on the rebel facility.

3 Swiveling on their bases, Golan Arms DF9 anti-artillery batteries hammer away at the advancing walkers, but to no avail. Snowspeeder pilots, too, find their lasers ineffective against the thick armor of the Imperial war machines. Raked by laserfire, Rogue Leader is hit, and Luke's gunner, Dak, is killed.

4 Following Luke's orders, Wedge Antilles and his gunner, Wes Janson, deploy Rogue 3's harpoon and tow cable against the AT-AT commanded by Brigadier General Nevar. The dangerous maneuver requires that the cable be wrapped around the legs of a walker, then severed at precisely the right moment.

5 Its four legs ensnared by the high-tension tow cable, Blizzard 2 crashes to the unyielding tundra, leaving the rear of its neck vulnerable to follow-up laser fire. With one walker dispatched, the rebels continue to wage their holding action, but are ultimately overwhelmed by the Empire's durable behemoths.

Han finds Luke and uses dead tauntaun to keep him warm

Luke staggers to freedom and has a vision of Obi-Wan

Luke slices arm off wampa and flees cave

Rogue 2 picks up transmission from Han Solo and reports back to Echo Base

Rebel snowspeeders searching for Luke split up as they fly over ridge

Rogue 2 picks up sensor readings and changes course

Luke and tauntaun fall prey to a male wampa

Probot first detects rebel base energy output

Probot detects and fights wampa hiding under snow dune

Large meteorite crater diverts probot

After destroying the AT-AT, Luke is picked up by a team member and brought back to Echo Base

MOUNT ISON • NORTH RIDGE • LANTEEL GLACIER • WAMPA'S ICE CAVE • CIRQUE GLACIER • HANGING VALLEY • CLABBURN

REBEL SHIELD SYSTEM

By dumping absorbed energy directly into the planet's interior, the rebels' planet-based shield withstands bombardments that would overwhelm ship shields. Only slow-moving ground-contact vehicles, like Imperial walkers, can traverse its outer surface. With the projector modules distributed throughout rebel territory, Veers targets the central power generator.

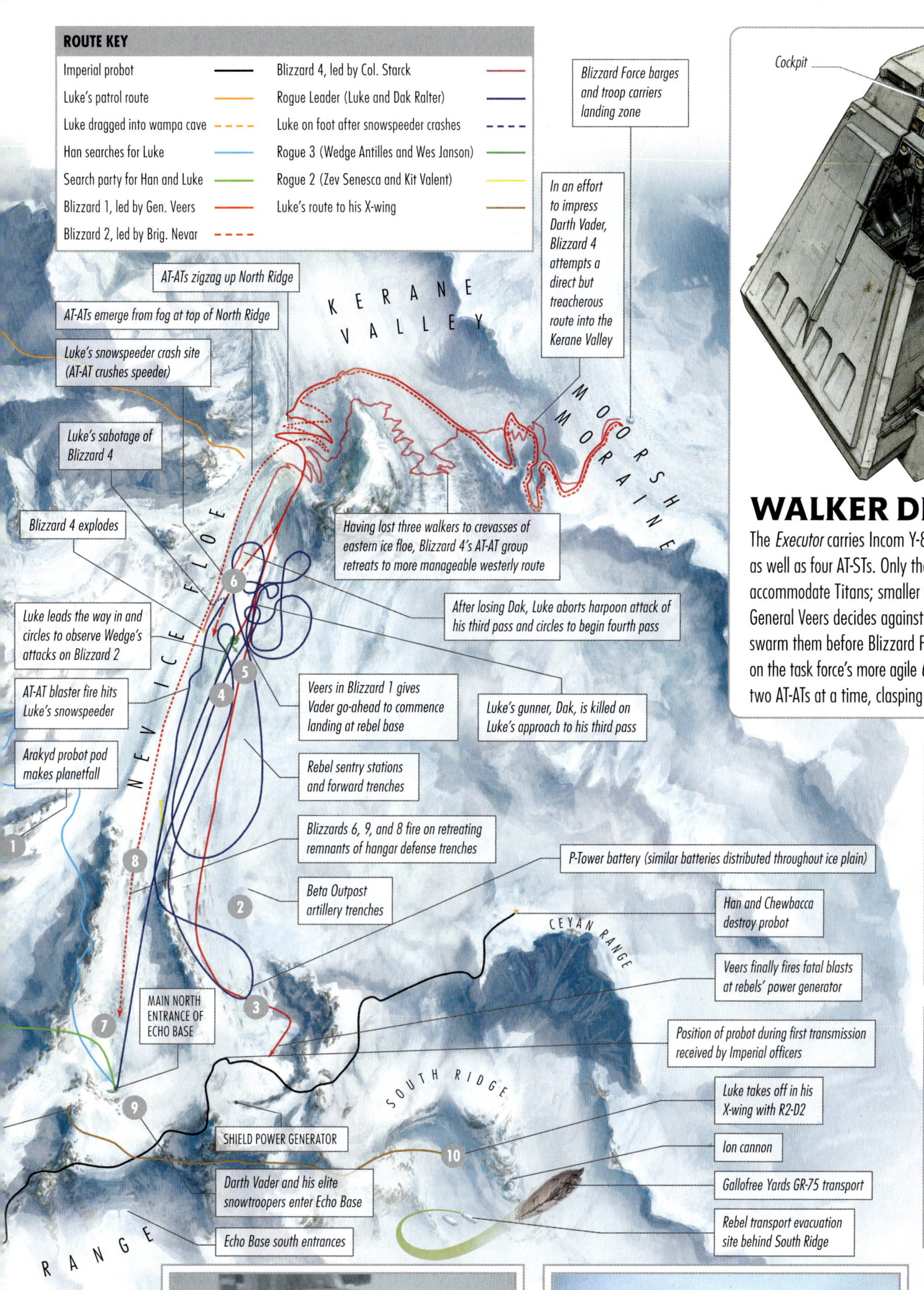

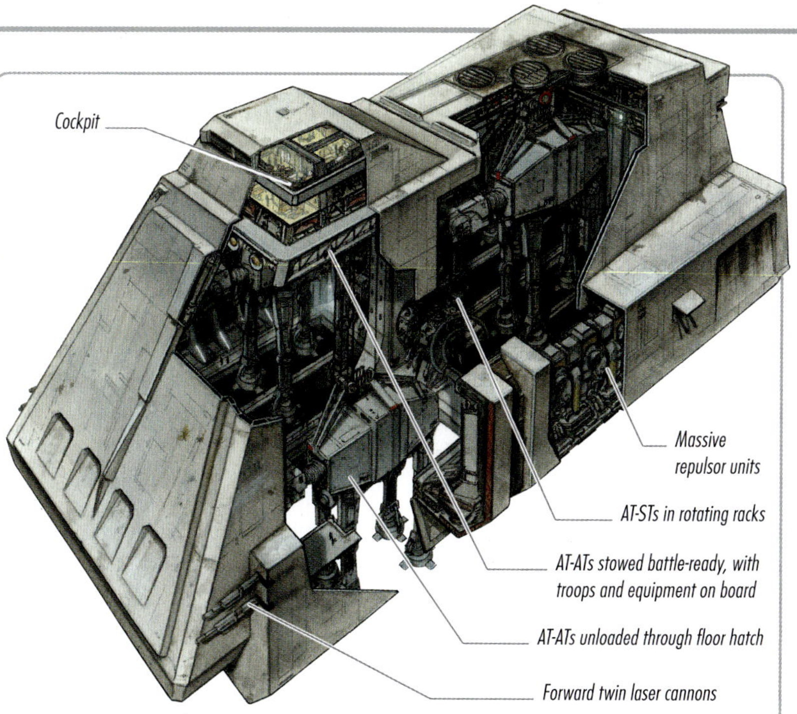

ROUTE KEY

Imperial probot	Blizzard 4, led by Col. Starck
Luke's patrol route	Rogue Leader (Luke and Dak Ralter)
Luke dragged into wampa cave	Luke on foot after snowspeeder crashes
Han searches for Luke	Rogue 3 (Wedge Antilles and Wes Janson)
Search party for Han and Luke	Rogue 2 (Zev Senesca and Kit Valent)
Blizzard 1, led by Gen. Veers	Luke's route to his X-wing
Blizzard 2, led by Brig. Nevar	

- AT-ATs zigzag up North Ridge
- AT-ATs emerge from fog at top of North Ridge
- Luke's snowspeeder crash site (AT-AT crushes speeder)
- Luke's sabotage of Blizzard 4
- Blizzard 4 explodes
- Luke leads the way in and circles to observe Wedge's attacks on Blizzard 2
- AT-AT blaster fire hits Luke's snowspeeder
- Arakyd probot pod makes planetfall

KERANE VALLEY

MOORSH MORAINE

Blizzard Force barges and troop carriers landing zone

In an effort to impress Darth Vader, Blizzard 4 attempts a direct but treacherous route into the Kerane Valley

Having lost three walkers to crevasses of eastern ice floe, Blizzard 4's AT-AT group retreats to more manageable westerly route

After losing Dak, Luke aborts harpoon attack of his third pass and circles to begin fourth pass

Veers in Blizzard 1 gives Vader go-ahead to commence landing at rebel base

Luke's gunner, Dak, is killed on Luke's approach to his third pass

Rebel sentry stations and forward trenches

Blizzards 6, 9, and 8 fire on retreating remnants of hangar defense trenches

Beta Outpost artillery trenches

P-Tower battery (similar batteries distributed throughout ice plain)

Han and Chewbacca destroy probot

CEYAN RANGE

Veers finally fires fatal blasts at rebels' power generator

Position of probot during first transmission received by Imperial officers

SOUTH RIDGE

Luke takes off in his X-wing with R2-D2

MAIN NORTH ENTRANCE OF ECHO BASE

Ion cannon

SHIELD POWER GENERATOR

Gallofree Yards GR-75 transport

Darth Vader and his elite snowtroopers enter Echo Base

Rebel transport evacuation site behind South Ridge

Echo Base south entrances

NEV ICE FLOE

RANGE

Cockpit

Massive repulsor units

AT-STs in rotating racks

AT-ATs stowed battle-ready, with troops and equipment on board

AT-ATs unloaded through floor hatch

Forward twin laser cannons

WALKER DROPSHIP

The *Executor* carries Incom Y-85 Titan dropships, which can accommodate four AT-ATs as well as four AT-STs. Only the largest Imperial warships have hangars massive enough to accommodate Titans; smaller ships, such as Star Destroyers, deploy single-walker barges. General Veers decides against using the Titans at Hoth, wary that rebel starfighters will swarm them before Blizzard Force can land outside the shield perimeter. Instead, he calls on the task force's more agile *Gozanti*-class cruisers. Escorted by TIEs, these freighters carry two AT-ATs at a time, clasping the walkers with their powerful ventral docking clamps.

10 At the evacuation site behind the South Ridge, the *Falcon* roars into Hoth's frozen sky and the final transport, *Bright Hope*, lifts off with the aid of starfighter pilots Wedge, Tarrin, and Janson. Luke trudges to where he and other survivors of the siege scramble into the cockpits of their X-wings.

9 Darth Vader and a squad of his elite snowtroopers blast their way into the base. Falling debris and the approaching enemy has kept Leia from reaching the last transport, but she, Han Solo, C-3PO, and Chewbacca manage to board the *Millennium Falcon* and escape the clutches of their dark nemesis.

6 Launching a magnetic grapple and cable into the underside of Blizzard 4, Luke hoists himself into the air and lobs a grenade inside the beast's belly. His single-handed victory grants the besieged rebels a short-lived moment of hope—but the Imperials' advance only becomes more determined.

7 After General Veers' AT-AT succeeds in destroying Echo's power generator, the rebels begin to retreat toward hidden tunnels in the mountainside. Deprived of energy, the base's defensive shield fails, opening it to direct enemy infiltration and bombardment from the orbiting Star Destroyers.

8 Veers orders the commanders of the remaining AT-ATs and the pilots of the All-Terrain scouts to overrun the trenches and capture as many rebels as possible. With Echo Base almost evacuated, the ion cannon's fire-control team sets the weapon to self-destruct and hurries to reach the last of the transports.

ECHO BASE

AFTER THE EVACUATION of Yavin 4, the Rebel Alliance embarks on a search for a planet or moon to serve as a new secret base of operations. Explorations by Luke Skywalker, Commander Narra, the Gigoran scout Purpruff and others lead to Hoth, a little-known ice planet near a major route in the Outer Rim. The command center is constructed over the course of two standard years, under brutal conditions. Rebel engineers and construction crews employ laser ice-cutting equipment to enlarge a series of natural caverns, excavate new ones, and fashion connecting corridors. Designated Echo Base for the cave's strange acoustics, the base is still being constructed when an Imperial probe droid plunges fatefully to Hoth's glacial surface…

ROUTE KEY
— Han and Leia's escape route

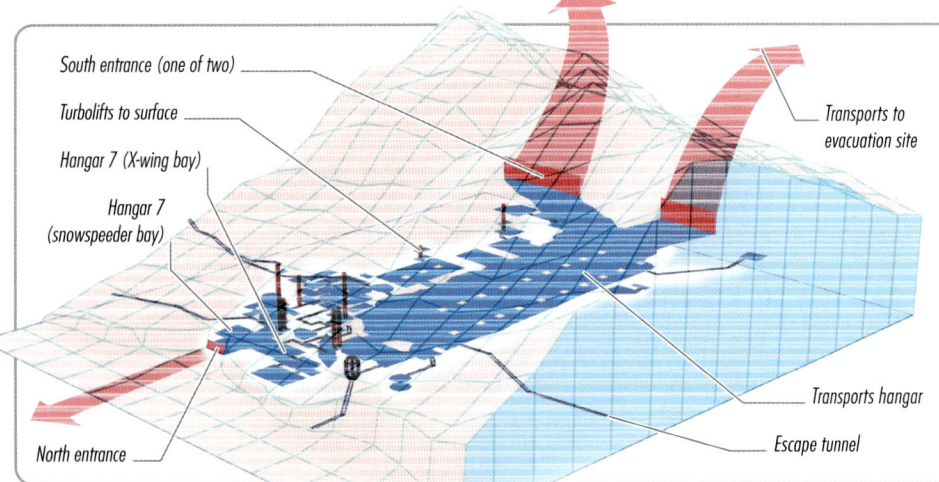

- South entrance (one of two)
- Turbolifts to surface
- Hangar 7 (X-wing bay)
- Hangar 7 (snowspeeder bay)
- North entrance
- Transports to evacuation site
- Transports hangar
- Escape tunnel

ICE MOUNTAIN HIDE-OUT

Several locations in Hoth's temperate zone were scouted and surveyed before a cavern-hollowed mountain in the southern Clabburn Range was judged suitable to serve as the hidden fortress the rebels had in mind. The Corp of Engineers fashioned interior spaces vast enough to house not only the Alliance's wings of starfighters, but also its tattered fleet of Gallofree Yards transports. Plasmold insulation and armored doors—of a different sort than those used on Yavin 4—help to shelter the base from the ferocity of Hoth's ice storms.

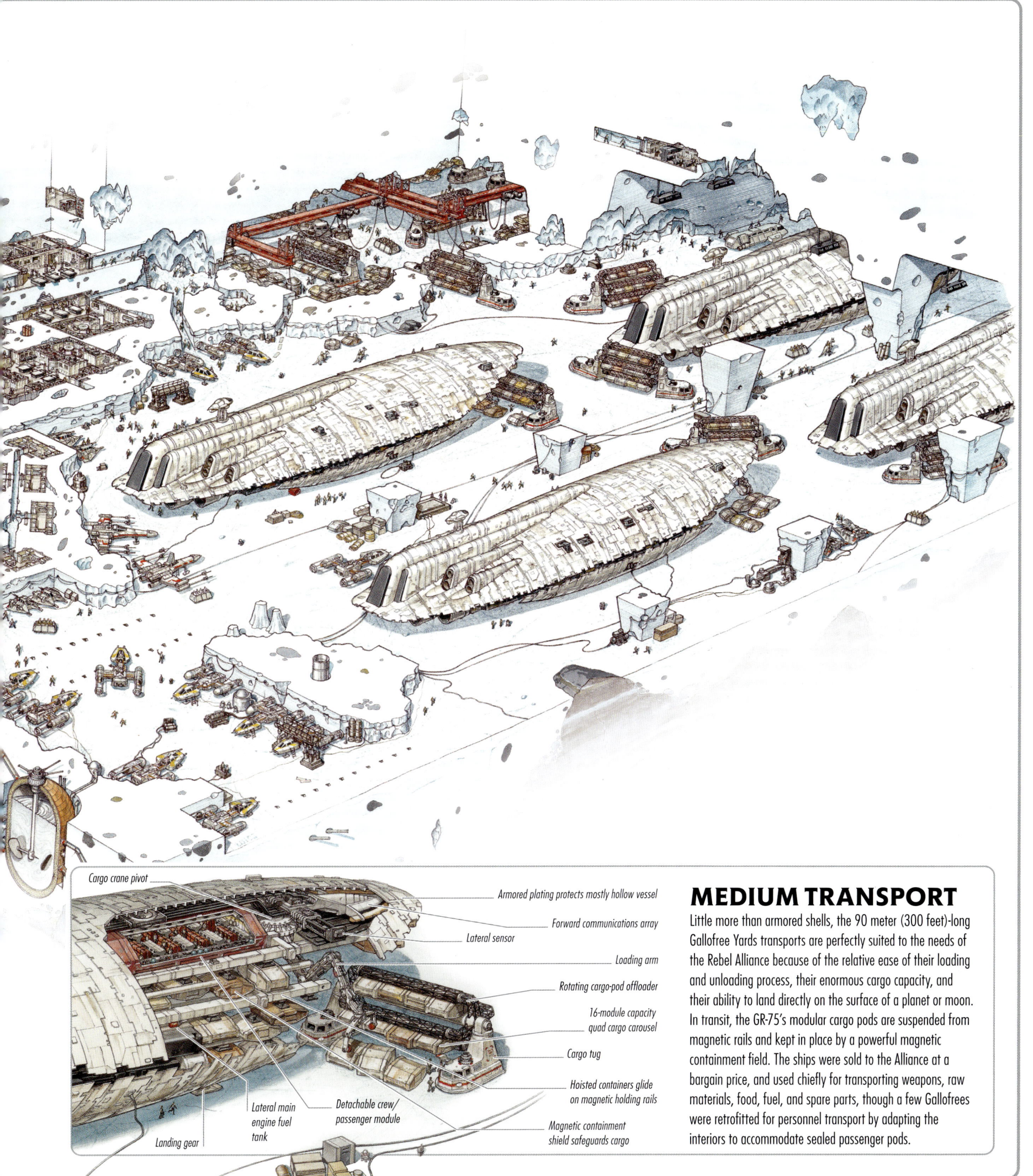

MEDIUM TRANSPORT

Little more than armored shells, the 90 meter (300 feet)-long Gallofree Yards transports are perfectly suited to the needs of the Rebel Alliance because of the relative ease of their loading and unloading process, their enormous cargo capacity, and their ability to land directly on the surface of a planet or moon. In transit, the GR-75's modular cargo pods are suspended from magnetic rails and kept in place by a powerful magnetic containment field. The ships were sold to the Alliance at a bargain price, and used chiefly for transporting weapons, raw materials, food, fuel, and spare parts, though a few Gallofrees were retrofitted for personnel transport by adapting the interiors to accommodate sealed passenger pods.

ECHO BASE CONTINUED

Snowspeeders and X-wings are stationed in North Hangar 7. Secret tunnels connect the hangar to several other, smaller, north entrances.

PREPARING FOR THE WORST

While essential for defense, the presence of the shield generator all but guarantees that Echo Base will eventually unmask itself to the Empire. Anticipating that an assault would be launched on the surface of Hoth, General Carlist Rieekan orders that heavy blast doors be installed in the north and south entrances, trenches be excavated on the glacial plains all around the base, and that ground-based anti-personnel batteries be embedded in the mountainside above the principal hangars and in the ice fields between artillery trenches.

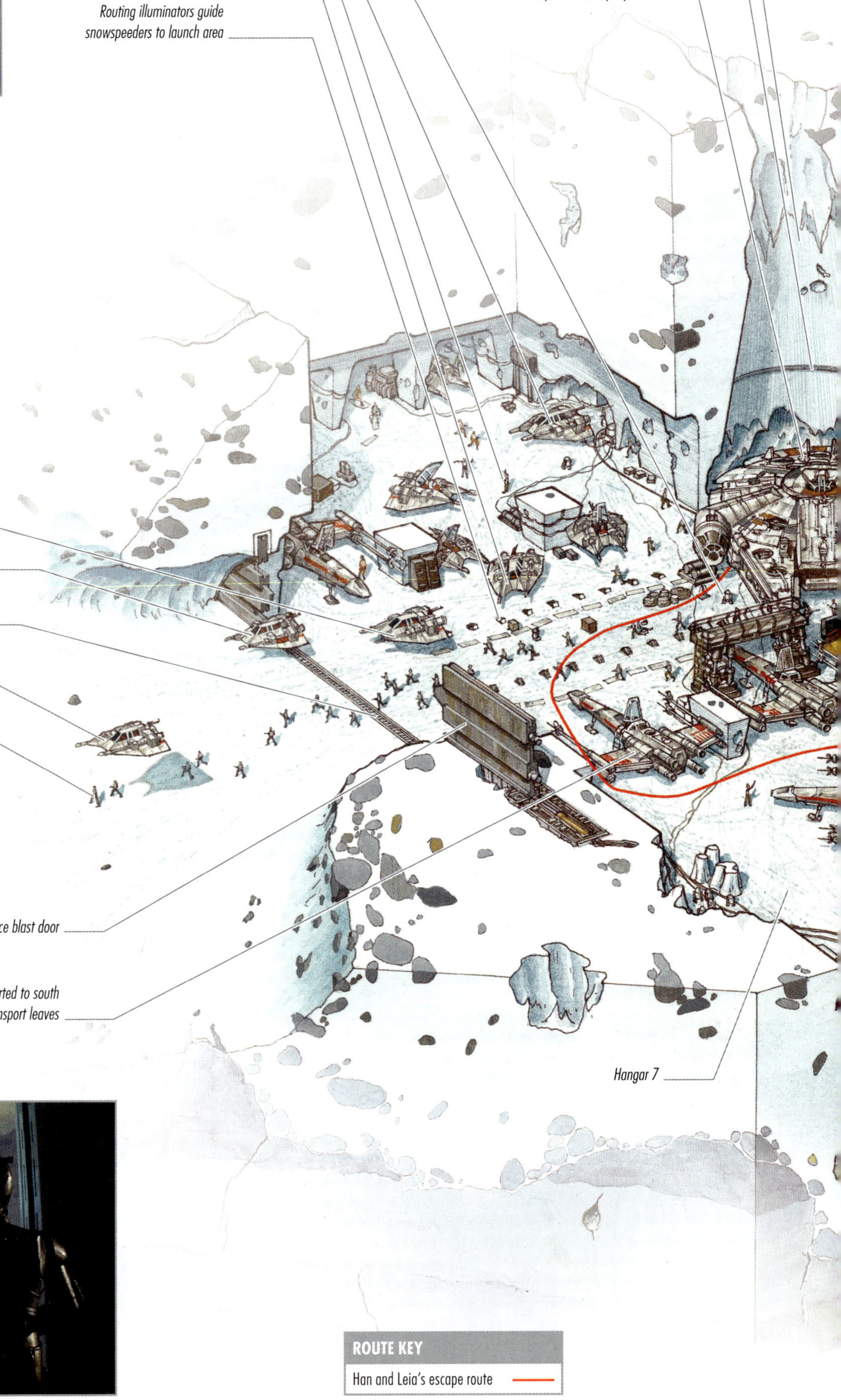

EMERGENCY CARE

The Rebel Alliance is careful to provide timely medical support for its valued troops. On Hoth, a well-equipped medical center provides first-rate response and triage for Echo Base's 7,500 combat personnel. Overseen by a medical command officer, the staff of 350 physicians and surgeons, augmented by some 120 specialized droids, remains on call to deal with any emergencies that might arise.

- R2-D2 searches for his counterpart
- Incom T-47 airspeeders modified to function on Hoth
- Air boss oversees starfighter launch
- "Hobbie" Klivian and Kesin Ommis in Rogue 4 snowspeeder
- Routing illuminators guide snowspeeders to launch area
- Sunlight filters into base through narrow crevasse in the surface ice
- Curved transparisteel window overlooks Hangar 7
- Millennium Falcon's hyperdrive has yet to be fully repaired
- Zev Senesca in Rogue 2 snowspeeder
- Wedge Antilles and Wes Janson in Rogue 3 snowspeeder
- Track for sliding door needs constant lubrication
- Luke Skywalker and Dak Ralter in Rogue Leader
- Major Dervis' infantry hurry to defensive trenches
- North entrance blast door
- Luke's X-wing will be transported to south entrance before last transport leaves
- Hangar 7

ROUTE KEY

— Han and Leia's escape route

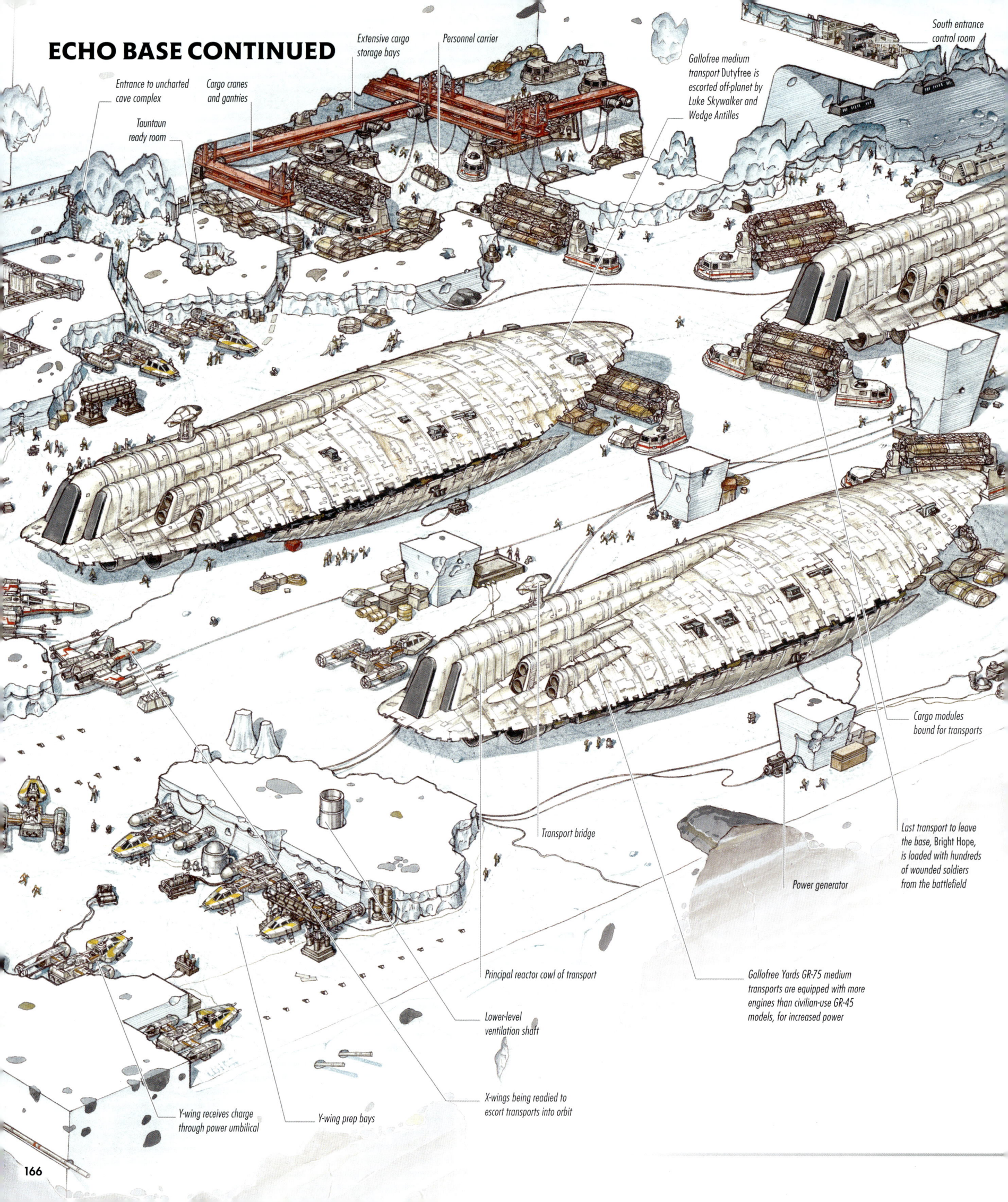

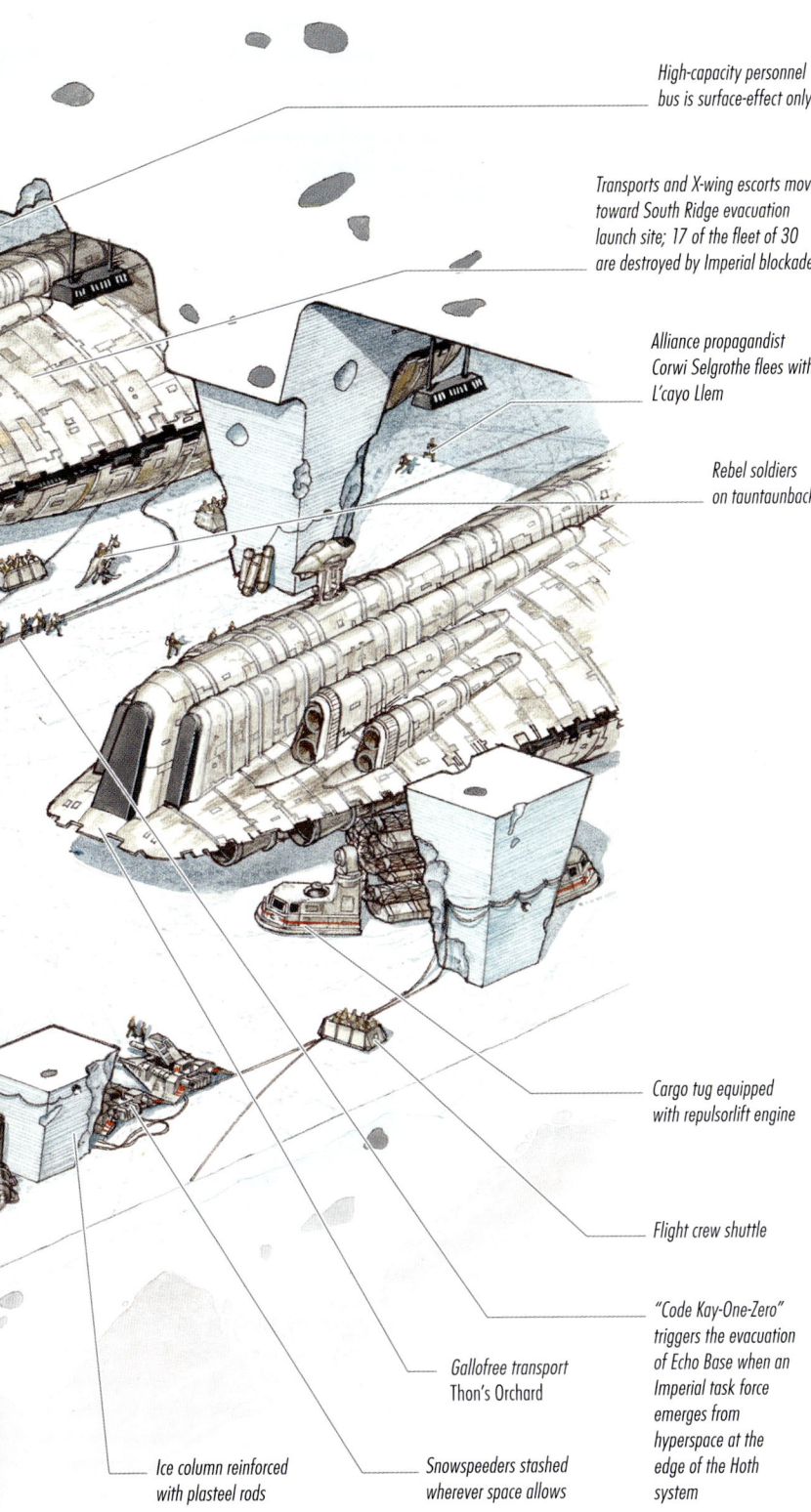

- High-capacity personnel bus is surface-effect only
- Transports and X-wing escorts move toward South Ridge evacuation launch site; 17 of the fleet of 30 are destroyed by Imperial blockade
- Alliance propagandist Corwi Selgrothe flees with L'cayo Llem
- Rebel soldiers on tauntaunback
- Cargo tug equipped with repulsorlift engine
- Flight crew shuttle
- "Code Kay-One-Zero" triggers the evacuation of Echo Base when an Imperial task force emerges from hyperspace at the edge of the Hoth system
- Gallofree transport Thon's Orchard
- Snowspeeders stashed wherever space allows
- Ice column reinforced with plasteel rods

ION BLASTS

Synchronized with a battle-theater shield generator, the Kuat Drive Yard v-150 ion cannon fires massive, charged-plasma shots powerful enough to penetrate the ray shielding of an Imperial Star Destroyer in orbit, neutralizing its weapons, shields, and engines—or, at the very least, disrupting control systems and ion drives. Drawbacks include a lengthy activation and targeting period, a low discharge rate of one volley per six seconds, and slow rotation as it aims.

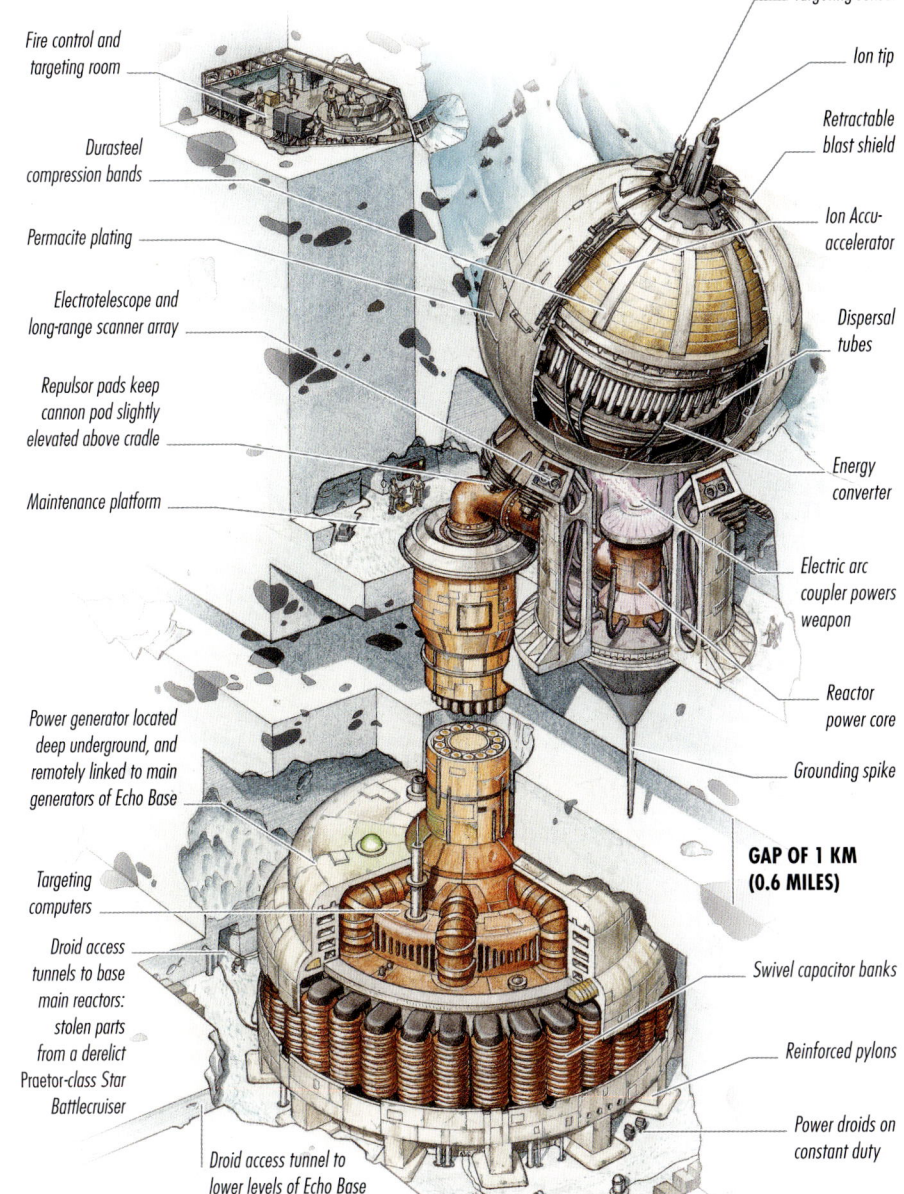

- Fire control and targeting room
- Durasteel compression bands
- Permacite plating
- Electrotelescope and long-range scanner array
- Repulsor pads keep cannon pod slightly elevated above cradle
- Maintenance platform
- Power generator located deep underground, and remotely linked to main generators of Echo Base
- Targeting computers
- Droid access tunnels to base main reactors: stolen parts from a derelict Praetor-class Star Battlecruiser
- Droid access tunnel to lower levels of Echo Base
- Targeting sensor
- Ion tip
- Retractable blast shield
- Ion Accu-accelerator
- Dispersal tubes
- Energy converter
- Electric arc coupler powers weapon
- Reactor power core
- Grounding spike
- **GAP OF 1 KM (0.6 MILES)**
- Swivel capacitor banks
- Reinforced pylons
- Power droids on constant duty

LIVESTOCK

At first, Hoth appeared to be almost devoid of large animals—which suited the rebels well. In fact, the ice world is home to a surprising variety of hardy species that have adapted to the harsh environment, including tauntauns and their chief predators, wampas. The latter are too ferocious to be domesticated, but tauntauns prove to be a great asset to the rebels while their X-wings and snowspeeders are undergoing special modifications. Hundreds of the reptilian "snow lizards" are rounded up and corralled inside the base, where their natural food of lichen and moss is carefully cultivated. Eventually, the creatures are trained for use as pack animals and patrol mounts.

DAGOBAH

NEAR DEATH FROM EXPOSURE to Hoth's sub-zero temperatures, the side of his face crushed by a giant wampa, Luke Skywalker has a vision of his mentor, Obi-Wan Kenobi. The Jedi Master orders him to go to the Dagobah system to complete his training under the guidance of Obi-Wan's former instructor, the diminutive Yoda. With a bewildered R2-D2 for companionship, Luke parts with Han Solo and Princess Leia to follow his destined course. Remote from known space routes, shrouded in cloud cover, but emitting massive life-form readings, Dagobah is a gloomy world of swamps and twisted trees, winged predators, and poisonous snakes. Seemingly engulfed by the planet, Luke's X-wing plummets to the surface…

1 Is this a dream or just a bad idea? Luke wonders aloud. His mind as foggy as his new environment, he leaves his crashed starfighter to marinate in the muck of one of Dagobah's black-water bogs and begins to take stock of the inhospitable world to which Obi-Wan has sent him.

2 While Luke can't help feeling that there is something strangely recognizable about haunted Dagobah, there is nothing even remotely familiar about the gnomish green creature who shows up to turn Luke and R2-D2's camp into his private playground.

3 In the creature's cramped dwelling, while torrential rain falls, Luke learns that he has in fact found Yoda. But the ancient Jedi Master and a ghostly Obi-Wan Kenobi disagree about whether Luke will be able to surrender his yearning for adventure and be properly trained in the ways of the Force.

4 Under Yoda's sometimes mystifying tutelage, Luke learns to perform superhuman tasks and will his body to levitate objects—including the astromech. With Yoda clasped to his back, Luke runs, leaps, and somersaults through Dagobah's riotous jungle, his strength flowing from the Force.

5 Deep within the cave-like root system of a colossal gnarltree—a domain of thick-bodied snakes and quick-tongued sleens—Luke has a precognitive vision of the true relationship with his evil adversary, Darth Vader. Strong with the dark side, the cave contains no more than what Luke has taken with him.

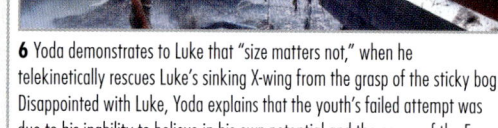

6 Yoda demonstrates to Luke that "size matters not," when he telekinetically rescues Luke's sinking X-wing from the grasp of the sticky bog. Disappointed with Luke, Yoda explains that the youth's failed attempt was due to his inability to believe in his own potential and the power of the Force.

7 A vision of Han and Leia imperiled on a city in the clouds persuades Luke to abbreviate his training and leave Dagobah—despite Yoda's admonition that, by doing so, Luke will likely destroy all for which Han and Leia have fought and suffered.

Gnarltree bridge over lagoon inlet

Yoda gathers galla seeds and sohli bark from areas surrounding his home

Spring-fed sweet water lagoon

Yoda's house

R2-D2 peers through the window of Yoda's dwelling

Yoda often gathers yarum seeds from the forest, avoiding the sharp webs spun by butcherbugs

Parasitic blackvine forms natural bridges

DISMAL AND DANGEROUS

Dagobah's bogs and lagoons are home to a host of creatures, including the swamp slug, which pulverizes its prey between thousands of tiny grinding teeth; the stealthy dragonsnake, whose razor-sharp claws are strong enough to incise alloy; and the quick-striking scrange, which uses its tusked tail to make short work of any creature that wanders into its reach. Smaller, but equally deadly, is the butcherbug, which spins slicing webs, and the morp, whose venom causes paralysis.

STRONG IN THE FORCE

During the Clone Wars, the Force spirit of Qui-Gon Jinn contacted Yoda, instructing the Jedi Master to travel to Dagobah in secret. Qui-Gon explained that the swamp planet was one of the purest places in the galaxy, made strong in the Force by its abundant life. There, Qui-Gon began to instruct Yoda in the mysteries of the cosmic Force and the Jedi Master experienced a vision of the Sith's triumph. After Order 66, Yoda sought refuge on Dagobah, learning how to retain his consciousness after death.

- Luke confronts vision of Vader
- Rusting remnants of Yoda's escape pod
- Many petrified gnarltrees
- Entire shoreline of peninsula is quicksand
- Luke leaves Yoda to reach cave entrance
- Entrance to cave located in immense gnarltree hollow
- Luke swings across boggy inlet using tree vines
- Good area for finding paludial fungi "yogurt plants"
- Trees weighed down with heavy nests built by jubba birds using mud scooped up from Dragonsnake Bog
- Enormous, predatory dragonsnake lurks just beneath bog waters
- Luke's X-wing landing trajectory causes swathe of broken branches
- Luke's training area
- R2-D2 is swallowed by dragonsnake and spat out again
- X-wing lands on edge of Dragonsnake Bog
- Yoda levitates Luke's X-wing from the bog and places it onto dry land
- Luke's temporary camp
- R2-D2 lands on firm ground after being spat out by dragonsnake

DRAGONSNAKE BOG

ROUTE KEY
- R2-D2's swamp walk
- Luke walks to a clearing and sets up camp
- Yoda takes Luke and R2-D2 back to his dwelling
- Luke's training circuit
- Luke in the cave

169

YODA'S HOUSE

HAND-BUILT OF MUD, gnarltree wattle, and stones, Yoda's house sits in the embrace of a giant gnarltree, atop a moss-covered knoll at the edge of a sweet water lagoon. The tiny dwelling comprises a sitting room, kitchen, and small sleeping loft, as well as windows and skylights with panes that may have been forged from precious gems—or perhaps from the transparisteel viewports of an abandoned escape pod. When Luke Skywalker is invited inside, he practically wears the miniature house like a shell. But Yoda is only amused by the young man's head-bumping attempts to make himself comfortable.

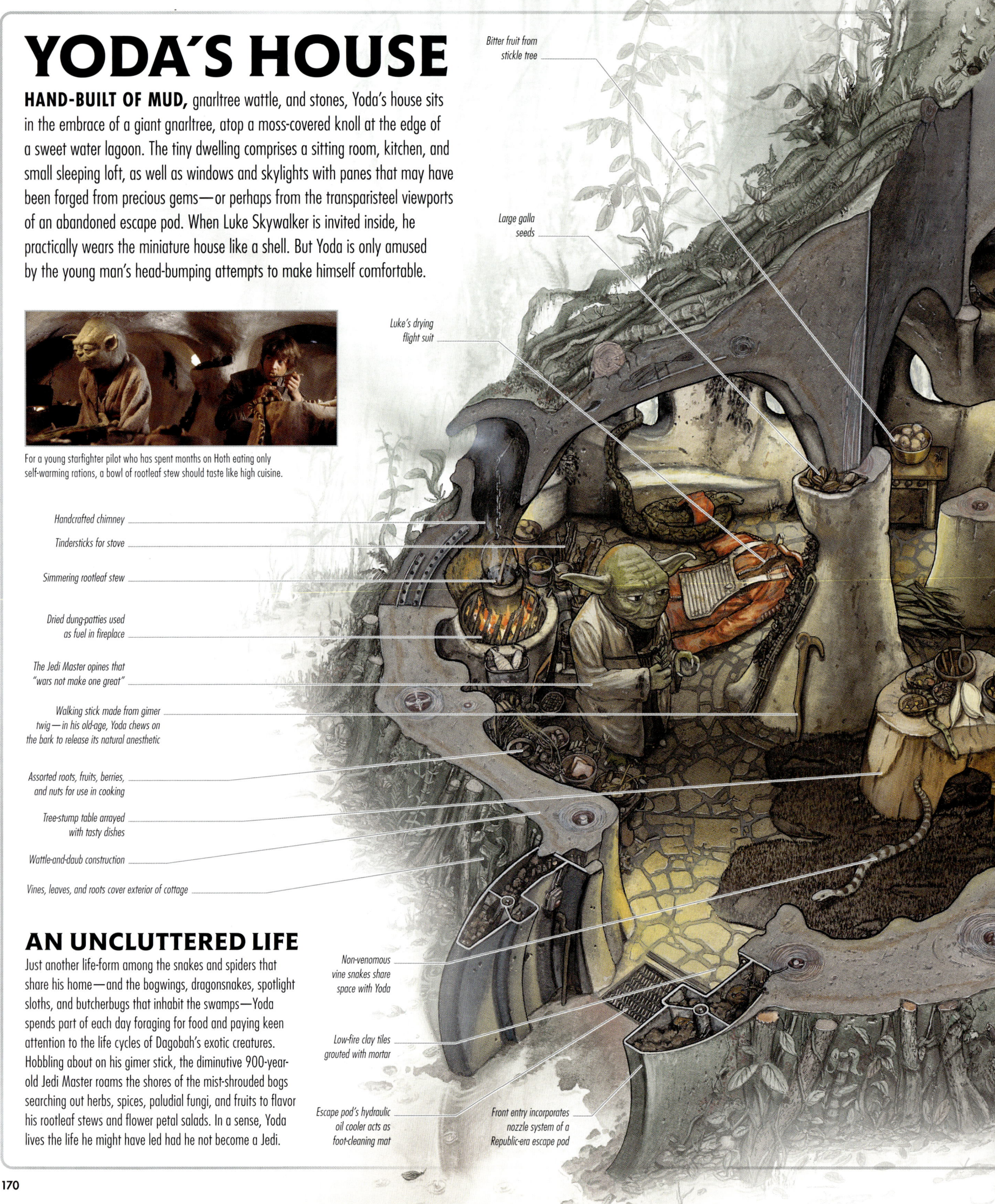

For a young starfighter pilot who has spent months on Hoth eating only self-warming rations, a bowl of rootleaf stew should taste like high cuisine.

AN UNCLUTTERED LIFE

Just another life-form among the snakes and spiders that share his home—and the bogwings, dragonsnakes, spotlight sloths, and butcherbugs that inhabit the swamps—Yoda spends part of each day foraging for food and paying keen attention to the life cycles of Dagobah's exotic creatures. Hobbling about on his gimer stick, the diminutive 900-year-old Jedi Master roams the shores of the mist-shrouded bogs searching out herbs, spices, paludial fungi, and fruits to flavor his rootleaf stews and flower petal salads. In a sense, Yoda lives the life he might have led had he not become a Jedi.

Callouts:
- Bitter fruit from stickle tree
- Large galla seeds
- Luke's drying flight suit
- Handcrafted chimney
- Tindersticks for stove
- Simmering rootleaf stew
- Dried dung-patties used as fuel in fireplace
- The Jedi Master opines that "wars not make one great"
- Walking stick made from gimer twig—in his old-age, Yoda chews on the bark to release its natural anesthetic
- Assorted roots, fruits, berries, and nuts for use in cooking
- Tree-stump table arrayed with tasty dishes
- Wattle-and-daub construction
- Vines, leaves, and roots cover exterior of cottage
- Non-venomous vine snakes share space with Yoda
- Low-fire clay tiles grouted with mortar
- Escape pod's hydraulic oil cooler acts as foot-cleaning mat
- Front entry incorporates nozzle system of a Republic-era escape pod

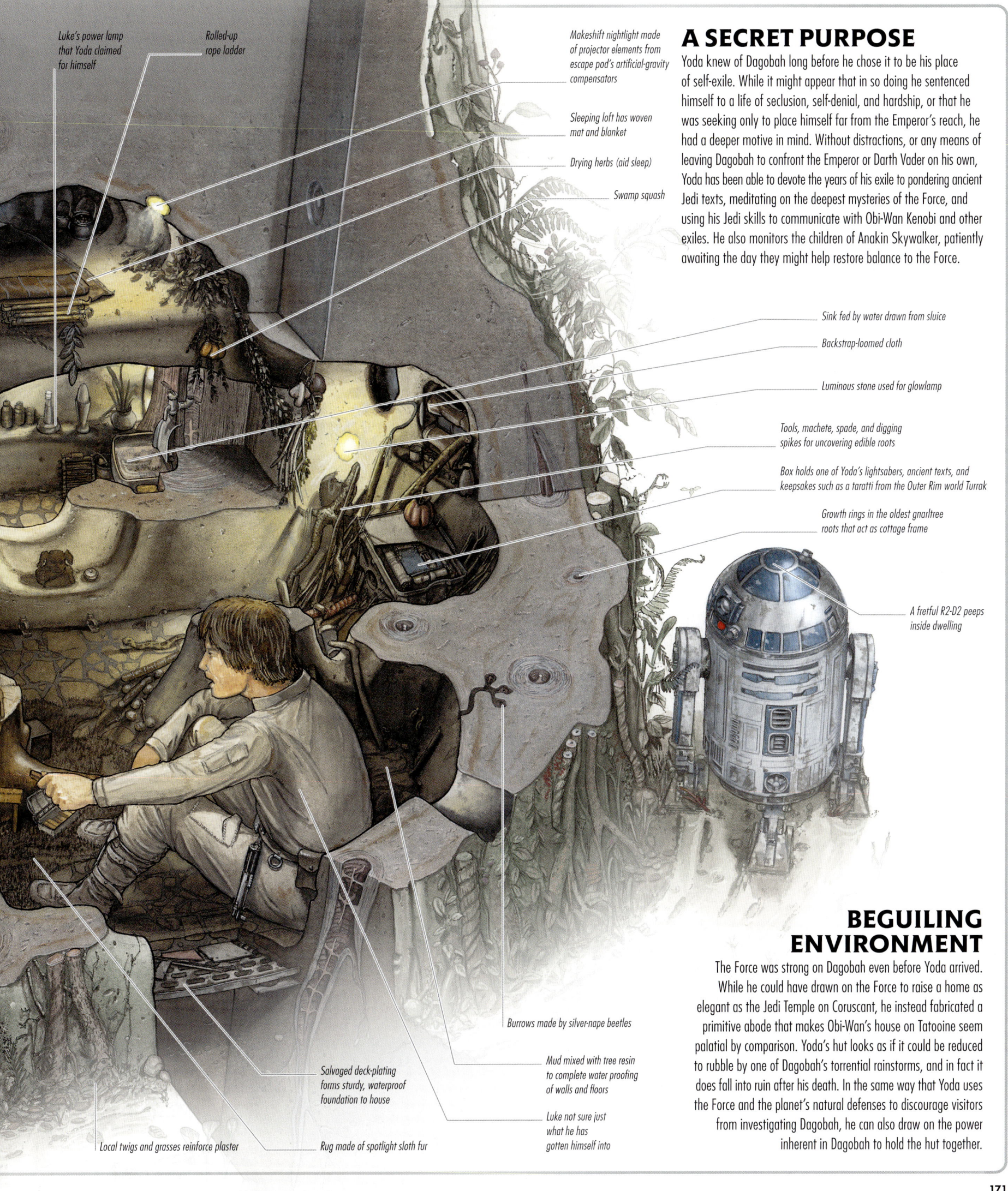

A SECRET PURPOSE

Yoda knew of Dagobah long before he chose it to be his place of self-exile. While it might appear that in so doing he sentenced himself to a life of seclusion, self-denial, and hardship, or that he was seeking only to place himself far from the Emperor's reach, he had a deeper motive in mind. Without distractions, or any means of leaving Dagobah to confront the Emperor or Darth Vader on his own, Yoda has been able to devote the years of his exile to pondering ancient Jedi texts, meditating on the deepest mysteries of the Force, and using his Jedi skills to communicate with Obi-Wan Kenobi and other exiles. He also monitors the children of Anakin Skywalker, patiently awaiting the day they might help restore balance to the Force.

BEGUILING ENVIRONMENT

The Force was strong on Dagobah even before Yoda arrived. While he could have drawn on the Force to raise a home as elegant as the Jedi Temple on Coruscant, he instead fabricated a primitive abode that makes Obi-Wan's house on Tatooine seem palatial by comparison. Yoda's hut looks as if it could be reduced to rubble by one of Dagobah's torrential rainstorms, and in fact it does fall into ruin after his death. In the same way that Yoda uses the Force and the planet's natural defenses to discourage visitors from investigating Dagobah, he can also draw on the power inherent in Dagobah to hold the hut together.

CLOUD CITY

FOUNDED BY ECCENTRIC INDUSTRIALIST Lord Ecclessis Figg of Corellia, Cloud City was originally known as Floating Home Mining Colony. Hovering at some 59,000 kilometers (37,000 miles) from Bespin's core, the installation is designed to extract rare tibanna gas from the lower atmosphere of the planet, which is then processed and packaged for shipment offworld. The facility is small by galactic standards, with its administrator, Lando Calrissian, hoping to turn a profit while avoiding scrutiny from the Mining Guild and the Empire. In recent years Lando has invited casinos to Cloud City, hoping to line his own pockets while providing further cover for the tibanna gas business.

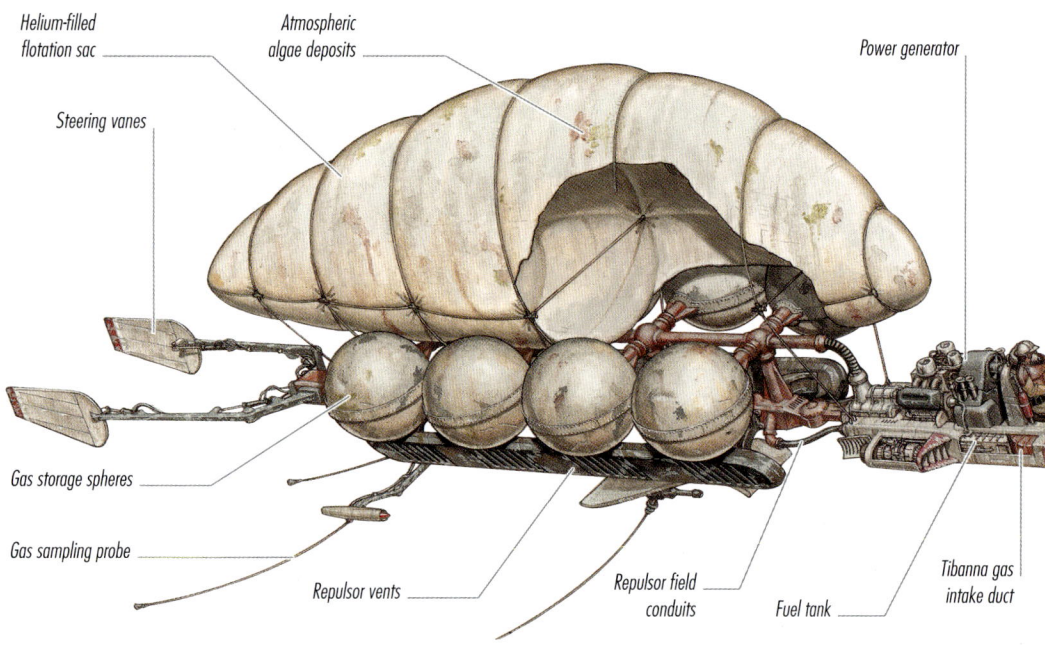

CHASING GAS STORMS

Gas prospectors have navigated Bespin's breathable upper atmosphere for many generations, and Cloud City still employs a legion of these freelance daredevils to pinpoint lush pockets of spin-sealed tibanna. Piloting their own jury-rigged craft through the clouds, prospectors seek to locate and exploit fresh eruptions of tibanna gas before the major contractors. Gas storms on Bespin are highly volatile and unpredictable, and, though the prospectors accept the risks for the sake of the sizeable profits, some pursuits are decidedly deadly.

FLOATING PARTNERSHIPS

Cloud City shares Bespin's extraordinary skies with smaller refineries. Kept aloft by massive repulsorlift generators, these mobile, automated facilities can re-orient themselves to draw tibanna from newly discovered pockets of gas. In general, however, these refineries handle surpluses from larger installations like Cloud City.

FRESH AIR

Constructed from materials mined from the Bespin System's innermost planet, Miser, Cloud City rises atop the 16 kilometer (10 mile)-wide mining structure. Its five million residents and visitors inhabit the planet's breathable upper atmosphere, known as the "Life Zone," which is replenished and shielded from the noxious lower atmosphere by a layer of airborne algae.

WATCH THE SKIES

With mining operations and tourism running unabated throughout Bespin's long year, the need for security is great. Stringent visa procedures are in place, and unidentified vessels are detected and intercepted long before they reach any of the docking platforms. A shield generator protects Cloud City from near-space bombardment and/or laser fire, but routine vigilance is overseen by the Wing Guard, which uses twin-pod cloud cars for patrol and emergency actions. These two-person fliers are equipped with blaster cannons and can sustain an average speed of 1,500 kph (930 mph). Employing both repulsorlifts and ion engines, the atmospheric airspeeders are also used as pleasure craft.

UNEASY REMINDER

The upper levels of Cloud City are designed to showcase the planet's two-hour-long sunsets and natural beauty. The white synthstone of Leia's chamber pays homage to the style of the planet Alderaan, the home of Lord Figg's wife. But this reminder of her destroyed planet does nothing to put Princess Leia at ease. Instead, it only heightens her sense that all is not right on Cloud City.

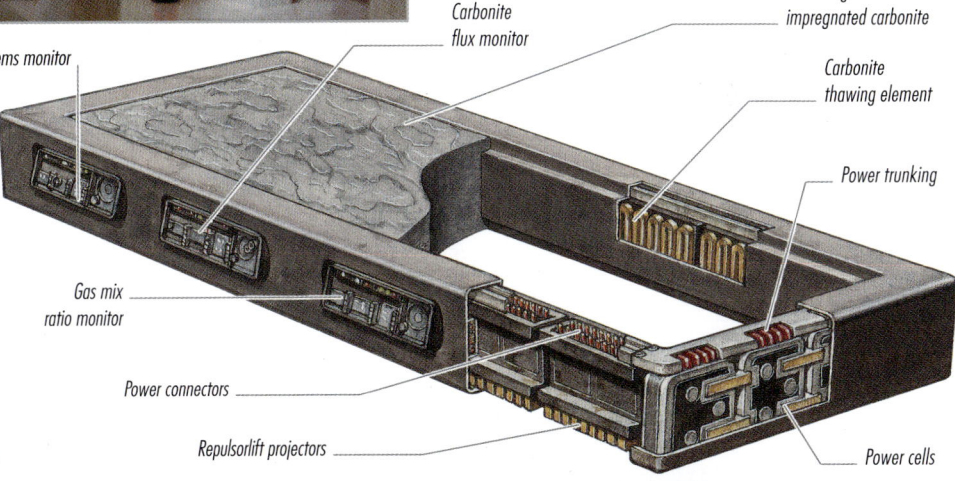

CARBONITE STORAGE REPULSOR SLED

Bespin Motors' carbonite sled is intended for use in conjunction with a carbon-freeze chamber for the safe transport of exotic gases that exist at high pressure, such as tibanna. Tibanna is used in starship weaponry, hyperdrives, and as a coolant around the gravito-active elements of repulsorlifts. Inside the sled's control frame, a quantity of gas is suspended within a super-strong block of carbonite. Lord Vader decides to use Han Solo as a test subject for the storage of a humanoid within carbonite. By this process, Vader hopes to immobilize his son, Luke Skywalker, for transport to the Emperor. As he is lowered into the freezing chamber, Han is injected to induce hibernation before carbonite infuses and solidifies throughout his body.

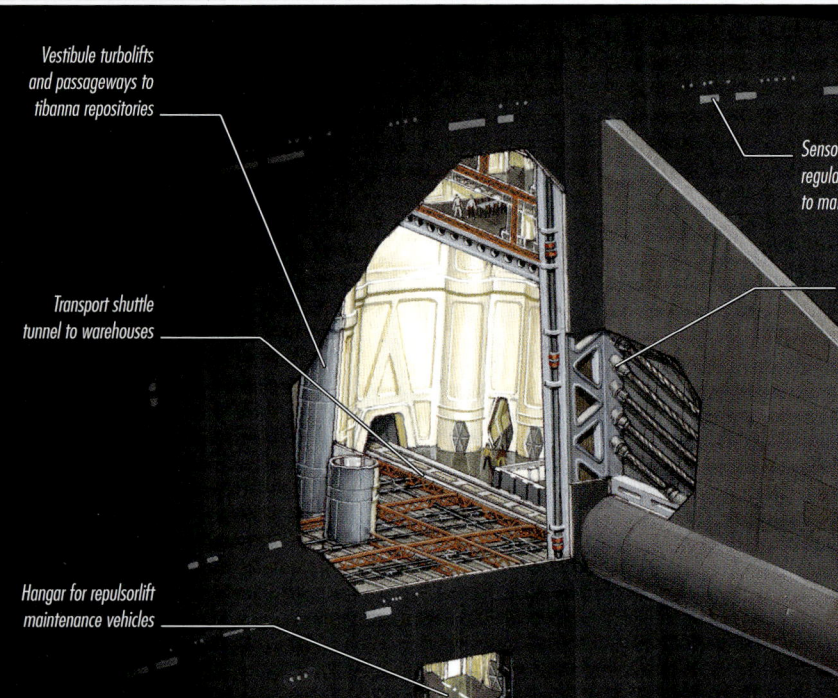

Vestibule turbolifts and passageways to tibanna repositories

Transport shuttle tunnel to warehouses

Hangar for repulsorlift maintenance vehicles

Sensor panels around shaft regulate low air pressure needed to maintain unrefined tibanna

Support cable anchor points

Narrow transportation tunnel connects processing vane to rest of facility

Single-track conveyor alternately transports empty carbon-block frames into vane and filled blocks out

High-tensile support cables

HARD-PRESSED WORKERS

The monotonous and sometimes dangerous work of mining and processing tibanna gas is performed by Ugnaughts—porcine humanoids native to the planet Gentes—who reside in the floating metropolis's labyrinth of humid, red-lighted work corridors.

PROCESSING VANE

DEEP INSIDE THE BELLY of Cloud City, Darth Vader takes advantage of one of the airborne facility's gigantic gas-processing vanes for his own evil ends. He makes sinister use of a carbon-freeze chamber—where tibanna gas is admixed with carbonite for flash-freeze preservation—by having Han Solo encased in carbonite and placed in the custody of bounty hunter Boba Fett. The Dark Lord then battles Luke Skywalker onto a sensor balcony suspended over a vast reactor shaft, in which tibanna is stored at low pressure before purification and stabilization. Luke is finally sucked out of the shaft through a network of gas-exhaust pipes and ends up dangling from the underbelly of Cloud City, desperately clutching a weather vane.

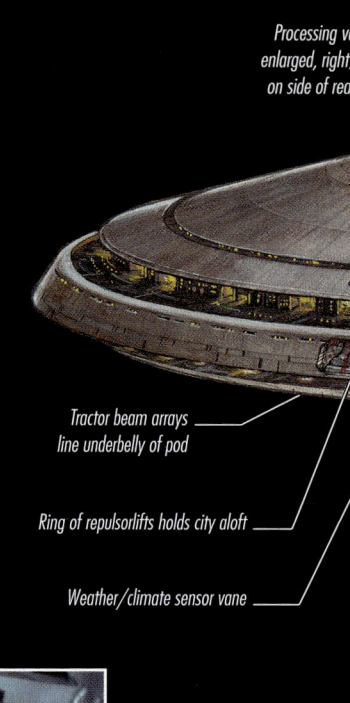

Processing vane (area enlarged, right) situated on side of reactor shaft

City level

Gas exhaust port into which Luke is sucked

Tibanna block warehouse and conveyors

Transport docking bays

Tractor beam arrays line underbelly of pod

Heavily shielded main power converter and distribution node

Ring of repulsorlifts holds city aloft

Weather/climate sensor vane

Tibanna gas shoots up reactor stalk and is ducted into reactor shafts at top for processing

Power conduits and converters line side of stalk

Ring of ducts around reactor bulb allows mined gases to enter reactor stalk from aperture in underside of bulb

SPIN-SEALED RICHES

Generators located along Cloud City's underbelly emit tractor beams that converge below the reactor bulb to create an energy funnel. This funnel mines tibanna from Bespin's lower atmosphere at depths of more than 23,000 kilometers (14,300 miles). The gas passes via an aperture in the underside of the reactor bulb (1) to the reactor stalk (2) and into smaller reactor shafts (3), where it filters into processing vanes. The manufactured gas outperforms the energy produced by competing gases in starship weaponry and hyperdrives.

Only just managing to keep ahold of the teetering sensor balcony in the reactor shaft, Luke refuses to accept Vader's offer of an alliance—or his revelation that he is in fact Luke's father.

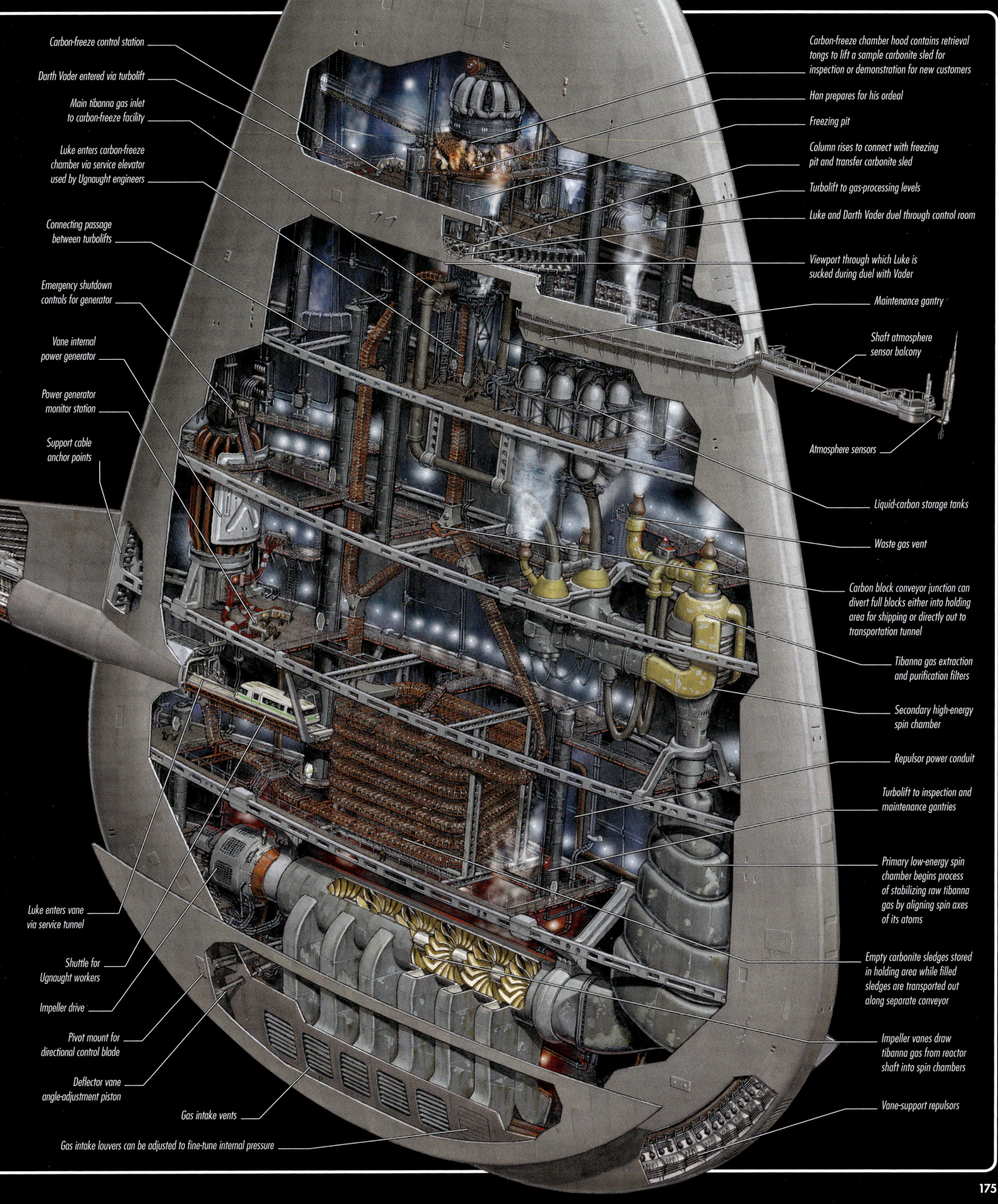

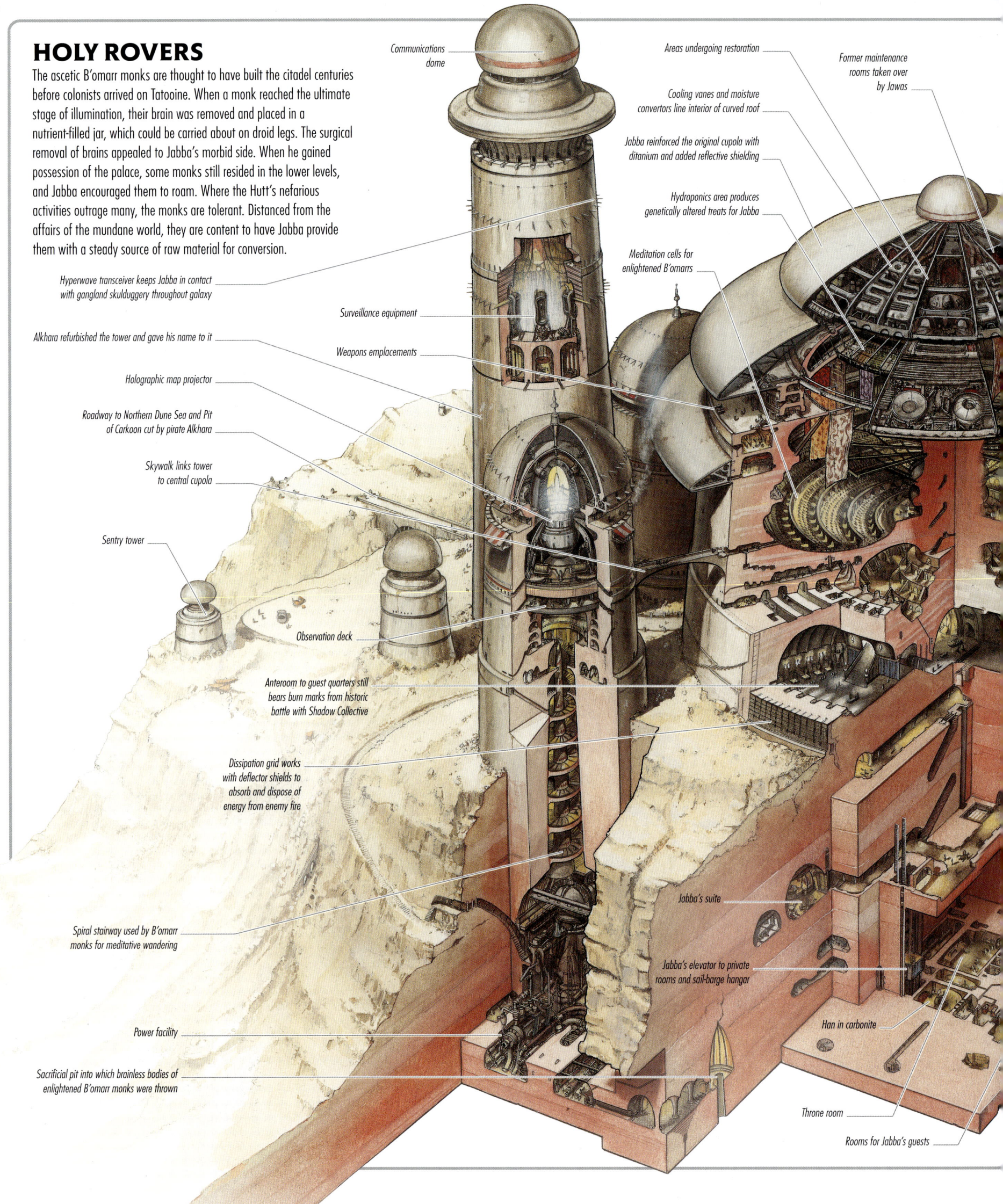

HOLY ROVERS

The ascetic B'omarr monks are thought to have built the citadel centuries before colonists arrived on Tatooine. When a monk reached the ultimate stage of illumination, their brain was removed and placed in a nutrient-filled jar, which could be carried about on droid legs. The surgical removal of brains appealed to Jabba's morbid side. When he gained possession of the palace, some monks still resided in the lower levels, and Jabba encouraged them to roam. Where the Hutt's nefarious activities outrage many, the monks are tolerant. Distanced from the affairs of the mundane world, they are content to have Jabba provide them with a steady source of raw material for conversion.

- Hyperwave transceiver keeps Jabba in contact with gangland skulduggery throughout galaxy
- Alkhara refurbished the tower and gave his name to it
- Holographic map projector
- Roadway to Northern Dune Sea and Pit of Carkoon cut by pirate Alkhara
- Skywalk links tower to central cupola
- Sentry tower
- Spiral stairway used by B'omarr monks for meditative wandering
- Power facility
- Sacrificial pit into which brainless bodies of enlightened B'omarr monks were thrown
- Communications dome
- Surveillance equipment
- Weapons emplacements
- Observation deck
- Anteroom to guest quarters still bears burn marks from historic battle with Shadow Collective
- Dissipation grid works with deflector shields to absorb and dispose of energy from enemy fire
- Areas undergoing restoration
- Former maintenance rooms taken over by Jawas
- Cooling vanes and moisture convertors line interior of curved roof
- Jabba reinforced the original cupola with ditanium and added reflective shielding
- Hydroponics area produces genetically altered treats for Jabba
- Meditation cells for enlightened B'omarrs
- Jabba's suite
- Jabba's elevator to private rooms and sail-barge hangar
- Han in carbonite
- Throne room
- Rooms for Jabba's guests

THIEVES AND MURDERERS

The bandit Alkhara was the first outsider to appropriate the B'omarr monastery for his own use. Among his legendary misdeeds, Alkhara had the members of a local police garrison murdered; he then, in turn, slaughtered the Sand People who had carried out the crime, thus initiating a blood feud between Tuskens and humans that exists to this day. Alkhara remained at the citadel for 34 years, before being driven off Tatooine by Jabba the Hutt.

SAIL BARGE HANGAR

Jabba is ferried across Tatooine in signature sail barges and skiffs designed by the Ubrikkian Corporation, but commissioned by architect Derren Flet. When it came to designing dungeons for the palace, however, Flet didn't fare nearly as well—he was executed for failing to take into account the number of beings Jabba would imprison, or the full extent of the Hutt's depravity.

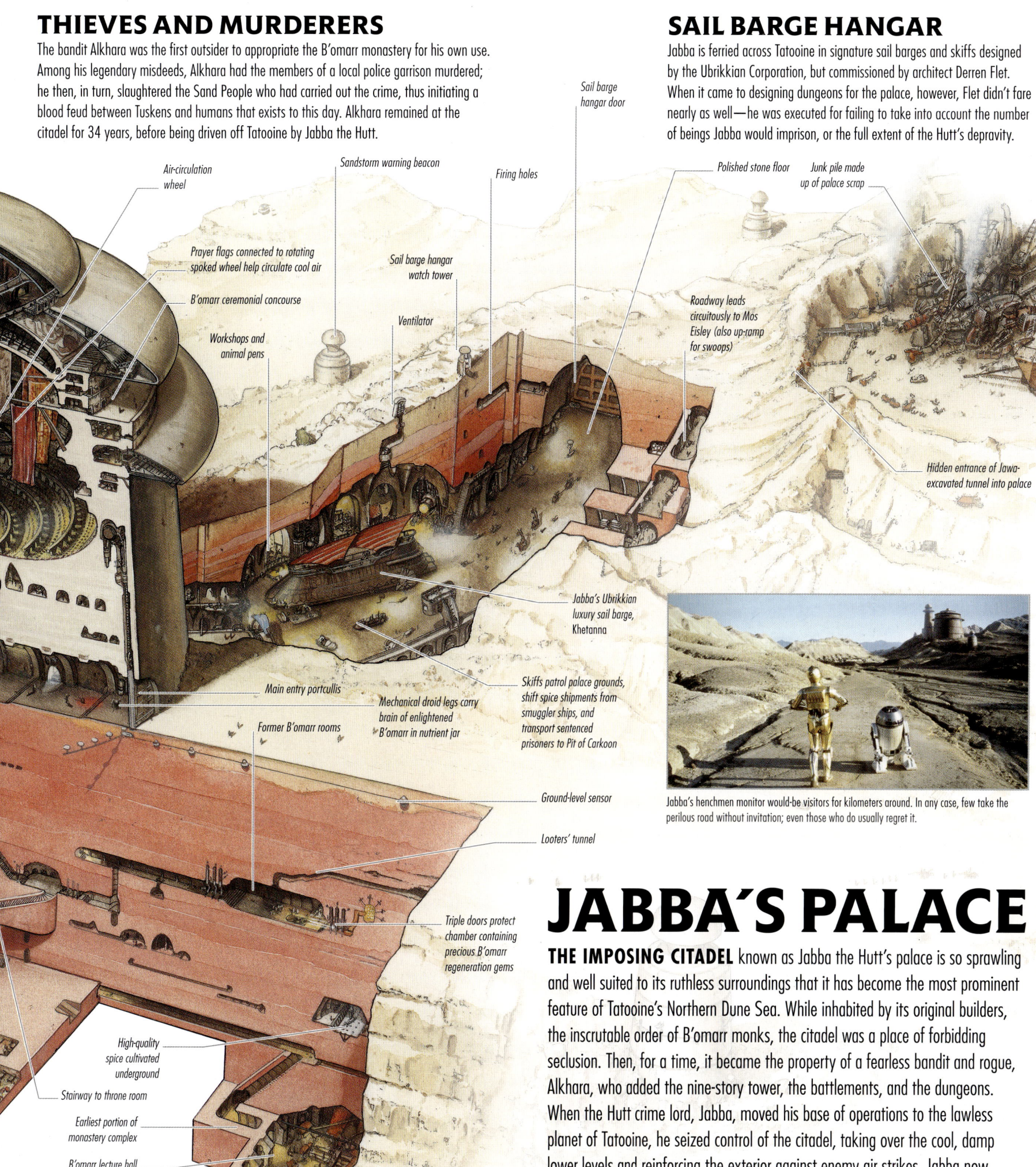

Jabba's henchmen monitor would-be visitors for kilometers around. In any case, few take the perilous road without invitation; even those who do usually regret it.

JABBA'S PALACE

THE IMPOSING CITADEL known as Jabba the Hutt's palace is so sprawling and well suited to its ruthless surroundings that it has become the most prominent feature of Tatooine's Northern Dune Sea. While inhabited by its original builders, the inscrutable order of B'omarr monks, the citadel was a place of forbidding seclusion. Then, for a time, it became the property of a fearless bandit and rogue, Alkhara, who added the nine-story tower, the battlements, and the dungeons. When the Hutt crime lord, Jabba, moved his base of operations to the lawless planet of Tatooine, he seized control of the citadel, taking over the cool, damp lower levels and reinforcing the exterior against enemy air strikes. Jabba now endows the palace with an atmosphere of unprecedented depravity and corruption.

JABBA'S THRONE ROOM

JABBA THE HUTT'S FONDNESS FOR murky underground places and theatricality leads him to convert a portion of the former B'omarr monastery into a presence, or throne, room, which he fills with his corrupt associates, cut-throat recruits, and sycophantic followers. At his command, the strains of music waft through the spicy air; dancers move across the stone floor; smugglers or weapons merchants who cross him are humiliated and thrown to the ferocious rancor beast—or a bounty hunter and his prisoner are admitted for audience.

THE HUTT'S HOUSE BAND

Made up of veteran local banders, the Max Rebo Band plays regularly for Jabba the Hutt, appearing at his palace or in his townhouse in Mos Eisley. The band's core consists of Max, Droopy McCool, and Sy Snootles; for high-profile gigs, Max supplements this ensemble, drawing on the talents of Joh Yowza, Barquin D'an, Doda Bodonawieedo, and Rappertunie, as well as drummers, backing singers, and dancers.

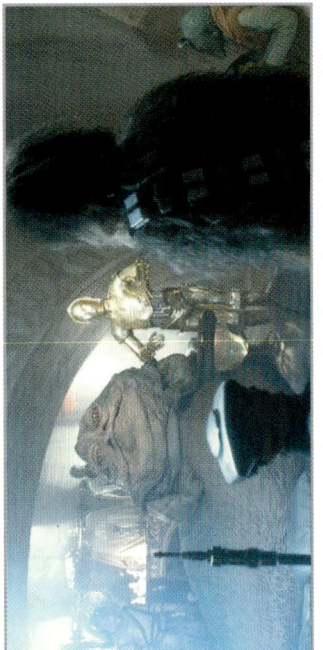

CORRUPT COURT

Only the most notorious smugglers and bounty hunters are allowed to consort openly in the throne room—those who have proved themselves adept at murder, mayhem, or crimes of high standing. Those of junior reputation room the vast palace, forced to make do with entertaining Jabba's subordinates, and are afforded less respect than Jabba's chief droids. It is into this intimidating atmosphere that Princess Leia, disguised as bounty hunter Boushh, enters.

From atop a colossal dais, Jabba the Hutt controls nearly everything in the throne room—including a trap door that leads to a rancor pit 7.5 meters (25 feet) below.

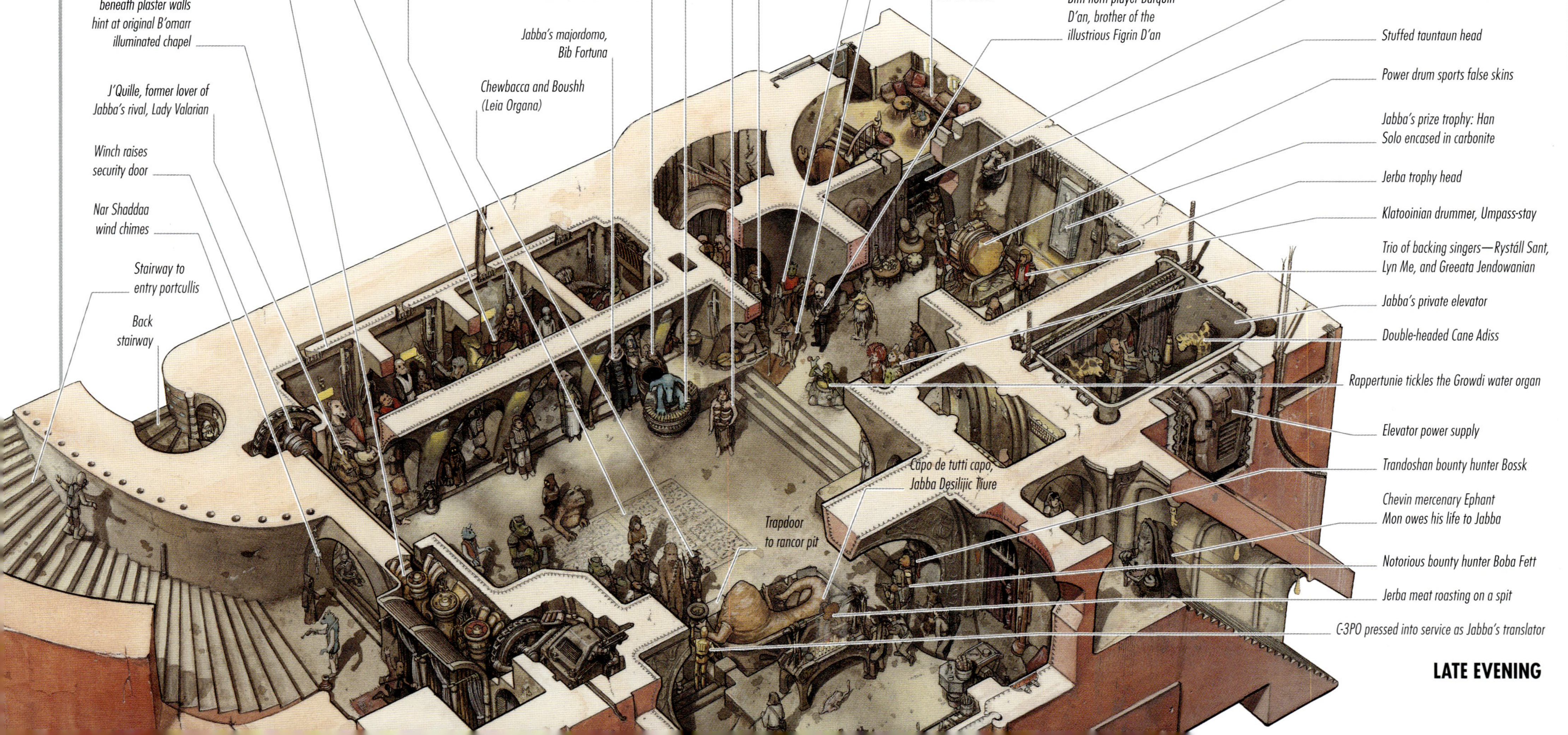

- Each cubicle hosts a hookah
- B'omarr pipe organ sealed behind false wall
- Glowing stones beneath plaster walls hint at original B'omarr illuminated chapel
- J'Quille, former lover of Jabba's rival, Lady Valarian
- Winch raises security door
- Nat Shaddaa wind chimes
- Stairway to entry portcullis
- Back stairway
- Rodian slitherhorn player Doda Bodonawieedo
- Singer Joh Yowza
- Private backstage loft for band
- Lando Calrissian, disguised as skiff guard Tamtel Skreej
- Dancer Yarna d'al' Gargan
- Band leader Max Rebo
- Jabba's Kowakian mascot, Salacious Crumb
- Jabba's majordomo, Bib Fortuna
- Chewbacca and Boushh (Leia Organa)
- Viewing grille to rancor pit below
- Trapdoor to rancor pit
- Bith horn player Barquin D'an, brother of the illustrious Figrin D'an
- Capo de tutti capo, Jabba Desilijic Tiure
- Entrance to droid elevator
- Stuffed tauntaun head
- Power drum sports false skins
- Jabba's prize trophy: Han Solo encased in carbonite
- Jerba trophy head
- Klatooinian drummer, Umpass-stay
- Trio of backing singers—Rystáll Sant, Lyn Me, and Greeata Jendowanian
- Jabba's private elevator
- Double-headed Cane Adiss
- Rappertunie tickles the Growdi water organ
- Elevator power supply
- Trandoshan bounty hunter Bossk
- Chevin mercenary Ephant Mon owes his life to Jabba
- Notorious bounty hunter Boba Fett
- Jerba meat roasting on a spit
- C-3PO pressed into service as Jabba's translator

LATE EVENING

EARLY NEXT MORNING

BOILER ROOM

In the Palace's underground labyrinth even the life of a droid is often forfeit. Captured, confiscated, or cajoled, a hapless droid will invariably find itself at the mercy of Jabba's malicious chief of Cyborg Operations, EV-9D9. A psychotic mechanical murderer of her fellow droids, she revels in torturing her charges or working them until their processors blow. A droid that survives to bear the brand of Jabba's Palace is a fortunate droid indeed!

RANCOR PIT

The underground levels of the palace are the haunt of exiled Jawas, B'omarr monks, and would-be burglars. Trusting in his lieutenants to police this brutal maze, Jabba confines his interest to the rancor pit, which is rumored to have been hollowed from a sacred B'omarr grotto, and is now littered with the regurgitated bones of the rancor's living repasts. After Luke Skywalker kills the hapless rancor, beastmaster Malakili is left despondent but eventually leaves to start a new life in Mos Pelgo with others seeking to escape their posts on Tatooine.

Unsuccessful at persuading Jabba to release Han Solo, Luke Skywalker uses the Force to draw a blaster belonging to one of Jabba's humanoid guards, Nizuc Beck.

Labels:
- Repair room, where C-3PO is fitted with a restraining bolt
- Room of Arches, home to colony of outcast Jawas
- Generator block
- 8D8, a humanoid droid devoted to EV-9D9
- Droid "assessment" room
- Captives awaiting torture
- Sadistic supervisor of cyborg operations, EV-9D9
- Droid-electronics repair room
- Droid corridor
- Droid elevator from throne room
- Chewie and hibernation-blind Han Solo, reunited
- Staircase between throne room and detention dungeon
- Heavy-duty doorway to secondary animal pen, where beasts that will fight the rancor are held
- Warden
- Tentacled prisoner
- Torture by blood-sucking worms
- Detention dungeon corridor
- Skull of Bib Fortuna's one-time competitor for the position of majordomo, Bidlo Kwerve — an early victim of the rancor
- Luke Skywalker
- Hapless Gamorrean guard Jubnuk
- Ancient stairway deliberately blocked to deter intruders
- Few know the rancor's name is Pateesa
- Armed assassins sent to steal Jabba's account records
- Ceremonial staircase in early B'omarr decorative style
- Spice thief worms eat way through rock fall
- Stairway to guard's quarters
- Stove
- Rancor pit gate mechanism
- Corridor to guard dormitories
- Chef Porcellus
- Refresher unit
- Obsolete pit droid
- Guards' quarters divided by curtain to reduce fumes from ancient stove
- Thief killed and eaten by predatory, rock-burrowing worms
- Malakili's sleeping quarters, equipped with now-unused stun device for controlling the rancor
- Rancor handler Malakili, former beast wrangler for the Circus Horrificus
- Scratches made by unhappy rancor
- Deceased B'omarr brains stored in wall niches of tomb
- Elevator used by Bib Fortuna to access entrance corridor
- Corridor to Jabba's private kitchens

BATTLE OF ENDOR

WHILE IT COSTS THE REBEL ALLIANCE many lives, Bothan spies furnish the following intelligence: the Empire is constructing a second Death Star near the isolated Forest Moon of Endor. The Alliance has to strike before the facility is operational—but the Bothans also report that the Death Star is protected by a massive defensive shield projected from a generator and dish network located on the surface of the Forest Moon. Thus, a desperate plan is hatched. Entrusting the *Millennium Falcon* to Lando Calrissian and Sullustan navigator Nien Nunb, Han Solo, Luke Skywalker, Princess Leia, and a team of Pathfinder commandos travel to Endor in a stolen Imperial shuttle, intent on destroying the shield installation.

1 Thanks to an old but serviceable Imperial code, the shuttle is allowed to land on the Forest Moon. The commandos set out for the shield-generator bunker, but are forced to engage a handful of Imperial scouts on speeder bikes. When two of the scouts flee, Luke and Leia take up the pursuit.

2 The 200-kph (124-mph) chase takes Luke and Leia on a zigzagging course through Endor's forest of mighty trees. Two more Imperials join the pursuit and Luke leaps onto the back of one of the bikes. He hurls the pilot into a tree, then drops back to deal with the second pair of scouts.

Leia swoops down from treetops, firing at a scout trooper with her blasters

Luke leaps off his speeder bike and uses his saber to slice control vanes off a scout trooper TK-151's bike as it passes

Luke's speeder bike hits tree

Scout trooper hits tree

Scout trooper begins firing at Leia

Leia falls from her speeder and is discovered by Wicket

Scout trooper looks back to see explosion of Leia's speeder bike before crashing into tree

Ewok trap

Lake Sui, home to Ewok stilt villages

Bright Tree Village

THE AFTERMATH OF VICTORY

The explosion of the second Death Star defies preconceived notions of physics, and miraculously a rain of apocalyptic debris doesn't hit the Forest Moon. The morning after the battle, rebel forces scramble to destroy an Imperial base on the far side of the moon. Within days, the Alliance is battling Imperial forces on a number of fronts, as moffs and Imperial commanders seek to carve out power in a rapidly fragmenting Empire.

3 Thrown from her speeder bike, Leia regains consciousness to discover that she has company: a furry Endor inhabitant, whose crude spear is taller than he is. After sharing rations with the Ewok, and allying with him to dispatch two more Imperial scouts, Leia accompanies Wicket to Bright Tree Village.

4 Chewbacca inadvertently leads Luke, Han, R2-D2, and himself into an Ewok net trap. The astromech's circular saw arm cuts effortlessly through the net, only to drop the prisoners to the ground and directly into captivity, at the hands—and spears—of Teebo, Paploo, and other Ewoks.

5 Deprived of their weapons, Luke, Han, Chewbacca, and the two droids are marched to Bright Tree Village high above the forest floor. Much to Han's dismay, the Ewoks treat C-3PO with reverential respect, having taken him for a deity—even though the droid's programming prohibits impersonation.

Ewok army and rebels cross strait of Lake Marudi using Ewok-made rope bridge

N 0   1 KM
   0   1 MILE

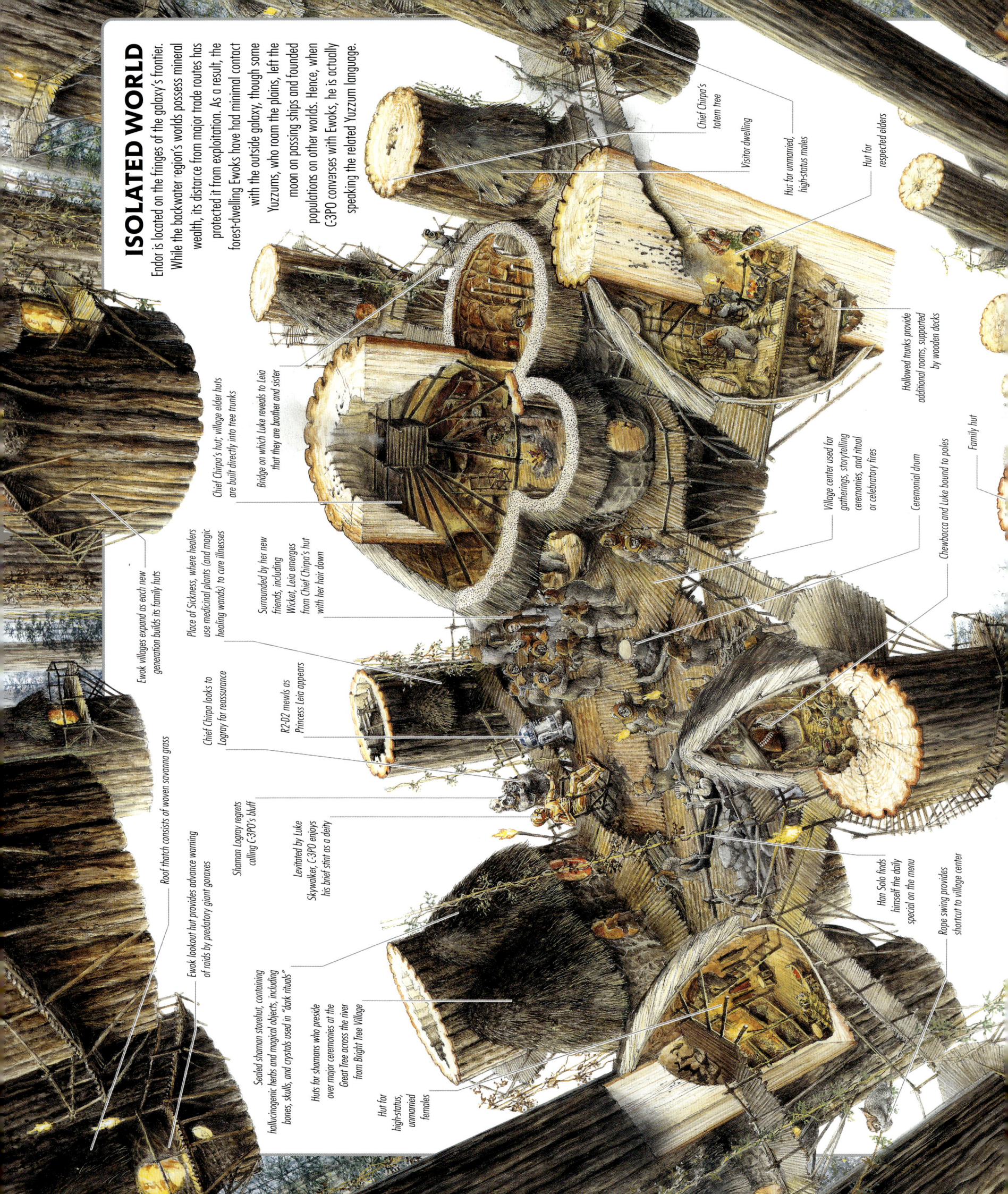

EWOK VILLAGE

THE SO-CALLED SANCTUARY MOON of the planet Endor is home to many tribes of Ewoks, who live for the most part above the forest floor in tree villages. Clusters of crude thatch-roof huts hug the trunks of the enormous conifer trees, and are linked to each other and to the forest floor by ingenious walkways, rope bridges, and swings. The central part of the village consists of the chief's and village elders' huts, with an open platform where ceremonies and meetings take place. Families, including unmarried females, live in clusters of huts arranged outside the village center, with unmarried males living a little further away.

The Ewoks love tall tales, music, and dance, and are quick to celebrate any occasion, such as the gentle capture of Luke, Han, Chewbacca, and R2-D2.

MAGICAL FOREST

The bark of the conifer provides the Ewoks with an insect repellent, and the strong boughs supply material for bows, spears, slingshots, and catapult arms. In addition, the Ewoks share a mystic bond with the forests, with village shamans serving as intermediaries between the trees and the tribes. At the birth of each new tribal member, a life tree seedling is planted, and the guardian tree and Ewok mature together. On death, the Ewoks believe an Ewok's spirit takes up residence in their tree.

- Endor's ancient trees are surprisingly resilient against the heat of Ewok fires
- The lively language of the Ewoks contains more than three dozen words for the conifers they refer to principally as "life trees"
- Unmarried males can be called upon to help defend the village against boar-wolves and other predators that prowl the forest floor below
- Principal walkway to village center

TREE HOME

Home to some 200 Ewoks, Bright Tree Village is situated approximately 15 meters (50 feet) above the forest floor. The trees in this part of the forest average only about 40 meters (130 feet) high, but the most ancient life trees elsewhere can exceed 1,000 meters (3,280 feet). Ewoks come down to ground level to forage for fruits and berries, and to hunt on wild ponies introduced to Endor by earlier human scouting parties. They also use smaller, native bordoks as beasts of burden.

- At certain times of year, colorful orchids bloom in crevices of bark
- Condor dragons have been known to perch in high branches
- Ewoks launch gliders from high in the canopy
- Food stored well above village huts
- Ewok village constructed in under-canopy
- Sentries and unmarried males live below village
- Forest floor covered with ferns, tree palms, and juicy matlberries

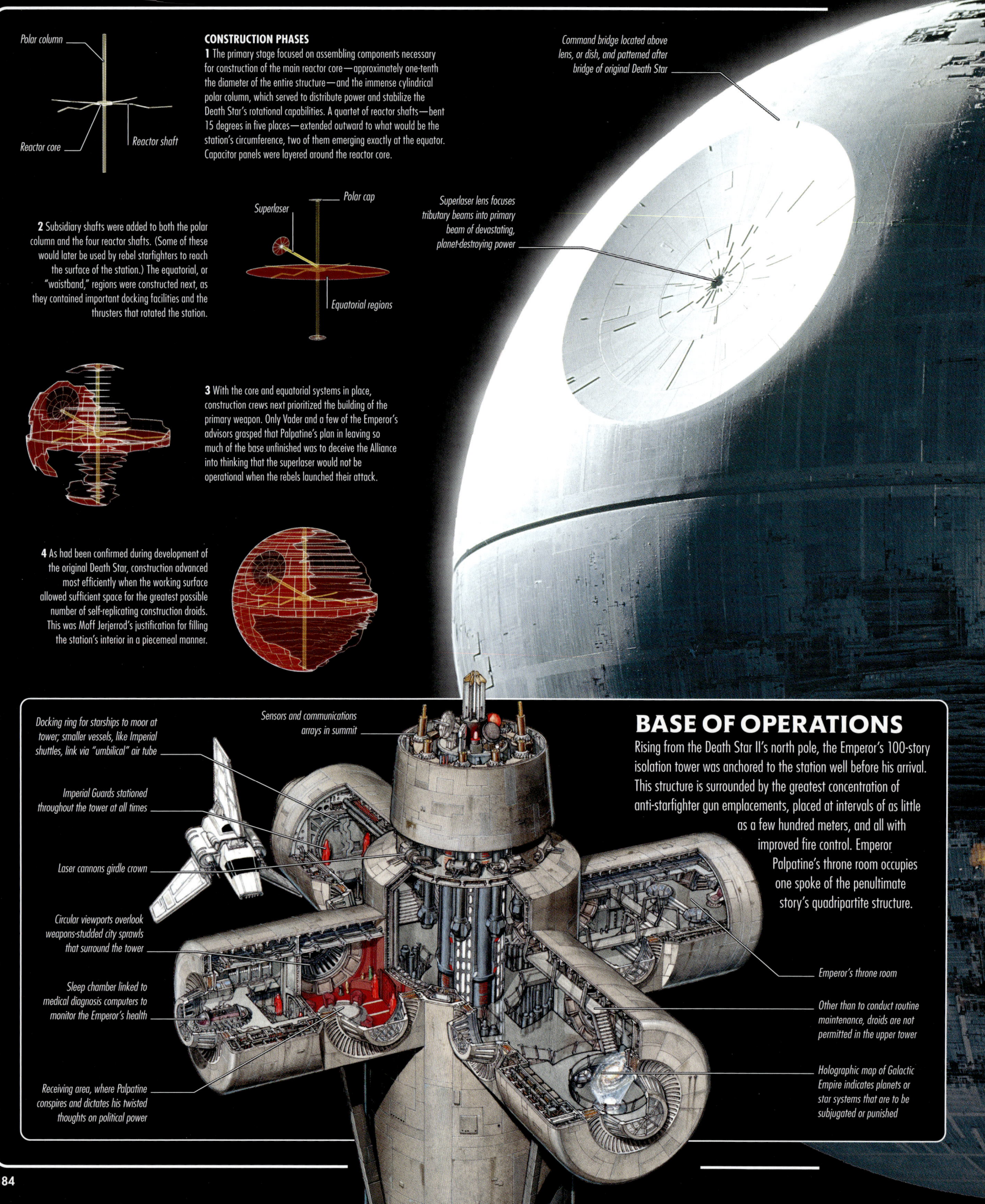

Polar column

Reactor core — Reactor shaft

CONSTRUCTION PHASES

1 The primary stage focused on assembling components necessary for construction of the main reactor core—approximately one-tenth the diameter of the entire structure—and the immense cylindrical polar column, which served to distribute power and stabilize the Death Star's rotational capabilities. A quartet of reactor shafts—bent 15 degrees in five places—extended outward to what would be the station's circumference, two of them emerging exactly at the equator. Capacitor panels were layered around the reactor core.

Superlaser — Polar cap

Equatorial regions

2 Subsidiary shafts were added to both the polar column and the four reactor shafts. (Some of these would later be used by rebel starfighters to reach the surface of the station.) The equatorial, or "waistband," regions were constructed next, as they contained important docking facilities and the thrusters that rotated the station.

3 With the core and equatorial systems in place, construction crews next prioritized the building of the primary weapon. Only Vader and a few of the Emperor's advisors grasped that Palpatine's plan in leaving so much of the base unfinished was to deceive the Alliance into thinking that the superlaser would not be operational when the rebels launched their attack.

4 As had been confirmed during development of the original Death Star, construction advanced most efficiently when the working surface allowed sufficient space for the greatest possible number of self-replicating construction droids. This was Moff Jerjerrod's justification for filling the station's interior in a piecemeal manner.

Command bridge located above lens, or dish, and patterned after bridge of original Death Star

Superlaser lens focuses tributary beams into primary beam of devastating, planet-destroying power

Docking ring for starships to moor at tower; smaller vessels, like Imperial shuttles, link via "umbilical" air tube

Sensors and communications arrays in summit

Imperial Guards stationed throughout the tower at all times

Laser cannons girdle crown

Circular viewports overlook weapons-studded city sprawls that surround the tower

Sleep chamber linked to medical diagnosis computers to monitor the Emperor's health

Receiving area, where Palpatine conspires and dictates his twisted thoughts on political power

BASE OF OPERATIONS

Rising from the Death Star II's north pole, the Emperor's 100-story isolation tower was anchored to the station well before his arrival. This structure is surrounded by the greatest concentration of anti-starfighter gun emplacements, placed at intervals of as little as a few hundred meters, and all with improved fire control. Emperor Palpatine's throne room occupies one spoke of the penultimate story's quadripartite structure.

Emperor's throne room

Other than to conduct routine maintenance, droids are not permitted in the upper tower

Holographic map of Galactic Empire indicates planets or star systems that are to be subjugated or punished

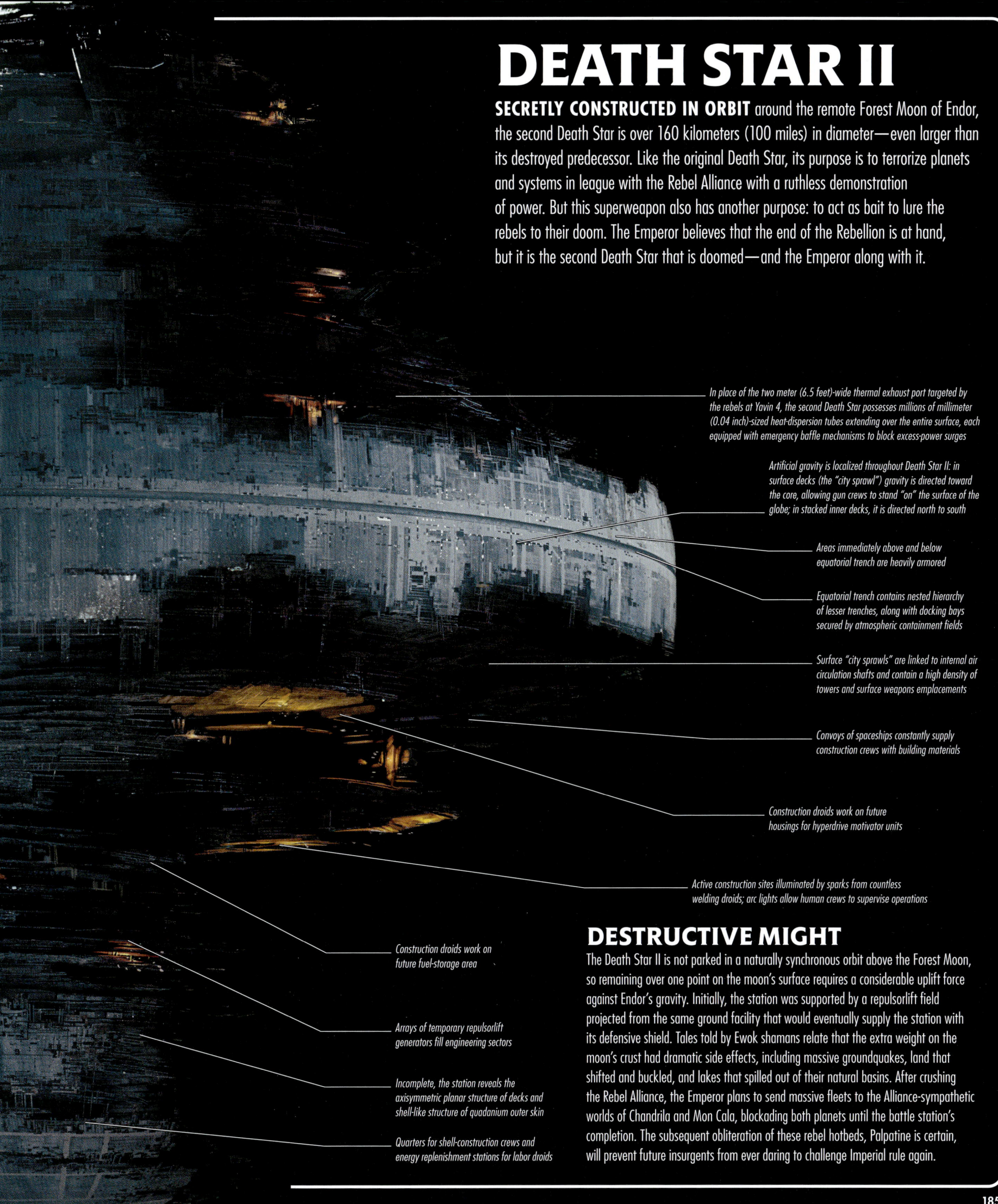

DEATH STAR II

SECRETLY CONSTRUCTED IN ORBIT around the remote Forest Moon of Endor, the second Death Star is over 160 kilometers (100 miles) in diameter—even larger than its destroyed predecessor. Like the original Death Star, its purpose is to terrorize planets and systems in league with the Rebel Alliance with a ruthless demonstration of power. But this superweapon also has another purpose: to act as bait to lure the rebels to their doom. The Emperor believes that the end of the Rebellion is at hand, but it is the second Death Star that is doomed—and the Emperor along with it.

In place of the two meter (6.5 feet)-wide thermal exhaust port targeted by the rebels at Yavin 4, the second Death Star possesses millions of millimeter (0.04 inch)-sized heat-dispersion tubes extending over the entire surface, each equipped with emergency baffle mechanisms to block excess-power surges

Artificial gravity is localized throughout Death Star II: in surface decks (the "city sprawl") gravity is directed toward the core, allowing gun crews to stand "on" the surface of the globe; in stacked inner decks, it is directed north to south

Areas immediately above and below equatorial trench are heavily armored

Equatorial trench contains nested hierarchy of lesser trenches, along with docking bays secured by atmospheric containment fields

Surface "city sprawls" are linked to internal air circulation shafts and contain a high density of towers and surface weapons emplacements

Convoys of spaceships constantly supply construction crews with building materials

Construction droids work on future housings for hyperdrive motivator units

Active construction sites illuminated by sparks from countless welding droids; arc lights allow human crews to supervise operations

Construction droids work on future fuel-storage area

Arrays of temporary repulsorlift generators fill engineering sectors

Incomplete, the station reveals the axisymmetric planar structure of decks and shell-like structure of quadanium outer skin

Quarters for shell-construction crews and energy replenishment stations for labor droids

DESTRUCTIVE MIGHT

The Death Star II is not parked in a naturally synchronous orbit above the Forest Moon, so remaining over one point on the moon's surface requires a considerable uplift force against Endor's gravity. Initially, the station was supported by a repulsorlift field projected from the same ground facility that would eventually supply the station with its defensive shield. Tales told by Ewok shamans relate that the extra weight on the moon's crust had dramatic side effects, including massive groundquakes, land that shifted and buckled, and lakes that spilled out of their natural basins. After crushing the Rebel Alliance, the Emperor plans to send massive fleets to the Alliance-sympathetic worlds of Chandrila and Mon Cala, blockading both planets until the battle station's completion. The subsequent obliteration of these rebel hotbeds, Palpatine is certain, will prevent future insurgents from ever daring to challenge Imperial rule again.

ELABORATE TRAP

From the start, it is the Emperor's plan to lure the rebels into a trap. By deliberately sabotaging supply convoys, Palpatine's agents delay construction of the second Death Star, thus creating the impression that it is vulnerable to attack. To bolster this subterfuge, Imperial agents see to it that Bothan spies are provided with disinformation regarding the state of readiness of the battle fortress' superlaser. The Emperor sees his plans nearing fruition: his forces will cripple the Alliance, and witnessing this disaster will leave the son of Anakin Skywalker vulnerable to the Sith's lures. In rapid order the Alliance will die and Palpatine will gain a younger, more powerful apprentice.

SITH STRONGHOLD

The throne room's design echoes that of Palpatine's headquarters in Coruscant's Imperial Palace, formerly the Jedi Temple. His receiving chamber's plush chairs and curious artworks belie the cold nature of the throne room beyond, and the Imperial Guards admit only those who have been summoned to audience.

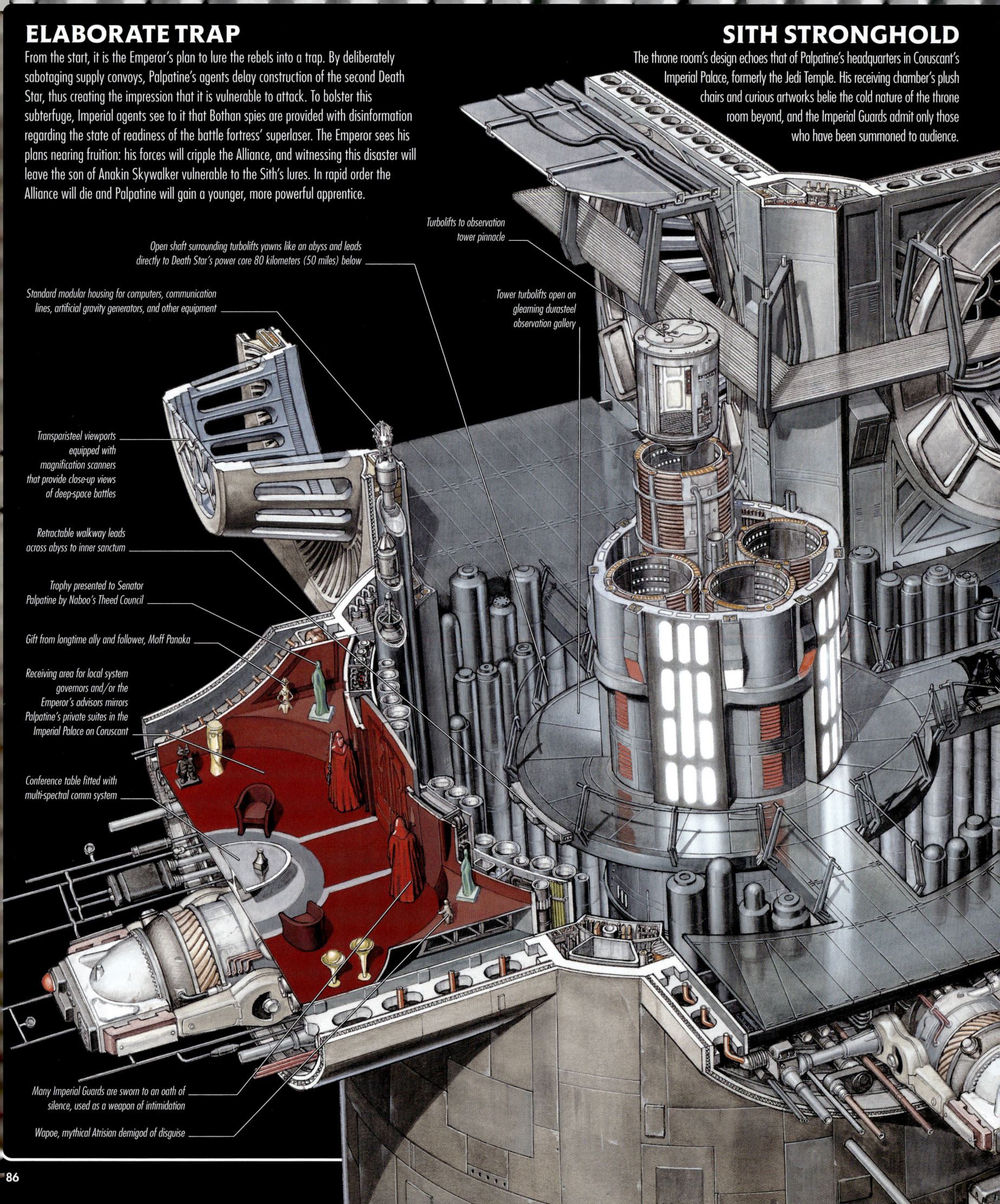

- Open shaft surrounding turbolifts yawns like an abyss and leads directly to Death Star's power core 80 kilometers (50 miles) below
- Standard modular housing for computers, communication lines, artificial gravity generators, and other equipment
- Turbolifts to observation tower pinnacle
- Tower turbolifts open on gleaming durasteel observation gallery
- Transparisteel viewports equipped with magnification scanners that provide close-up views of deep-space battles
- Retractable walkway leads across abyss to inner sanctum
- Trophy presented to Senator Palpatine by Naboo's Theed Council
- Gift from longtime ally and follower, Moff Panaka
- Receiving area for local system governors and/or the Emperor's advisors mirrors Palpatine's private suites in the Imperial Palace on Coruscant
- Conference table fitted with multi-spectral comm system
- Many Imperial Guards are sworn to an oath of silence, used as a weapon of intimidation
- Wapoe, mythical Atrisian demigod of disguise

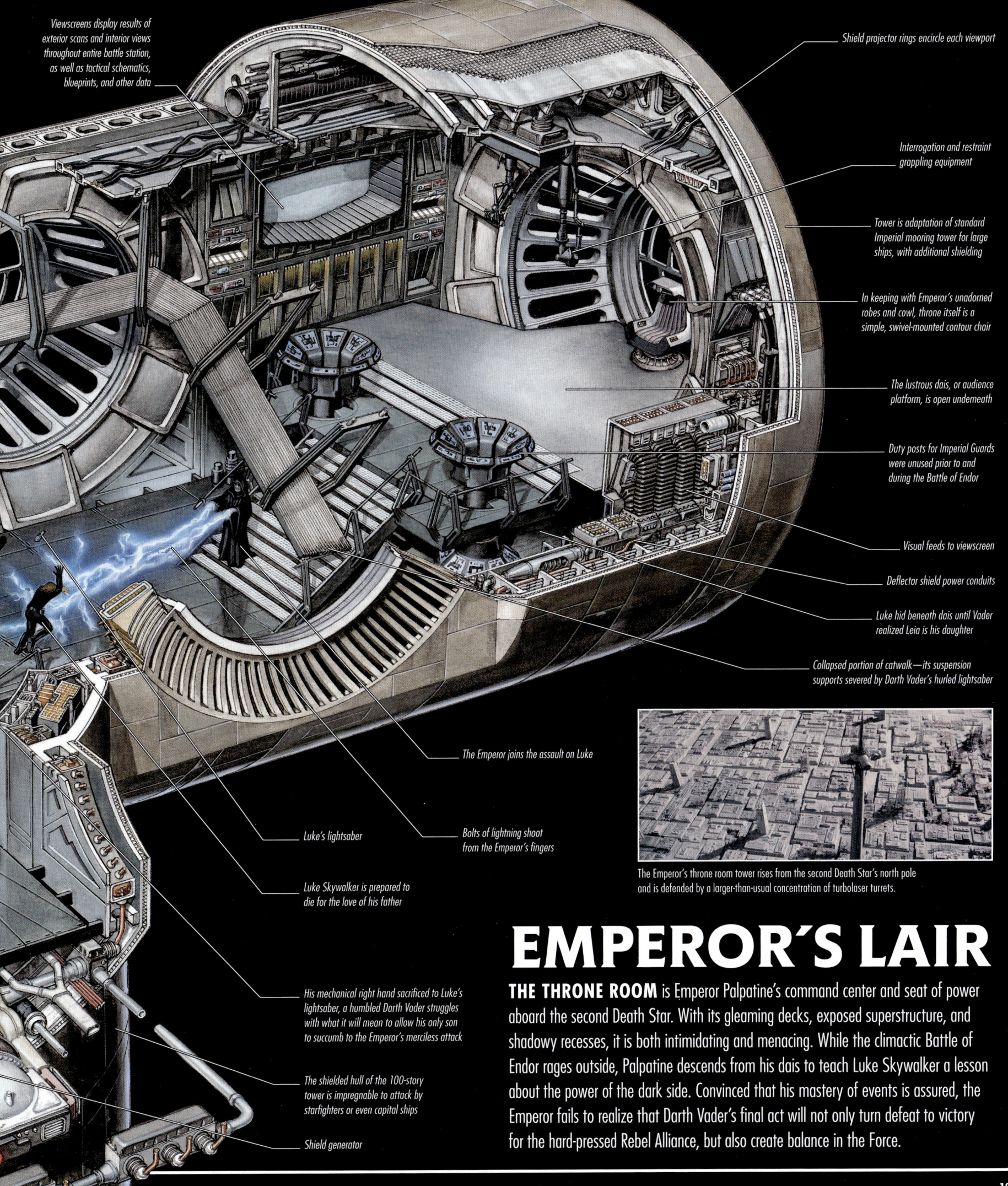

EMPEROR'S LAIR

THE THRONE ROOM is Emperor Palpatine's command center and seat of power aboard the second Death Star. With its gleaming decks, exposed superstructure, and shadowy recesses, it is both intimidating and menacing. While the climactic Battle of Endor rages outside, Palpatine descends from his dais to teach Luke Skywalker a lesson about the power of the dark side. Convinced that his mastery of events is assured, the Emperor fails to realize that Darth Vader's final act will not only turn defeat to victory for the hard-pressed Rebel Alliance, but also create balance in the Force.

EXECUTOR COMMAND TOWER

RAISED ON A THICK STALK above the *Executor's* dorsal technoscape, the 285 meter (935 feet)-wide command tower is practically a ship in its own right. It houses a profusion of vital components, including shield generators, communications systems, and sensor arrays, as well as officers' quarters, briefing rooms, and escape pods for the vessel's upper-echelon commanders. Just above the centerline of its forward face sits the command bridge. Standing on the bridge of this gigantic warship, its commander can call on almost unimaginable power, in the process embodying both the glory and wrath of the Empire.

Ship crew stationed at consoles below the Executor's command bridge walkway toil under the withering scrutiny of Lord Vader.

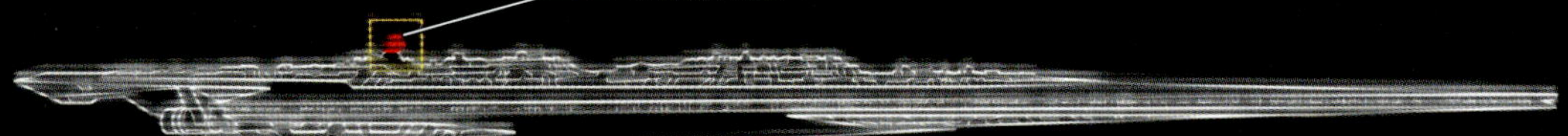

FATAL FLAW

With its gleaming command walkway and 2 meter (6.5 feet)-tall transparisteel viewports, the *Executor's* bridge provides unobstructed views of quarries and kills. The ship's shielding—driven by the power of its massive reactor—makes such displays of Imperial arrogance possible. Yet the vessel is not impregnable. At Endor, pounded mercilessly by the capital ships of the Rebel Alliance flotilla, the ship's shields fail. At that moment, the rebels are able to strafe the command tower—and with the *Executor's* navigation suite in ruins and defensive guns losing coordination, a careening A-wing destroys the bridge.

- Command tower
- Bridge tower's main computer deck
- Tracking array controls and processors
- Atmosphere tanks
- Surge capacitor
- Power relays
- Local-area shield projector vanes
- Hyperwave transceiver coils
- Long-range scanners feed targeting information to the ship's weapons systems
- Stabilizer beams
- Power feeds
- Command tower generator
- Port and starboard power trunking
- Comm/scan power modulator
- Turbolift clusters
- Officers' mess
- Life-pod launcher tubes
- Escape hatch
- Heat-sink panels

- High-pressure gas mix in chamber aids oxygen absorption by scarred lungs
- Transfusion inlets/outlets
- Diagnostics and life-support computers
- Dedicated servos lift helmet and mask
- High-bandwidth communications consoles
- Air tubes to compressor, which provides gas mix
- Data feeds

MEDITATION CHAMBER

Darth Vader has the *Executor* equipped with a hyperbaric pod—or meditation chamber—for his own use during space voyages. Inside the spherical chamber, he is free to rid himself of the fearsome mask he has chosen as his brand, and to allow his horribly scarred face and head to feel fresh air. While his artificial breathing mechanisms are maintained and recharged, Vader exercises his severely damaged lungs, aided by a high-pressure air mix in the chamber.

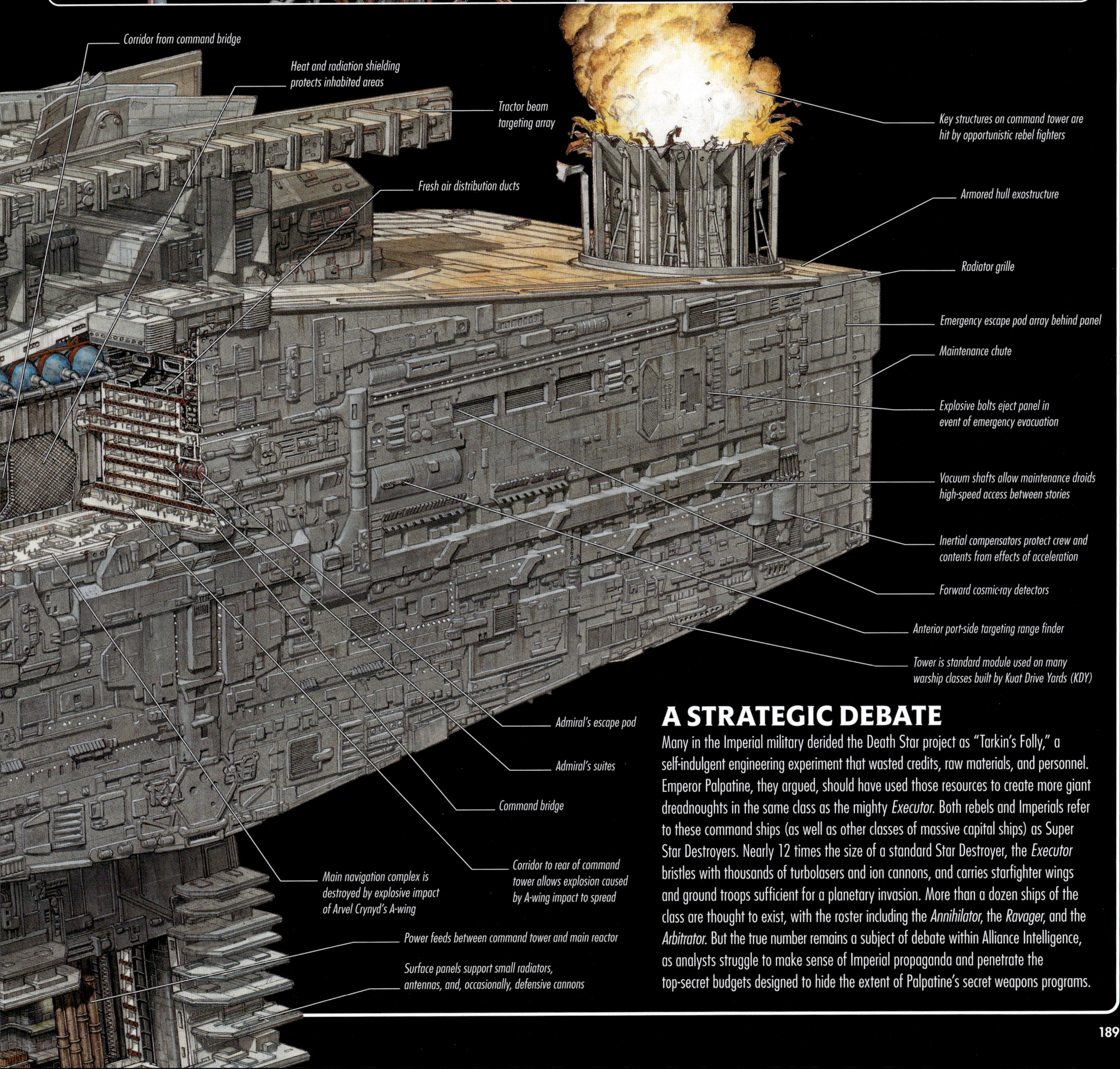

- Corridor from command bridge
- Heat and radiation shielding protects inhabited areas
- Tractor beam targeting array
- Fresh air distribution ducts
- Key structures on command tower are hit by opportunistic rebel fighters
- Armored hull exostructure
- Radiator grille
- Emergency escape pod array behind panel
- Maintenance chute
- Explosive bolts eject panel in event of emergency evacuation
- Vacuum shafts allow maintenance droids high-speed access between stories
- Inertial compensators protect crew and contents from effects of acceleration
- Forward cosmic-ray detectors
- Anterior port-side targeting range finder
- Tower is standard module used on many warship classes built by Kuat Drive Yards (KDY)
- Admiral's escape pod
- Admiral's suites
- Command bridge
- Corridor to rear of command tower allows explosion caused by A-wing impact to spread
- Main navigation complex is destroyed by explosive impact of Arvel Crynyd's A-wing
- Power feeds between command tower and main reactor
- Surface panels support small radiators, antennas, and, occasionally, defensive cannons

A STRATEGIC DEBATE

Many in the Imperial military derided the Death Star project as "Tarkin's Folly," a self-indulgent engineering experiment that wasted credits, raw materials, and personnel. Emperor Palpatine, they argued, should have used those resources to create more giant dreadnoughts in the same class as the mighty *Executor*. Both rebels and Imperials refer to these command ships (as well as other classes of massive capital ships) as Super Star Destroyers. Nearly 12 times the size of a standard Star Destroyer, the *Executor* bristles with thousands of turbolasers and ion cannons, and carries starfighter wings and ground troops sufficient for a planetary invasion. More than a dozen ships of the class are thought to exist, with the roster including the *Annihilator*, the *Ravager*, and the *Arbitrator*. But the true number remains a subject of debate within Alliance Intelligence, as analysts struggle to make sense of Imperial propaganda and penetrate the top-secret budgets designed to hide the extent of Palpatine's secret weapons programs.

THE NEW REPUBLIC

In the time after the Battle of Endor, the Alliance to Restore the Republic transitions itself to the New Republic, the earnest stewards of the galaxy. Recovery and restoration efforts unfold across the stars under this new regime, aiding worlds especially afflicted by the Empire's tyranny like Kashyyyk, whose forests and inhabitants suffered greatly under occupation. Imperial remnants hold out in the Unknown Regions and on the fringes of the galaxy, causing unrest on worlds such as Nevarro. In even more remote places in the galaxy, a new stormtrooper program takes shape and the dead Emperor's contingency plan unfolds. The hidden Sith world of Exegol produces clones of Palpatine, such as the enigmatic Supreme Leader Snoke, who is used to twist the mind of the impressionable Ben Solo, the Force-sensitive son of Han Solo and Leia Organa.

On Ossus, Luke Skywalker's hard-earned Jedi temple crumbles and Ben falls to darkness, becoming Kylo Ren. Under Snoke's leadership and with an all-new army of stormtroopers, the First Order forms with the express directive to spread order to the galaxy. While the New Republic relies on diplomacy out of fear of triggering another war, a Resistance forms with the hope of defending the galaxy against this latest threat. At the forefront of the movement is none other than Leia Organa, who is eager to find her long-lost brother, Luke Skywalker, in the hopes that they can save Ben and defeat this new evil together. After the First Order uses their superweapon, the Starkiller, to destroy the entire Hosnian system where the New Republic government is residing, the Resistance scrambles their fighters before their base on D'Qar becomes the next target. With the help of a recently deserted stormtrooper called Finn and a scavenger from Jakku named Rey, the Resistance successfully destroy Starkiller Base and acquire a portion of a map leading to Luke's location.

This leads to the discovery that through his careful scheming, the dead Emperor lives again! Pulling the strings once more, Palpatine reveals his ultimate plan to use his Final Order fleet, which is equipped with planet-killing weapons, to destroy any and all worlds not loyal to him, making an example out of Kijimi. This ruthlessness inspires the galaxy to rise up, with Rey and the redeemed Ben Solo taking on Palpatine, and ace pilot Poe Dameron and Finn leading the charge against the fleet. In the end, the Resistance and people from across the galaxy win the fight against evil by showing their oppressors that they're stronger when they stand together.

THE MANDALORIAN AND THE CHILD

Early into the New Republic era, an Imperial remnant comes into conflict with a local bounty hunter named Din Djarin, who is in possession of an asset they require. The asset in question is a special child called Grogu, to whom Djarin quickly becomes attached. The Imperial remnant attacks Nevarro City in order to retrieve the child, using flamethrowers to intimidate and burn down buildings. In the end, Djarin protects and saves Grogu.

NEVARRO

SITUATED IN THE OUTER RIM, Nevarro maintains significance in the galaxy thanks to its proximity to a popular trade route called the Hydian Way. The planet is made up of lava fields and oceans, appearing bruised and scarred from space. With much of Nevarro covered in volcanic terrain, residents make the most of places they can comfortably inhabit, such as its capital, Nevarro City. Throughout most of history, Nevarro has gone unnoticed, but in the early years of the New Republic, the capital becomes a boom town.

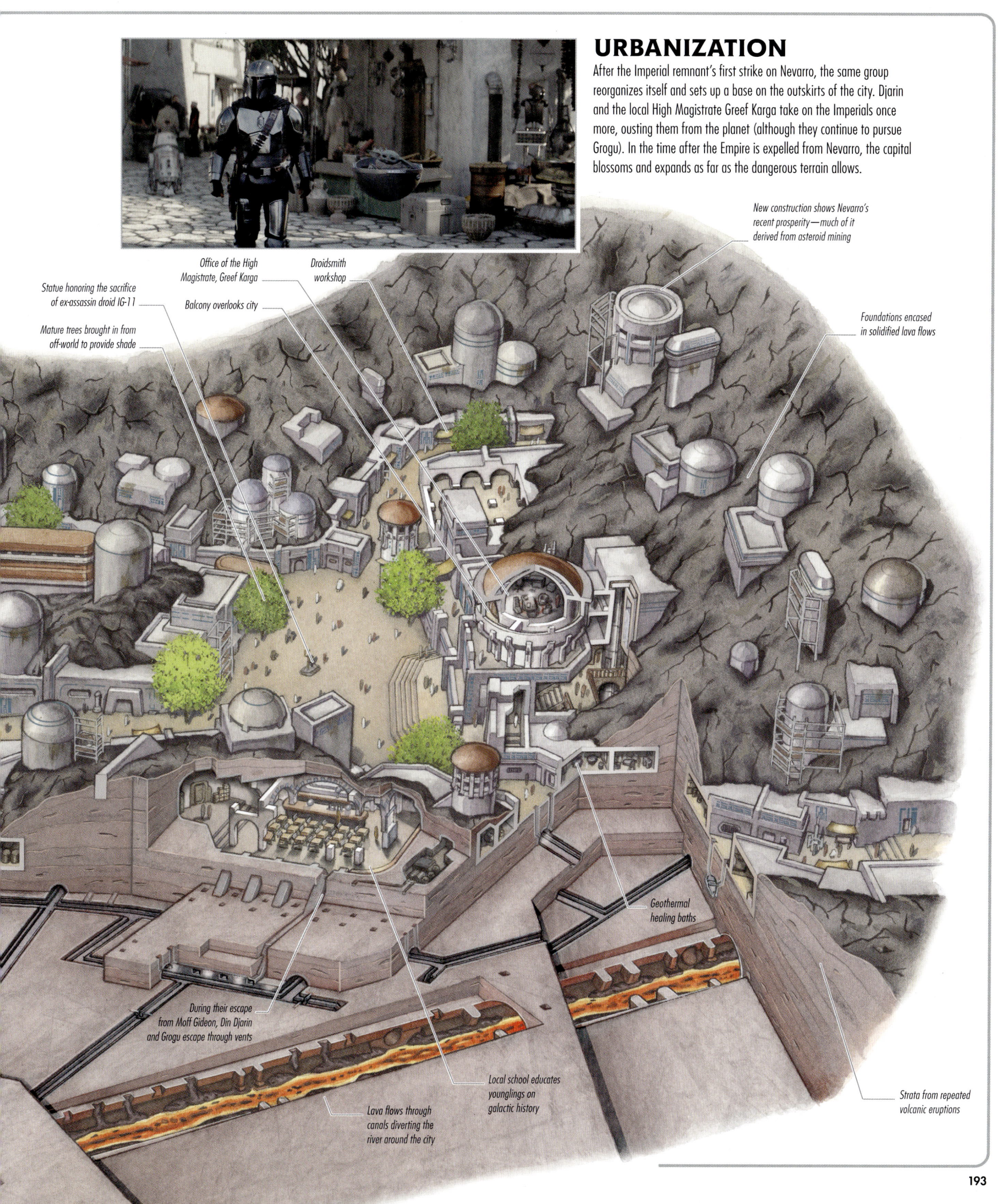

URBANIZATION

After the Imperial remnant's first strike on Nevarro, the same group reorganizes itself and sets up a base on the outskirts of the city. Djarin and the local High Magistrate Greef Karga take on the Imperials once more, ousting them from the planet (although they continue to pursue Grogu). In the time after the Empire is expelled from Nevarro, the capital blossoms and expands as far as the dangerous terrain allows.

- Office of the High Magistrate, Greef Karga
- Droidsmith workshop
- Statue honoring the sacrifice of ex-assassin droid IG-11
- Balcony overlooks city
- Mature trees brought in from off-world to provide shade
- New construction shows Nevarro's recent prosperity—much of it derived from asteroid mining
- Foundations encased in solidified lava flows
- Geothermal healing baths
- During their escape from Moff Gideon, Din Djarin and Grogu escape through vents
- Local school educates younglings on galactic history
- Lava flows through canals diverting the river around the city
- Strata from repeated volcanic eruptions

JAKKU

A FORLORN WORLD on the edge of settled space, Jakku is a bleak desert globe notable as the site of the Empire's last stand a year after its defeat at Endor. As the battle raged, stricken warships used their tractor beams to lock onto their foes, dragging them down to the surface. A generation later, these wrecks form the Starship Graveyard, picked over by scavengers searching for technology to salvage. Besides scavengers, Jakku is home to religious orders craving solitude, conspiracy theorists peddling wild tales about lost Imperial secrets, and desperate beings seeking to start new lives or escape past misdeeds.

THE GRAVEYARD

The Graveyard is an eerie place, with shattered ships protruding from the sand like silent sentinels, surrounded by the bleached bones of their long-dead crews. The wrecks range from the vast bulk of the mighty Super Star Destroyer *Ravager*, lying broken on its back, to the scattered remains of countless starfighters. Jakku's scavengers lead a perilous existence inside the cavernous hulls, searching for intact components amid razor-sharp metal, spilled toxins, cracked reactors, and unexploded munitions.

ROUTE KEY
- Poe's route
- Finn's route
- BB-8's route
- The Pilgrims' Road
- Rey's route from home to Graveyard
- Rey's route from Graveyard to Niima
- *Millennium Falcon's* escape route

1 Tuanul village is attacked by First Order forces looking for clues to the location of Luke Skywalker. They capture Resistance pilot Poe Dameron, and massacre the villagers.

2 Deep inside the wreck of a crashed Star Destroyer, a scavenger named Rey finds a valuable capacitor bearing, and adds it to her haul of tech to trade at Niima Outpost.

3 Having finished scavenging for the day, Rey returns from Niima Outpost to the wrecked Imperial walker that she calls home, and eats her evening meal.

4 Poe Dameron's droid, BB-8, escaped the massacre at Tuanul, and has made his way to the dunes near Rey's house. Rey rescues him from a surly Teedo scavenger.

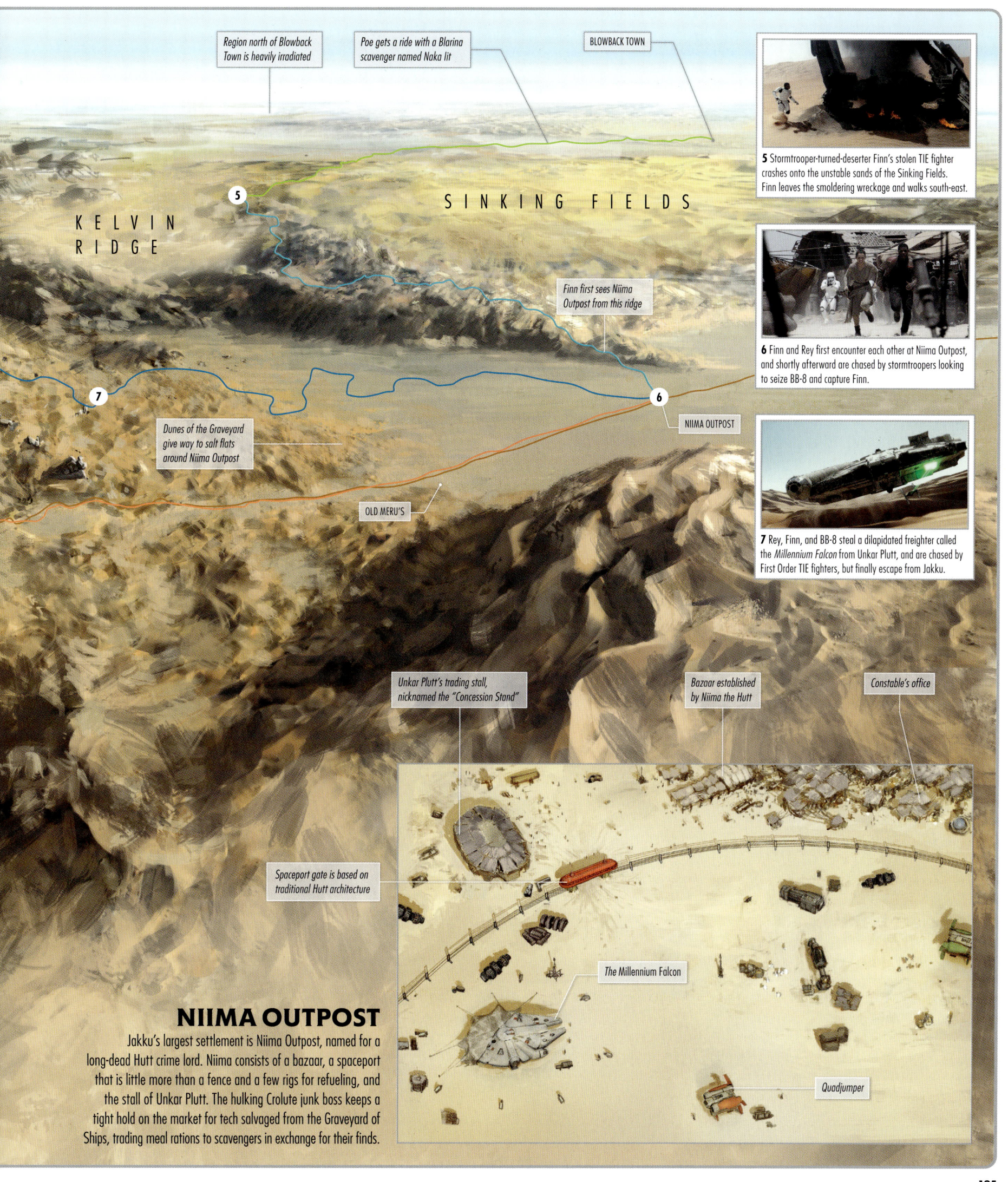

Region north of Blowback Town is heavily irradiated

Poe gets a ride with a Blarina scavenger named Naka Iit

BLOWBACK TOWN

5 Stormtrooper-turned-deserter Finn's stolen TIE fighter crashes onto the unstable sands of the Sinking Fields. Finn leaves the smoldering wreckage and walks south-east.

KELVIN RIDGE

SINKING FIELDS

Finn first sees Niima Outpost from this ridge

6 Finn and Rey first encounter each other at Niima Outpost, and shortly afterward are chased by stormtroopers looking to seize BB-8 and capture Finn.

Dunes of the Graveyard give way to salt flats around Niima Outpost

NIIMA OUTPOST

OLD MERU'S

7 Rey, Finn, and BB-8 steal a dilapidated freighter called the *Millennium Falcon* from Unkar Plutt, and are chased by First Order TIE fighters, but finally escape from Jakku.

Unkar Plutt's trading stall, nicknamed the "Concession Stand"

Bazaar established by Niima the Hutt

Constable's office

Spaceport gate is based on traditional Hutt architecture

The Millennium Falcon

Quadjumper

NIIMA OUTPOST

Jakku's largest settlement is Niima Outpost, named for a long-dead Hutt crime lord. Niima consists of a bazaar, a spaceport that is little more than a fence and a few rigs for refueling, and the stall of Unkar Plutt. The hulking Crolute junk boss keeps a tight hold on the market for tech salvaged from the Graveyard of Ships, trading meal rations to scavengers in exchange for their finds.

REY'S HOME

REY HAS MADE a home for herself in a toppled Imperial walker in Jakku's Goazon Badlands. The downed AT-AT has been stripped of its valuable components and now serves as shelter for the capable scavenger. Rey lives in the troop compartment, which is simultaneously her kitchen, bedroom, and workroom. To defend against intruders, she has welded the AT-AT's hatches shut, coming and going through the auxiliary hatch in the walker's belly. Buried sensors alert her to visitors, but Jakku's scavengers mostly stay away, wary of traps she's reportedly installed in her home and her willingness to use the quarterstaff she carries for self-defense.

- Rey's speeder
- Battle damage covered by curtain
- Speeder garage formed from empty engine compartment
- Salvaged Y-wing flight computer
- Troop seating
- Lamps crafted from nightwatcher-worm casings by Tuanul village artisan
- Hammock woven by Rey as a child
- Rey has welded this escape hatch shut
- Auxiliary belly hatch serves as front door
- Stove
- Electroshock traps rigged to entrance passage
- Solar array crafted from TIE fighter parts
- Eksoan power generator links to homemade solar array

CASUALTY OF WAR

While in Imperial service, the AT-AT Rey now calls home was designated Hellhound 2, and formed part of the military complement of the Star Destroyer *Interrogator*. Rey discovered this information in the craft's troop manifest, but has never found any sign of what happened to the stormtroopers, pilots, or their commanders—they, like so many others, were apparently casualties of the chaotic Battle of Jakku decades earlier. Rey has salvaged fuel cells from the AT-AT's laser-cannon energizer and from two wrecked speeder bikes, then wired them to scavenged TIE solar panels. This homemade power system feeds her home's generator, though the cobbled-together system requires constant maintenance.

SCAVENGER'S WORK

While at home, Rey spends most of her time at her workbench. She prefers cleaning and refurbishing parts here to using Unkar Plutt's washing tables in Niima Outpost because the junk boss charges for the use of his facilities. By working at home, Rey can gain more portions in exchange for her salvage, lessening Unkar's power over her. Rey's work area also includes an old Y-wing computer that she uses to study ship schematics, run flight simulations, and practice alien languages and droidspeak.

Rey reacts angrily when she discovers a Teedo capturing an astromech near her home. Jakku's Teedos have always respected her territory and kept out of it. Rey knows if she doesn't protest this one's intrusion, she'll soon have problems.

As well as its remote location, Rey chose Hellhound 2 as her home because its heat shielding has remained largely intact. This allows her to work within its interior without being cooked by the heat of a Jakku day.

- Top hatch with cryptographic lock protects head, where Rey keeps her most valuable items
- Cooling unit for perishables
- AT-AT pilot control panel
- Medium blaster cannon
- Teedo
- Water barrels (hidden to prevent theft)
- Class II heavy laser cannon
- Fuel storage
- Motion sensors hidden in pile of junk
- Neck is crushed and impassable
- Valuable parts from ankle drive motors salvaged and traded with Unkar Plutt
- Knee joint cover
- Rey likes to rest in shade created by AT-AT's foot
- Terrain sensors in foot have been removed and repurposed as motion sensors
- Scavenged rebel pilot's helmet

After eating a meager meal of rations and inspecting the AT-AT's systems, Rey allows herself a few minutes to sit in the cool evening. Soon it will be time to return to her workbench. But for a little while, she lets herself dream, imagining that tomorrow will be the day that she escapes Jakku.

MAZ'S CASTLE

THE GALAXY HAS no shortage of strange watering holes, but Maz Kanata's fortress might be the strangest. The diminutive Kanata has welcomed visitors to her home on the planet Takodana for centuries, offering them a safe haven from pursuers and a respite from galactic quarrels. Maz offers her visitors food and drink, room and board, medical assistance, repairs to droids and starships, loans and appraisals, entertainment, and information. Her castle also serves as a hub for deal-making, with everyone from pirates and smugglers to information brokers and diplomats striking agreements at her tables. Deals are witnessed and sealed by ME-8D9, an ancient protocol droid who enforces the castle's rules and ensures that Maz gets her cut of any bargain struck within her halls.

THE RULES

Visitors to the castle will notice a simple warning posted in numerous galactic languages: NO FIGHTING. Those who violate this principal commandment will find themselves turned away the next time they visit, and Maz has a long memory. The castle's other rules are unwritten but passed down to new visitors: one night's food, drink, and shelter are free to all, with no questions asked. After that, you have to pay—and cheaters may find themselves rethinking their lives in Maz's dungeons. Maz has seen galactic regimes rise and fall, and insists on keeping Takodana neutral ground as conflicts engulf the galaxy beyond her castle's walls.

"DON'T STARE"

Maz's castle is an overwhelming place for new arrivals. Musicians, poets, and artists take turns on the stage; laughter, boasts, and curses rise from the gambling tables as sabacc cards are thrown down and chance cubes tumble; and the kitchens conjure up cuisine and grog suitable for countless species' digestive systems. And that's just the public spaces of the castle: away from prying eyes, pirate captains search for brave young deckhands, explorers and fortune-hunters barter secret hyperspace routes, and those seeking illegal solutions to underworld problems find no shortage of helpers. Meanwhile, spies of every affiliation gather information for their masters.

STORIES AND SECRETS

Maz sees every visitor as a source of stories, delighting in the experiences of grizzled war heroes and wide-eyed young dreamers alike. Her castle's storehouses and vaults overflow with objects that have piqued her interest over the centuries: antique weapons wielded by lost heroes, indecipherable poems from extinct species, icons of vanished religions, and maps to dead worlds. Maz protects objects that speak to her, guided by a certainty that one day her relics will call out to other searchers.

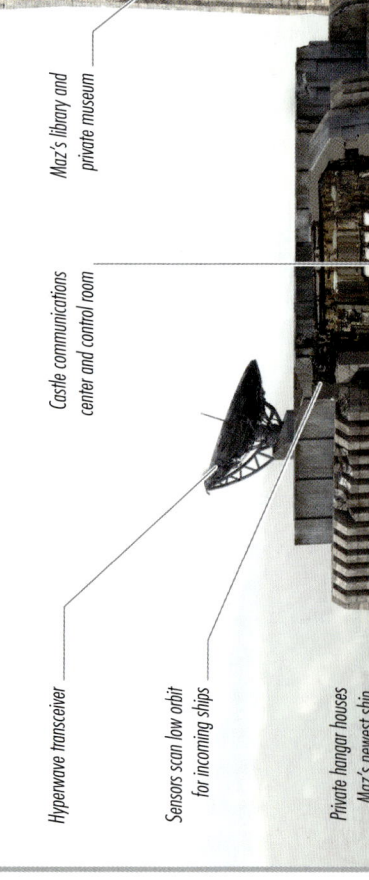

Ancient power generators in tower collect energy from Takodana's storms

Laboratory rented by Thromba and Laparo, Frigosian cryptosurgeons—Maz prefers not to ask what they use it for

Maz's quarters

Statue of Maz is a (relatively) recent addition to the castle, a gift from a former husband

Private banquet hall

Private casinos

Prayer flags hung by deep-space explorers

Rumors of strange beasts in the surrounding forests keep guests within the castle walls

Maz's library and private museum

Castle communications center and control room

Hyperwave transceiver

Sensors scan low orbit for incoming ships

Private hangar houses Maz's newest ship, the Epoch Swift

FIRST ORDER ASSAULT

Maz's castle is built on the site of an ancient battle between the Jedi and the Sith. For centuries the powers of the galaxy have respected its neutrality, sparing its stone halls and soaring towers from war. In its determination to annihilate the New Republic and destroy the Resistance, the First Order ignores this tradition, sending TIE fighters to blast the castle to rubble. Standing among her shocked guests, Maz calmly vows to clean up the mess and continue as she always has.

Labels: Maz's office; Observation deck; Main kitchen, staffed by Strono "Cookie" Tuggs; Bar serving counter; Storage room; Castle sub-level; Crypt containing Luke Skywalker's lightsaber; Castle's lowest level is largely untouched since time of Jedi occupation; Sealed crypt containing remains of fallen Jedi; Holding cell for those who break Maz's rules; Ancient defensive passageways; Han Solo, Rey, Finn, and BB-8 walk toward castle entrance; Flags include padracing pennants and Mandalorian war banners; Spa and sauna; Water filtration system and brewery; Guest dormitories; Premium guest suites.

RESISTANCE BASE

REBEL PILOTS DISCOVERED D'Qar prior to the Battle of Yavin, but the remote planet only housed a small Alliance outpost during the Galactic Civil War. Seeking a home for her new Resistance movement, Leia Organa remembered D'Qar and sent engineers to expand the facility. Much of the base is underground, with the jungle planet's thick foliage hiding the facility from the air and sensor countermeasures concealing power leaks and other evidence of its presence. Remembering the Alliance's near-extinction on Hoth, Leia has insisted on portable equipment that can be evacuated ahead of an attacking First Order fleet.

The Resistance base's resemblance to the famed rebel headquarters on Yavin 4 appeals to Leia and the other rebel veterans on her staff.

- Sturdy earthworks protect upper hangars
- Ventilation shaft
- Medcenter staffed by Doctor Kalonia
- Base command center with holographic command interface
- Command center entrance concealed in ruins
- Memorial wall in base records names of Resistance personnel lost in conflict
- Subterranean maintenance hangars used for major refits and storage
- Personnel quarters
- Upper hangars used for simple repairs and loading of ordnance
- Poe Dameron's customized T-70 X-wing, Black One
- Hangar elevator lowers ship to maintenance level

LIVING WORLD

D'Qar lacks intelligent life but teems with other varieties: huge trees rise from its steamy jungles, great flocks of avians darken the skies, and the night is alive with the howls of creatures and the thrum of insects. The base occupies a small footprint, both to avoid detection and to keep from disturbing the harmony of this lush refuge. The jungle is relentless, with fast-growing tree roots squeezing through seams in base corridors and chambers. Leia finds such intrusions strangely comforting: nature continues to thrive even as the galaxy descends into conflict.

REBELS ONCE MORE

After the Battle of Endor, Princess Leia Organa was hailed as a rebel hero. But she soon found herself shut out of the New Republic she had fought to restore. Her protests about disarming the fleet were dismissed as paranoia, while her warnings about the First Order's intentions were derided as warmongering. Convinced that a new darkness threatened the galaxy, Leia gathered former Alliance compatriots—many of them also sidelined by a new generation of New Republic leaders—and formed the Resistance.

- D'Qar vegetation had to be cleared when base was first reoccupied
- Mountain conceals observation post
- Long-range sensor tower
- Hyperwave transceiver
- The Millennium Falcon
- Pipeline from deep-level fuel reservoir
- Vober Dand, Chief of Ground Logistics Division
- Encrypted nav-beacon
- Portable power generator
- Boxes contain starship components for rapid repairs
- Sensor jamming array masks base's sensor signature
- Proton torpedoes ready for loading
- Jury-rigged speeders are used to transport personnel and munitions

FIRST ORDER MILITARY

FOR MANY YEARS, the First Order has been secretly amassing a vast military, waiting patiently for the day when it could launch a devastating surprise attack and destroy its enemies. That day has now come. Across the Unknown Regions, stormtroopers prepare for battle and fleets of warships gather. With the New Republic deluded into thinking the First Order poses no threat, the First Order stands poised to conquer an unsuspecting galaxy.

LEGIONS REBORN

The First Order's stormtroopers are not the poorly trained garrison troops that made up large parts of the Imperial army. Constantly drilled and indoctrinated from birth, these are soldiers at the peak of effectiveness. They are equipped with the finest weaponry and have been taught to regard the New Republic with a hatred bordering on the fanatical. The creation of new stormtroopers clearly violates the Galactic Concordance treaty between the New Republic and First Order, but by the time the Republic realizes it has been deceived, it will be far too late.

STAR DESTROYERS

The First Order made the construction of new shipyards within the Unknown Regions a priority, and within a relatively short time these yards were producing huge new capital ships. While the fleet does not rival the Old Empire in terms of numbers, the ships themselves are a significant improvement. The *Resurgent*-class, as they have been named, are much larger than an Imperial Star Destroyer, carry more starfighters and stormtroopers, have improved defenses, and utilize advanced kyber-crystal-augmented weaponry. They outgun anything in the New Republic fleet by a considerable margin.

ASSAULT LANDERS

First Order strategists argue that the Empire's use of shuttles as troop transports was at best a compromise, and its lack of dedicated assault landers was a serious flaw that resulted in unnecessary casualties. To rectify this, the First Order uses an advanced lander designed from the outset for combat drops into hostile territory. The Atmospheric Assault Lander (AAL) is more heavily shielded and armored than an Imperial shuttle, and can land and deploy its troops far more rapidly.

STARKILLER BASE

The crowning achievement of the First Order is Starkiller Base. This immense, planet-scale facility is half military command center and half superweapon. Construction has taken many years and consumed vast resources, but the base is now ready for its terrifying unveiling to the wider galaxy. With a single shot, the Starkiller has the power to destroy the entire New Republic government and military command, leaving the First Order free to sweep to its inevitable—and crushing—victory.

TIE FIGHTERS

Although more advanced versions of TIE fighter, like the TIE Interceptor, had entered production by the time the Empire fell, the First Order believed that the original TIE design held ample opportunities for upgrades. Sienar-Jaemus Fleet Systems, a First Order-controlled successor to the infamous Sienar Fleet Systems, was given the task. The addition of shields and more efficient components transformed the TIE into the TIE/fo—a far more versatile and capable fighter. To complement it, the First Order also commissioned a more powerful variant, featuring a heavy weapons turret, two pilots, and a hyperdrive system. This fighter, dubbed the TIE/sf, is reserved for the use of elite Special Forces personnel.

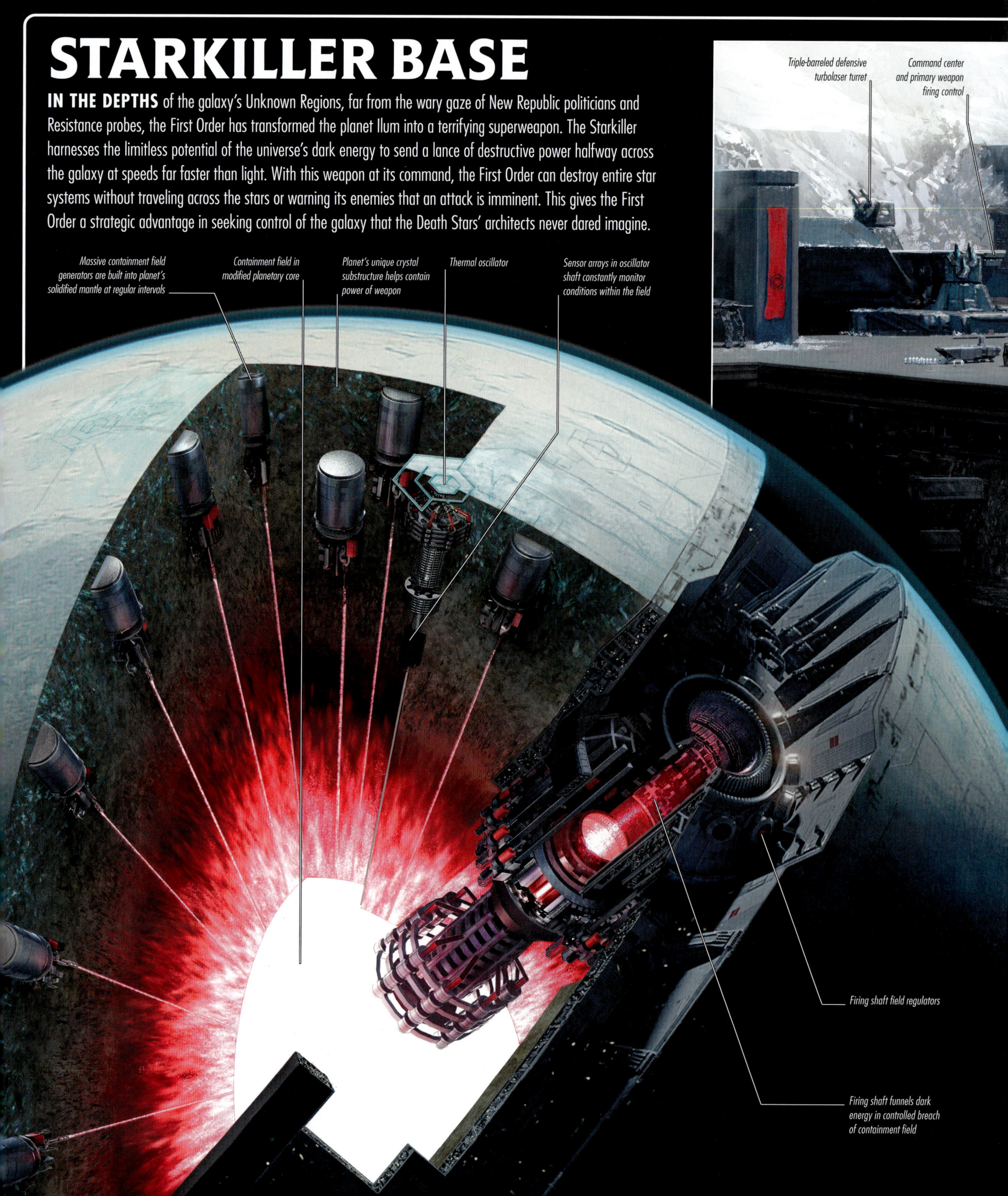

STARKILLER BASE

IN THE DEPTHS of the galaxy's Unknown Regions, far from the wary gaze of New Republic politicians and Resistance probes, the First Order has transformed the planet Ilum into a terrifying superweapon. The Starkiller harnesses the limitless potential of the universe's dark energy to send a lance of destructive power halfway across the galaxy at speeds far faster than light. With this weapon at its command, the First Order can destroy entire star systems without traveling across the stars or warning its enemies that an attack is imminent. This gives the First Order a strategic advantage in seeking control of the galaxy that the Death Stars' architects never dared imagine.

- Massive containment field generators are built into planet's solidified mantle at regular intervals
- Containment field in modified planetary core
- Planet's unique crystal substructure helps contain power of weapon
- Thermal oscillator
- Sensor arrays in oscillator shaft constantly monitor conditions within the field
- Triple-barreled defensive turbolaser turret
- Command center and primary weapon firing control
- Firing shaft field regulators
- Firing shaft funnels dark energy in controlled breach of containment field

Assembly chamber where Kylo Ren and General Hux contact Supreme Leader Snoke

Rostrum from which Hux addresses First Order personnel

Banner with First Order symbol

Parade ground/landing platform

Main hangar

TIE fighters in conveyor mechanism to parade ground level

Interrogation room where Rey is held

Stormtrooper barracks

Officers' quarters

Maintenance hangar

A FATEFUL ORDER

The First Order's Supreme Leader Snoke is infuriated when he learns that BB-8 and the map to Luke Skywalker will likely soon be in the hands of the Resistance. Eager to prevent Skywalker's return, Snoke agrees to General Armitage Hux's proposal to unveil the Starkiller by destroying the New Republic capital of Hosnian Prime. Hux predicts this vicious attack will cripple the New Republic and force the Resistance to respond, revealing its hidden base of operations and giving the Starkiller its next target.

Addressing a rally at Starkiller Base's command center, General Hux declares that the last day of the Republic is at hand, and the galaxy's star systems will soon bow to the First Order.

FIERCE MACHINE

The Starkiller weapon draws on decades of secret Imperial research into harnessing the potential of dark energy. A collector on one side of the planet gathers dark energy from a host star and redirects it into the planetary core. There, this energy is bound by a containment field created by a combination of the planet's magnetic field and unique crystal substructure, and artificial forces regulated by a thermal oscillator. A breach is then opened in the field, funneling the dark energy into a shaft on the planet's other side. This escaping energy takes a form of an astonishingly powerful beam that tunnels through hyperspace itself, its lethal force undiminished even after traveling halfway across the galaxy. A planet is a barely adequate vessel for containing such terrifying power; even the Starkiller's normal operations destabilize the crust of its host, breeding groundquakes and atmospheric disturbances that boil up into vicious storms.

The dark energy collection process is awe-inspiring to witness—vast sheets of flame are drawn down into the planet's core, and smoke and steam rise into the sky from the region around the collector.

STARKILLER BASE CONTINUED

PERILOUS PLAN

The Resistance attack on Starkiller Base exploits weaknesses in the weapon's construction. First, Han Solo approaches at supralight speeds in the *Millennium Falcon*, slipping through the planet's energy shield. It takes Han's phenomenal instincts as a pilot—and a fair measure of Corellian luck—to survive this perilous passage. Han, Chewie, and Finn then target the shield control room, forcing Captain Phasma to bring the shields down so the Resistance's X-wings can attack the weapon's thermal oscillator. But the oscillator's armored housing proves impervious to aerial bombardment; only after Chewie uses detonators to blow a hole through the housing is the oscillator vulnerable to Poe Dameron's attack run. With the oscillator destroyed, Starkiller Base's containment field ruptures, causing the freed dark energy to shatter the planet and engulf its fragments.

Black Leader engaging TIEs of "Tarkin's Revenge" fighter wing

Surrounding region is constantly patrolled by snowtroopers

Armored housing built to withstand any attack

Defensive turbolasers mounted on casing unleash a wall of laser bolts at attacking ships

Trench system holds conduits that link thermal oscillator to containment field generators

Entry to oscillator is controlled remotely as an additional security measure

Anti-ship missile batteries

Poe uses this trench as cover for his final attack run

Thermal oscillator sits in center of vast trench network

KEY TO THE WEAPON

A complex network of generators maintains the containment field inside Starkiller Base's planetary core, linked by conduits in a web of surface trenches. Keeping this field continuously intact would require massive amounts of energy and generate waste heat that would overload the system. Instead, the field oscillates, with each generator cycling on and off as needed. The hexagonal thermal oscillator is the heart of this system, monitoring conditions in the containment field and thermally regulating the generators to preserve stability. When the thermal oscillator is destroyed, the containment field weakens and then fails catastrophically.

Rey and Finn watch confrontation between Han and Kylo

Han Solo confronts Kylo Ren on bridge over oscillator shaft

Dent caused by ineffective proton torpedo impact

Control vanes in oscillator's interior regulate the containment field, allowing it to hold back the forces inside the planet

Communications relay allows oscillator to be controlled remotely from base command center

TIE/sf space superiority fighter

Resistance pilots have been told to expect at least 80% casualties

STOLEN WORLD

Starkiller Base was once Ilum, a remote world sacred to the Jedi Order and reached by secret routes. The Empire ruthlessly strip-mined Ilum for its kyber crystals, which it used in the Death Stars' superlasers. Before fleeing into the Unknown Regions, the founders of the First Order secured research logs from the secret Imperial labs that had tested these experimental weapons. With its location revealed, Ilum became the heart of a new secret empire, as the First Order harvested its kyber crystals for use in its war machine before turning the ruined planet into a mobile weapons platform.

Oscillator cooling system

Sensor feeds from deep-level monitoring systems in oscillator shaft

Oscillator shaft is hundreds of kilometers deep

Dampening chambers absorb harmful spikes of dark energy moving up shaft from planet core

AHCH-TO

A PRIMEVAL OCEAN WORLD deep in the galaxy's Unknown Regions, Ahch-To is the site of the first Jedi temple. Ahch-To's location was lost eons ago and most scholars dismissed it as a myth, but Luke Skywalker is convinced it is real and holds the key to understanding how a reborn Jedi Order might best serve the Force. Luke finds Ahch-To with Lor San Tekka's help, but by now his dream of a new Jedi Order has been shattered. The lonely planet becomes the site of his exile, with Luke cutting himself off from the rich currents of the Force that flow so powerfully there.

ANCIENT DUTIES

Ahch-To's temple island is populated by birdlike Lanais, which are distantly related to the ubiquitous porgs. An order of female Lanais known as the Caretakers lives in a hillside village, maintaining the Jedi structures and attending to the planet's now-rare pilgrims—an eons-old charge passed down from matriarch to matriarch. Lanai males spend most of their lives at sea, returning each month for a celebration known as the Festival of Return and giving the Caretakers a respite from their ancient duties.

Beaches where nightkelp is gathered

Blowhole leading to mirror cave

Luke spearfishes from these cliffs

SEA OF PALLASKEA

1 Both the light and dark side of the Force are powerful on the temple island. The Jedi temple is a vergence of the Force's positive energies and a focal point for meditation.

2 The temple's light is opposed by a dark side vergence, a cave of mirrored obsidian in which an unwary Jedi may experience strange visions and the pull of the dark side.

3 The tension between these two powerful vergences attracted the first Jedi, who built stone huts and lived simple lives spent in contemplation of the dual aspects of the Force.

SEEDS OF THE JEDI

Little remains of the first Jedi temple save time-worn meditation plinths, a font depicting the legendary Prime Jedi, and a vertiginous ledge where long-dead Jedi once connected with the Force. Not far away, the hollowed-out trunk of an ancient uneti tree contains a reading chamber and sacred Jedi texts gathered by Luke. The Jedi Master decides to burn the library to end a ceaseless cycle of galactic upheaval, but his resolution falters and the books remain intact.

GALACTIC LUXURY

The sprawling Canto Casino and Racetrack sits at the top of a hill overlooking the rest of Canto Bight. It offers wealthy visitors a choice of casinos, with the Crescent Royale the most prestigious. Gaming tables feature everything from hazard toss to Zinbiddle, as well as fathier racing, a luxury hotel, music venues, spas and saunas, boutiques and bespoke services, and 22 restaurants ready to satisfy the palate of any known sentient galactic species.

1 After escaping from jail, Rose and Finn find themselves in the casino's fathier stables, where they convince the urchins who care for the animals to help stage a diversion.

2 The freed fathiers instinctively head for the track, with Rose and Finn clinging to Vermilion, the herd's matriarch. But then Vermilion makes a hard right across the infield.

Sand Sisters' convent is now pied-a-terre for anonymous Bonadan arms dealer

Piazza Molbro is often closed for fetes

Court of the Sand Sisters is popular for trysts

Workers District

Canto Bight Yacht Club

Landing apron used by yachts

ROUTE KEY
Fathier route ———

FATHIER CHASE

ROSE AND FINN TRAVEL to Canto Bight to find the Master Codebreaker in hopes of saving the Resistance, and are plunged into a glittering world in which the galactic super-rich indulge their passions with little thought for those whose lives have been upended by war. Arrested for leaving their shuttle abandoned on the beach, Finn and Rose escape from jail and make an audacious break for freedom on the backs of fathiers forced to race for gamblers' amusement. It's a night that even the most jaded galactic tourist will never forget witnessing.

Ubialla Gheal's nightclub is very popular

Canto Casino

Racetrack is attached to casino

3 The fathiers smash through the picture window of Ganzer's Grotto and rampage through the casino, scattering gamblers before racing out into the streets of Canto Bight.

4 Vermilion knows where to go, and Rose and Finn hang on tight as the herd pounds down Cabranga Street, wrecking luxury speeders with Canto Bight's police hot on their tails.

Canto Bight Piazza is noted for its Alderaanian chinar trees

5 To evade the police speeders, the fathiers veer off into a warren of narrow alleyways. Rose and Finn can only cringe as the headroom shrinks dangerously.

Blue Wall bar

Sewers connect Canto Bight jail with casino complex

Silken Parlor spa

Café Raduli

Tagge Pavilion

6 A vertiginous leap carries the fathiers to the lower districts' rooftops, drawn to the scent of the grass they can sense beyond the city's noise and stench.

Country retreat owned by Big Sturg Ganna

7 The fathiers crash through the skylight of Zord's Spa and Bathhouse, startling clients paying top Cantocoin for zero-g massages and other restorative pampering.

Klang's Place is a dive rarely visited by tourists

9 Finn exults as the fathiers near the shuttle he and Rose used to reach Cantonica, but his glee turns to despair when blasts from the police speeders turn the craft into a fireball.

Kessen's Alley is notable for its illegal speeder-mod shops

8 The fathiers leap over the city wall and reach the beach. With the city's tumult behind them, they sprint through the sand on a beautiful moonlit night.

10 Vermilion and several of the herd survive a perilous race up the cliff face to the grassy fields on the plateau above. The herd scatters as the police continue their pursuit.

Office of Neepers Panpick, P.I.

11 "NOW IT'S WORTH IT"

Rose and Finn find themselves trapped at the edge of a cliff with police speeders in search of them. Facing the prospect of another arrest and reincarceration, Finn muses that it was worth it to tear up Canto Bight and shake up the sensibilities of its jaded clientele. But Rose finds a quieter note of triumph. She removes Vermilion's saddle and tells the fathier matriarch to go, hoping she and the rest of the herd have enjoyed their brief respite from the racetrack's abuses.

CRAIT

BAIL ORGANA SECRETLY establishes an outpost on the salt-encrusted planet Crait in the early days of the Rebellion, only to have his daughter Leia stumble across it. The Rebel Alliance fortifies Crait as a base after the Battle of Yavin, but abandons its efforts when the Alliance's presence is discovered by an Imperial squad. Years later, a wary Leia chooses not to share Crait's location with the New Republic, keeping it—and a handful of other former rebel bases—secret, in case the political winds blow in a direction she doesn't like. Following the Resistance's retreat from D'Qar, Crait beckons as a refuge for her freedom fighters.

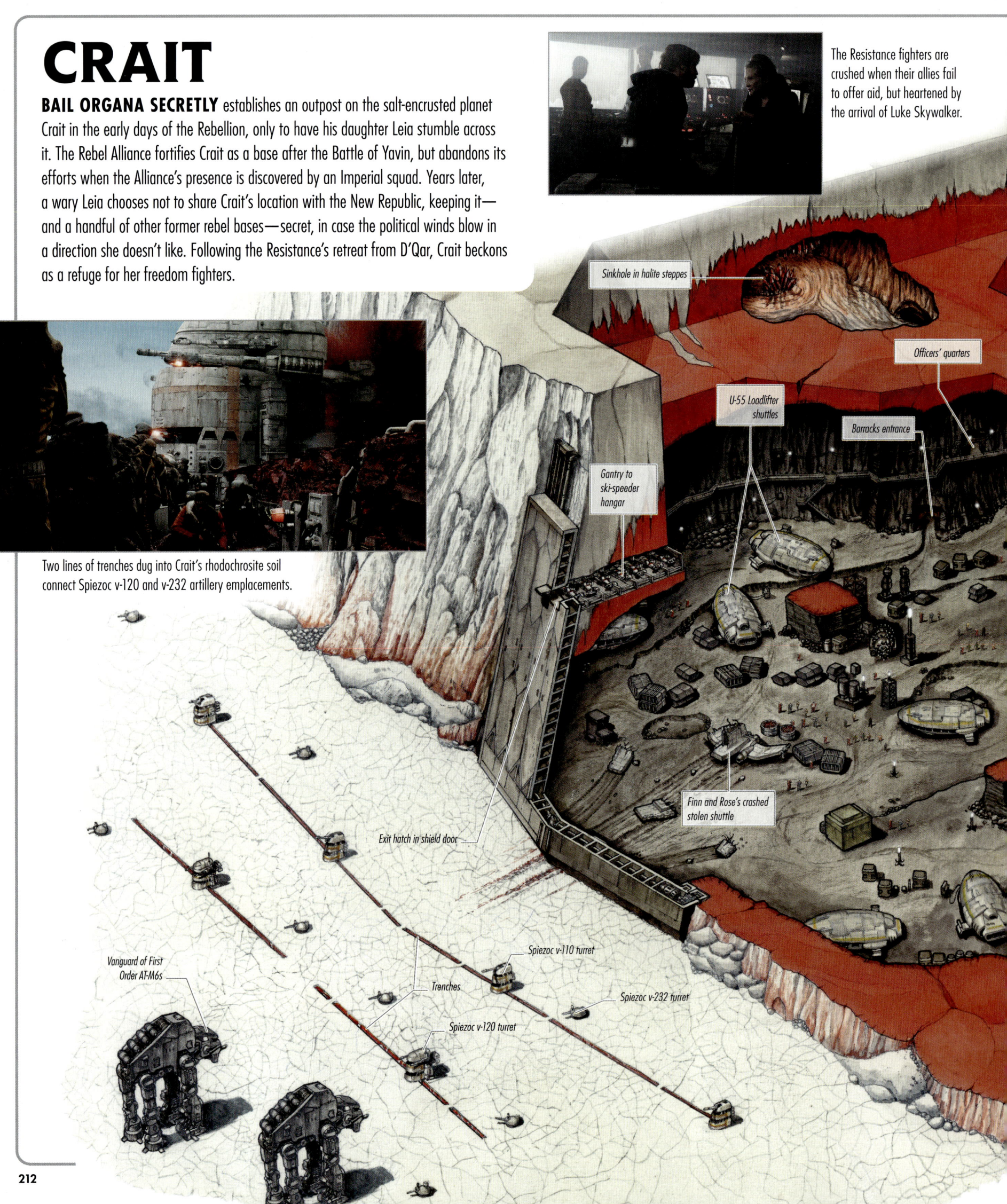

The Resistance fighters are crushed when their allies fail to offer aid, but heartened by the arrival of Luke Skywalker.

Two lines of trenches dug into Crait's rhodochrosite soil connect Spiezoc v-120 and v-232 artillery emplacements.

- Sinkhole in halite steppes
- Officers' quarters
- U-55 Loadlifter shuttles
- Barracks entrance
- Gantry to ski-speeder hangar
- Finn and Rose's crashed stolen shuttle
- Exit hatch in shield door
- Vanguard of First Order AT-M6s
- Trenches
- Spiezoc v-110 turret
- Spiezoc v-232 turret
- Spiezoc v-120 turret

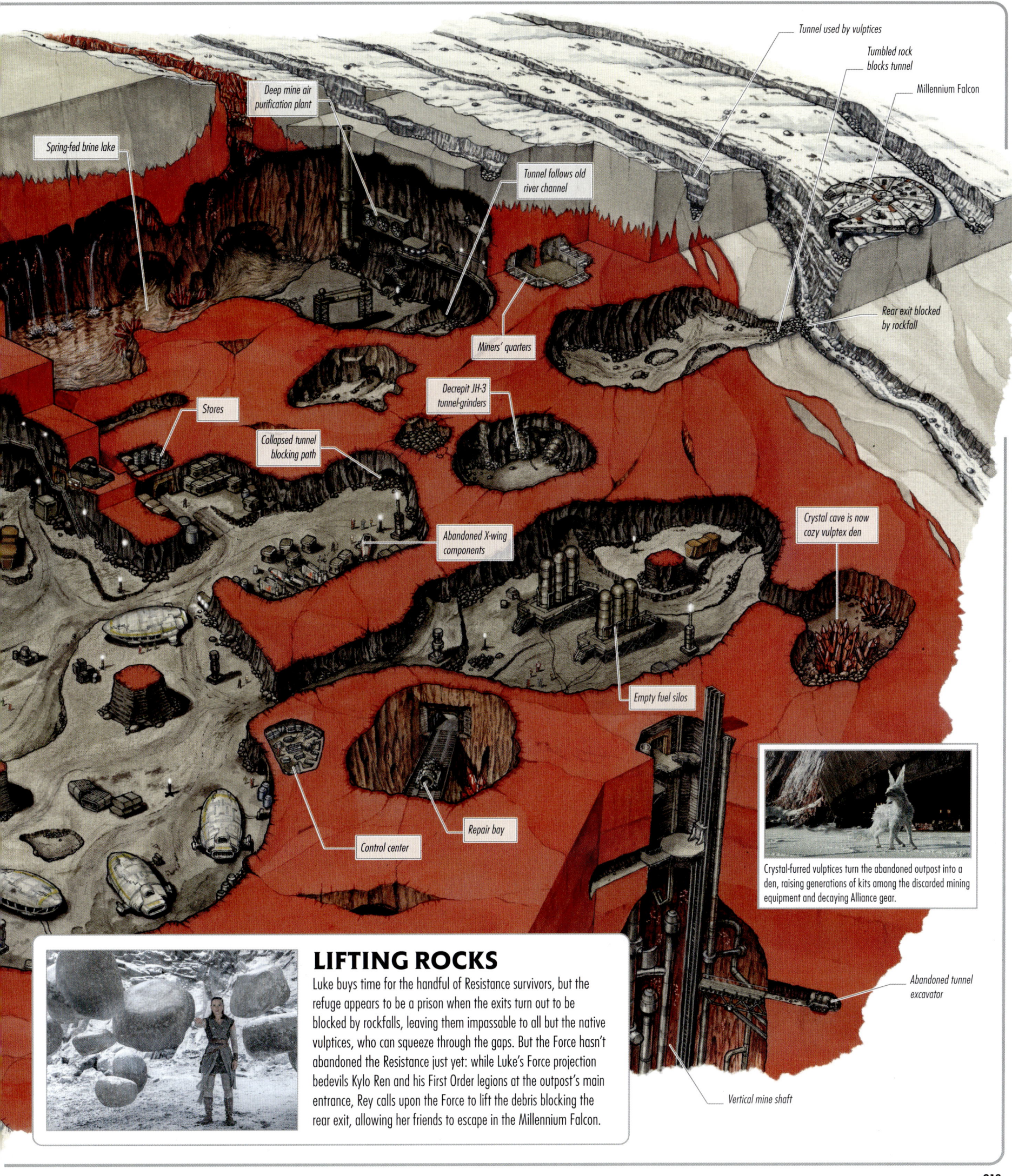

BATTLE OF CRAIT

CRAIT'S DEFENSES include a shield generator, blast doors, and artillery batteries—meager protection against a First Order assault force led by hulking AT-M6s. The Resistance activates the old rebel outpost's shields, which forces the invading First Order army to deploy beyond the protective perimeter and advance overland to engage the enemy, just as the Empire did decades earlier on Hoth. But Kylo Ren's forces have something in their arsenal that Darth Vader lacked—a "battering ram" cannon packing experimental superlaser technology, and dragged across the bright salt flats by AT-HH tug walkers. The Resistance launches rickety ski speeders in a desperate attempt to destroy the cannon before it can be towed into firing range, while ground troops and personnel trapped in the dark, dreary outpost hold out hope that Leia Organa's allies in the Outer Rim will respond to her distress call in this, the Resistance's most desperate hour.

6 Aerial Assault
First Order TIEs join the fray, blasting apart the lightly armored ski speeders.

10 In Range
The cannon fires on the mine. Finn ignores Poe's entreaties and tries to close to point-blank range, but is knocked off course and saved by Rose.

4 Sky Eye
Kylo Ren and General Hux supervise the First Order advance from a shuttle hovering above the battlefield.

IN THE TRENCHES

To slow down the First Order advance, Poe Dameron sends crews to the old artillery batteries installed by the Alliance and orders ground troops into the trenches to thwart a possible advance by snowtroopers and soften up the enemy's line of walkers. But the batteries prove ineffective against the walkers, and Ren keeps his infantry in reserve for the final assault, instead deploying TIE fighters to strafe the trenches and the helpless troops within them. With the artillery emplacements shredded by cannon fire, the surviving Resistance troops have no choice but to fall back and prepare for a last stand in the tunnels of the outpost.

5 Remorseless March
The First Order's AT-M6 and AT-AT walkers march toward the Resistance base largely untouched by the Resistance gun batteries.

The Resistance troops find the Spiezoc batteries' controls caked with rhodochrosite and encrusted with salt, but the robust fire-control systems remain functional despite decades of disuse.

AERIAL ATTACK

The Resistance hastily repairs 13 ski speeders and forms an ad hoc squadron that blasts across the salt flats—mono-skis slice through the white crust as they go, sending up gaudy plumes of crimson soil. But while long-ago rebel techs did wonders outfitting the craft with laser cannons and additional armor, the ski speeders are no match for the walkers or TIEs. Despite the Resistance pilots' bravery, speeder after speeder disintegrates in a barrage of First Order fire.

8 Lured Away
The TIEs pursue the Falcon, freeing the ski speeders to continue their run against the cannon.

11 Showdown
A new arrival enters the fray: Luke Skywalker emerges from the mine to confront Kylo Ren, giving the Resistance time to escape.

2 Trenches
The old rebel trenches offer the Resistance ground troops only minimal cover from enemy fire.

9 Change of Plan
As the Resistance's losses mount, Poe realizes the attack is suicidal and orders a retreat.

3 Mine Defenders
The Resistance manages to get 13 ski speeders airborne to defend the Crait base.

7 Nick of Time
The arrival of the Millennium Falcon saves Rose from being shot down by a trio of TIEs.

1 Blast Door
A massive, armored blast door renders the mine base invulnerable to conventional laser blasts.

Leia's fighters retreat, but an unlikely defender walks out of the outpost to face down the whole First Order... armed only with a laser sword. Using the Force to project his image across the galaxy from Ahch-To fatally weakens Luke Skywalker, but buys crucial time for the Resistance survivors.

SITH CITADEL

RESIDING ON THE HIDDEN world of Exegol, this ancient, trapezoid-shaped citadel is the heart of Palpatine's resurgent Sith empire, featuring a gladiatorial arena, a spiritual cathedral, Sith statuary, and various technologies that maintain the structure. Following the rise of the First Order, the dead Emperor's return is broadcast across the galaxy from the antennas atop this building. With this announcement comes the reveal of Palpatine's Final Order, an enormous fleet of Star Destroyers constructed beneath the world's surface, each equipped with planet-destroying weapons.

EXEGOL

The Sith world of Exegol lies within the Unknown Regions, hidden behind the Galactic Barrier (a maze of dangerous space phenomena). The planet is only reachable via the so-called Red Honeycomb Zone, which was charted eons ago and the route then concealed by the Sith. The planet's turbulent atmosphere is statically charged, causing frequent storms and lightning strikes. In addition to the Sith citadel, the planet's surface includes the Hōsk desert, the Hon Zdawl plateau, and the Sadow escarpment.

HALL OF STATUES

The main hall beneath the citadel houses oversized statues of Sith acolytes, some of whom hold lightsabers with their blades pointed downward. This stance, sometimes attributed to fallen lords of the Sith, is symbolic of their fight against death having ended. Other statues show Sith holding miscellaneous artifacts significant to their lifetime, or posing with their hands pressed together in faith. Although Sith are not necessarily friendly to each other in life, they can be very respectful of their dead, especially those who forged great paths for future generations.

Weathering from the charged dust particles in Exegol's atmosphere has deteriorated the statues' surfaces, blurring the details of the huge stone carvings.

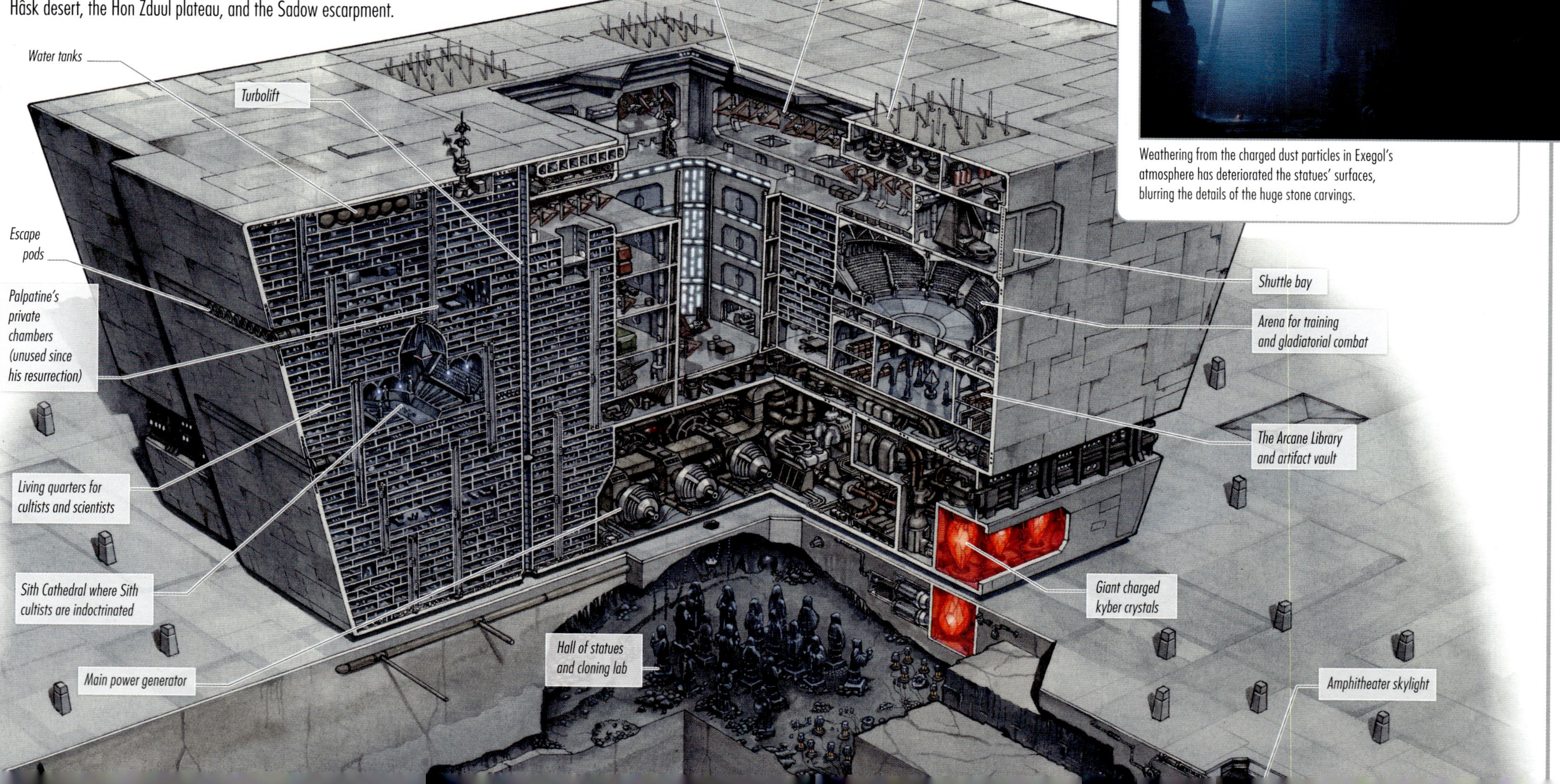

- Amphitheater skylight
- The Arcane library and artifact vault
- Arena for training and gladiatorial combat
- Shuttle bay
- Giant charged kyber crystals
- TIE daggers in launch racks
- Comms antennas
- Central hangar access door
- The lightning-like spikes of the Throne of the Sith were carved by the lightsabers of ancient Sith Lords, symbolising the sinister powers of those who sit upon it.
- Turbolift
- Water tanks
- Escape pods
- Palpatine's private chambers (unused since his resurrection)
- Living quarters for cultists and scientists
- Sith Cathedral where Sith cultists are indoctrinated
- Main power generator
- Hall of statues and cloning lab

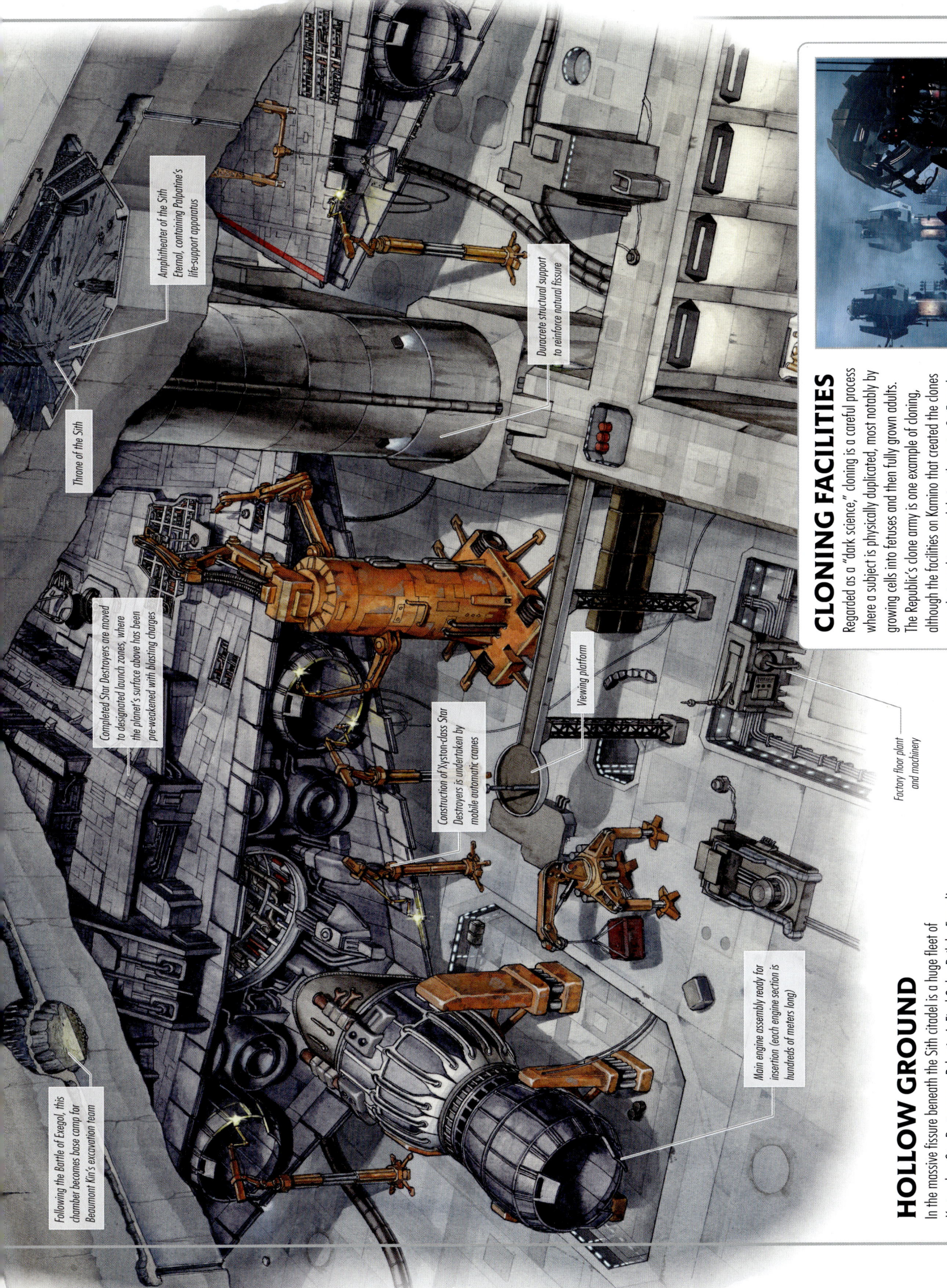

HOLLOW GROUND

In the massive fissure beneath the Sith citadel is a huge fleet of Xyston-class Star Destroyers—Palpatine's Final Order. Built by Exegol's inhabitants, an undocumented number of cultists loyal to the Sith, these destroyers are launched via a navigational signal broadcast to them from a central relay. At least one ship is able to deploy prior to the Final Order's official launch, destroying the planet of Kijimi with its superlaser.

CLONING FACILITIES

Regarded as a "dark science," cloning is a careful process where a subject is physically duplicated, most notably by growing cells into fetuses and then fully grown adults. The Republic's clone army is one example of cloning, although the facilities on Kamino that created the clones were destroyed to conceal their evil secrets. On Exegol, these secrets are the foundation for some of Palpatine's most wicked machinations, including creating clones and "strandcasts" of himself to serve as vessels or experiments.

DEATH STAR RUINS

THE SECOND DEATH STAR'S FINAL resting place is the moon of Kef Bir in the Endor system. After it exploded above the nearby Forest Moon, pieces of the battle station were hurled in every direction. While some wreckage still remains floating like a specter in space, other pieces become caught in Kef Bir's gravity well, the debris plunging into the raging oceans below. There, the Death Star II is at the mercy of the salty waves, deteriorating slowly over decades. Despite the vast depths of the ocean, the outline of the superlaser array disk emerges from the waters like a twisted mountain of durasteel.

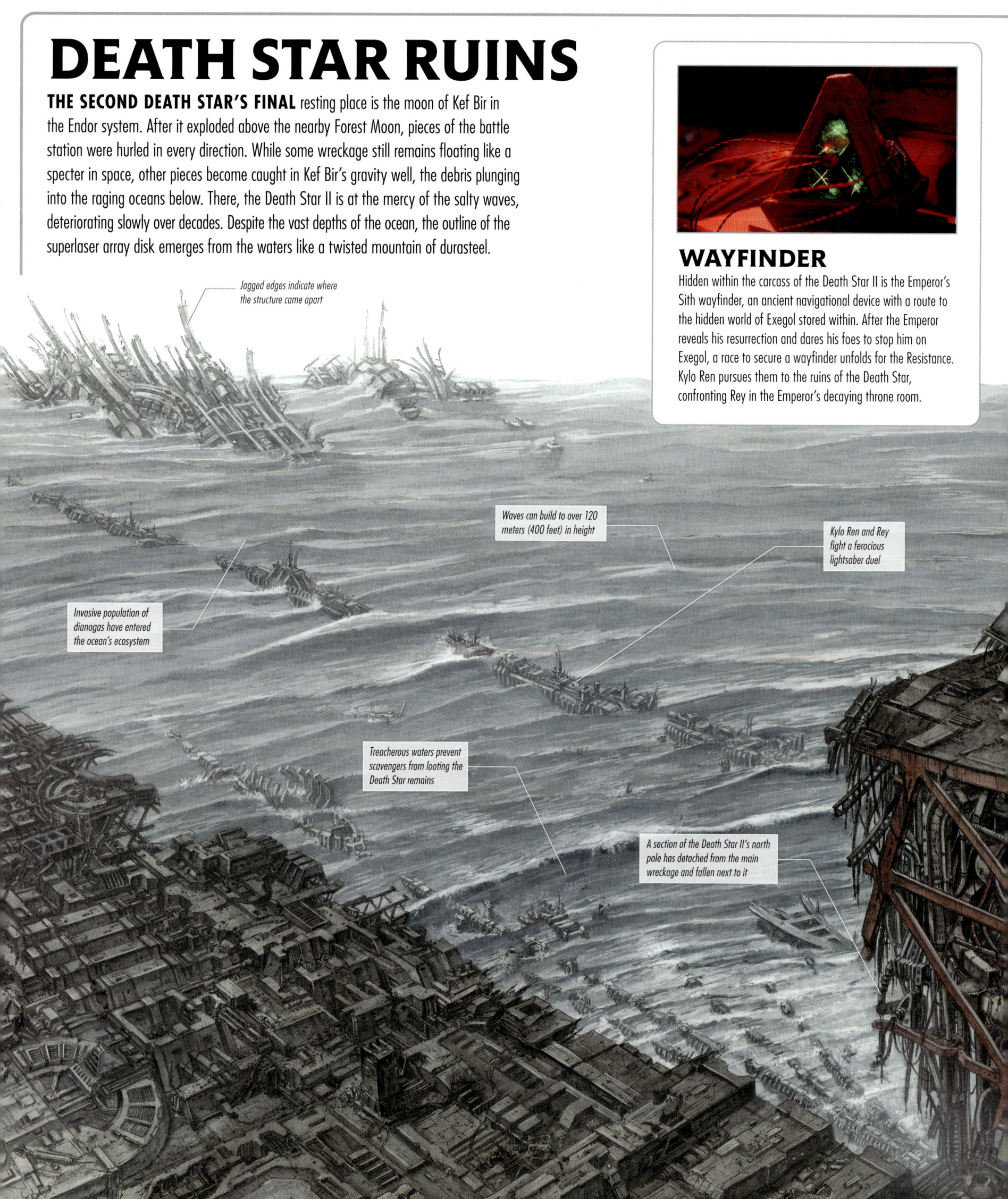

WAYFINDER

Hidden within the carcass of the Death Star II is the Emperor's Sith wayfinder, an ancient navigational device with a route to the hidden world of Exegol stored within. After the Emperor reveals his resurrection and dares his foes to stop him on Exegol, a race to secure a wayfinder unfolds for the Resistance. Kylo Ren pursues them to the ruins of the Death Star, confronting Rey in the Emperor's decaying throne room.

Jagged edges indicate where the structure came apart

Waves can build to over 120 meters (400 feet) in height

Kylo Ren and Rey fight a ferocious lightsaber duel

Invasive population of dianogas have entered the ocean's ecosystem

Treacherous waters prevent scavengers from looting the Death Star remains

A section of the Death Star II's north pole has detached from the main wreckage and fallen next to it

KEF BIR

Known as the "Ocean Moon of Endor," Kef Bir also features islands of grasslands. Like its neighbor the Forest Moon, few in the galaxy knew of Kef Bir's existence until after the Galactic Civil War. In later years, the moon becomes a sanctuary for First Order stormtroopers who have deserted. They cohabit the moon with the local flora and fauna, as well as invasive species that arrived with the remnants of the Death Star. With no signs of native intelligent life, these settlers begin to define locations on Kef Bir, naming features such as the Cliffs of Dead Empire, which overlook the Death Star ruins.

DUEL OF THE DYAD

Uniquely connected through the Force, Rey and Kylo Ren form a so-called dyad with opposing goals. While Rey seeks to defeat the evil on Exegol, Kylo envisions usurping it. After Kylo destroys the wayfinder that Rey has located within the Death Star ruins, a ferocious lightsaber duel unfolds. The fight culminates with Rey mortally wounding Kylo, only to reverse the damage by healing him. Rey escapes, leaving behind a conflicted Kylo.

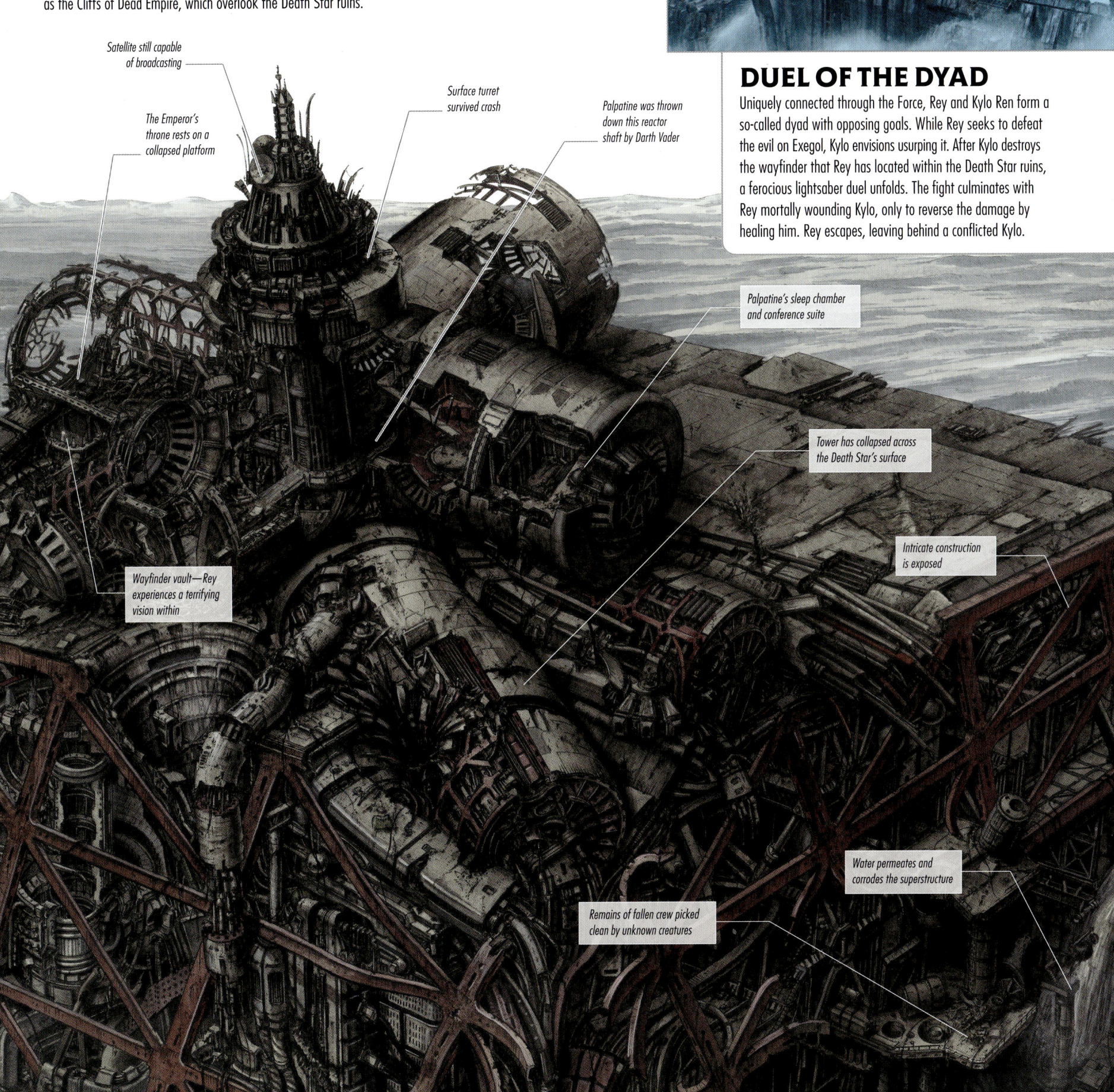

- Satellite still capable of broadcasting
- The Emperor's throne rests on a collapsed platform
- Surface turret survived crash
- Palpatine was thrown down this reactor shaft by Darth Vader
- Palpatine's sleep chamber and conference suite
- Tower has collapsed across the Death Star's surface
- Intricate construction is exposed
- Wayfinder vault—Rey experiences a terrifying vision within
- Water permeates and corrodes the superstructure
- Remains of fallen crew picked clean by unknown creatures

INDEX

A
Ahch-To 17, 208–209
Alderaan 126, 157, 173
Alkhara 177
Alliance *see* Rebel Alliance
Allie, Stass 114
Amidala, Padmé 8, 49, 120
    on Coruscant 66, 67, 68, 85
    on Geonosis 88, 89, 90, 97, 98, 99
    on Naboo 29, 54, 55, 62, 63, 74–75, 84
    on Polis Massa 122, 123
    Royal Starship 28, 61, 62
Andor, Cassian 134, 141, 159
Antana, Soara 72
Antilles, Wedge 160, 164
assault landers 203
assault ships 93

B
bacta tank 143
BB-8 194, 195, 205
Beckett, Tobias 130, 131, 132–33
Beggar's Canyon 38, 146
Ben's Mesa 38
Berenko, Omar 74, 75
Bespin 16, 172–75
Bestine 151, 153
Binks, Jar Jar 56, 59
Blizzard Force 160–61
B'omarr monks 176, 177, 178, 179
Boonta Eve Classic 38, 40, 41
Bothan spies 180, 186
Boushh 178
Bravo Flight 57
Bright Hope 161, 167

Bright Tree Village 180–83
B'thazoshe Bridge 83

C
C-3PO: on Endor 180–81, 182–83
    on Geonosis 88, 89
    on Hoth 161
    on Tatooine 36, 146, 147, 149, 151, 152, 153, 178, 179
Calrissian, Lando 172, 180
Canto Bight 17, 210–11
Canto Casino and Racetrack 210
Cantonica 17, 210–11
carbon freezing 173, 174–75
Carbonite Storage Repulsor Sled 173
the Caretakers 209
Cato Neimoidia 115
Chalmun's Spaceport Cantina 152, 153, 154–55
Chewbacca 114, 130, 131, 180, 183, 206
Chirpa 181, 182
Christophsis 18
City Bigspace 25
Claatuvac Guild 111, 112, 113
Clabburn Range 162
clone troopers 92–93, 94
Clone Wars 8, 18, 72, 97, 100–101, 102, 110, 114–15, 117, 125
clones 12, 76, 77, 78, 80–81, 217
Cloud City 172–75
Cloud-Riders 130–31
coaxium 128, 130–31
Coco Town 65
Commerce Guild 95
core ships 87, 95, 96
Core Worlds 46, 47, 122
Corellia 15, 126, 128–29
Coronet City 15, 128–29
Coronet Spaceport 85, 128

Corporate Alliance 111
Coruscant 14, 46–53, 64–73, 84
    Battle of Coruscant 100–101
    entertainment districts 65, 70
    Federal District 47, 48–49, 52, 65, 67
    Galactic Senate 47, 50–51
    Imperial Senate Building 138–39
    Jedi Temple 52–53, 72–73, 102–103
    Medcenter 124–25
    Outlander Club 70–71
    sectors 68
    skylanes 64–69
    spaceport 85
    speeder chase through 66–69
    the Works 65, 125
Crait 17, 212–13
    Battle of Crait 214–15

D
Dagobah 16, 168–71
Dameron, Poe 194, 206, 214
Dantooine 158
dark energy 205
Death Star 8, 15, 17, 126, 137, 144, 145, 156–57
Death Star II 17, 126, 180–81, 184–85
    construction 17
    Emperor's throne room 184, 186–87
    ruins 218–19
Dex's Diner 65
Djarin, Din 192, 193
docking bays 84, 108, 109, 152
Dooku, Count 89, 97, 98–99
Dowager Queen 153
D'Qar 17, 191, 200–201
Droid Control Ship 26–27, 57
droid factories 86, 87, 88–89, 121
droids 26, 27, 39, 66, 73, 83, 85, 119, 152, 162, 179

battle droids 55, 59, 62, 63, 86, 87, 94, 96, 97
buzz droids 101
droidekas 94, 96
dwarf spider droids 94, 96
hailfire droids 95, 97
spider droids 95, 96, 97, 114
vulture droids 100, 101
drones 88, 89, 90, 91
dropships 161
Durant, Rio 130, 131

E

Echo Base 161, 162–67
Eellayin 122
Empire 8
    Imperial Senate Building 138–39
    installation on Endor Moon 181
    Scarif 144–45
Endor 17
    Kef Bir 218–19
Endor, Forest Moon of 16
    Battle of Endor 180–81
    Death Star II 185
    Ewok village 182–83
Erso, Jyn 141, 145, 159
Ewoks 180–83
Executor 161, 188–89
Exegol 8, 17, 191, 216–17, 218

F

fathier chase 210–11
Felucia 114
Ferrix 15, 126, 134–35
Fett, Boba 87, 174
Fett, Jango 77, 78, 79, 87, 89
Figg, Lord Ecclessis 172, 173
Final Order 17, 216, 217
Final Protector 140
Finn 191, 195, 206, 207, 210–11, 214
First Order 8, 191, 194, 200, 201, 202–207, 216, 219
    Battle of Crait 214–15
    Maz's Castle 199
    military 202–203
    Starkiller Base 17, 204–207
Fisto, Kit 96
the Force 168, 169, 171, 208, 209
Forest Moon *see* Endor, Forest Moon of

G

Galactic Civil War 8, 17, 126, 160
Galactic Empire *see* Empire
Galactic Republic *see* Republic
Galactic Senate *see* Senate
Gallofree Yards transports 162, 163, 166
gaming 70–71, 154, 198, 210
Gardulla the Hutt 36, 41
gas refineries 172
    processing vane 174–75
the Gathering 17
Geonosis 14, 86–99, 157
    Battle of Geonosis 18, 96–97
    Dooku's hangar 98–99
    execution arena 90–91
    Republic Army 92–93
    Separatist forces on 94–95, 96, 98
Gideon, Moff 16
gnarltrees 168, 170, 171
Goazon Badlands 196
Graveyard of Ships 194–95
Great Grass Plains 22, 23, 57
    Battle of the Great Grass Plains 58–59
Great Jedi Purge 18
Great Temple (Yavin 4) 158–59
Grievous, General 100–101, 107, 108
Grogu 192, 193
Gungans 20–25, 56–59
Gunray, Nute 55, 115
gunships 93, 111

H, I

hangars 161, 177
    Dooku's hangar 98–99
    Geonosis 87
    Jedi Temple 72
    Mos Espa arena 44, 45
    Theed Hangar 28–29, 60, 61, 62
Hellhound 2 196, 197
hive galleries 87
HoloNet relay station 110
Hosnian Prime 205
Hoth 16, 126, 160–67
    Battle of Hoth 160–61
    Echo Base 162–67
Hutt, Jabba the 44, 146, 152
    at Mos Espa Arena 40, 41
    Jabba's palace 176–79
Hutt family 30, 82
Hutt Flats 39
Hux, General Armitage 205, 214
Ilum 17, 204–207
InterGalactic Banking Clan 95, 115
Interrogator 194, 196
Invisible Hand 100–101
ion cannons 167

J

Jakku 16, 194–97
    Battle of Jakku 194, 196
    Niima Outpost 194, 195, 197
    Rey's home 196–97
    Starship Graveyard 194–95
    Tuanul village 194, 196
Jawas 30, 35, 38, 82, 146, 147, 151
Jedha 15, 140–41
Jedha City 140–41
Jedi Order 8, 46, 52–53, 121
    Ahch-To 208
    Clone Wars 114
    Great Jedi Purge 18
    High Council 52, 72, 100, 102
    Jedha 140–41
    Knights 52, 72, 103
    Masters 72, 102
    Order 66 111, 114
    Padawans 72, 102, 103
Jedi Temple 47, 52–53, 102–103
    Analysis Rooms 73, 103
    Archives 73, 102, 103
    databanks 72
    hangars 72
    holomap rooms 52
    Jedi councils 53
    meditation chambers 72, 102
    operations 72–73
    Temple Spire 53
Jestefad 116, 117, 118
Jett's Chute 39
Jinn, Qui-Gon 23, 56, 60, 151, 169
Junda, Cere 140
Jundland Wastes 83, 146–47, 148, 151, 152

K

Kachirho 111, 112, 114
Kallidahin 122
Kamino 14, 76–81, 217
    air-to-sea transport 77
    landing platforms 77, 78
    Tipoca City 76, 77, 78–81
Kaminoans 76–81
Kanata, Maz 16, 198–99

Karga, Greef 16, 193
Kashyyyk 15, 110–15, 191
    battles on 114–15
    wroshyr trees 112–13
Kef Bir 17, 218–19
Kenobi, Obi-Wan 23, 56, 156, 171
    Ben's house 151
    on Coruscant 66–69, 70, 100–101
    on Geonosis 87, 89, 90, 97, 98–99
    on Kamino 77, 81
    on Mustafar 120–21
    on Tatooine 146–47, 152, 153, 154
    Theed generator 60
    on Utapau 107, 108
Kessel 15
    Kessel mines 132–3
Kessoline 133
Ki-Adi-Mundi 115
Koon, Plo 115
Krennic, Orson 142, 145
kyber crystals 17, 140, 156, 207

L

LAAT/C 92
Laguna Caves 38
Lake Country 74–75
Lanais 209
landing ships 55
landspeeders 147, 152
Lars, Beru 147, 148–49
Lars, Cliegg 82, 83, 149
Lars, Owen 147, 148–49
Lars, Shmi 36, 82, 83
Lars homestead 147, 148–49
lava 116, 117, 120, 121, 142, 143
    mining 118–19
Lefrani 117, 120
Leia, Princess see Organa, Leia
Lianorm Swamp 22, 23
Livet Tower 23
Local Dig 122
locap plants 24
Loneozner, Laze "Fixer" 150
Lothal 126

M

Madine, General Crix 181
Mai, Shu 114
Malastare 42, 44
Massassi 158, 159
Maul, Darth 49, 60
Max Rebo Band 178
Maz's castle 198–99
Mid Rim 110, 140
Millennium Falcon 156, 157, 159, 160, 161, 180, 195, 206, 213
mining: on Bespin 172–73
    on Geonosis 89
    on Kessel 132–33
    on Mustafar 116, 118–19
    Pau City 109
    on Tatooine 30, 37
moisture farming 30, 82, 146, 147, 148–49, 150, 153
Moloch 128, 129
Mon Cala 185
Moorsh Moraine 160
Mos Eisley 147, 152–53
    Chalmun's Spaceport Cantina 152, 153, 154–55
Mos Espa 30, 31, 32–33, 152
    Anakin's hovel 36–37
    docking bays 84
    Mos Espa Arena 40–45
    race circuit 30, 38–39
    Watto's junkshop 34–35
Mothma, Mon 138
Mushroom Mesa 31, 38
Mustafar 15, 116–21
    architecture 121
    duel on 120–21
    mining 118–19
    Vader's castle 142–43
Mygeeto 115

N

Naboo 14, 20–25, 74–75
    Battle of Naboo 28, 58–59, 60–61
    invasion of 54–61
    Theed 60–63, 84
    Theed power generator 60–61
Narkina 5 15, 136–37
Nass, Boss 24, 25
Neimoidians 26, 27, 54, 55, 87
Nest, Enfys 130, 131
Nevarro 16, 192–93
New Republic 8, 191, 199, 201, 202, 205, 212
Nihil 18
Niima Outpost 194, 195, 197
Northern Dune Sea 40, 177
Nu, Jocasta 73

O

observation ships 80
offices: Galactic Senate 51
    Palpatine's Senate office 104–105
Order 66 111, 114, 169
Organa, Leia 8, 126, 171, 191
    Cloud City 173
    on Crait 17, 212–13, 214
    on D'Qar 17, 200–201
    on Endor Moon 180–91
    on Hoth 161
    on Tatooine 178
Ossic architecture 107, 108–109
Ossus 102, 191

Otoh Gunga 21, 22, 24–25, 57
Outer Rim 20, 30, 46, 76, 82, 86, 100, 106, 116, 122, 144, 146, 192, 214
Outlander Club 70–71
Ozzel, Admiral Kendal 160

P

Padawans 72, 102, 103
Palpatine, Emperor 8, 18, 21, 61, 125, 126, 189
    Clone Wars 100, 101
    Chancellor's podium 50, 51
    on Coruscant 48, 49
    Death Star II 184, 185, 186–87
    Exegol 216–17
    Final Order 191
    Imperial Senate Building 138
    Senate building office 104–105
Panaka, Captain 23, 56, 59, 62, 63
Paonga, Lake 22, 24
Pathfinders 181
Pau City 107, 108–109
Pau Sinkhole 107, 109
Pau'ans 106, 107, 108–109
Phasma, Captain 206
Pit of Carkoon 146
plasma 20, 21, 24, 25, 59, 60, 61
Plutt, Unkar 195, 197
podracers and podracing 30, 31, 32, 33, 35, 38–45, 70, 82
    Mos Espa Arena 40–45
Poggle the Lesser 87
Polis Massa 18, 122–23
POW camps 63
prisons, Narkina 5 136–37
Project Stardust 137
Pyke Syndicate 15, 132

Q, R

Qi'ra 128, 129
R2-D2: on Dagobah 168–71
    on Endor Moon 180–81, 182–83
    on Geonosis 89
    on Tatooine 36, 45, 146, 147, 149, 152, 153
rancor pit 179
Ravager 189, 194
Rebel Alliance 8, 126, 187
    Battle of Endor 180–81
    Crait 212–13
    Death Star 156
    Echo Base 162–67
    Scarif 144–45
    Yavin 4 158–59
Ren, Kylo 191, 207, 213, 214, 218, 219
Republic 8, 26
    Battle of Geonosis 96–97
    Clone Wars 100–101, 114
    Republic Army 92–93

Resistance 8, 191, 201, 210
   on Crait 212–15
   D'Qar base 200–201
   Rey 191, 213
   on Jakku 194–97
   on Kef Bir 218, 219
Rieekan, General Carlist 164
Rook, Bodhi 144, 145
Royal Naboo Security Forces 28, 61, 62
Royal Starship 28, 61, 62

S

Sand People *see* Tusken Raiders
sandcrawlers 82, 147
sandstorms 33
Scarif 15, 144–45
Se, Nala 77
Sebulba 32, 38, 39
Secura, Aayla 114
Senate 8, 47, 50–51
   apartments 48
   Battle of Geonosis 92
   Chancellery Secretariat 104
   Senate building 50–51, 65, 104–105
Separatist Alliance 8, 18, 87, 88, 89
   armies 94–95, 114, 115
   Battle of Geonosis 92–93, 96–97
   Clone Wars 100–101
Separatist Council 107, 115, 116, 120
shield generators 58, 59, 180–81
Sidious, Darth 17, 18, 49, 54, 117, 121, 125, 186, 218
sinkholes 107, 108, 109
Sith 8, 103, 117, 121
   artifacts 105, 124, 125
   citadel on Exegol 17, 216–17
   Death Star 156
   hall of statues 216
   wayfinder 218
skyhoppers 146
skylanes 64–69
skyscrapers 48, 67
skytunnels 68
Skywalker, Anakin 8, 18, 23
   on Coruscant 66–69, 70, 85, 100–101, 124, 125
   on Geonosis 88, 89, 90, 97, 98
   Jedi Temple massacre 102, 120
   on Mustafar 120–21
   on Naboo 62, 74–75
   podracing 32, 38–39, 45
   on Tatooine 32, 36–37, 82–83
   see also Vader, Darth
Skywalker, Luke 8, 17, 126, 191, 205
   on Ahch-To 208–209, 215
   in Cloud City 173–75
   on Crait 212, 213
   on Dagobah 168–71
   on Death Star II 186–7
   on Endor Moon 180–83, 187
   on Hoth 160–61, 162, 164
   in Jabba's palace 179
   on Tatooine 146–53
Snoke, Supreme Leader 191, 205
snowtroopers 161, 164, 214
Solleu River 23, 62
Solo, Ben 191
Solo, Han 191
   on Bespin 173–75
   coaxium heist 130, 131, 132–33
   on Corellia 128–29
   Death Star 156, 157
   on Endor Moon 180–83
   on Hoth 161
   on Starkiller Base 206
   on Tatooine 152
sonic cannons 95
Space Fighter Corps 29
spaceports 73, 74, 84–85, 152–53
SPHA-Ts 93, 96, 97
Squad Seven 100, 101
Star Destroyers 159, 160, 194, 203, 216, 217
starfighters 72
Starkiller Base 17, 191, 203, 204–207
Starship Graveyard 194–95
stilt-cities 76, 77, 78–79
stormtroopers 191, 195, 219, 202–203
Su, Lama 81
Super Star Destroyers 188–89, 194

T

Takodana 16, 198–99
Tarkin, Grand Moff 157, 189
Tatooine 14, 30–45, 82–83, 84, 146–47
   Anakin's hovel 36–37
   Ben Kenobi's house 151
   Chalmun's Spaceport Cantina 152, 153, 154–55
   death and burial on 83
   Jabba's palace 176–79
   Lars homestead 82, 148–49
   Mos Eisley 152–53
   Mos Espa 32–33, 84
   Naboo 82–83
   podracing 30, 31, 38–45
   Tosche Station 150
   Watto's junkshop 34–35, 82
Techno Union 96, 116, 117, 118, 120, 157
Teedos 197
Tekka, Lor San 208
Theed 21, 23, 54, 55, 56, 59, 62–63, 74
   Funeral Temple 23
   power generator 60–61
   Theed Hangar 28–29, 60, 61, 62
   Theed Palace 20, 23, 55, 75
   Theed Spaceport 84
tibanna gas 172–75
Tico, Rose 210–11, 214
TIE fighters 203, 206, 207, 214, 215
Tipoca City 76, 77, 78–81
Tosche Station 150
Trade Federation 26, 29, 50, 54, 56, 57, 59, 61, 62, 63, 75, 87, 89, 95, 96, 97, 157
transports 55, 59, 68, 92, 147, 152, 161, 162, 163, 166, 167
Tuanul village 194, 196
Tusken Raiders 30, 31, 39, 41, 82, 83, 146, 147, 154, 177

U, V, W

Ugnaughts 174
Ultimo Vista 68
Umbara 18
underwaterways 22, 74
Unduli, Luminara 114
Unknown Regions 202, 203, 204, 208, 216
Utai 106, 107, 109
Utapau 14, 106–109
   Pau City 107, 108–109
Vader, Darth 117, 121, 124, 125, 153
   bacta tank 143
   castle on Mustafar 142–43
   in Cloud City 173–75
   on Endor Moon 181
   on Executor 189
   on Hoth 160, 161, 165
   see also Skywalker, Anakin
Val 130, 131
Vandor 15, 130–31
Varykino 74, 75
Veers, General 160, 161
Vermilion 210–11
volcanoes 116, 118, 192
Vos, Quinlan 114
vulptices 213
Vuutun Palaa 26
Watto 32, 34–35, 36, 82
Wawaatt Archipelago 111, 112, 114
Wesell, Zam 66–69, 70
Western Dune Sea 82, 151
White Worms 128
Windu, Mace 92, 96–97
Wiyentaah 122
Wookiees 15, 110, 111, 114, 115, 154
   wroshyr trees 112–13

X, Y

Xelric Draw 32
Yavin 4 16, 162
   Battle of Yavin 126
   Great Temple 158–59
Yoda 16, 23
   on Dagobah 168–71
   on Geonosis 92, 93, 96–97, 98
   on Kashyyyk 111, 112, 114

Senior Editors Matt Jones and David Fentiman
Project Art Editor Chris Gould
Editor Kathryn Hill
Designers Toby Truphet, Samantha Richiardi, Christopher Ibbitt
Production Editor Siu Yin Chan
Senior Production Controller Laura Andrews
Managing Editor Emma Grange
Design Manager Vicky Short
Publisher Paula Regan
Art Director Charlotte Coulais
Managing Director Mark Searle

For Lucasfilm
Senior Editor Brett Rector
Creative Director Michael Siglain
Art Director Troy Alders
Story Group Leland Chee, Pablo Hidalgo, Phil Szostak, and Kate Izquierdo
Asset Management Chris Argyropoulos, Jackey Cabrera, Elinor De La Torre, Gabrielle Levenson, Michael Trobiani, and Sarah Williams

This book was made with Forest Stewardship Council™ certified paper – one small step in DK's commitment to a sustainable future. Learn more at www.dk.com/uk/information/sustainability

First published in Great Britain in 2025 by
Dorling Kindersley Limited
20 Vauxhall Bridge Road,
London SW1V 2SA

The authorised representative in the EEA is
Dorling Kindersley Verlag GmbH. Arnulfstr. 124,
80636 Munich, Germany

Page design copyright © 2025 Dorling Kindersley Limited
A Penguin Random House Company

© & TM 2025 LUCASFILM LTD.

10 9 8 7 6 5 4 3 2
002–339394–Mar/2025

Material in this book previously published in:
Inside the Worlds of Star Wars Episode I © & TM 2000 LUCASFILM LTD.
Inside the Worlds of Star Wars Attack of the Clones © & TM 2003 LUCASFILM LTD.
Inside the Worlds of Star Wars Trilogy © & TM 2004 LUCASFILM LTD.
Star Wars Battles that Changed the Galaxy © & TM 2021 LUCASFILM LTD.

All rights reserved.
No part of this publication may be reproduced, stored in or introduced into a retrieval system, or transmitted, in any form, or by any means (electronic, mechanical, photocopying, recording, or otherwise), without the prior written permission of the copyright owner.

A CIP catalogue record for this book
is available from the British Library.

ISBN 978-0-2416-5805-5

Printed and bound in China

www.dk.com
www.starwars.com